Praise for *Away 1*
A History of Sout

D0430600

"The inhabitants of *Away Down South* come at us thick and fast, benighted and bemused, roaring down some unpaved back-country road, pedal to the metal. If this sounds like a breathless rendition of Southern history by an academic who loves to name names, it certainly is. Still, no one remotely interested in the South will be able to resist this book, and readers are bound to learn from Cobb's enormous erudition."—Ira Berlin, *The Washington Post Book World*

"In this comprehensive, thoughtful, and utterly fascinating account, Cobb stalks the elusive mind—or rather minds—of the South. I don't use the word 'masterpiece' often, but it's the right word here."—John Shelton Reed, author of *My Tears Spoiled My Aim: And Other Reflections on Southern Culture*

"In this riveting read, Cobb charts the twisting, shifting history of Southern identity and how folks, Southern and non-Southern, have thought about the region.... Hopefully, he has a sequel planned."—*Publishers Weekly*

"If South-gazing is your bag, *Away Down South* is your book.... With C. Vann Woodward's death, Cobb is perhaps our best historical interpreter of the South and this may be his best book, better even than his fine book about the Mississippi Delta.... Not only has he done his homework, he has reflected deeply and the result is mature (as in good wine), mellow, stylish and tasty."—Edwin M. Yoder Jr., *Weekly Standard*

"A special treasure for all of us who have loved, studied, and tried to understand the South, a wonderfully complicated part of our country which—despite the changes chronicled in Jim Cobb's fine work—still more than any other region, thinks of itself as being different and special. *Away Down South* provides not only context and perspective but Cobb's own unique and powerful insights into the South's inherent contradictions."—Hamilton Jordan

"If you want to know what makes the South tick, you might well look to James C. Cobb for insight. For that matter, if you want to understand the inner workings of the contemporary United States, *Away Down South* would be a good place to start."—John Egerton, author of *The Americanization of Dixie: The Southernization of America*

"A tour de force from one of the South's premier historians. James Cobb shows, with characteristic wit and acuity, how a distinctive regional identity from the time of Jamestown to the Iraq war depended not just on how white and black southerners thought of themselves, but also on what others thought of Dixie."—Anthony J. Badger, author of *The New Deal: The Depression Years 1933–1940* and co-author of *Race in the American South*

Also by James C. Cobb

Redefining Southern Culture:
Mind and Identity in the Modern South

Georgia Odyssey

The Mississippi Delta and the World:
The Memoirs of David L. Cohn (editor)

The Most Southern Place on Earth:
The Mississippi Delta and the Roots of Regional Identity

The Selling of the South: The Southern Crusade for
Industrial Development, 1936–1980

Industrialization and Southern Society, 1877–1984

The New Deal and the South (co-editor)

Perspectives on the American South (co-editor)

Away Down South
A History of Southern Identity

James C. Cobb

OXFORD
UNIVERSITY PRESS

Oxford University Press, Inc., publishes works that
further Oxford University's objective of excellence
in research, scholarship, and education.

Oxford New York
Auckland Cape Town Dar es Salaam Hong Kong Karachi
Kuala Lumpur Madrid Melbourne Mexico City Nairobi
New Delhi Shanghai Taipei Toronto

With offices in
Argentina Austria Brazil Chile Czech Republic France Greece
Guatemala Hungary Italy Japan Poland Portugal Singapore
South Korea Switzerland Thailand Turkey Ukraine Vietnam

Copyright © 2005 by James C. Cobb

Published by Oxford University Press, Inc., 2005
198 Madison Avenue, New York, NY 10016
www.oup.com

First issued as an Oxford University Press paperback, 2007
ISBN-13: 978-0-19-531581-3
ISBN-10: 0-19-531581-2

Oxford is a registered trademark of Oxford University Press

The Library of Congress has cataloged the hardcover edition as follows:

Cobb, James C. (James Charles), 1947–
Away down South : a history of Southern identity / James C. Cobb.
p. cm.
Includes bibliographical references and index.
ISBN-13: 978-0-19-508959-2
ISBN-10: 0-19-508959-6
1. Southern States—Civilization.
2. Group identity—Southern States—History.
3. Southern States—Race relations. I. Title.
F209.C597 2005   975—dc22   2005017126

1 3 5 7 9 8 6 4 2
Printed in the United States of America
on acid-free paper

In Memory of
Modena Vickery Cobb
1910–1989

Contents

Acknowledgments

WRITING A PROPERLY INCLUSIVE ACKNOWLEDGMENT is difficult for any author, let alone one whose book was more than a decade in the making. Although he contributed, however unwittingly, to elongating the process, I must thank Sheldon Meyer, the original editor for this project, for his suggestion that what began as a book on southern identity since the publication of W. J. Cash's *The Mind of the South* in 1941 must first offer some understanding of where Cash was coming from. This ultimately meant a trip all the way back to the unfamiliar terrain of the late eighteenth century, but it also meant, I hope and trust, a much better and more valuable book. For his patience and faith that this would be the case, I must also thank Peter Ginna, who inherited me and my project from Sheldon and stuck with me until we got it into print. And to Joellyn Ausanka, my production editor, "Bless your heart!"

A number of people have read and commented on parts of the manuscript, including the late Numan Bartley, whose loss grieves me sorely. He was everything anyone could ask for in a mentor or a friend. I am similarly indebted for the feedback provided by Thomas Dyer, Emory Thomas, Robert Haws, and Michael Kwass. John Inscoe generously lent me book after book from his disheveled but voluminous library. Craig Pascoe, Jenny Brooks, and Angie Thompson provided crucial research assistance.

A National Endowment for the Humanities Fellowship for Individual Research afforded me an invaluable year of freedom from classroom responsibilities in 2002–2003. Some of the most important and easily the most enjoyable work on this book came in May–June 2002 courtesy of a Residence Fellowship at the Rockefeller Foundation's Study Center at Bellagio, Italy. We are deeply grateful to the center's director, Ms. Gianna Celli, and her entire staff for such an enriching and productive experience. No part of our time in Bellagio was more rewarding than hanging out with fellow historians Fred Anderson and Drew Cayton, who always managed to convince me that the problems with my work were minimal compared to theirs.

As usual, I am indebted most of all to my family. Our son Ben makes us prouder every day, and his wonderful wit and amused tolerance of his aging and eccentric parents lightens our hearts. Throughout our thirty-six years of marriage, Lyra Cobb has meant everything to me, but never more so than in the last few years, when she offered her unqualified love and support even as she suffered the loss of her father and wrestled with a number of crucial personal challenges and obligations of her own.

Whatever else may be said of this book, few will deny its ambition. It seems fitting, therefore, that it should be offered in tribute to the person who instilled in me the determination and drive (my strongest suits by far) to undertake such a project. "*Can't* never did anything, Jimmy," she used to say, and I have recalled those words countless times over the years when I had myself almost convinced that I had set my sights too high or overestimated my abilities. Her example spoke to me even more authoritatively than her words, however. Here was a woman with eleven years of formal education who spent the prime of her life on a played-out farm where ends didn't always meet and never traveled more than 100 miles from home until she was in her sixties. Yet her grasp of history and current affairs was encyclopedic and sure, and her love of language and poetry both pure and profound. A skilled seamstress and cook, she was also a natural mechanic and a more accomplished and exacting carpenter than any man I ever saw. She always demanded his best effort from her son, but once she knew she had gotten it, that was always good enough for her.

Not all the reviewers of this book may find my best effort satisfactory, but I am confident that the person whose opinion always mattered most to me would have. Otherwise, I would not have dedicated it to the memory of my mother, Modena Vickery Cobb.

Away Down South

Introduction

WHEN WE SANG "DIXIE" in assembly at my elementary school in the early 1950s, I always wondered why we were saying "away down South" when we were already in Georgia, about as "down South" as you could get. I would have been really confused, I'm sure, had I known then that this song, which a bunch of southern white kids were belting out with such fervor, was supposedly written by an Ohioan of Irish descent and first performed in blackface on Broadway in 1859. Only years later would I understand that the initial popularity of "Dixie" among New Yorkers had reflected an already well-established tendency among northern whites to see the South as a primitive and exotic land distinctly apart from the rest of America. The subsequent metamorphosis of this otherwise unremarkable little minstrel ditty into the favorite marching anthem, first of fire-eating secessionists and then of fire-breathing segregationists, testified as well to the readiness of white southerners to embrace and defend even the most controversial aspects of their region's distinctiveness.

As the civil rights movement unfolded, "Dixie" soon evoked a vision, not of happy darkies on the plantation but of decidedly unhappy rednecks waving the Confederate flag and spewing contempt for national authority. In fact, an accumulated panorama of appalling and indelible imagery, from a beaten and bloated Emmett Till to the raw brutality of Selma, presented the South as not just what Howard Zinn in his 1964 book, *The Southern Mystique*, had called "the most terrible place in America," but a place that hardly seemed part of America at all. This was the white South captured so brilliantly by W. J. Cash in his 1941 classic, *The Mind of the South*, a savagely racist, intellectually stunted, emotionally deranged society unwilling to admit it was sick, much less heal itself.

By the end of the 1960s the crudely coded race-baiting and angry anti-intellectualism that had propelled a defiant Alabama governor George C. Wallace to impressive showings in northern presidential primaries had begun to suggest that the land "away down South" might not be as distant as many

Americans preferred to believe. When I entered graduate school in 1969, however, I found southern historians still largely intent on isolating and illuminating the aberrant historical processes behind the sinister regional malignancy that seemed to pose such an up-close and deadly serious threat to the nation's loftiest ideals and aspirations. Thus, as a fledgling scholar, rather than concern myself "indiscriminately with everything that occurs within the South," I was obliged, as David Potter had recently admonished, "to identify and investigate the distinctive features of southern society" by exploring "points where the conditions of the southern region might differ from those of other regions." Historians had actually been searching for the sources of southern distinctiveness long before Potter's pronouncement, suggesting possible explanations such as dedication to white supremacy, a peculiar climate, a decidedly un-American historical experience, and, in Potter's own case, a unique "culture of the folk," rooted in life on the land.[1]

However, after occupying myself with this exercise for the better part of a decade, it finally dawned on me that, instead of examining southern differences with "other regions," as Potter had suggested, historians and other critical observers typically defined southern peculiarities solely in relation to "the North." In this usage, the North actually represented not simply another region or even, as William Faulkner's Charles Mallison put it, a "geographical place" at all but an "emotional idea" of the remainder of a triumphantly superior America both literally and figuratively beyond and without the ever-problematic South. Struck by the irony of this comparison, C. Vann Woodward had first pointed out in 1953 that in the world at large it was the inspiring, larger-than-life idea of northern accomplishment and virtue, rather than the dreary reality of southern failure and guilt, that seemed exceptional. By that time, however, as Edward L. Ayers has noted, a persistent focus on the North-South polarity had long since transformed "a relative situation" into "an absolute characteristic." Not only had southern cultural identity become "a fiction of a geographically bounded and coherent set of attitudes to be set off against a mythical non-South," but, one might add, that mythical non-South had become virtually synonymous with the idea of America itself.[2]

The inclination both to make invidious comparisons between the South and the North and to see the latter as the normative standard for the entire nation dated back well before the civil rights era to the earliest days of American independence when, as Joyce Appleby has written, the first post-Revolutionary generation of Americans had inherited "the responsibility for explicit articulation of what the United States stood for." From the outset, a widely dispersed, overwhelmingly rural population and the absence of incentives in a plantation-based society for the investments in public education needed to develop significant literary or journalistic institutions had effectively consigned the southern states to the periphery of popular communication in America. Despite the crucial roles of prominent southerners in securing America's independence and drafting its fundamental documents of state, with the infant nation's literary and publishing core already fixed firmly in the Northeast, it was hardly surprising that, even in its embryonic phase, the dominant vision of American character emphasized northern sensibilities and perceptions.[3]

One of these perceptions, and a difficult one to dismiss, was that the major impediment to constructing an inspiring and credible identity for a nation supposedly committed to the principles of liberty, equality, and democracy was a southern economy, society, and culture shaped and sustained by human bondage. As the leaders of the young republic struggled to gain the acceptance and respect of other nations, northern architects of national identity soon realized that their vision of America would not only be much simpler to construct but also much easier to look at and far more emphatic and unequivocal in meaning if they simply focused on what they saw, or sometimes chose to see, in the states above the recently drawn Mason-Dixon line.

The exclusion of the southern states from this northernized image of America did not mean that they played no role in its construction, however. Traditionally, "identity" has been defined as the condition of being simultaneously both "one's self or itself *and not another*." [Emphasis added.] Typically, the creation of any sort of group identity, be it regional, national, ethnic, or otherwise, has required what Susan-Mary Grant called a "negative reference point," against which it may be defined in stark and favorable contrast. Noting that Europe and the West once used the Orient as the "other" against which they identified themselves, David Jansson saw a similar process at work in the United States, a kind of "internal orientalism" that built and sustained a "privileged national identity" by consigning most of the undesirable traits exhibited by Americans to "the imagined space called 'the South.'"[4]

During and immediately after the Revolution, England had served as the primary negative reference or "other" for the new American nation. However, the dramatic political differences and the great physical distance between the United States and its rejected parent nation soon suggested the need for a more proximate and vivid source of opposition and contrast, a need that the southern states, with their increasingly controversial labor system; archaic social customs; and staple-crop, export economy, seemed well suited to supply. The muskets of the American Revolution had hardly fallen silent before northern novelists, scholars, journalists, and other popular writers (who sometimes wrote authoritatively about places they had never visited and described scenes they had never witnessed) began constructing a vision of America that was based almost exclusively on the northern model and used the southern states primarily as an example of what the nation was not and must never become.

By the eve of the Civil War, amateur historian George Bancroft had already laid down the story of America as primarily the story of the Northeast, especially New England. The separation between the South and the nation only widened under the strain of antebellum sectional conflict, while the North's military triumph in the Civil War further secured its role as the true symbol of American society. In the wake of the war, other northern historians followed Bancroft's lead, conveying what Jack P. Greene called an "implicit belief that the main line of American political and cultural development ran not from Jamestown but from Plymouth to the present." In doing so, they also nurtured "the comforting illusion that slavery, that blatant anomaly in republican and egalitarian America, had never been central to American culture but . . . only a marginal institution confined to the cultural peripheries of the colonial British American world." Meanwhile, "the history of the South and southerners" stood only as "a negative example of what America had to overcome before it could finally realize its true self."[5]

In the minds of many, of course, it was the South that must overcome its history in order to find its "true self" and join the North in the mainstream of American society. Even in the 1830s, the ever-perceptive French visitor Alexis de Tocqueville was already predicting that the northern states would provide "the common standard to which the whole nation will one day be assimilated." Some 150 years after de Tocqueville, Carl Degler explained that "the story of America has been perceived as the triumph of freedom, national unity and equality, the acquisition of wealth, the growth of great urban centers, and the ethnic diversification of the population." Because these defining components of the nation's identity were "obviously northern in character," the challenge of "Americanizing" or bringing a backward Dixie up to national standards has therefore been seen largely as a matter of what Richard N. Current called "northernizing the South." Accordingly, many of those who have explored the discrepancies between South and North have done so with an eye toward not simply understanding them, but, insofar as possible, eliminating them as well.[6]

Reacting in a way that held profound implications for their identity as a group, white southerners often insisted that *their* society was the true embodiment of the American spirit, and proceeded, by steadfastly and often blindly resisting what they saw as northernization for well over a century, to define themselves primarily in opposition to the North. When they were unable to turn back the (essentially northern) Republican political challenge of the 1850s, they took up arms against their countrymen in defense of slavery. In the wake of defeat and occupation, they succeeded in rolling back the northernizing initiatives of Reconstruction and then moved to construct a "New South" dedicated to emulating the North's industrial achievements without allowing northern social and political influences to undermine the regional autonomy of southern whites. To that end, they vociferously and sometimes violently resisted the federally mandated but North-inspired destruction of the Jim Crow system.

Not all southern white opposition to northernization centered on race, of course; the North also represented the combined forces of an intrusive, unsettling, faith-and-tradition-shaking modernity as well. Still, because they had made their racial supremacy the cornerstone of their regional identity, it also became the cornerstone of their resistance to northern intrusions in general. As a result, many white southerners were actually plunged into an identity crisis in the wake of Jim Crow's long-awaited demise, especially when, amid revelations of racial and economic imperfections of its own, their once-formidable nemesis and idealized counterpoint, the North, began to disintegrate before their very eyes.

But what of southern blacks? Although not all of the North-South contention was about race, recalcitrant white southerners had insisted that segregation was the essence of the "southern way of life," and many of the whites, northern and southern, who committed themselves to destroying that system seemed to agree. This definition of southern identity effectively excluded the South's black residents in much the same way that both black and white southerners had been "othered" out of the construction of American identity. Even as slaves, African Americans had been major contributors to the southern cultural synthesis, and the narratives of escaped or freed bondsmen had challenged both the regional and national mythology of contented slaves laboring for benign and indulgent masters. When emancipation came, African Americans' celebrations of their freedom and heritage served notice of their determination to offer an alternative version of southern identity. This determination flowered during the post–World War I Harlem Renaissance but truly began to flourish only when the burden of Jim Crow had finally been lifted, as many southern blacks began to assert their identities as southerners and to embrace the South as their homeland. As black southerners grew increasingly comfortable in acknowledging their ties to the region, they also began to explore the commonalities between the sources of their southernness and the sources of their blackness as well.

Be it real or imagined, however, the most common foundation of group identity is a shared sense of a common past, and despite their mutual attachments to the South, black and white southerners clearly differed on how southern history should be represented or remembered. While black leaders worked to establish civil rights memorials and other monuments to African American achievement, they often clashed with whites over public displays of the Confederate flag and other historical symbols frequently associated with black subjugation. As the twenty-first century began to unfold, both groups faced the challenge of constructing a new cooperative southern identity for the future while still struggling to reconcile their conflicting visions of the past.

Identity has been used so often to interpret (or justify) so much that it has become something of a cliché whose perceived explanatory muscle actually conceals a fair amount of conceptual flab. By the mid-1970s critical observers were already describing identity as a word "driven out of its wits by over use," and Philip Gleason concluded in 1982 that it had grown both diffuse in meaning and subject to "increasingly loose and irresponsible usage." Moreover, Gleason added, "a good deal of what passes for discussion of identity is little more than portentous incoherence, and the historian should not be intimidated into regarding it as more than that."[7]

Having ventured into what is now, more than twenty years later, a much larger and, if anything, even more "portentous" theoretical thicket of literature on identity only to emerge bleary eyed, brain befogged, and not much the wiser for it all, I have decided to banish discussions of scholarly treatises on identity to the notes and simply explain how I have approached the question of identity in this book. I want to emphasize first of all that, as it appears here, identity typically refers to a *perception* of reality rather than to reality itself. Identity may, of course, be grounded in verifiable fact, but as the case of the South demonstrates all too well, it is often a mixture of the unvarnished and the varnished or even the whitewashed truth. The matter of perception versus reality is compounded by the fact that, historically, identities have not existed in isolation, but always in relation to other perceived oppositional identities against which they are defined. Hence, there could have been no South without a North and regardless of reality, the perception of significant differences between these two was vital to sustaining the identity of either. Things get even more complicated here, for this has not always been a purely reciprocal process. The idea of a "North" as a fundamental source of identity and an object of attachment has been far less important historically to Americans above the Mason-Dixon line than has the idea of a "South" to those who lived below it. Simply put, where southerners (regardless of race, to some extent) have staked their claim to a distinctive regional identity defined in contrast with the North, northerners have been more likely to characterize their own identity as simply "American" and define that in contrast with the South.[8]

Because it was cast in opposition to the values of a more modern and morally and economically powerful America, the idea of a distinctive southern regional identity has, it seems, always been living on borrowed time. The reality that, over the course of nearly a century and a half of fading away, the South has staged what George B. Tindall called "one of the most prolonged disappearing acts since the fall of Rome" is less a commentary on the stubbornness of its identity than on the way we have defined and perceived that identity in the first place. Lexicographers tell us that "identity" is "the state or fact of remaining the same one, as under varying aspects or conditions." In my view, however, the experience of the South affords proof enough that identity is not a fixed and immutable condition, but as Lawrence Levine suggests of culture, an ongoing interactive "process" in which adaptability, rather than resistance, to change is more often than not the real key to survival.

The history of southern identity is not a story of continuity *versus* change, but continuity *within* it. For example, as Edwin Yoder points out, there have been roughly as many New Souths as "French constitutions and theories of the decline of Rome." Henry Grady and the architects of the first postbellum "New South" swore undying fealty to the social and political values of the antebellum "Old South" in order to show that their plan to restructure the region's economy would not lead to the northernized "No South," first invoked by George W. Cable in 1882. Yet by the middle of the twentieth century, the heralds of a newer and improved New South clearly envisioned a region that looked less like the Old South and more like America. More than fifty years and several more New Souths later, however, it requires no great exertion to find vestiges of the Old South still flourishing in what many insist is now the irrevocably assimilated and indistinguishable No South so long sought by some and resisted by others.[9]

This matter is muddled even further by the fact that the apparent waning of southern distinctiveness over the last generation reflects more than the internal changes that moved the South closer to the perceived American mainstream. There were also external changes, such as the exposure of racism as more than a southern problem and the national resurgence of political, social, and cultural conservatism that have seemed to move the mainstream toward the South.

The foregoing suggests why the reader who picks up this book looking for a definitive pronouncement as to whether "the South" still exists as a distinctive region is destined to put it down disappointed. There is no telling how many times in thirty years of banquet speeches I have been asked this question, to which even the most informed and responsible "Yes" or "No" reply must still be so conditional and subjective as to be practically meaningless. I have long sensed that the most appropriate response to this query is "It depends on who's asking—and when and why," and in short, that is why I have written this book.[10]

I hasten to point out that what I am offering here is *a* history rather than *the* history of southern identity. I make no claim that what I have done is totally inclusive or definitive. On the other hand, I do believe this book offers a useful chronologically comprehensive historical framework for understanding the origins and evolution of an ongoing effort, now into its third century, to come to terms with the South's role as both a real and imagined cultural entity separate and distinct from the rest of the country. Because southern distinctiveness has so often been defined in opposition to our larger national self-image, this enduring struggle with southern identity has actually become not only a sustaining component of southern identity itself, but as we shall see, of American identity as well.

1

Cavalier and Yankee

THE ORIGINS OF SOUTHERN "OTHERNESS"

LIKE ALL QUESTIONS OF IDENTITY, the point at which "southern" began to convey sociocultural as well as geographic distinctions is largely a matter of perception. Initially, the American colonies were most likely to be divided between the "eastern" colonies of New England and the "southern" ones, which included the remainder stretching from New York all the way down to Georgia. Gradually, however, New York, New Jersey, Pennsylvania, and Delaware became the "middle" colonies, leaving "southern" to apply only to Virginia, the Carolinas, and Georgia.[1]

Jack P. Greene has argued that, prior to the Revolution, these latter colonies were anything but "a peripheral, much less [a] deviant area." Accounting for nearly two-thirds of the value of the products of the thirteen colonies between 1768 and 1772, they were squarely "in the mainstream of British-American development." Still, however brightly the southern colonies may have shone in the British imperial firmament, they were destined to follow a path of development that differed significantly from the one taken by their immediate neighbors to the north.[2]

In fact, as Peter Coclanis has argued, this process of North-South divergence had actually gotten under way by the midpoint of the seventeenth century, as institutionalized reliance on slave labor and plantation-based production of tobacco for export combined to send the South "down a path never followed in temperate colonies in the North." The growing dominance of plantation agriculture with its economies of scale and the attendant concentrations of wealth led to what Coclanis called a "pinched and niggardly institutional development" in areas such as transportation, urban growth, education, and even religious organization.[3]

These conditions stood in stark contrast with the New England and Middle colonies, where climate, soils, and terrain precluded the production of a profitable export crop comparable to southern tobacco or sugar, and thus obviated the need for a large slave labor force. As a result, inhabitants of the northern colonies were obliged to pursue a more diversified approach to agricultural and industrial development. They also concentrated on areas like transportation and trade and adopted flexible entrepreneurial strategies that could be adapted quickly to shifts in the patterns of regional, national, and international commerce. Although the Middle colonies fared better economically than those in New England, on the whole, as the Revolution approached, the northern colonies enjoyed both urban expansion and stable urban-rural interactions that produced a relatively broader and more balanced prosperity than the southern colonies had achieved. These northern colonies also provided much greater public access to "an array of social, educational, political, cultural, and institutional entitlements" than could be found in the top-heavy, plantation-predicated economy and society of their southern neighbors.[4]

Citing these emerging differences in economic, political, and social orientation, historian John Richard Alden argued that by the end of the colonial era there was already a "First South," which was "crudely a unit with interests and views opposed to those of the rest of the Union." In reality, these regional dissimilarities are much more obvious in retrospect than they were to most Americans in 1776, especially since, as Greene has also suggested, until they began their agitation against the Crown, each of the American colonies remained "a discrete and largely self-contained political environment" arguably more closely connected to London than to "any of its immediate neighbors in America."[5]

Ultimately, however, in the process first of cooperating to resist oppressive British colonial policies, then fighting together for independence and then drawing and redrawing the blueprint for self-government, close observers in both the northern and southern states had become increasingly aware of some distinctions between their societies. Responding to his friend the Marquis de Chastellux's drafts of his observations about differences he had observed among the peoples of the several American states, Thomas Jefferson affirmed the contrasting characters and temperament that separated the people of the North from the people of the South. "In the North," Jefferson wrote, "they are, cool, sober, laborious, independent, jealous of their own liberties, and just to those of others, interested, chicaning, superstitious and hypocritical in their religion. In the South they are fiery, voluptuary, indolent, unsteady, jealous for their own liberties, but trampling on those of others, generous, candid, without attachment or pretensions to any religion but that of the heart."[6]

"These characteristics," Jefferson insisted, grew "weaker and weaker by gradation from North to South and South to North, insomuch that an observing traveler, without the aid of the quadrant may always know his latitude by the character of the people among whom he finds himself." In keeping with contemporary scientific thought, Jefferson ascribed these differences in regional traits to climate, although he allowed that "peculiar circumstances" had given New York "the character which climate would have given had she been placed on the South instead of the North side of Pennsylvania," while "other circumstances may have occasioned in Virginia a transplantation of a particular vice foreign to its climate."[7]

Chastellux was not entirely persuaded by Jefferson's climatic interpretation of regional traits. In his view, Jefferson's Virginians differed from those who lived north and east of the Chesapeake "not only in the nature of their climate, soil, and agriculture, but also in that indelible character which every nation acquires at the moment of its origin, and which by perpetuating itself from generation to generation, justifies this great principle, that everything which is partakes of what has been." Despite the presence of large numbers of whites "living in miserable huts" whose "wane [*sic*] looks and ragged garments bespoke poverty," Chastellux insisted that Virginia's general social and political demeanor would "always be aristocratic" not simply because of any distinction attached to owning slaves but because "the sway held over them nourishes vanity and sloth." Hence, Chastellux believed, unlike New England, which had rebelled against British rule "through reason and calculation," Virginia had simply "revolted through pride."[8]

Chastellux professed reluctance to comment on the states south of Virginia because he was not sufficiently acquainted with them, but he did observe that North Carolina had been settled by Scotsmen "brought thither by poverty rather than by industry." South Carolina, he thought, "owes its existence to its seaports," especially the cosmopolitan city of Charleston, where "manners are polished and easy" and "the inhabitants love pleasure, the arts and society" so that the environment is "more European than the rest of America." Despite the best efforts of governments or individuals, Chastellux believed the peculiar temperaments of the American regions "can never be entirely changed" so that future readers of his accounts would always be able to find "traces of their former character."[9]

Chastellux was not the first foreign observer to emphasize regional distinctions among Americans. These differences had been apparent to British observers even before the upstart colonists had demanded their independence. In 1765 London philanthropist Dr. John Fothergill divided the "British Inhabitants of North America" into "two sorts; those who lived in the northern part

of the continent and those who inhabit the Southern." The former area stretched
from Nova Scotia to northern Maryland, the latter from southern Maryland
to Georgia. In Fothergill's view, the inhabitants of the northern colonies lived
"like our lower English farmers," and their industry, thrift, and modest accu-
mulations and expectations contrasted starkly with the inclinations of their
slaveholding neighbors to the South toward "Idleness and Extravagance" and
their constant searching for "every means of Gratifications." The southern colonists, Fothergill thought, had more in common with the "West Indians" than
with their neighbors to the North.[10]

This Caribbeanized representation of the South was still much in evidence
in 1810 when a touring French dignitary contrasted the "bold and enterprising [sic]" residents of the northern states with the "heedless and lazy" people
of the South and observed that American manners seemed "entirely changed"
below the Potomac, where they were "strongly tinctured with those of the West
Indies." With so much of the nation's literary and publishing activity concentrated in the North, northern writers attempting to sketch the emergent American national character had little if any firsthand knowledge of the southern
states and often drew heavily on foreign travelers' descriptions and depictions
of the region. As a result, with its hierarchical social system and its dependence on plantation slavery, the South also stood out in many of these accounts as more like the northernmost outpost of what latter-day comparative
theorists have called the "extended Caribbean" or the "American tropics" than
the southernmost portion of the United States.[11]

In J. Hector St. John de Crevecoeur's fictional *Letters from an American
Farmer*, which appeared in 1782 before American nationhood was officially
finalized, the narrator, "Farmer James" of Pennsylvania, believed "Charles-
Town" [South Carolina] with its barbarous institutions and traits, especially
slavery and the cruelty and self-indulgence of its wealthy planters, bore a certain resemblance to Lima, Peru. Because "both are Capitals of the richest provinces in their respective hemisphere," he reasoned, "you may therefore
conjecture that both cities must exhibit the appearances necessarily resulting
from riches."[12]

Charleston's slaveholding elite enjoyed "all that life affords most bewitch-
ing and pleasurable, without labour, without fatigue, hardly subjected to the
trouble of wishing." They sustained this lifestyle, Crevecoeur observed, by using
their gold, "dug from the Peruvian mountains," to send ships "to the coast of
Guinea." There, the allure of their gold sparked "wars, murders and devastations in some harmless, peaceable, African neighborhood, where dwelt inno-

cent people who even knew not but that all men were black." They would soon learn better, however, when they were dragged back to Charleston in chains to labor for their callous, self-indulgent masters in the "most diffusive misery and wretchedness" for the remainder of their days.[13]

Farmer James conveniently avoided reference to the likelihood of northern ownership or command of the slave-bearing vessels, but he was forced to concede that, to his infinite dismay, the institution of slavery was not yet peculiar to the South. He nonetheless insisted that the lot of northern slaves was far "different . . . in every respect" for they were, "truly speaking, a part of our families." In order to emphasize the particular barbarity of southern—as opposed to northern—slavery, he offered a chilling description of a condemned slave, left in a cage hanging from a tree, his eyes pecked out by birds and his flesh being devoured by insects, still alive but praying for death.[14]

Speaking through Farmer James, Crevecoeur hoped to portray "the American" as a "new man." In order to present the distinctive character of the new nation in the sharpest relief, however, he had set the southern states apart from the remainder of the Union, especially "sober, laborious and religious" New England, suggesting that they were still burdened with the social, cultural, and economic vestiges of colonialism, which the northern core states of the republic had now cast off and moved safely beyond. In doing so, Crevecoeur linked the southern states more closely to a host of foreign colonies to their south than to their fellow states to the north where the true essence of the new American nation could be discerned.[15]

Ratification of the Constitution had brought the sense of a stronger central government, which, so many northerners expected and many southerners feared, boded well for northern economic as well as political fortunes. Northern interests generally fared quite well in early national era political conflicts ranging from the passage of a tariff to protect northern manufacturing, to funding of the national debt (by one northerner's contemporary estimate, nearly three-fourths of the benefiting note-holders resided in Massachusetts, New York, and Pennsylvania), creation of the National Bank (which greatly strengthened the hand of northeastern bankers), and the initial placement of the nation's capital in New York, which lay to the north of some 70 percent of those who would travel there to serve in Congress.[16]

Moreover, thanks to rapid expansion of manufacturing and commerce, as the eighteenth century drew to a close, the share of the total wealth in the United States produced by the northern states had for the first time surpassed that of the southern states. Buoyed by an enhanced feeling of national destiny and confident of their region's preeminent role in shaping it, participants in the northern-based American print culture continued to offer readers a steady diet of the South as an oppositional "other" situated within the nation's physical boundaries but embodying everything the United States was not "about." Writers like Crevecoeur and New England lexicographer Noah Webster occasionally drew criticism for offering such "splenetic observations respecting the southern states, while not a *single good quality* is attributed to them." In the main, however, as Jennifer Rae Greeson argued, the 1790s brought more literary and journalistic treatments of the South as what Edward Ayers described as "the Latin America of North America." These portrayals served up consistent images of a "swampy" and "disease-ridden" region whose early settlers had been motivated solely by greed and the lust for material gain. The result had been an altogether predictable descent into "iniquity, aristocracy and luxury" and the "drunken, lascivious, lazy, gluttonous and violent" behavior so woefully characteristic of the inhabitants of the South.[17]

According to one writer's account of "A Georgia Planter's Method of Spending His Time," the typical southerner rose at six, knocked back "a dram of bitters to prevent the ill effects of the early fogs," whipped a slave with his "rattan whip," and met with his overseer. By eight, his day's labors done, he returned to the plantation house to be greeted by "a tribe of young negroes in the primitive state of nakedness." After breakfast, he headed to the nearest tavern whence he remained until late in the afternoon before returning home to dine, bringing along, of course, a coterie of friends from the tavern with whom he just might share a drunken midnight hunt if the moonlight was sufficient for it.[18]

Greeson notes that in the literature and popular press of this era, northern writers consistently employed a first-person/third-person "we"/"they" dichotomy in describing southerners. Because the southern states supposedly embodied the backwardness and crudity that the more civilized northern states rejected out of hand, they actually seemed to represent a threat to national progress, integrity, and resolve. Lamenting the incursion of cockfighting, thought to be one of the worst of southern manly vices, onto the New York scene, an alarmed correspondent to *New York Magazine* warned in 1791, "We are again assaulted—the enemy is within." The spread of these practices, he predicted, "will lead us gradually into habits of intemperance and therefore rob the entire nation of the honour which we formerly acquired."[19]

With the likelihood of war with France looming large at the end of the 1790s, the South's proximity and similarity to the French West Indies led a number of nervous northern observers to see it as a suspect spot in the line of national defense. Reports of French plans to invade South Carolina using black troops transported by ship from Guadeloupe and Santo Domingo circulated throughout the North. There were also innuendos about traitorous southerners plotting a slave uprising similar to the one that had raged in Santo Domingo from 1791 to 1795. "It is certain," wrote a contributor to the *Pennsylvania Gazette* in July 1789, "that the [French] Directory count much on a revolution in their favor in the South, and have employed some means to let loose the Negroes to compleat [*sic*] their purposes."[20]

A prime literary example of the South as a sort of backdoor conduit through which the insidious influences of the greedy, materialistic, and depraved colonial world might invade and even topple the young republic was Royall Tyler's 1797 novel *The Algerine Captive*. Tyler used the recently concluded and extremely embarrassing capture and enslavement of more than 100 American sailors by Algerian pirates to suggest how the South's vices, particularly its devotion to slavery and lust for unearned wealth, could debilitate and embarrass the nation as a whole. The novel's protagonist, Dr. Updike Underhill, heads to "one of the states southward of Philadelphia" to make his career and fortune. He is immediately repulsed by scenes such as a "parson in his canonicals" first beating his tardy slave as he strode toward his church, then after taking the pulpit for an eleven-minute sermon, leading the way as his congregation made off to a much-anticipated horse race, at which the parson held so many of the wagers that "the sleeve of his cassock was heavy laden, with the principal bets."[21]

When the disapproving Underhill signs on as the physician on a slave ship, he does so unwittingly, knowing only that it will sail first to London with a load of tobacco, then on to Africa, and back via Barbados to South Carolina. (By having the vessel depart implausibly from a southern port directly to London instead of via New England or mid-Atlantic ports, he absolves the northern states from any responsibility for the infamous triangular trade in slaves, tobacco, and rum.) In the end, despite his innocence and good intentions, Underhill is captured and enslaved by the Algerians, suffering a great injustice brought on by the sins of the southerners whose ignorance and immorality he so thoroughly rejects.

It was no mere coincidence that Tyler, a Harvard-educated Bostonian, made Underhill a native of New Hampshire and had him attribute his extreme discomfiture in the slave South to "a certain staple of New England which I had with me, called conscience." The inclination to present New England as both the moral and intellectual center of the new nation was a recurrent theme in

early writing about the American character. Even as he lauded the piety and
industry of New England, Crevecoeur had damned Maryland and Virginia
with faint praise as "two of our finest provinces," while suggesting that many
of their most affluent and prominent citizens were descended from people
who had been transported there as felons.[22]

Chastellux had also looked most favorably on New Englanders, whose sole
motive in settling in North America had been "escape from the arbitrary power
of their monarchs" who had imposed on them "the double tyranny of despotism and intolerance." Unlike their southern countrymen, the people of New
England were not "adventurers" but simply men enjoined by doctrine to embrace equality and to respect industry, who "labored to live" and wished only
"to live in peace." As Robert Kelley noted, by the early national era, many of
New England's "Yankees" saw themselves as "the only truly 'American' people
and conceived of the nation in their own image."[23]

New England writers consistently portrayed New Englanders as the salt of
America's earth and the true and worthy embodiment of the country's character and virtue. In fact, well before the end of the eighteenth century, the
region's self-confident intellectual and political leaders had mounted an impressive effort to cast it as the fountain from which all of the nation's blessings
would ultimately flow. A pioneer in this campaign was Jedidiah Morse, whose
late-eighteenth-century volumes on American geography shamelessly touted
New England as what Joseph A. Conforti called "a civic model for the early
republic." In the end, Morse's crusade to establish New England as "America's
America" led him, like Crevecoeur, Royall, and others, to set up the South as
just the opposite, what Conforti called "an alien, un-American territory."[24]

Despite Morse's limited firsthand knowledge of the region, as Conforti observed, "The real and imagined South of Morse's geographics functioned as
the anti-image of sober, republican, New England." While he praised New
Englanders as "a hardy race of free, independent republicans" who lived without "temptations to luxury" in a "happy state of mediocrity," Morse found in
the people of Maryland a "disconsolate wildness" and an indolence and inac-
tivity that he attributed to "solitude and slavery." Morse scoffed at Virginia's
status as the "ancient dominion" and its ostensible role as leader of the new
nation. On a visit to Williamsburg, he had seen "no trade—no amusements,
but the infamous one of gaming—no industry, and very little appearance of
religion," save for "the mingled effusions of piety, enthusiasm, and supersti-
tion" characteristic of popular ignorance and a "poorer sort of people."[25]

In South Carolina, Morse encountered a culture of "luxury, dissipation, and extravagance" among the white inhabitants who "too generally want that enterprise and perseverance, which are necessary for the highest attainments in the arts and sciences." Morse's contemporary, lexicographer Noah Webster, shared his view of the South as an inferior and alien society and summed up his own feelings when he brooded, "O, New England! How superior are thy inhabitants in morals, literature, civility and industry." Not surprisingly, at this point some New England children were even being taught "New England is my nation," alongside "Christ is my salvation," and to sing "Rule New England" to the tune of "Rule Brittania." Overall, Martin Bruckner found the school texts used in the early Republic attempting to inculcate a "North-South gradient of moral-ethnic distinction" designed to "ascribe moral value to local places" and "privilege white Americans living in the North over those in the South."[26]

Perhaps a bit too mindful of the outcome of the Civil War, many historians have blamed white southerners for introducing the virus of sectionalism into the American body politic and praised their northern adversaries for their selfless devotion to the Union. Peter Onuf has shown, however, that it was not southerners but New Englanders who were the nation's most "precocious sectionalists." Some delegates had expressed their suspicions of the aims of their New England colleagues during the Constitutional Convention in 1787, but with representatives from Virginia siding with those from Massachusetts and Pennsylvania more often than with those from South Carolina, a discernibly "southern" voting pattern was difficult to establish. Moreover, during the more sectionally charged congressional conflicts of the 1790s, New England representatives clearly stuck together more consistently than did their counterparts from the southern states.[27]

As the nineteenth century began, with no room to expand and its population already trickling off to the West, New England seemed to be staring marginalization squarely in the face. Accordingly, behind their nationalistic façade, the region's Federalists were actually dedicated to sectional interests that could best be served by a central government powerful enough to protect and advance their trade and shipping interests at home and abroad. They grew increasingly frustrated after the election of Thomas Jefferson in 1800, which ushered in a Virginia dynasty that would dominate the presidency for the next quarter century. Although it seemed to escape the notice of many New Englanders, the reign of the "perfidious Virginians" was actually sustained by an intersectional party, a fact that may have also retarded the growth of a distinctively southern political mind-set. In any event, the threat of secession that

hung over the 1814 Hartford Convention's call for a radical restructuring of
the constitution in order to protect the interests of New England showed that
regional self-consciousness was yet another category in which the nation's
southernmost states seemed to lag behind its northernmost.[28]

With the American experiment in republicanism predicated largely on the
sovereign rights of the individual states and their equal access to the levers of
governmental power, it was hardly surprising to find northern or southern
spokesmen cloaking their sectionalist agendas in nationalist rhetoric. Although
the early champions of New England did not win an outright acknowledgment of their subregion as the vital essence of the new nation, what Eve
Kornfield has called "the New Englandization of American culture" was a "pervasive and invisible" *fait accompli* outside the southern states by 1800. Southern and western cultures might be acknowledged, but only as "regional"
phenomena while "New England culture was American culture." At the very
least, the energy and conviction of New England's cultural supremacists helped
to inspire and nurture what would eventually become a broader "northern"
vision in which the northern states became synonymous with America and
the southern ones its polar opposite.[29]

A survey of the *Pennsylvania Gazette* in the years between 1778 and 1799
shows eighty-eight references by northern sources to the "southern states" as a
distinct region, but only thirteen such references by northerners to the "northern states." A close reading of these entries suggests not the weakness of any
sense of northern sectional interests, however, but an inclination simply to
conflate those interests with the interests of the nation as a whole. Even as they
linked the effort to become a "truly independent people" to "mercantile intercourse" between the northern and southern states and the "honorable dependence of the United States on one another," many northerners clearly did so
anticipating that the most profitable aspects of this interdependency would
accrue to them.[30]

Because nature itself had practically consigned the southern states to the
production of certain agricultural staples, the "eastern states may grow rich by
transporting those productions to foreign markets," one northern commentator predicted. Suggesting a vision of the South transformed from a British
colony to a northern one, a Philadelphian observed, "Should the new congress
pass suitable laws to protect American manufactures, the middle and eastern
states may become a Great Britain, with respect to arts and manufactures, to
the southern states. From them they may receive raw materials and return
them in manufactures of all kinds. By these means the ties of commerce and

interest will be added to the ties of government, to preserve a perpetual union of the States." When the "manufacturing society" of Philadelphia acquired two machines for spinning and carding cotton, local industrialists urged their southern brethren to "pay the most unremitting attention to the cultivation of COTTON, to which their soil, their climate, and the nature of their population, are all adapted."[31]

The reference to the "nature" of the southern population suggested that the good manufacturers of Philadelphia might not be unduly troubled by the thought of profiting from the labor of slaves, even though slavery was illegal in Pennsylvania itself. Meanwhile, a number of southern planters of the post-Revolutionary era insisted that slavery was an unwanted legacy of British colonialism of which they would gladly be shed if only some practicable means of doing so could be devised. Despite such protestations, however, slavery was securely fixed as an integral component of southern identity well before the cotton boom triggered by the invention of the cotton gin in 1793.[32]

Racial as well as social considerations had helped to make this so, but slavery's most tangible hold on southern whites was economic. Large slaveholdings did not translate in 1800 into the great wealth that they would represent a half century later, but all else being equal, any southerner who owned slaves was better off financially than one who did not, even if the owner, like a certain Mr. Jefferson of Monticello, was not particularly adept at managing them either as labor or as capital. Although Jefferson is recalled as one of Virginia's leading advocates of emancipation, save for his proposed Ordinance of 1784, which would have banned slavery from the western territories after 1800, he directed most of his energies against outlawing the further importation of slaves into Virginia, a move that only enhanced the value of the slaves held by planters like Jefferson himself. In 1782 when the Virginia legislature passed a law allowing private manumission of slaves, Jefferson, whose approximately 200 bondsmen and 10,000 acres of land marked him as one of the wealthiest men in the state, made no move to take advantage of the statute.[33]

Despite his allegedly poor head for figures, Jefferson clearly understood that his slaves were at least as valuable as property as they were as a source of labor. He confided to his farm manager that he considered "a woman who brings a child every two years as more profitable than the best man of the farm. What she produces is an addition to capital, while his labors disappear in mere consumption." Complaining constantly of mounting financial obligations, Jefferson refused to "willingly sell the slaves as long as there remains any prospect of paying my debts with their labor." He was "governed solely by views to their happiness," Jefferson explained, and therefore it would be "worth their while to use extraordinary exertions for some time" to enable him to put them "ultimately on easier footing . . . the moment they have paid the debts due from the estate, two-thirds of which have been contracted by purchasing them." Apparently, however, even through "extraordinary exertions" his bondsmen never succeeded in paying for themselves. In 1822, four years before his death, his slaveholdings had increased to 267. Farther South, the story was much the same. A recent survey suggests that between 1740 and 1809 slaves accounted for approximately 70 percent of the wealth in South Carolina and Georgia, with planters enjoying significant capital gains due to the rising value of their human property.[34]

Although some northerners seemed more sympathetic to those who owned slaves than to the slaves themselves, there were a number who had always found slavery troubling, and the fact that steps had been taken to abolish it in every state north of Pennsylvania by 1804 only served to set the southern states even further apart from the northern ones. It was certainly true, as one northern observer later noted, that slavery established "a very marked line of distinction between the States, which tolerate it, and those which do not." Slavery lay at the heart not just of differences in economic and social organization between North and South but of the moral, philosophical, and temperamental distinctions that allowed northern spokesmen and representatives to cast America as their society writ large—fluid, innovative, proud of its accomplishments but dedicated to self-improvement and eager to confront the future.[35]

Despite the prominent role played by southerners in rationalizing and securing American independence and in drafting the defining documents and filling the highest positions of leadership in the new nation, the slaveholding South was simply too much tied to the past, too wedded to hierarchy, and too wary of innovation and reform to make it much of a competitor as a potential role model for the new nation. In fact, some northern observers had begun to wonder if there was any place at all in their vision of American identity for such an aberrant society. By 1823 New Yorker Gerrit Smith could remark on the almost "national difference of character between the people of the Northern and the people of the Southern states" without acknowledging, as Joyce Appleby noted, "that Northerners imaginatively thought of their 'nation' as the United States, leaving the South with its peculiar institution and a particular regional culture."[36]

It is impossible to tell how many Americans would have agreed in 1823 that the distinctions between the North and the South were more on the scale of national than regional dissimilarities, but Smith's observations reflected the heightened awareness of North-South differences that had emerged in the decade following the War of 1812. Southern enthusiasm for the conflict itself had contrasted sharply with New England's opposition. It soon became apparent, however, that the war had stimulated the expansion of northern manufacturing even as its costs helped to bring on the Panic of 1819, a severe recession that pitted the debtor states of the South and West against the National Bank and the creditor states of the East. On the heels of the Panic came the conflict over the admission of Missouri to the Union as a slave state in 1820, jangling like a "firebell in the night," as Jefferson portentously described it. Two years later, news of the Denmark Vesey slave insurrection plot in Charleston rekindled the specter of Santo Domingo, bolstering northern critics who assailed the degradation and barbarity engendered by slavery, while convincing many southern slaveholders that no one in the North truly understood or could ever understand the perils and predicaments that they faced on a daily basis.[37]

The earliest attempts to explain what the new republic was all about had extolled its potential as a global showplace for democracy, justice, and human unity and happiness. As the nation's fiftieth birthday came and went, disappointment that this potential clearly remained unfulfilled, coupled with fears that it might never be, lent a greater sense of urgency to the effort to construct a satisfying and sustainable sense of the national character even as the widening North-South divide underscored the difficulties of doing so. By the 1820s seekers after the American essence struggled to construct what Appleby called a "unifying story" of national identity, without simply "characterizing the nation in a way that failed to account for the alternate ideals of the South."[38]

Some even attempted to present the contrasts between the people of the northern states and those of the southern states as a potential source of national strength and vitality. A writer for the *North American Review* boasted in 1822 that "in no one country on the face of the globe can there be found a greater variety of specific character than is at this moment developed in these United States of America." Yet he hardly struck a blow for cultural unity when he suggested to his New England readers that possibly even beyond the Hudson, but certainly beyond the Potomac, lived "a different race of men." He reaffirmed this perception when he asked if there was "any assimilation between the highminded, vainglorious Virginian, living on his plantation in baronial

state, an autocrat among his slaves, a nobleman among his peers, and the active, enterprizing [*sic*] moneygetting merchant of the East, who spends his
days in bustling activity among men and ships, and his nights in sober calculations over his ledger and day-book?"[39]

By the 1830s writers eager to explain why the inhabitants of the northern
states and those of the southern states appeared to be so different in values
and temperament had begun to seize on the idea that the people of the two
regions were simply heirs to the dramatically different class, religious, cultural, and political traditions delineated by the English Civil War. The northern states were populated, so many believed, by the descendants of the
middle-class Puritan "Roundheads" who had routed the defenders of the mon-
archy, the aristocratic Cavaliers, supposedly of Norman descent, who had then
settled in the southern states. Historian David Hackett Fischer has argued that
the "cavalier thesis" may have some validity for Virginia at least. Although some
75 percent of the colony's immigrants consisted of indentured servants and
landless whites, in the mid-seventeenth century it had served for a time as
what one contemporary observer had called "the only city of refuge left in His
Majesty's Dominions . . . for distressed cavaliers." Some of these Royalist refu-
gees had been recruited by Virginia's governor, William Berkeley, who favored
them with political office and grants of large estates, thereby positioning them
for places of political leadership and influence.[40]

Although exceptional, the example of Virginia was quickly written large.
Not only was the Cavalier legend appropriated by a number of over-proud
South Carolinians, but it even cropped up in depictions of Louisiana. By the
Civil War, southern propagandists were asserting matter-of-factly that "this
cavalier or Anglo-Norman element that had presided at the founding of the
original Southern colonies entered largely into the new populations; . . . mingling the refinement of the courtier with the energy of the pioneer." They also
credited the "Cavalier element" with "predominating in southern civilization
and giving tone to southern society and character to southern politics."[41]

The Cavalier-Puritan dichotomy also struck the fancy of numerous northern as well as foreign observers, such as Louis Philippe, who simply noted in
1835, "You have the Puritans in the North and Cavaliers in the South, Democracy with its leveling rod, and Aristocracy with slavery raising its haughty head
in the other section and creating a social elegance, a superiority of breeding
and race." The Cavalier became a familiar figure in publications like *Godey's
Lady's Book*, which featured stories of women smitten by even the mere fantasy of a Virginia man "who belongs to one of the noblest Cavalier families."[42]

John Pendleton Kennedy's 1832 novel, *Swallow Barn*, ranks as the defining literary contribution to the enduring image of a southern planter-cavalier. Set in the Virginia Tidewater, it chronicled life on "Swallow Barn," the cozy plantation kingdom of one Frank Meriwether, "a very model of landed gentlemen." Possessed of a "great vanity of manners and a genuine benevolence of disposition," Meriwether is likely to treat "any genteel stranger" in the vicinity to "a week's hospitality." All in all, Swallow Barn is "a very agreeable place," for Meriwether is "a kind master, and considerate toward his dependants [*sic*], for which reason, although he owns many slaves, they hold him in profound reverence, and are very happy under his dominion."[43]

Despite its occasionally celebratory tone, *Swallow Barn* was also gently and affectionately satiric. Frank Meriwether is well read and "a most discomfiting antagonist in the way of dates and names," though not so formidable when it comes to ideas and concepts. He is long-winded and somewhat closed-minded, and though he prides himself on being a "high-churchman," he is "only a rare frequenter of places of worship." When he is drawn (much against his will) into discussions of scripture, he has trouble distinguishing between Peter and Paul. Finally, despite his resources and his leisure, as a "thorough-bred Virginian," he seldom ventures beyond Richmond, which for him is indisputably "the centre of civilization."[44]

When he discussed Virginia's history, however, Kennedy himself largely played it straight, declaring that colonial pioneer John Smith had been, "according to the ancient laws of chivalry, . . . a Chevalier tres hardie." Virginia's colonial population, he believed, had been dominated by "gentlemen of good name and condition, who brought within the confines a solid fund of respectability and wealth." The Virginia environment had allowed for an expansion of the English spirit of liberty, and thus the Virginia planter had evolved into an even more appealing aristocrat than his ancestors. Two centuries in the Old Dominion, Kennedy concluded, had "gradually matured the sober and thinking Englishman into that spirited, imaginative being who now inhabits the lowlands of this state."[45]

In retrospect, it is easy enough to recognize *Swallow Barn* as a clever mixture of sentiment and satire, but to those less acquainted with the region or unaware of the author's intent, it served as a more literal portrait of historical and contemporary reality. The *North American Review* seemed to take Kennedy at his word in calling Meriwether "the thorough-bred Virginian." *New England Magazine* picked up on the "gentle satire" of *Swallow Barn* but nonetheless treated it as an essentially accurate "still life" portrait of the plantation South.[46]

In its first two years of publication, 1831 and 1832, *New England Magazine* also offered relatively appealing sketches of South Carolina, Virginia, and Kentucky, paying tribute to "the great number of intelligent cultivators who live on their plantations after the fashion of the old English country gentlemen" and suggesting that "a similar class would be of advantage in New England." Such sympathetic sentiments were by no means uncommon among northern observers of the South in the 1820s and 1830s. In 1828 James Fenimore Cooper ventured that, proportionately, the South had "more men who *belong to the class of what is termed the class of gentlemen*" than "any other country of the world."[47]

The allure of the Cavalier ideal for northern readers might seem surprising, especially since the southern planter's aristocratic airs and indulgences had been so repugnant to some earlier northern writers, but the surging egalitarianism of the Jacksonian era seemed to spark a certain "hankering after aristocracy," as William R. Taylor put it, among more affluent, better-educated Americans in general. Beyond that, where the early moral arbiters of New England Puritanism had thought it a good thing to aspire to better one's station in life through industry and thrift, there was growing concern about a national obsession with the accumulation of wealth by any means available. This encouraged many Americans, North and South, to regard the laid-back planter-aristocrat as an appealing symbol of a bygone era when idealism and respect for tradition had supposedly trumped the lust for money and material luxuries. In some quarters, a French visitor's observation that "a Bostonian would go in search of his fortune to the bottom of Hell," while "a Virginian would not go across the road to seek it" now seemed less flattering to the former and critical of the latter than perhaps it had in 1815. After all, the stereotypical southerner had much to offer that the stereotypical dollar-chasing Yankee did not, including "honor and integrity, indifference to money and business, a decorous concern for the amenities, and a high sense of civic and social responsibility." As Lorman Ratner put it, "living close to nature and at the same time displaying all the social graces," the planter-Cavalier appeared to be "the ideal citizen of a republic of virtue."[48]

In embracing the Cavalier legend, however, Americans concerned about the rapid democratization of political and economic influence revealed their anxieties that their country's days as "a republic of virtue" might well be numbered. In the South, where the inhabitants of the interior appeared to be wresting economic and political control from the Tidewater and the Low Country regions of Virginia and South Carolina, novelists and commentators (who hailed primarily from the older, more settled areas) often painted disturbing portraits of a society in decline. By 1851 even the Baltimorean John Pendleton Kennedy was bemoaning the fact that Virginia was losing the distinctive "mellow, bland, and sunny luxuriance of her home society," especially the "thriftless gayety of the people" and "that over-flowing hospitality which knew no ebb."[49]

In the eyes of many, the old planter-Cavaliers were doomed not just by the rise of the backcountry and the concomitant expansion of a crude upstart brand of democracy, but by their own naiveté, thriftlessness, and affinity for cards or horses or whiskey or, quite often, all three. In James Kirke Paulding's *Westward Ho!* the much admired Tidewater aristocrat Colonel Cuthbert Dangerfield lacks any sense of financial responsibility or capacity for self-discipline. He refuses even to keep books on his planting operations and has no idea how much he owes, how much he earns, or even how many acres or slaves he owns. Proclaiming himself "utterly incapacitated" for the task of managing his own affairs, he rejects assurances that "a few years of saving will set all right," explaining "I don't know how to save" and insisting that so long as he stays in that vicinity, he must continue to keep his horses and his hounds and to maintain his reputation for extravagant hospitality.[50]

Perhaps thinking of Thomas Jefferson, among others, John Randolph believed that Virginia had more than its share of these "kind hearted . . . and guileless" men "who, so long as they could command the means by sale of their last acre, or last negro, would have a good dinner, and give a hearty welcome to whomsoever chose to drag in to eat, friend or stranger, bidden or unbidden." It was just such men, Randolph contended, who had thoughtlessly surrendered Virginia's claims to its western lands with no thought to the future needs of their state.[51]

For all the expressions of sympathy for the southern gentleman who "is generous to a fault with his property, is fond of gaiety and pleasure and generally dislikes the routine of business," the perception of the planter-Cavalier as not quite up to the demands of a rapidly changing contemporary world suggested someone who, however noble, was also flawed, someone whose admirable intentions were often neutralized by ineffectual behavior. The old planters might be gracious hosts and gifted orators, but for all their talk of honor and pride, they were often of little use in a real crisis. "In disastrous periods," complained William Gilmore Simms, "they fold their arms, in stupid despair." For Simms, the hesitant and indecisive planter was but a latter-day embodiment of Shakespeare's Hamlet, "whose native hue of resolution/Was sicklied o'er by the pale cast of thought." Evoking Freudian imagery when Freud was still in knee pants, Mary Boykin Chesnut noted later in her Civil War diary, "Our planters are nice fellows, but slow to move; impulsive but hard to keep moving. They are wonderful for a spurt, but that lets out all their strength, and then they like to rest." As Taylor concluded, whatever they may have said, many southerners actually believed less in the Cavalier than "in the need for him."[52]

The same might have been said of many non-southerners as well. Although northern observers had seemed to find much to admire in him, in the long run the figure of the planter-Cavalier both reflected and reinforced what was by then an already long-standing sense of the South as not simply a distinct subset of American society, but a world and a way of life not only apart but behind. Emphasizing the exotic Caribbean flair and Europeanized culture of Charleston, a northern correspondent cautioned readers that "the Carolinian is very different from the Yankee." Instead of contenting himself with living like "a patriarch of old" the Carolina aristocrat would do well to spend "a year's residence" in New England, whose "neat villages, flourishing farms, and . . . gainful employment of machinery" simply underscored the idleness and slovenly appearance of his "own district."[53]

In an 1842 short story that appeared in *Godey's*, a northerner's trip to Savannah conveyed the impression of the last days of a crumbling Latin American colonial empire. The "mould and rust" fostered by the tropical dampness of the local climate "imparted an air of remote antiquity to its buildings," while outside the city the abandoned remains of a once-grand plantation estate sat at the intersection of several lanes lined with oaks. Draped with silvery Spanish moss, the oaks themselves seemed like "the solemn ruins of a temple of nature." For all its romance, as the rest of the nation moved ahead, the image of the planter-Cavalier presiding grandly over his semi-feudal subtropical fiefdom also symbolized not just a society rooted in the past but one sinking into stagnation and decline.[54]

Northern writers were quick to contrast southern stasis with northern dynamism. One journalist compared the small, rocky-soiled, climatically challenged but nonetheless dynamic state of Massachusetts with warm and fertile South Carolina, which was "now growing old and poor, . . . deficient in roads . . . and almost wholly destitute of the local markets of towns and factories necessary to support in prosperity her farmers." There was also Virginia, "at once old and yet undeveloped," with little to commend it save "that ancestral pride, which the children of broken down families retain to the last, when every other relic of greatness has departed."[55]

As Susan-Mary Grant has noted, "the image of the South as a land of decaying splendor was typical by the 1840s." Even as many northerners had been caught up in the myth of the planter-Cavalier, the previous decade had also brought a steadily intensifying and expanding chorus of northern antislavery rhetoric, and in the future it would be much more difficult for other Americans to ignore the link between slavery and southern backwardness. As one proceeded southward, Gouvernor Morris of Pennsylvania had charged at the Constitutional Convention in 1787, "every step you take thro' ye. great region of slaves presents a desert increasing, with ye increasing proportion of these wretched beings." In reality, however, Morris was less directly concerned with the condition of these "wretched beings" than his words might indicate. Under the plan of counting each bondsman as three-fifths of a person for purposes of apportioning congressional seats, Morris complained, the southerners who enslaved them, "in defiance of the most sacred laws of humanity," would benefit from it politically at the expense of "the Citizen of Pa. or N. Jersey who views with a laudable horror, so nefarious a practice."[56]

Early northern commentators on southern deficiencies had often tempered their critical remarks with expressions of sympathy for the gracious, kindly planter-Cavalier victimized by his own admirable, though archaic, personal values and what Bishop Benjamin H. Whipple called the crippling "incubus of slavery." However, even those who portrayed the planter as a victim rather than a victimizer believed that being a master over slaves had imbued him with some less than admirable qualities, not the least of them being laziness. The touring Frenchman who in 1810 had found southerners "heedless and lazy" had explained that their "trade is entirely given up to foreigners, and agriculture abandoned to the slaves, whilst the proprietor, under the stately name of planter, attends to nothing but his pleasures."[57]

In the widely read chronicles of his travels in the South during the 1850s, Frederick Law Olmsted pointed to the white southerner's dislike of labor as "the grand distinction between him and the Northerner," who "finds his happiness in doing." The southerner's aversion to exertion meant that "he has much less curiosity than the Northerner, less originating genius, less inventive talent, less patient and preserving energy." All of this resulted, Olmsted concluded, from the southern planter's habit of "habitually leaving all matters not either of grand and exciting importance, or of immediate consequence to his comfort, to his slaves."[58]

Slavery weakened the planter not only by freeing him from labor but by tempting him to immoral and abusive behavior. Ralph Waldo Emerson had been inclined initially to see the planter as a victim whose "misfortune is at least as great as his sin," but his mounting outrage over slavery led him ultimately to denounce the slaveholder as "a spoiled child of his unnatural habits," dominated by the "love of power, the voluptuousness of holding a being in his absolute control." Elsewhere, because its plantations were "little less than Negro harems," the *New York Tribune* insisted, the South was "a perfect puddle of amalgamation."[59]

Not all this amalgamation was sexual. Northern and foreign travelers in the antebellum South remarked frequently and often critically on the amount of time young white southerners spent in the care and company of blacks. Meant to instill wisdom and moral virtue, slave folk tales were a vital part of the informal education of both white and slave children and helped to establish what became the vaunted southern storytelling tradition. Likewise, African belief in the spirituality of the natural environment reinforced white southerners' reverence for certain familiar places. Other influences, such as foodways and speech patterns, are even more obvious in retrospect. Utilizing previously unpublished narratives of former slaves compiled by the WPA in the 1930s, scholars have now managed to provide important insights into slavery as it was actually experienced by the slaves themselves. This has been a development of only the last thirty years or so, however. At the middle of the nineteenth century, the slave perspective on slavery was available only in a scattering of accounts of former slaves. These were generally published at the urging or with the support of northern abolitionists who reasoned that the most compelling indictments of the system seen increasingly as the centerpiece of southern life would come from those who had experienced it firsthand. These narratives of escaped slaves revealed that, for all the romantic portraits drawn by southern whites, plantation life consisted of little but unrelenting toil and suffering for blacks.[60]

As a former slave, Frederick Douglass was "utterly astonished" by travelers' accounts that interpreted slave singing as "evidence of their contentment and happiness." He found it "impossible to conceive of a greater mistake. Slaves sing most when they are most unhappy. The songs of the slave represent the sorrow of his heart; and he is relieved by them only as an aching heart is relieved by its tears." When slaves did manifest genuine signs of merriment, Douglass added, "It only proves to my mind that though slavery is armed with a thousand stings, it is not able entirely to kill the elastic spirit of the bondman."[61]

During the year he had been hired out to "Mr. Covey," Douglass himself received an average of one whipping a week for the first six months, as he was made to drink "the bitterest dregs of slavery," working day and night in "all weathers. It was never too hot or too cold, it could never rain, blow, hail, or snow too hard for us to work in the field." Covey was able to buy but one slave, and he freely admitted that he had purchased a woman "for a *breeder*." Having already given birth to a child, she had proven her fertility, and thus found herself chained each night to one of Covey's hired male slaves for an entire year, at the end of which she gave birth to twins, delighting her owner with this "addition to his wealth."[62]

Offering another view of the sexual exploitation of slave women, in an 1853 letter to the *New York Tribune*, Harriet Jacobs told not only of her own two children, sold away "at the early ages of two and four years old," but the tragic tale of her sister, who at age fourteen had fallen prey to her mistress's new husband. When the girl's mother tried to intervene, he had her jailed and threatened to sell her unless her daughter yielded to his advances. To save her mother, Jacobs's sister relented, bearing two children whose resemblance to their father eventually aroused the jealousy of her mistress, which, in turn, led to the poor woman and her children being sold away. Once they were gone, the lord of the household had then simply turned his attention to another fourteen-year-old slave girl, "for the slaveholder seldom takes a white mistress, for she is an expensive commodity, not as submissive . . . more apt to be tyrannical; and when his passion seeks another object, he must leave her. . . . But not so with the poor slave victim, that he has robbed of everything that can make life desirable; she must be torn from the little that is left to bind her to life, and sold by her seducer and master, caring not where, so that it puts him in possession of enough to purchase another victim."[63]

Escaped slaves also exposed the hypocrisy behind the professed piety of many slaveowners. John Brown recalled a Jones County, Georgia, planter who was also a Methodist minister. Yet, he was quick and merciless with the whip, gave his slaves no meat, and never fed them at all until noon and then not again before nine in the evening. "He was reputed to be a very bad master," Brown observed sarcastically, but "a good preacher."[64]

The bitter pain of separation when family members were sold was also a recurrent theme in these accounts. Charles Ball's mother was sold to one slave trader and his siblings to another, while he and his father were kept on separate plantations in Calvert County, Maryland. He never forgot the day when he was taken from his mother, who pleaded piteously for his new master to buy her and her other children until her new owner snatched Charles from her arms and proceeded to whip her and drag her away. "Young as I was," Ball recalled fifty years later, "the horrors of that day sank deeply into my heart, and even at this time . . . the terrors of the scene return with painful vividness upon my memory." Angry white southerners charged, sometimes correctly, that such ostensibly firsthand accounts were either fabrications or had been carefully edited by radical abolitionists to reflect more negatively on slavery, but the vehemence of their responses was, in many cases, quite likely a reflection of how closely to home these narratives actually hit.[65]

Ironically, the portrait of slavery that seemed to hit closest to home was a work of fiction by a white author, Harriet Beecher Stowe's *Uncle Tom's Cabin*, which appeared in 1852, and as Taylor observed, "probably did more than any other book ever published to alter the American image of the South." No mere abolitionist propaganda tract, Stowe's novel was actually quite complex. She insisted that her aim was not to inflame northern opinion against the South so much as to convince southerners themselves that slavery was cruel and unjust. Accordingly, Stowe's treatments of many of the principal white characters in her story sometimes seemed as sympathetic and romanticized as anything any white southerner might have written. Stowe's depictions of the physical environment evoked the familiar Latin American image of the South as what Joseph Conforti called "an exotic, semitropical land of moral laxity and indulgence." She contrasted the typical New England farm house with its "clean-swept grassy yard" and "air of order and stillness" and its rooms where "everything is once and forever rigidly in place" to Louisianan Augustine St. Clare's "ancient mansion built in that odd mixture of Spanish and French style . . . in the Moorish fashion" with its "voluptuous" almost jungle-like courtyard overgrown with fragrant trees and blossoming shrubbery.[66]

Likewise, "Miss Ophelia," the New England cousin of the happy-go-lucky, indecisive St. Clare, is his temperamental counterpoint, "a living impersonation of order, method, and exactness." Miss Ophelia's parents had been sorely troubled by her plans to journey to the foreign, foreboding South, her mother declaring her sojourn to Louisiana "equal to going to the Sandwich Islands, or anywhere among the heathen," and, indeed, Miss Ophelia herself finds St. Clare's place "rather old and heathenish."[67]

Even New Englanders could be corrupted by slavery, however. Stowe's villain, Simon Legree, is originally from Vermont, and Stowe held nothing back in her portrayal of him as a brutal, rapacious, sexually predatory polar opposite of Tom's previous owners. Legree's house is likewise the antithesis of the stereotypically warm and inviting plantation house. Littered, barren, decaying, its walls decorated only by Legree's obsessive financial calculations, it is more occupied than lived in by Legree and his mulatto mistresses.

Vermont was the first New England state to ban slavery, and northerners concerned about its expansion saw a sobering message in a Vermonter's apparent seduction by this despicable southern institution. However, Legree had been reduced to his degraded state not by the exotic allure of slaveholding so much as by the same greed that fueled modern capitalism but was supposedly anathema to the typical slaveowner. In fact, Stowe's critique proved so devastating because it stripped the slaveholding system of its genteel, anti-capitalist pretensions and revealed it as little different from the northern factory system where a brutally imposed productivity was often an absolute necessity for survival.

Stowe's novel showed that even the oft-invoked kind, indulgent, and impractical master who was supposedly indifferent if not hostile to considerations of monetary gain was not immune in the least to the raw dollars-and-cents realities of slavery and the slave trade. George Shelby, the son of the debt-ridden first master who has just sold Tom, tells the slave trader who bought him, "I should think you'd be ashamed to spend all of your life buying men and women and chaining them like cattle." Rejecting this high-minded rebuke, the trader retorts, "So long as your grand folks wants to buy men and women, I am as good as they is . . . 'tant any meaner sellin' on em than 'tis buyin'."[68]

Regardless of how honorable and decent their owners might be, poorly managed plantations were doomed to fail, and for their enslaved workers, who were, after all, only "so many *things* belonging to a master," there were no guarantees against falling into the hands of ruthless men like Simon Legree. For the slaves, the kindness of today's master offered no protection against the brutality of tomorrow's. Tom's second owner, the sympathetic and kindly St. Clare, is stabbed to death before he can fulfill his promise to his dying daughter, "Little Eva," to set Tom free. In the wake of her husband's death, the pampered and selfish Marie St. Clare wastes no time in selling Tom, who then becomes the property of Legree.[69]

When George Shelby finally comes to buy Tom back, he arrives just in time to witness his faithful former slave's death from multiple beatings at the hands of Legree and his drivers. Enraged, he threatens to "go to the very first magistrate and expose you," but Legree only mocks him and dares him to do so. At once, Shelby sees "the force of his defiance," for "there was not a white person on the place, and in all southern courts, the testimony of colored blood is nothing." Earlier, commenting on a slave woman who was whipped to death, St. Clare observes, "It's commonly supposed that the property interest is a sufficient guard in these cases. If people choose to ruin their own possessions, I don't know what's to be done." In her "concluding remarks" to the novel, Stowe asked what the response would be if "the laws of New England were so arranged that a master could *now and then* torture an apprentice to death."[70]

In *Uncle Tom's Cabin*, Stowe broke new ground by having her black characters express their feelings about slavery, and in doing so, she confronted southern whites with the reality that their slaves might indeed feel kindly toward them and still yearn passionately to be free. When St. Clare asks Tom if he doesn't feel that he has been better off being the slave of a kind master than to have been free, Tom responds without hesitation: "No *indeed*, Mas'r St. Clare. . . . Mas'r's been too good; but . . . I'd rather have poor clothes, poor house, poor everything, and have them *mine*, than to have the best, and have them any man's else."[71]

Several commentators have noted that Tom showed quiet strength but few "aggressive male traits" when, in the words of one commentator, he is "forced to deal with the grasping realities of the dominant patriarchy." In fact, his piety, sensitivity, loyalty, and stoic acceptance of the "brutality and oppression" that he endures personally make him seem, by traditional mid-nineteenth-century gender expectations, like a female character.[72]

Clearly, Stowe's portrait of slavery bore heavily on southern women. Nearly a decade after the book was published, Mary Boykin Chesnut and her companions in Richmond still wondered, "Are our men worse than the others? Does Mrs. Stowe know? You know what I mean?" As the discussion turned to miscegenation, one participant noted that at least by making Legree a bachelor, "Mrs. Stowe did not hit the sorest spot." Proclaiming her own hatred for slavery, Chesnut sketched a hypothetical planter as "a magnate who runs a hideous black harem with its consequences under the same roof with his lovely white wife, and his beautiful and accomplished daughters. . . . He holds his head as high and poses as the model of all human virtues to these poor women. . . . From the height of his awful majesty, he scolds and thunders at them, as if he never did anything wrong in his life." One of Chesnut's friends knew of such a planter whose wife and daughters "play their parts of unsuspecting angels to the hilt" and "profess to adore their father as the model of all earthy goodness." Another added cynically, "Well, yes. If he is rich, he is the fountain from which all blessings flow."[73]

It is important to note that these comments were offered for the benefit of Mary Chesnut's tight circle of intimate female friends only. Public admissions that northern criticisms of southern slave society might have some validity would have been rare indeed among most white southerners long before 1861. As a group, southern leaders had been slower than their New England counterparts to adopt a profoundly sectionalist posture. However, the hostile northern reaction to South Carolina's move to nullify the Tariffs of 1828 and 1832 and the rising clamor after 1830 for the abolition or geographic restriction of slavery forced many southerners to acknowledge for the first time that their values and priorities might be fundamentally at odds with those of other Americans. There was also what Charles S. Sydnor called an expanding and increasingly bitter conviction among them "that their interests were seldom respected by the rest of the nation and that the fabric of their way of life was being destroyed." Aware of their exclusion from the northernized vision of American identity, but unwilling to abandon slavery and the culture and lifestyle it sustained, white southerners would only grow progressively more defensive and hostile. Turning inward upon themselves, they would withdraw into the same idyllic "dream world" of the southern plantation fantasy that many of them had earlier viewed with skepticism and reserve, demanding, as Sydnor put it, that "others accept their castle in the sky as an accurate description of conditions in the South."[74]

2

The South Becomes a Cause

MANY NORTHERNERS had seemed to find the romantic legend of the planter-Cavalier a pleasurable escape from the disconcerting tumult of Jacksonian Era popular politics and other potentially destabilizing encroachments of modernity on their own lives. By the middle of the nineteenth century, however, ardor for the southern fantasy had waned considerably (for the time being at least) among whites in the North, giving way to a vision of the South as not merely a benign aberration from the American norm but an invasive, potentially mortal threat to the nation's health and progress.

As early as 1837, abolitionist Angelina E. Grimké, who had long since abandoned her native Charleston, had seen the sexual licentiousness bred by slavery exerting "a wide and destructive influence on Northern character . . ." and "corrupting the very heart's blood of the nation." By the 1850s a growing number of northern critics saw slavery and the slaveholding South in general as both a smudge on the nation's character and a serious challenge to the northern-inspired national ideals of progress and self-improvement. In fact, the early effort to illuminate southern shortcomings in order to demonstrate that New England should serve as the model for national identity had evolved by the 1850s into what Susan-Mary Grant has called a broader "northern nationalism," also "predicated on opposition to the South" in order to "define and defend a specifically northern ideology that in time, many hoped, would become truly national."[1]

In the view of one northern editor, the absence of "enlightened enterprise" and the "enervating influence of Slavery" had not only impoverished southerners spiritually but had also "stripped them of almost all of the distinguishing traits of the American identity." When Ralph Waldo Emerson's friend Samuel Hoar was expelled from South Carolina after investigating the alleged seizure of free negroes from Massachusetts on ships in southern harbors, Emerson scoffed that the Palmetto State was to America what Algiers was to Turkey, Calabria to Naples, or Alsatia to London—"We must go there in disguise with pistols in our pockets, leaving our pocketbooks at home, making our wills before we go."[2]

In reality, however, the South's differences with America were defined largely in terms of its differences with the North. The leaders of the South seemed "like dwarfs by the side of the giants of the North," one editor declared. Others sometimes lapsed into using "the North" and "the United States" interchangeably, and the *Massachusetts Quarterly Review* simply declared that the North was primarily responsible for the nation's growth and success. Moreover, its people alone embodied "the American sentiment, the American idea" and had "the spirit of the nation on their side." Despite such celebrations of northern superiority, after the Kansas-Nebraska Act reopened the prospect of slavery north of 36° 30' in 1854 and the Dred Scott decision banned the exclusion of slaveholding from the territories in 1857, the Scottish traveler James Stirling could not help wondering, "With a minority of states, with less than a third of the white population, how is it that the South has managed to appropriate to herself so large a share of official influence and executive power?"[3]

Northern leaders had been asking themselves the same question for some time. As early as 1801, one resentful federalist had seen "a spirit of domination ingrafted on the Southern people," and others were soon urging their compatriots to "resist the encroachments of Southern despotism." Josiah Quincy had charged in 1804 that the country was run by a southern planter elite, and by 1856 he was insisting that John Quincy Adams was the only president since 1800 who had not been subject to their influence. Not only had a southern slaveholder occupied the White House for more than two-thirds of the nation's history, but southerners had enjoyed a comparable advantage as speakers of the House and presidents pro tem of the Senate, while the Supreme Court had always had a southern majority.[4]

By the 1850s northern politicians were charging that through its efforts to thwart the ambitions of the other states, an entrenched "Slave Power Conspiracy" was actually threatening the future of the entire nation. A leading proponent of the Slave Power thesis, William H. Seward cited everything from the three-fifths compromise to the wars to secure Florida, the Louisiana Territory, Texas, and the Southwest for slavery expansion, to southern designs on Cuba and Central America as proof of his point. Speaking for the "great states of the North," the *New York Times* warned in 1857 that "the feeling is growing deeper in the northern heart with every passing year, that our character, our prosperity, and our destiny are most seriously involved in the question of the separation or extinction of slavery."[5]

The best means of curbing the influence of the Slave Power South seemed to lie in forging the popular and numerical majorities enjoyed by the free states into a unified, politically cohesive "North." While the southern and northeastern states had still shown some notable similarities in 1800, over the first half of the nineteenth century the latter had become significantly more urban and industrial and their leaders increasingly averse to the expansion of slavery. Meanwhile, as the South and the Northeast grew apart, the emerging midwestern states gravitated toward the economic and political orbit of the latter, finding markets for the products of their farms in the great cities of the East while providing attractive outlets for the East's industrial products, surplus investment capital, and rapidly expanding populations.

Throughout his long political career, New England's eloquent champion Daniel Webster had, as Merle Curti wrote, "cleverly associated national interest with all the policies which his opponents declared to be sectional in character—tariffs, internal improvements . . . and restriction of the disposal of public lands in the West." In September 1848, however, reflecting on the formation of the "Free Soil" party by northerners opposed to the expansion of slavery and on the heated congressional debates on the same question, Webster spoke openly and hopefully of the potential emergence of "a North." By this, he meant a northeastern-midwestern alliance "strong in opinion and united against slavery."[6]

Historian Larry Gara has argued that Webster got his wish with the rise of "a self-conscious North" after the 1848 election. Others thought the political North coalesced a few years later when passage of the Kansas-Nebraska Act triggered widespread alarm and outrage among northerners opposed to the expansion of slavery. In June 1854 the *Springfield Republican* exulted that "a determination that henceforth there shall be a North" had "sprung up through the Northern states." Noting the strikingly concentrated northern support for the defeated John C. Fremont in 1856, one editorialist consoled his readers with the thought that although the Republicans had not elected a president, "they have what is better, a North."[7]

In the wake of Abraham Lincoln's election in 1860, secessionists like Georgia's Henry L. Benning would charge that "the . . . Republican party has now become the North." Certainly, the emergence of a North was at once cause and effect of the rise of the Republican party, which both drew on and orchestrated what Susan-Mary Grant called "a distinct antisouthernism." The Republicans' "stock-in-trade," as Richards observed, consisted of attacking the arrogant planter elite presiding over the southern Slave Power conspiracy. Because their

party was, as David Potter put it, "totally sectional in its constituency," Republican leaders had little incentive to cultivate southern voters, especially when attacks on the smug, self-serving southern slavocracy were so crucial to their efforts to forge their northern constituency into an energized and united whole. "The creation of such a powerful enemy," Grant observed, "lent cohesion to the conglomerate of disparate forces that composed northern society" and "gave northerners a focus for their fears and a scapegoat for their problems."[8]

The Republicans may well have come together to defend the North from the southern Slave Power conspiracy, but party strategists quickly decided that with the North's electoral and congressional majorities unified behind them, they must take the offensive. In order to secure northern influence (and thereby further the aims and interests of the nation as well), the South must be "northernized." As early as 1845 Seward was arguing that it should be left up to "the free and vigorous North and West to work out the welfare of the country and drag the reluctant South up to participate in the same glorious destinies." It was "the inevitable destiny of the South to be molded by the North," a northern writer boasted in 1849, and three years later a Cincinnati journalist called for "the introduction upon Southern territory of the Northern system of life." Such presumptuousness prompted one southerner to observe that northerners appeared to feel that "the landmarks of 'Mason and Dixon'" were "the very outposts of all civilization and progress." Another warned that there was "one ideal of Southern character, and another of Northern" and suggested that "the peculiar institution" was one of but very few barriers "that prevent us from becoming completely Yankeefied."[9]

As Eric Foner wrote, there was no doubt that many Republicans believed the South was "an alien and threatening society whose values and interests were in fundamental conflict with those of the North" or that what Foner called the "Republican critique of the South" was essentially a northern critique of the South. David Potter has argued that the rhetoric of American nationalism came easily to Republican lips because, with a growing majority behind them, they realized that northern sectional interests would soon be dominant within the Union. Thus, northerners could "support the Union for sectional reasons," while southerners clearly could not. Conflating northern interests with national interests, Republican leaders held that "The whole mentality and flavor of southern life" was not only "antithetical to the North," but with its decadence, indolence, and devotion to slavery, it was also, as Foner put it, "an intolerable hindrance to national achievement."[10]

Owing to the steady westward migration of New Englanders, on the eve of the war one observer noted that "almost every free state has its New England within its border." Not only did these New England expatriate outposts become the locus of early Republican zeal in the Midwest, but the overall Republican plan for rigidly prescribed social, moral, and economic reform of the South gave off more than a whiff of what Robert Kelley called a "revitalized New England imperialism." The same was true of Republican designs abroad. The United States, Seward believed, had a mission "to renovate the condition of mankind" by spreading its "experiment in self-government" throughout the world, and he and other Republican leaders insisted that only by accepting "the superiority of the political, social and economic institutions of the North" could the nation hope to prove "that democratic institutions were self-sustaining." In particular, Foner argued, Republicans like Seward saw their crusade against slavery "as one part of a world-wide movement from absolutism to democracy, aristocracy to equality, backwardness to modernity, and their conviction that the struggle in the United States had international implications did much to strengthen their resolve."[11]

The Republican depiction of where the South stood in relation to the rest of the world and the rest of the nation in 1860 was adopted by many postbellum historians at least in part because it helped them make sense of the origins, course, and outcome of the Civil War. Eric J. Hobsbawm maintained that because "the overwhelming consensus of bourgeois liberalism" saw slave societies "as contrary to history's march, morally undesirable, and economically inefficient," the "currents of history ran dead against" the South. Yet at the height of the antebellum English textile boom, as Barrington Moore, Jr., has argued, "the plantation operated by slavery was no anachronistic excrescence on industrial capitalism," but "an integral part of this system and one of its prime motors in the world at large." By the 1820s the South had become the world's premier supplier of cotton, and by the late antebellum period, more than three-fourths of its cotton was being exported. Not only was cotton the leading American export in the antebellum period, but when cotton was combined with the two other leading southern staples, tobacco and rice, the South, with just over a third of the nation's population (free and slave), accounted for well over half of the value of American exports during the 1850s.[12]

The South's prominent position in the world economy not only encouraged southern leaders to oppose the protective tariff and other measures disadvantageous to the export trade, but it reinforced their predispositions toward a belief in southern superiority or even invincibility. When he proclaimed in 1858 that "Cotton is King" and "No power on earth dares to make war on it," South Carolina's James Henry Hammond actually sounded fairly moderate in comparison to another southerner who insisted that without southern cotton "England would topple headlong and carry the whole civilized world with her, save the South." Such assertions may seem altogether ludicrous in retrospect, but at the peak of England's textile expansion, the loss of southern cotton, which then accounted for nearly 80 percent of its cotton imports, would obviously have smarted quite a bit.[13]

The problem for the King Cotton cohort was that, even as Hammond was making his coronation speech, the English textile boom was not only past its peak but drawing to an end. Whether a continuation of strong British demand for cotton would have spurred northern marketers and processors to be more aggressive in seeking a compromise with the South or helped to bring the much-yearned-for British recognition of the Confederacy is a matter of pure conjecture. Then again, so is the presumption of slavery's imminent obsolescence in the Western world. The adaptability of other rigidly hierarchical and undemocratic social and political systems to a host of economic and technological innovations should remind us that, although the "currents of history" may well have run "dead against" the slave South, the speed of those currents and the size of the swath they cut has proven anything but constant across time and space.[14]

The antebellum South's actual standing in relation to the rest of the United States is also open to interpretation. Between 1800 and 1860, the portion of the labor force engaged in agriculture had dropped from 70 to 40 percent in the North while holding constant at 80 percent in the South, and on the eve of the Civil War, both New York and Pennsylvania each accounted for more than twice the manufactured goods produced by all of the soon-to-be Confederate states combined. Although its manufacturing sector seemed far less anemic when compared to the Northwest, or even Continental Europe, the South's economy lacked diversity because, as one observer put it, "to sell cotton in order to buy negroes—to make more cotton to buy more negroes, 'ad infinitum' is the aim and direct tendency of all operations of the thoroughgoing cotton planter."[15]

This concentration of investment in slaves explained why planters owned only 12 percent of southern manufacturing stock in 1860 even though the profits of southern manufacturers exceeded the national mean in both 1850 and 1860, averaging an estimated 26 percent profit in the latter year. Although the general reluctance of southern slaveholders to move more of their capital into the manufacturing sector may have reflected some apprehension about the social and political consequences of industrialization, it just as likely revealed a simple preference for plantation agriculture, not merely as a lifestyle choice but as a stable as well as socially appropriate means of making a comfortable living. Not only were planters averaging an estimated 10 percent return per annum, but during the 1850s, as Gavin Wright has pointed out, "the capital gains from rising slave prices [alone] were sufficient to make financial successes of all but the most incompetent slaveholders." The investment behavior of southern planters may seem conservative by the standards of our own day, but it was nonetheless far too remunerative to constitute proof of either a "backward" or a "pre-capitalist" economic mind-set. After all, again thanks in part to the soaring slave prices of the 1850s, on the eve of the Civil War, large-scale southern slaveholders accounted for some 60 percent of the nation's richest men.[16]

Here again, filtering one's retrospective on the antebellum South through the outcome of the Civil War can be risky. The fact that the relative absence of heavy industry crippled the southern war effort from the start may well indicate that overzealous secessionists were foolish to goad their so obviously overmatched fellow southerners into a war with a nascent industrial Goliath. Still, southern planters can hardly be faulted for failing to predicate their investment behavior over several generations on the possibility that they might one day go to war against their countrymen. After all, a great many of the North's factories had been constructed not to provide war readiness but to process southern cotton.[17]

By no means were all the differences between North and South economic. Approximately 17 percent of the South's free adult population was illiterate in 1860, in contrast to only 6 percent in the North. Compared to the North, the South was similarly deficient in newspapers, magazines, and other publications, as well as voluntary associations and similar indicators of widespread civic involvement. Beyond these were what Edward Pessen called "profound differences" in "climate, diet, work habits, uses of leisure, speech and diction, health and disease, mood habits, morals, [and] self-image . . . [and] labor systems."[18]

Bertram Wyatt-Brown has argued that perhaps the most crucial difference between North and South was not reflected in economic or social statistics but in the white South's retention of a masculine behavioral code rooted in an older European tradition of "honor" in which a man's actions must be "ratified by community consensus." In the North, where "honor" simply referred to "domestic and civic virtue," the Puritan emphasis on individual conscience and guilt was a primary influence on personal conduct. In the South, however, a more "primal," communally derived concept of honor provided the "keystone in the arch of social order," and the white male's power, prestige, and reputation for manliness in the eyes of others were the crucial influences on his behavior. Ultimately, Wyatt-Brown concluded, "it was this discrepancy between one section devoted to conscience and to secular economic concerns and the other to honor and to persistent community sanctions" that led white southerners "to calculate the value of union when their claims to respect were met in the North with skepticism, condescension, and finally, contempt."[19]

Regardless of whether the behavior patterns Wyatt-Brown cited were quite as peculiarly southern as he suggested, Pessen was surely safe in arguing that the North and the South did not go to war primarily as a result of the "differences in their cultures and institutions." Rather than nonacquisitive gentlemen of leisure with little concern for wealth, profits, and losses, like their northern adversaries, southern planters "depended heavily on outside trade, participated enthusiastically in a money economy and sought continuously to expand their operations and their capital." Yet, because for white southerners expanding both "their operations and their capital" meant acquiring more slaves, they were determined to secure slavery's economic and political future. Meanwhile northern whites (as represented by the Republican party) moved to curb what they saw as the slave South's inordinate political influence and prevent it from interfering with the settlement of the new states by the free farmers, artisans, and laborers who would supply the foodstuffs and provide the markets for the industrial cities of the Northeast. (Here again, the Republican party's socioeconomic blueprint for the emerging free states was based on the New England model as well.) In the end, Pessen concluded, two "relatively rich, powerful, aggressive and assertive communities" came to blows primarily because they believed their "inevitably opposed but similarly selfish interests" could not be reconciled within the Union.[20]

Still, their increasingly heated disagreements over the intractable, emotionally charged issue of slavery seemed to lead many southerners and northerners to exaggerate their other cultural and institutional differences to the point of concluding that, as one southerner put it, "they cannot longer exist under the same government." Unwilling to embrace the northernized "values of the nation at large," as William R. Taylor explained, southern whites had simply proceeded "to invent others, . . . which had even less relevance to the Southern situation." As they observed efforts to make the interests of the North seem synonymous with those of the entire nation, white southerners not only developed a greater sense of their own distinctiveness, but they even managed, as Taylor put it, "to reshape this acknowledged difference into a claim of superiority."[21]

Architects of new group identities typically base their claims to distinctiveness and superiority on the vision of a glorious communal past. The more venerable that past, the better, for it is usually harder to exalt events and deeds that can actually be recalled clearly than those that must simply be imagined. Going into the struggle for independence, leaders of the American colonies had little in the way of such a peculiar past on which to draw because they could not dig very far into their history without exposing a common historical taproot with the people from whom they now wished to separate. In the case of the antebellum South, too little time had elapsed by the 1850s to afford much in the way of a regional past distinctly apart from the national one, but otherwise, all of human history, Great Britain's included, was fair game. With no suitable contemporary role models available to them, the architects of a separate and superior southern identity simply looked back, as Jack Greene put it, to "an idealized version of the sharply stratified patronage societies that had characterized early modern Europe and, southerners liked to emphasize, many of the great civilizations of antiquity."[22]

Rollin G. Osterweis explained that "the cult of Greece" had been an important component in European romanticism, and it also flourished in the minds of southern intellectuals who, seeking a respectable precedent for "the establishment of a free state based on a slave proletariat," seized on the example of Periclean Athens. Not only did ancient Greece provide a useful model of a slave society that developed a refined and thoughtful landed class, but its great philosopher Aristotle had placed slavery within a natural human hierarchy, where some would dominate and some would remain in perpetual subjection. The South's spiritual kinship with ancient Greece became a pet theme of orators and politicians like John C. Calhoun, some of whom, as Caroline Winterer put it, "cast the North as an overweening Sparta to the South's more democratic Athens," while others made the North play "a licentious Athens to the South's more socially conservative Sparta."[23]

This reverence for Greek antiquity also revealed itself in the emergence and spread of "Greek Revival" architecture, reflected in both public buildings and private dwellings. As some historians saw it, the Greek Revival movement in the South produced a "nationalistic architecture" whose imposing columns suggested "a paternalistic and chivalrous society, aristocratic rule, and hierarchical rigidity" and made "virile collective statements about southern cultural and economic attainment." The Greek model drew praise not only in the South but throughout the nation from the opponents of an emergent modernity seen as tilting America toward materialism and mobocracy. It held special significance, of course, for whites in a rural slave society who saw themselves facing the determined onslaughts of an insidiously modern, free-labor North.[24]

In the final analysis, however, as Osterweis observed, "The Southern ideal was the belted knight, not the Athenian in toga and sandals." A tiny kernel of truth that quickly sprouted into a popular legend, the notion that white southerners were descended from the Norman barons through the English Cavaliers rather than the Puritan Roundheads who had settled the North had first gained currency in the 1830s. It was beside the point, of course, that outside Virginia, few southerners could show evidence of Cavalier descent or that perhaps even fewer Cavaliers could have legitimately claimed Norman descent. Under the steadily rising pressures generated by escalating sectional tensions, by the 1850s the Cavalier legend had become for more literate and affluent white southerners what James McPherson called "the central myth of Southern ethnic nationalism."[25]

As early as 1835, Louis Phillipe had warned that the Puritan-Cavalier polarity meant that Americans "as a people, have conflicting interests and ambitions and unappeasable jealousies." Two years later another writer warned, "there can be no true affinity between the Roundhead and the Cavalier," and shortly thereafter, another referred to the "far-descended antipathy between the Round-head and the Cavalier."[26]

James Kirke Paulding had anticipated the danger posed by such conflicting ideologies and temperaments in his 1844 novel, *The Puritan and His Daughter,* which spun the tale of Virginia Cavalier Hugh Tyringham and his Puritan neighbor, Harold Harbingdon. "Seldom have two men been brought together into close contact with more points of dissimilarity," Paulding wrote, as he contrasted Harbingdon's "stiff sobriety, colloquial precision and staid abstinence," so cold that it would "take ten summers in Virginia to thaw him out," with Tyringham's "frank speech and manners" and "the convivial habits of the cavalier." As the story unfolds, the intense mutual antipathy between Tyringham and Harbingdon very nearly leads to the deaths of Tyringham's son and Harbingdon's daughter before the couple ultimately strikes a symbolic blow for tolerance by becoming man and wife.[27]

For some, however, the "antithesis between the Puritan and the Cavalier" was the substance as well as the symbol of "the utter incompatibility of the civilizations of the two sections." The differences between Puritan and Cavalier and, therefore, North and South, had become not simply a matter of region, class, or culture but of race. When J. Quitman Moore listed "the five fundamental facts" that distinguished "Southern civilization," he placed "the Norman race" first, ahead of "domestic servitude, agricultural occupation, tropical climate and staple production." Not only were the high-born Cavaliers of the South clearly superior to the Puritan commoners of the North, but, so Moore claimed, "Among the races descended from the great Caucasian stock, the Norman is the august head and central representative power." Elsewhere, a "distinguished gentleman of Alabama" assured readers of the *Southern Literary Messenger* that the South had been settled and governed by "persons belonging to the blood and race of the royal family . . . a race distinguished in its earliest history for its warlike and fearless character, a race in all times since renowned for its gallantry, chivalry, gentleness and intellect."[28]

Not all the proponents of the Puritan-Cavalier polarity as a matter of race were southerners. Unitarian clergyman John Gorham Palfrey turned the southern version of the Puritan-Cavalier legend on its head, insisting that it was the "Roundhead founders of Massachusetts" who represented the true "noble and gentle blood of England." The "Anglo-Saxon race" that had settled the North was "farther advanced in civilization, more enterprising and persevering, with more science and art, with more skill and capital," while the southern Cavaliers were "poor gentlemen, broken tradesmen, rakes and libertines, footmen, and such others as were much fitter to spoil and ruin a Commonwealth than to help to raise or maintain one."[29]

At the middle of the nineteenth century, "race" and "nation" were often used synonymously, and the belief that their ethnic ancestry was distinct from and superior to that of their Yankee antagonists led some upper-class southerners to speak interchangeably of themselves as both. A Virginian asserted in 1863 that "the Saxonized maw-worms creeping from the Mayflower . . . have [no] right to kinship with the whole-souled Norman British planters of a gallant race." From such sentiments it was not such a great leap to a

Louisianan's insistence that the Civil War was "a war of *Nationalities* . . . a war of alien races . . . Cavalier and Roundhead no longer designate parties, but *nations*, whose separate foundations were laid on the Plymouth Rock and the banks of the James River."[30]

In addition to mounting sectional tensions, the zeal of the southern upper classes for the Cavalier legend had also been stoked by the enormously popular writings of Sir Walter Scott, especially his 1820 novel *Ivanhoe*. Scott's Waverly novels presented Scotland's struggles against English oppression in a way that seemed to evoke the South's struggles against the North, which was supposedly populated, after all, by the "Saxon" descendants of the very Englishmen who had wronged Scotland so terribly. Scott's *Ivanhoe* was set in medieval England, and it was replete with chivalrous, jousting knights, although, ironically, the hero was actually one of the defeated Saxons whose Norman conquerors came across as arrogant and cruel. Scott's reference to dashing knights as "The Chivalry" had caught the fancy of many upper-crust southerners who also adopted his term "Southron" to describe themselves despite the fact that it had sometimes been used by the Scots as a somewhat disparaging reference to those who lived south of their border.[31]

In later years, Mark Twain would even blame Scott for secession, noting the white South's affliction with "the Sir Walter disease" and insisting that the novelist "had so large a hand in making Southern character . . . that he is in great measure responsible for the War." Scott's influence should not be discounted, but Twain may have gone a bit too far. Although the Cavalier legend had indeed "diffused into the discourse of Southern nationalism," by 1860 southerners could also draw on numerous contemporary examples, both fleshy and bloody, of ethnic nationalism in nineteenth-century Europe. The Greeks were struggling against the Turks, and the Hungarians against the Habsburgs. Meanwhile, the *Richmond Enquirer* insisted in 1863 that "the cause of Poland is the same cause for which the Confederates are now fighting . . . against that crushing, killing union with another nationality."[32]

Michael O'Brien has taken southern romanticism more seriously than Twain, arguing that it took root so rapidly and firmly in the southern white imagination because of its "special appeal for those who thought themselves on the periphery." The white southerner's sense of alienation from the larger society had, in turn, fostered a sense of membership in a smaller community, one obliged not only to defend itself against northern attacks on slavery and southern economic and political interests, but to counteract the destabilizing forces unloosed by the region's relatively slower but still significant move toward economic modernity. (O'Brien points out that, save only for Great Britain and the North, the South was urbanizing and industrializing more rapidly than any other Western society.) Romanticism's preoccupations with nostalgia, loss, and impending tragedy gave it a particular resonance among white southerners, but their crusade for "self-justification" quickly confronted them with a dilemma that would bedevil their ideological heirs for a full century thereafter. They were far more comfortable exalting a glorious, imagined past than celebrating a disturbing and undeniably real present that suggested to many of them how far the white South had actually strayed from its ancestral ideals.

Nowhere was this contradiction more apparent than in the attitudes and arguments of those who aggressively propounded the merits of slavery. Radical proslavery advocate George Fitzhugh argued that slavery was a "natural" outgrowth of human inequality and that as a slave society the South was much closer to nature than the cruel, exploitive, mercenary, and competitive industrial society of the North. The northern "free laborer," Fitzhugh often insisted, was "more of a slave than the negro," because he worked both "longer and harder for less allowance" and had to contend with "the cares of life" when his work was finally done. In contrast, "the Negro slaves of the South are the happiest and, in some respects, the freest people in the world," spending "the balance of their time . . . in perfect abandon," enjoying "contentment with the present, and confident assurance of the future."[33]

It is difficult to comprehend how Fitzhugh and other proslavery spokesmen could make such claims when they were well aware of abundant evidence to the contrary. Fitzhugh himself even confessed to a friend that he saw "great evils in slavery, but in a controversial work I ought not to admit them." Others in the proslavery contingent lamented the "disgusting spectacle" of "half-starved, meanly clad, overworked slaves," and William Gilmore Simms condemned "the illicit and foul passions of some among us, who make their slaves the victims and the instruments alike of the most licentious passions." When the outspoken defender of slavery James Henry Hammond conceded that "some intercourse . . . does take place" between masters and slave women, he knew whereof he spoke, having fathered a daughter by a slave woman and another child by that same daughter.[34]

There is no denying Hammond's hypocrisy or the moral repugnance of the proslavery argument in general. Yet, those who made the case for slavery as a positive good seemed to do so based on slavery not as a contemporary reality, but as they imagined it had been when the right people with the right values had presided over it. What Hammond described as "our ancient system" contrasted sharply with the "cold, calculating ambitious world" of the mid-nineteenth century in which the South appeared to be succumbing to the same "modern," excessively democratic, crassly acquisitive bourgeois impulses that had long ago corrupted northern society.[35]

Fitzhugh was not simply trying to rebut northern abolitionists when he offered up an idealized composite of the southern slaveholder as "lofty and independent in his sentiments, generous, affectionate, brave and eloquent . . . superior to the Northerner in every thing but the art of thrift." He also meant to rebuke those southern whites who seemed oblivious or indifferent to the appearance in their midst of what he sarcastically called a new "aristocracy" of parvenus "with more of privilege, and less of public spirit, than any that we meet with in history." Elsewhere, shortly before boosting slavery as a vital part of "the divine plan for promoting the general progress of civilization," Simms had published *The Sword and the Distaff* (later retitled *Woodcraft*), in which he told the melancholy tale of "Lieutenant Porgy," a Revolutionary patriot and rice planter whose hard-nosed but socially inferior overseer rebukes him both for his inattention to "what's useful in this world" and for his devotion to such "flummery" as "music and poetry and the soul" and other things that "don't make the pot bile."[36]

Perhaps the best evidence of the contradictory self-critical impulse embedded within the dogma of southern superiority came from Daniel R. Hundley. A patrician lawyer who was prouder of his Virginia ancestry than his Alabama origins, Hundley achieved a certain highly selective sense of critical detachment from his native region during his training in law at Harvard and his residence in Chicago thereafter. Published in 1860, his *Social Relations in the Southern States* offered an unlikely mixture of pure propaganda and subjective social criticism. Hundley insisted that he had written to answer "the persistent misrepresentation of the South by the various journals and unscrupulous demagogues of the free states." Accordingly, he presented the familiar portrait of the southern planter as aristocratic, graceful, honorable, manly, and well-spoken, exuding "that much coveted *savoir faire*, which causes a man to appear perfectly at home, whether it be in a hut or a palace." A consummate outdoorsman, the southern gentleman was therefore a stark contrast to the Yankee radicals who spent all their time indoors, their minds possessed by "Spiritualism, and every other blind function of the hour," their bodies "unsound" and their "secretions . . . altogether abnormal."[37]

As Fred Hobson has pointed out, Hundley's depiction of the gentleman was in a sense a wishful self-portrait as well. As an heir to the Virginia Cavalier tradition, he saw himself as an anomaly in a contemporary southern society increasingly beset by the likes of money-grabbing "Yankees" and the South's own Yankeefied "model storekeepers." Hundley reserved his bitterest contempt, however, for the "Cotton Snob," who sought to insinuate his way into the ranks of the chivalry by flaunting his recently acquired wealth and indulging himself in all of the latest fashions, talking all the while of "'my niggers.' (Observe, a Southern Gentleman rarely if ever says *nigger*.)" His boasting and bravado akin to "the senseless braying of the ass that is simply robed in the lion's skin," the tasteless, ill-bred Cotton Snob was giving the true southern gentleman a bad name. Yet, now that Cotton was "King," Hundley sneered, "the New Order of Chivalry is the Cotton Snob." Here again was the planter-Cavalier as an admirable figure, the best and strongest man that southern slave society could produce but, sadly, no match for the lesser men with lesser values and baser motives who were rising to the top.[38]

One of the most effective antidotes to such skepticism or uneasiness about the present or the future is a healthy dose of divine sanction. Despite the perception that the South has always qualified as the nation's "Bible Belt," estimates suggest that fewer than one in ten southerners were church members as late as the 1820s. In the ensuing decades, however, as the population shifted further into the interior, the growing appeal of the more emotional and evangelical sects like the Baptists and the Methodists became apparent. In Virginia, the Carolinas, and Georgia the aggregate membership in these two denominations swelled by 70 percent between 1820 and 1850, more than doubling the combined population growth rate of these states. By 1860 nearly three-fourths of the South's churchgoers attended either the Baptist or the Methodist church.[39]

Preaching humility and repentance and condemning pride in one's earthly accomplishments and possessions, the evangelicals had found a receptive audience among the South's common whites, but its headstrong, honor-obsessed planters presented a bigger challenge. In fact, Christine Heyrman has argued that the evangelical churches rose to true prominence in the region at least in part by acquiescing to the prerogatives, interests, and impulses of its male slaveholders. As Edward R. Crowther has shown, however, preacher and planter actually "needed one another," the preacher craving the ultimate validation of his status and influence that only the planter could provide, the planter seeking the "moral defense" of his hegemony as husband, father, and slave master that only the preacher could offer.[40]

Both the southern Methodists and Baptists broke with their northern brethren and sisters over the slavery issue in the 1840s. Not only did they largely abandon their criticism of slavery, but southern evangelicals moved from arguing that the Holy Scriptures did not prohibit human bondage to declaring that they actually ordained it. Baptist minister and slaveholder Iveson Lewis Brookes insisted that "every intelligent man of the South making a philosophical investigation into the institution of Negro slavery with the Bible in his hand . . . must come to the conclusion with me that it is God's institution," and the learned Presbyterian clergyman James Henry Thornwell assured slaveholders that they enjoyed "the sanction and protection of the divine word." Such rhetoric was virtually indistinguishable from the proclamations of proslavery politicians like James Henry Hammond, who declared slavery "the greatest of all the great blessings which a kind Providence bestowed on our glorious region" or the planter who believed that slavery had "the sanction of God, and upon that sure foundation and none other, we would have it rest."[41]

If the clergy, as God's agents, saw slavery as his instrument, then its northern critics were by definition occupying what some southern clerics called "an anti-Christian position," characterized by "free-thinking and contempt of the Bible." In the eyes of the Reverend Thornwell, the South's "friends of order and regulated freedom" were pitted against the "atheists, socialists, communists, red republicans [and] Jacobins" of the North. "From the pulpit and the hustings," as W. J. Cash wrote, "ran the dark suggestion that the God of the Yankee was not God at all but Antichrist loosed at last from the pit." It was small wonder that in the wake of the war, when asked who had crucified Christ, a young southern girl responded immediately, "O, yes, I know . . . the Yankees."[42]

Meanwhile, intent on assuring white men that evangelical Christianity was not incompatible in the least with the notions of patriarchy and aggressive masculinity that fueled their overheated sense of honor, some ministers cast themselves as bold and courageous warriors who practiced what Heyrman called a "muscular Christianity" (based on "the conviction that Jesus Christ, for all his charity, held no communion with sissies"), and they did not shrink from mixing it up with bullies and blasphemers when the need arose. The ultimate aim may have been to win the allegiance of wealthy and influential white men and "spiritualize the culture of honor" in the bargain, but instead, Heyrman believed, "the strategy of making evangelicalism appear aggressive and militant lent itself . . . to the spiritualizing of all assertions of southern manliness, militancy, and masterly prerogative."[43]

Needless to say, such an attitude did little for the cause of sectional compromise. Wholly dedicated to the cause of slavery, the aforementioned Reverend Brooks exhorted white southerners to Christian service "in defence [*sic*] of our dearest interests against the fanatical encroachments of the North and the world." Well before Alabama seceded, nearly 100 of its Methodist preachers circulated a statement calling for the South to "assert her independence" and vowed to preserve their honor "unsullied," And none of the eighteen ministers who served as delegates to the various state secession conventions favored remaining in the Union under prevailing conditions. Making "political speeches" and penning "fiery poems and articles," a Georgia minister admitted he went "wild with war fever" in 1861. As Heyrman summed it up, "Baptists and Methodists rose steadily to defend slavery in the 1830s, secession in the 1850s, and the holy cause of upholding both with force in 1861."[44]

Evangelical faith not only rallied white southerners to arms but helped to consecrate the Confederacy as a Christian nation. "A pure Christianity" lay at the heart of the Confederate revolution, one zealot insisted, "and Providence is using the South for the grand work of its preservation and extension." Confederate president Jefferson Davis actively nurtured this impression by proclaiming official days of public prayer and fasting, and the clergy often seemed to reciprocate by equating submission to God with submission to Confederate authority.[45]

By the 1850s the defense of slavery had encouraged a more hierarchical view of human society posited on the belief that, as Crowther observed, "Jehovah himself preferred stratification to social leveling." For some prominent clergy as well, creating a southern nation meant reversing the democratizing trends that were often associated with northern degeneracy. Damning democracy as the bastard child of Satan and his Yankee mistress, they declared it time, "to talk less about the rights of the people and more about the rights of God" and to "learn the virtue of reverence—and the lesson of respecting, obeying, and honoring authority, for authority's sake." Confederate doctrine made spiritual deference synonymous with social and political deference as what Drew Gilpin Faust called "an elite of planters, clergy, politicians and intellectuals led the movement to create a shared public culture and to produce consent to the terms of its rule."[46]

The sense of urgency surrounding this move testified abundantly to the Confederate elite's doubts that efforts to ground southern identity in a ro-

mantic vision of ancient Greece or Cavalier chivalry had fostered a broadly compelling sense of cultural unity among southern whites in general. In the wake of
Italy's political unification, one skeptical official supposedly pointed to enduring geographic and cultural divisions and the absence of a strong nationalist
sentiment and concluded, "We have made Italy, now we must make Italians." A
similar challenge awaited would-be architects of southern nationalism who, as
they set about to "make" southerners, found themselves with a long way to go, a
short time to get there, and some major obstacles in their way.[47]

Not the least of these was the weakness of the South's common schools in
comparison to the North's. Only 35 percent of the South's white children were
enrolled in school in 1860 as compared to 72 percent outside the region, where
the average school year was also 70 percent longer. This deficiency could be
traced in part to the simple reluctance of planters who educated their own
children privately to part with tax dollars in order to school the offspring of
the yeomanry. As sectional tensions grew and some signs of class apprehen-
sions began to emerge as well, many planters also worried that an expanded
school system might foster dissatisfaction and unrealistic ambitions among
their slaveless white brethren. William R. Taylor concluded that because education had long been seen as primarily "northern" in both origins and purpose, the South's white elite chose to "withhold it from almost everyone." In
the long run, however, the absence of an extensive public educational system
also meant the absence of the institutional structure that was so readily available in the North for inculcating and confirming regional loyalties. Beyond
that, the relatively small urban population, a per capita circulation for newspapers and magazines that was less than half the northern rate, and an illit-
eracy figure roughly three times the northern average further complicated the
process of "making southerners."[48]

Because the North seemed to represent a common enemy against which a
southern nation might be both unified and defined, would-be southern nationalists had long demanded, in the words of a *Richmond Enquirer* editorial
in 1855, "the declaration of our independence of the North in commercial,
literary and other matters of equal importance." It made little sense, an Alabama editor agreed, to quarrel with the North for political advantage and benefits "while we feed our minds on her literature, and our bodies on her luxuries,

and clothe them in her manufactured goods." "Were we practically independent," the New Orleans *Daily Crescent* contended, "we could afford to laugh to scorn" the "ravings" and "threats" of "the fanatics of the North."[49]

Although some southern industries did show noticeable growth in the 1850s, efforts to persuade white southerners to purchase only goods made in the South generally came to little. The same was true of the campaign to get farmers to diversify their crops. Advocates of agricultural self-sufficiency made little headway against entrenched habit and the relatively high cotton prices of the 1850s. Southern rights advocates also urged their fellow southerners not to hire northern teachers or to send their sons to northern colleges where they might be exposed to the "incendiary teachings of fanatical professors" who were "implacable enemies of the South and of its patriarchal institutions." At the peak of the secession crisis, some southern students did withdraw from northern schools, but there was hardly a wholesale exodus. Southern enrollment at the University of Pennsylvania had peaked in 1840 at 281, but there were still 222 southerners studying there in 1860. At Princeton, the number of southerners in the student body stood at 134 in 1848 and 114 in 1859. Suffice it to say, although it was widely endorsed in principle, southern cultural and economic self-sufficiency ultimately proved a doctrine infinitely more preached than practiced. As David Potter pointed out, those who dedicated themselves to creating "a sense of cultural separateness by self-conscious means . . . spent much of their time complaining that the South would not accept their cultural program."[50]

Efforts to promote greater solidarity among southern whites simply fell prey in large part to white indifference, but there was some outright resistance as well. Intrastate political conflicts over the pluses and minuses of slavery and the inordinate political influence of the slaveholding class had erupted periodically between representatives of plantation and small farming areas, especially in the Upper South, throughout the earlier part of the century. Such dissent had been ever more assiduously discouraged or suppressed as the sectional crisis deepened, but some nonslaveholding whites had begun to grow politically restive during the 1850s as skyrocketing slave prices seemed to shut the door on their aspirations to climb into the planter class.

In *The Impending Crisis of the South*, published in 1857, North Carolina native Hinton Rowan Helper boldly insisted that the brunt of slavery's oppression actually fell not on the slaves but on the slaveless southern yeomanry, whom it "cast into the dismal abodes of extreme ignorance, destitution, and misery." Helper sounded much like the aspiring southern nationalists of his day when he declared his "active desire to . . . elevate the South to an honorable and powerful position among the enlightened quarters of the globe." He also condemned the bitterly ironic spectacle of southerners entering the world "swaddled in Northern muslins" and departing it, "shrouded in Northern cambric . . . borne to the grave in a Northern carriage, entombed with a Northern spade, and memorized [*sic*] with a Northern slab!" Helper explained this abject dependence on the hated North quite differently from most of his contemporaries, however. As he saw it, the South was deplorably and inexcusably inferior to the North "in a commercial, mechanical, manufactural, financial, and literary point of view" solely because of "*Slavery*."[51]

Egregiously distorting data from the 1850 census, Helper asserted that New York was wealthier than any seven southern states and that the North's hay crop was more valuable than the South's annual harvest of cotton and its other major crops combined. He also blamed the depressed value of southern land on slavery and calculated that its "aiders and abettors" owed the South's slaveless farmers more than $7.5 billion on this account alone. Because such wealth as the South produced had been gobbled up by its large slaveowners, he argued, white yeomen must organize politically, impose an immediate tax of $60 per slave on these greedy and selfish planters, and boycott slaveholding merchants as well. Should the slaveholders, "more criminal than common murderers," try to use force against them, Helper felt confident that "the Negroes, . . . in nine cases out of ten, would be delighted with the opportunity to cut their masters' throat." Finally, he warned the "terror engenderers of the South" that should you "succeed in your treasonable attempts to take the South out of the Union today, we will bring her back tomorrow—if she goes away with you, she will return without you."[52]

Needless to say, like others who had criticized slavery and slaveholders (in language far more moderate than his), Helper had no choice but to take up permanent residence above the Mason-Dixon line. Even so, unprecedented vituperation rained down in absentia on this "vile wretch" who was assured that should he ever return to North Carolina, his expressed wish to die in his native state would be granted on the spot. Although some states made it a crime to possess a copy of *The Impending Crisis*, there is little reason to think that even if they had gotten their hands on it, nonslaveholding whites would have been swayed by a book whose language was so intemperate that it had to be toned down even before it could be reissued as a Republican political tract in 1859. Still, Helper's effort to inflame class resentments rekindled long-standing anxieties about the declining influence of the planter governing class and the destabilizing effects of political and social democratization on southern white society. [53]

These anxieties were much in evidence during the debates over the state constitution in Virginia and elsewhere in the Confederacy, as conservatives argued for restricting the franchise to taxpayers or reducing the number of elective offices. In the end, however, more pragmatic heads generally carried the day by pointing out that the slaveless common whites who made up two-thirds of the South's free population might not respond enthusiastically when called on to fight for an institution in which they had no immediate interest by a government that had just disfranchised them. Similar arguments prevailed against a proposal to feature a figure of a "Cavalier" on the official seal of the Confederacy in order to "indicate the origin of southern society." Such pragmatic nods to democracy notwithstanding, many champions of the Confederate cause remained unrepentantly hierarchical in their social and political thinking. Near the midpoint of the war, Frank H. Alfriend argued that "the *South needs no labouring class,* other than her *slaves.*" Clearly fearing the rise of the "easily deceived" white masses, he warned in rhetoric most un-Jeffersonian that the South was vulnerable to "the vandalic inundations of Agrarian democracy," especially if the North succeeded in imposing "the pernicious doctrine of the Declaration of Independence, that all men are born free and equal."[54]

Those who made the final decisions about Confederate political and governmental institutions and symbols had little time for deliberation. In this sense, much like American nationalism, which, as Don H. Doyle has observed, had not only "emerged within an independence movement in search of an ideology" but "had to be constructed, and quickly, in the maelstrom of war," Confederate nationalism would have to be assembled on the fly. The resemblance did not end here, however. For all their insistence that they were forging a new nation, when the time came to establish a self-governing southern state, the leaders of the Confederacy chose to ground its political identity in what they saw as the fundamental principles on which the United States itself had been founded. Modeling the rationale for southern independence on the rationale for American independence that had, in turn, provided the foundation for American national identity, the architects of Confederate identity claimed that they were simply withdrawing from "a federation of sovereign states that now had abused their rights." Because southerners were merely following the example of those who inspired the American Revolution, their struggle against northern tyrants and bullies was therefore comparable to the American struggle against British tyrants and bullies. Jefferson Davis added that the South's abrupt departure from the Union was not a rejection so much as a reassertion of the principles on which that Union was founded: "We have changed the constituent parts but not the system of government."[55]

This much was evident in the Confederate constitution in which, as Alexander Stephens pointed out, "all the essentials of the old Constitution, which have endeared it to the hearts of the American people, have been purveyed and perpetuated." Save for the explicit protection it provided for slavery, the Constitution of the Confederacy amounted to what historians have described as "largely a copy" and even "a parody" of the Constitution of the United States. Beyond that, the original flag of the Confederacy, the "Stars and Bars, " looked so much like the United States flag that a separate battle flag soon had to be devised to prevent southern troops from firing on their own men. Although "Dixie" became the acknowledged anthem of the Confederacy, southern songsters also borrowed freely from the tunes and lyrics of familiar American patriotic ditties. At least one prominent Confederate thought the new nation should be called "the Republic of Washington," and its leaders placed an imprint of George Washington on its great seal and on one of its postage stamps. Jefferson Davis, "our second Washington" to some Confederates, was sworn in as their president near a statue of the first Washington on the latter's birthday in 1862.[56]

For the Confederates, Doyle observed, "the father of the country they were leaving became the stepfather of the country they were inventing." Confederate leaders might have responded that they were not kidnapping Washington so much as rescuing his principles from the scrap heap where their northern antagonists had discarded them. In fact, their core message seemed to be that the new southern nation would not really be an original creation but simply a restoration of the American republic as they believed its founders had actually envisioned it. Historian Reid Mitchell observed that while "the power of borrowed symbols to compel loyalty is severely limited," the Confederates "had no choice; they had to use American symbols because they regarded themselves as the true Americans."[57]

As a result, combatants on each side in the Civil War drew on a "pervasive American identity" to justify their actions against each other. The Ohio lieutenant who saw himself fighting for "the rights garenteed [sic] in the Declaration of Independence" sounded little different from the Virginia officer who described the Confederate struggle against the Yankees as the "second War for American Independence." This self-perception of white southerners as the true defenders of American ideals (which is, in some ways, still with us today) had emerged in part as a response to the efforts of northern politicians and propagandists to claim this title for themselves. It became a key theme for patriotic orators in the South during the late antebellum era, and it may explain why many Confederate soldiers and civilians, in the early years of the war especially, continued to observe the Fourth of July and Washington's birthday holidays, claiming they had even more right to do so than their northern adversaries.[58]

Kenneth Stampp has concluded that in clinging to their American heritage, the leaders of the Confederacy simply confessed at the outset "rather pathetically to the speciousness of southern nationalism." In reality, he argued, "except for the institution of slavery, the South had little to give it a clear national identity." Alexander Stephens seemed to concede as much when he pointed out on numerous occasions that the Confederacy's real claim to distinctiveness lay in making slavery, "African inequality and subordination, and the equality of white men, the chief corner-stone of the Southern Republic." Nation-building typically entails a lot of preaching to the choir, but although Stephens's remarks hardly came as a revelation to southern slaveholders, his effort to make slavery synonymous with "the equality of white men" was aimed at nonslaveholding whites. The goal of slave ownership might have slipped beyond their economic reach, but, lest they be tempted to listen to the preachings of Helper and a number of northern abolitionists as well, they should understand that the institution of slavery was all that stood between them and a swift and irreversible descent into the unthinkable humiliation of economic, political, and social equality with blacks. The argument that slavery automatically bestowed a fundamental equality on all whites simply by virtue of their skin color hardly squared with efforts to restrict voting and office-holding to more affluent Confederates, of course, but consistency is hardly the sine qua non of national identities.[59]

One difficulty in assessing the vitality of southern nationalism is that, for the most part, those who have written about it have not only employed widely varying definitions but have tended to use "nation" and "nation-state" or "nationalism" and "patriotism" interchangeably. Despite its failure to gain official recognition as such abroad, the Confederacy was indisputably a separate nation-state complete with its own government, constitution, official boundaries, and army. Well in advance of the flood of recent writing on nation-building, however, David Potter observed in 1963 that "in psychological terms, a nation exists only subjectively, as a convergence of men's loyalties; without this convergence there would be no nation."[60]

Potter's approach seems particularly appropriate, for, as we will see, southern white loyalties appeared to focus much more intensely on the Confederate military cause than on the Confederate nation-state itself. Unless the would-be nation has held what Ernest Renan called "a daily plebiscite," however, determining whether a state of nationhood has actually been achieved or maintained requires exhaustive research into the intensity and extent of sometimes elusive feelings of ethnic, cultural, or historical kinship and common allegiance within a discrete population. Even then, depending on their respective definitions of a nation, two scholars might well review the same evidence and reach precisely the opposite conclusions. There is a world of difference, for example, between Benedict Anderson's rather uncomplicated vision of a nation as "an imagined political community" and David A. Bell's "sovereign political community grouping together people with enough in common . . . to allow them to act as a homogeneous, collective person."[61]

In addition to inconsistent criteria and terminology, there is the matter of changes in popular attitudes over time. Despite fire-eater William Lowndes Yancey's talk of inspiring a shared "southern heart" or instructing a common "Southern mind," a great many and possibly most Confederate soldiers marched off to war in 1861 inspired less by a broadly abstract allegiance to their new nation-state than by what Bell describes as an "emotional attachment to a place thought of as 'home.'" When a northern soldier said he was fighting for his "country," he typically meant the Union or the United States. For a southern soldier, however, "my country" could refer not to the Confederacy or even to the South but to his own particular geographic and emotional realm of existence and experience, whether he defined that as his state or his local community, or simply "the loved ones who call upon me to defend their homes from pillage." As one South Carolinian explained before the war, "I go first for Greenville, then for the Greenville District, then for the up-country, then for South Carolina, then for the South, then for the United States, and after that I don't go for anything." Compared to such a detailed hierarchy of specific local allegiances, a Georgia private's insistence that "if I can't fight in the name of my own state, then I don't want to fight at all" seemed almost cosmopolitan.[62]

In his study of the "flag culture" of the Confederacy, Robert E. Bonner has also traced the evolution of southern popular allegiances during the war. Although we might quibble with his terminology, Bonner has offered a useful

distinction between nationalism, which he associates with support for "an independent, indivisible, and fully sovereign nation-state," and patriotism, seen
as "emotional loyalty to a government-led collective effort." If Bonner's analysis of the meaning of the Confederate flag is correct, patriotism and nationalism were by no means synonymous within the Confederacy, and if anything,
the strength and focus of the former may ultimately help to explain the weakness of the latter. The St. Andrew's Cross battle flag design (derived from the
x-shaped cross on which St. Andrew was crucified) was born of the combat-
inspired demand for a standard less likely to be confused with that of the enemy. It proved immensely popular among the white citizenry as well, and
according to Bonner, its placement in one corner of the otherwise pure-white
"stainless banner" that supplanted the Stars and Bars as the official flag of the
Confederacy in 1863 signified the "fundamentally military nature of [south-
ern] collective purpose." Emblazoning the Confederacy's official seal with the
martial image of Washington as a mounted officer leading the war for American independence conveyed a similar meaning.

What quickly became known as the "Southern Cross" flag, intoned General
P. G. T. Beauregard, had been "consecrated by the best blood of our country on
so many battlefields." It celebrated both military valor and Christian martyrdom to a holy cause, but, unlike the Stars and Bars, which had suggested a
resurrection of the founding principles of the American republic, the new flag
offered no vision of what the Confederacy represented or promised to become.
Moreover, although the second official banner of the Confederate nation-state
flew on some major public buildings, it was not nearly so widely displayed on
the home front as the Stars and Bars had been, and the battle flag itself was
seldom seen when troops were not present.[63]

While it no doubt helped to instill a patriotic "loyalty to a government-led
collective effort," the Southern Cross flag both reflected and reinforced a far
stronger and more enduring attachment to the collective effort than to the
government that led it. Wartime disaffection with the politicians charged with
oversight of a faltering military cause is hardly unusual, but the Confederate
government had irritated many of its citizens both by its assumption of cen-
tralized power on the one hand and its failure to prosecute the war effort more
effectively or to respond to the needs of the home front on the other. It was far
easier to form attachments to military heroes like Lee, Jackson, and the dashing Jeb Stuart than to the bickering, self-aggrandizing politicians who often
seemed bent on undermining the noble cause for which, at their behest, others were suffering and dying in large numbers.[64]

Gary W. Gallagher has argued that as the war progressed "the national strivings of the Confederacy came to center on the Army in Virginia." This intense but narrowly concentrated emotional investment in the original military effort itself may well have contributed to the relatively feeble resistance put up by whites on the Confederate home front. Certainly, "with the country's identity intertwined with that of its regular armies," Bonner contended, "most people accepted the fact that hopes for Confederate independence, however fiercely defended during war, would expire with defeat on the battlefield." A Confederate major seemed to speak for the overwhelming majority of his contemporaries when he admitted, "My last hope died within me when General Lee surrendered."[65]

Scholars have long argued that establishing a nation-state as a duly constituted political absolute may be much easier than molding those living within that nation-state into a "nation." Beyond that, the experience of the Confederacy suggests as well that the inhabitants of a nation-state may actually come together as a nation for reasons other than a strong common allegiance to the nation-state itself. Despite his emphasis on the convergence of human loyalties as the prerequisite for forming a nation, Potter concluded that "once the nation has been institutionalized, men tend to regard the institution itself as transcendent—a thing on which the loyalties of men ought to converge simply because it does exist." The loyalties of white southerners, however, had actually converged not primarily on their nation-state but on their common struggle against the North, which had, in turn, actually led to the destruction of their nation-state before it could become truly institutionalized. For all this, before we pin the failure of the Confederacy on the failure of southern nationalism, we should note that nationalism has caused a lot more wars than it has won. The outcome of the American Revolution is testimony enough that strong feelings of unity and kinship with one's countrymen or of dedication to one's government are not necessarily prerequisites for victory, even in a war where the odds against success are at least as great as those that confronted the Confederates.[66]

Regardless of whether the wartime weakness of Confederate nationalism (defined as widespread support for the Confederate nation-state) contributed significantly to the Confederacy's defeat, it seems clear that the Confederacy's defeat contributed to the postwar strength of southern patriotism (defined as loyalty to the collective southern white cause). The architects of Confederate nationalism believed they had built a nation when they framed a new government and sent their troops off to war with hearty assurances of a glorious victory. Yet, it took a fierce four-year conflict ending in a bitter and ignominious defeat to forge anything approaching the sense of unity and common grievance and cause that the white South's leaders had tried to instill before its ill-fated struggle for independence began. Noting that Beaufort, North Carolina, had once been a Whig stronghold with notable unionist proclivities, Judkin Browning found that after three years of Union occupation, local whites were "more firmly sympathetic with the Confederacy at the war's end than they had ever been during the heady days of secession."[67]

Likewise, W. J. Cash argued in 1941 that it was really "the conflict with the Yankee that created the concept of the South as something more than a matter of geography, as an object of patriotism . . . in the mind of the Southerners." For the first time, perhaps, they had developed what Bonner called "a patriotism across state lines." Local allegiances remained strong, but, as Cash put it, Confederate veterans appeared to have forgotten that they had gone out initially "to die merely for Virginia or Carolina or Georgia." After four years of common struggle against the North, they not only responded to the term "Southern" with an emotion once reserved for "Virginia or Carolina or Georgia," but they were much more acutely conscious "of the line which divided what was Southern from what was not." As a broadly held communal perception, "the South" was born for a great many white southerners not in Montgomery or even in Charleston harbor, but, as Robert Penn Warren observed, "only at the moment when Lee handed Grant his sword" at Appomattox, and it was only thereafter that the "conception of Southern identity truly bloomed."[68]

Reflecting on the impact of France's defeat in the Franco-Prussian war, Ernest Renan concluded that "suffering in common unifies more than joy does." Carlton J. H. Hayes agreed that "A people may be more united and nationalistic through grief over defeat than through celebration of triumph." The postbellum mind-set of many white southerners underscores these observations. Bertram Wyatt-Brown explained that "like Ireland, Poland, Finland [and] Bohemia," the white South found "a new unity in the fury of war and the resentment of defeat." Raised in an expatriate Savannah family living in Paris, novelist Julian Green recalled that his mother made her offspring "the children of a nation which no longer existed but lived on in her heart. . . . We were eternally the conquered but unreconciled—rebels, to employ a word dear to her." As William Pfaff observed, Green's mother "could as well have been a

Pole of the Partitions, or of the totalitarian diasporas, or a White Russian, or a Scot across the waters, follower of a maladroit king."[69]

In general, white southerners directed their unifying sense of resentment and grievance not against the United States itself but against the North, which, so they believed, had seized control of the national government and used its armies and instrumentalities to visit all manner of suffering and indignities on them. The refusal of a number of southern whites to celebrate the Fourth of July again for many years after the war did not mean that they no longer saw themselves as Americans. Rather, they now associated the rhetoric, rituals, and symbols to which they had once given their whole-hearted allegiance with the northern armies who had invaded and then occupied their homeland and the Reconstruction-era politicians who had seemed bent on humiliating them and turning their world upside down. Diehards like Edmund Ruffin might go (or, in his case, send themselves) to their graves proclaiming their "hatred for the entire Yankee race," but hating "the Yankees," as Kenneth Stampp pointed out, "was not quite the same as hating the Union." David Potter concluded that "southern loyalties to the union were never really obliterated," but owing to the conflict with the North, they were simply "eclipsed by other loyalties with which, for a time, they conflicted." Even E. Merton Coulter, the incompletely reconstructed southern historian of both the Confederacy and Reconstruction, agreed. White southerners shared too much of a "common heritage" with other Americans, Coulter concluded, and "four years were not sufficient to hallow" the Confederate nation-state as "an undying ideal." Hence southern whites were quick to abandon their hastily constructed separatist state and eager to "resume their position in the old government."[70]

The widespread assumption among white southerners that they should be allowed to do just that with minimal restriction or delay was in part a reflection of their dogged insistence that they had not left the Union voluntarily, but had been forced out by the North. When it appeared that some northerners were intent on blocking their return to the Union until they consented to the total destruction of the Confederacy's cornerstone of white supremacy, white southerners renewed the battle against further "northernization" with a passion that seemed at times every bit as intense as their commitment to the Confederate cause itself.[71]

In the struggle against Congressional Reconstruction, some southern whites would even embrace the guerilla and terrorist tactics that they had foresworn in 1865. The effort to overthrow Reconstruction actually drew much of its energy and inspiration from a new postbellum ethos of southern white identity grounded in the failed movement for southern independence. The term "Lost Cause" was familiar to antebellum southern devotees of Sir Walter Scott, because it referred to the prolonged struggle to restore the Stuart monarchs of Scotland to their rightful position as rulers of England as well. The last "Jacobite" uprising, led by Charles Edward Stuart, had shown some prospect of success before it was finally crushed at Culloden in 1746, assuring "Bonnie Prince Charlie" of his place in the legendary Lost Cause of Scottish nationalism and later inviting white southerners to see Gettysburg as the South's Culloden.[72]

In its southern translation, as first popularized in Edward A. Pollard's 1866 book of the same name, the "Lost Cause" ethos not only defended secession and glorified the society that white southerners had gone to war to preserve, but actually transformed their tragic military defeat into a tremendous moral triumph. As Emory M. Thomas explained, "The Lost Cause mythology held that the southern cause was not only undefiled by defeat but that the bloodbath of war actually sanctified the values and mores of the Old South." Proponents of the Lost Cause quickly pieced together a remarkably seamless historical justification of the actions of southern whites before and during the war. Though foisted on the South by the British with the assistance of northern slavetraders, in the hands of southern planters, slavery had actually been a benign, civilizing institution. Furthermore, the South's antebellum planter aristocrats had supported secession not to preserve slavery but to secure nothing more than the individual and state rights granted by the Constitution. This abrupt dissociation of the Confederacy from slavery came not only from Jefferson Davis but also Alexander Stephens, whose repeated insistences in 1861 that slavery was the very "cornerstone" of Confederate nationality were suddenly forgotten as he explained matter-of-factly that the Civil War had not been "a contest between the advocates or opponents of that peculiar institution."[73]

Neither the audacity or the immediacy of such revisionism seemed to trouble the apostles of the Lost Cause, who reiterated the contentions of Davis and other Confederate leaders that they had left the Union via the same path and in adherence to the same principles that had led their forefathers to create it in the first place. Faced with a Yankee invasion, they had little choice but to take up arms in defense of both their homeland and their honor. Showing none of the skepticism or ambivalence that could be found in some antebellum literary treatments, devotees of the Lost Cause celebrated the Cavalier legend uncritically. Tennessean Ethel Moore praised the brave soldiers who had defended "the traditions and memories of the old-time South—the sunny South, with its beautiful lands and its happy people, the South of chivalrous men and gentle women, the South that will go down in history as the land of plenty and the home of heroes." The defenders of the South had failed to repulse the Yankee aggressors. Yet their steadfast resistance in the face of the North's overwhelmingly superior numbers of men and machines of war had not only wiped out any reason for shame over their defeat but allowed them to emerge from the conflict with at least some of their pride intact and their sense of honor affirmed.[74]

The ultimate symbol of the Lost Cause was the aristocratic Cavalier who, despite antebellum-era skepticism about his true mettle, had apparently proven himself a worthy and honorable warrior. With his impeccable aristocratic credentials, Robert E. Lee, who epitomized the gallant knight who had led his men "on a field of chivalry more glorious than any since the Round Table," became synonymous with the Lost Cause to a large number of whites in the South and ultimately in the North as well. The knightly image of Confederate heroes seemed even more appropriate as southern clergymen repeatedly likened them to Christian crusaders who had fought a holy war against the cruel, greedy Yankee infidel.[75]

This analogy did raise a rather troublesome question, however. If, as so many of its adherents had claimed, the Confederate crusade was undertaken to fulfill the true will of God, why had it failed so abysmally? Admitting that their cause had not, in fact, been just or righteous would have been too emotionally devastating for white southerners, especially at a time when their hated conquerors were in the process of subjecting them to the humiliation of Reconstruction. A far more palatable explanation held that, like all human events, the war had actually played out precisely as God had planned all along. The Episcopal bishop of Georgia, Stephen Elliot, insisted that "God's people must always be tried," and his successor, John Beckwith, concurred that, as Christians, "it is part of our destiny to suffer." Embracing an analogy that, ironically enough, black ministers had long offered to their people ("God try Abra'am. He try his people *now*"), white clergymen likened white southerners to the children of Israel and "the God of Israel" to "the God of the Southern Confederacy," explaining that "for wise purposes" God sometimes allowed his people to undergo "apparent defeat."[76]

The use of "apparent" was revealing, for many ministers and politicians alike saw the South's military failure as a "baptism in blood" that, as historian John B. Boles put it, actually "presaged moral triumph." "In God's good time," a Virginia minister predicted in 1889, a new generation of southern heroes would don the knightly armor of righteousness and "vindicate the principles which must ultimately triumph," and like Jesus himself, the inscription on a Confederate monument promised the southern cause would one day celebrate "a joyful resurrection."[77]

The cult of the Lost Cause fused the belief that the white South was destined to "rise again" with what Warren called a "mystique of prideful 'difference,' . . . and defensiveness" that became an integral element of postbellum southern white identity. This fusion was much in evidence throughout Edward A. Pollard's *The Lost Cause* (1866) and *The Lost Cause Regained* (1868). Reviving the antebellum rhetoric of southern distinctiveness and superiority, Pollard even suggested that northern hostility to the South was rooted in "the conviction that the Northern man . . . was coarse and inferior in comparison with the aristocracy and chivalry of the South." Indeed, despite this defeat "the Confederates have gone out of this war with the proud, secret, deathless, *dangerous* consciousness that they are THE BETTER MEN, and that there was nothing wanting but a change in a set of circumstances and a firmer resolve to make them the victors."[78]

Pollard seemed to imply at several points that another Civil War might be a real possibility, but his primary purpose was to rally white southerners to a renewed ideological struggle against the North, one in which there were still "noble victories to be won, memorable services to be performed, and grand results to be achieved." Stressing the urgent need for unity and political activism, Pollard pointed out that even as *The Lost Cause* went to press in 1866, the "extreme Black Republican party at Washington has sought to disfranchise the Southern people, to force negro suffrage on the South" and to secure "the means of governing the Southern states as conquered and subjugated territories." Such actions were not only vindictive but also unjust because the Civil War had not established racial equality or black suffrage nor, save for invalidating secession, had it destroyed the constitutional principle of State Rights. These things that the war had not resolved, white southerners must "still cling to, still claim, and still assert in them their rights and views." "There may not be a political South," Pollard insisted, "yet there may be a social and intellectual South." Therefore, even as they tried to fend off further ravages at the hands of those seeking to northernize their society, southern whites must begin to counterattack with a "war of ideas."[79]

Two years later, with congressional Reconstruction well under way, Pollard offered his battle plan for such a war, insisting "the true cause fought for in the late war has not been 'lost' immeasurably or irrevocably, but is yet in a condition to be 'regained' by the South on ultimate issues of the political contest." Upon reflection, Pollard had joined Davis and Stephens in concluding that white southerners had not fought to preserve slavery as a right of property or as a "peculiar institution of labor." Rather, slavery had served primarily as "a barrier against a contention and war of the races," and "the true question" of the war was "the supremacy of the white race, and along with it the preservation of the political traditions of the country." If the white South managed to "defeat the Radical Party" and "secure the supremacy of the white man," it would actually triumph "in the true cause of the war, with respect to all its fundamental and vital issues."[80]

The "true hope of the South" lay therefore in forging political alliances against the Radical Republicans based on "the natural affections of race" with conservative Democrats and other northern whites in order to restore white supremacy and thereby preserve "the dearest political traditions of our country." Here Pollard simply reasserted the claim that the South had left the Union not to destroy it, but to defend the fundamental principles on which it had been founded. "The Union, as it was," he insisted, "is the true and logical expression of that 'Lost Cause' which the country is in the prospect of regaining or of losing forever." Perhaps taking his cue from Pollard, the former Confederate Henry Watterson preached a message of national reconciliation based on white supremacy to northern and southern audiences, proclaiming that by virtue of the common "vestal fire of our Anglo-Saxon race," white Americans were the world's most "homogeneous" people. On the other hand, Watterson argued, "the negro is an African in Congo or in Kentucky, in Jamaica or in Massachusetts."[81]

A combination of Lost Cause propaganda and Pollard's political plan proved the means by which the white South would eventually manage to overthrow Reconstruction and restore both racial and political home rule for southern whites. In South Carolina, for example, former Confederate general Wade Hampton made the Lost Cause the symbolic centerpiece of his 1876 bid to claim the governorship and bring Radical Reconstruction to an end in that state. Hampton's strategists capitalized on his credentials as an aristocratic planter and Confederate hero to turn the gubernatorial contest into an opportunity to reopen the conflict of 1861–65 and achieve a different result.

Hampton's campaign skillfully orchestrated Lost Cause images of the Christian knight doing battle with a Yankee infidel over the sanctity and purity of South Carolina, represented by attractive young white women reminiscent of the lovely, virginal plantation belle. Hampton's victory meant, one journalist wrote, that South Carolina had been restored, and the state had been "re-baptized with the blood of some of her bravest and best." With northerners still dominating national politics, as W. Scott Poole has argued, the Lost Cause provided white southerners with much more than a "prop for flagging self-esteem." It also served as "a grammar of recalcitrance and as a vehicle for the white southern conservative ethos." In 1877, with the end of Reconstruction at hand, Jefferson Davis revealed the motivational value of the Lost Cause when he conceded that although "we may not hope to see the rebuilding of the temple as our fathers designed it ... we can live on praying for that event and die with our eyes fixed on the promised land."[82]

As the spiritual and ideological core of the effort to restore the white South to the Union on their own terms, the Lost Cause quickly became for white southerners what David Blight called a source of "emotional fuel and suste-nance." It also offered, as Boles put it, "a means by which many postbellum white southerners found self-identity." It was to that very end that Pollard had rallied white southerners in 1866 to defend both their cultural heritage and their racial and political interests, warning that "it would be immeasurably the worst consequence" of the region's military defeat, "that the South should lose its moral and intellectual distinctiveness as a people, and cease to assert its well-known superiority [sic] in civilization, in political scholarship, and in all standards of individual character over the people of the North."

3

The New South and the Old Cause

SOME WHITE SOUTHERNERS may have managed to emerge from the Civil War and Reconstruction with their sense of cultural superiority to their northern conquerors intact, but even those capable of such a leap of faith could not deny the bitterly painful economic realities that confronted them. The war had removed slavery as the most distinctive feature of southern life, but in almost all other categories related to progress or prosperity, the disparities between the two regions were far greater in 1870 than they had been a decade earlier. Northern industrial potential was now on track toward realization, its engines stoked by heavy government spending and what Peter Coclanis has called "a greater and more embracing commitment to policies and values conducive to capitalism and industrialization."[1]

As northern wealth grew by 50 percent during the 1860s, southern wealth had declined by 60 percent. Other physical and material setbacks aside, emancipation alone meant the loss of an estimated $3 to $4 billion in slave property that had been the primary basis for securing agricultural credit in the antebellum era. There was also the challenge of adapting southern agriculture to a free labor system in an age of flagging world market demand for cotton. The region's postbellum economic plight seemed to underscore not just the wisdom but the absolute necessity of capitalizing on its abundance of cheap labor and raw materials to build an industrialized "New South" whose wealth and power would soon not just rival but surpass that of the North.[2]

At first glance, such an idea might seem wholly irreconcilable with the Lost Cause and its celebration of an idyllic antebellum plantation kingdom. Although the Lost Cause ethos responded to the emotional, racial, and political needs of many white southerners, it offered no solutions to the postbellum economic crisis threatening the entire region. Not only did the architects of the New South step forward with a much-needed plan for economic revitalization, but in large measure they also embraced the fundamental social and political tenets of the Lost Cause. Despite some early objections from Lost

Cause purists, the two ideologies were eventually fused into what Paul M. Gaston has called the "New South Creed," a powerful synthesis that provided a blueprint not only for sustaining a distinctive identity for many southern whites but for reclaiming their lost status and autonomy as well.[3]

In the rhetoric of mid-twentieth-century southern liberals, the term "New South" implied a region so thoroughly transformed and cleanly disconnected from its past that it would in reality be not so much a "'New' South" as what George Washington Cable had referred to in 1882 as a "'No' South," fully assimilated and essentially indistinguishable from the rest of American society. (Formed in 1944, the liberal, activist Southern Regional Council even titled its official magazine *The New South*.) The original New South was conceived quite differently, however. Its proponents vowed to use industrial development to northernize their region's economy while doing their best to restore and then to uphold the most definitively "southern" ideals of the Old South, especially its racial, political, and class hierarchies. Defeated and embittered, southern whites drew determination and hope from the New South's promises of an affluent golden age just ahead. They also found pride and reassurance in its celebration of a carefully constructed golden age behind, the glorious and heroic heritage of the Old South and the Lost Cause. Thus, as David R. Goldfield has observed, much like "Bismarckian Germany," the New South "marched forward to modernity, while looking to the past for its inspiration and guidance."[4]

Antebellum manufacturers like Daniel Pratt of Alabama and William Gregg of South Carolina had long touted the benefits of industrial expansion, and publications like J. D. B. DeBow's *DeBow's Review* preached the gospel of industrialism as well. As we have seen, amid the mounting sectional tensions of the 1850s, aspiring southern nationalists had preached the gospel of economic diversification and self-sufficiency in order to free the South from its "economic vassalage" to the North. In the wake of the war, DeBow and a number of other antebellum economic leaders endorsed industrialization as the only "true remedy" for the South's ills and flatly declared, *"We have got to go to manufacturing to save ourselves."*[5]

Despite losing over 1,900 slaves, Paul Cameron was still the richest man in North Carolina at the end of the Civil War. In addition to owning 30,000 acres of land, Cameron had been involved in improving transportation and promoting industrial development in the antebellum era, and in 1868, nearly two decades before Henry Grady's famous New South speech, he advised his friends that "Not until the South shall hammer and plane, stitch and grind and bring the plow, loom, and anvil close to each other will it become self-dependent and *independent*."[6]

Unlike Cameron, many of the most energetic and effective spokesmen for the New South's industrial ideal were too young to have achieved prominence before the Civil War. The baby-faced Grady was the son of an Athens, Georgia, merchant, and he had married into a cotton manufacturing family before he became the editor of the *Atlanta Constitution* in 1880. One of the few New South proponents with direct ties to the old plantation order, Daniel Augustus Tompkins sprang from a wealthy South Carolina planting family and went on to become president of three cotton mills, director of three others, and owner of three newspapers. Richard H. Edmonds was born on a small farm in Virginia in 1857, and he became the New South's leading industrial propagandist when he began publishing the *Manufacturer's Record* in 1881.[7]

Journalistic connections were clearly a pervasive thread at the upper echelons of the New South movement. Though he was born in England, Francis W. Dawson served in the Confederate army before becoming "the voice of Manchester to the New South" as editor of the *Charleston News and Courier*. Tennessee native Henry Watterson was the son of a well-known lawyer and antebellum industrial advocate who went on to become editor of the *Louisville Courier-Journal*. Although Dawson and Watterson were among the few influential New South advocates who had actually fought in the Civil War, from P. G. T. Beauregard to John B. Gordon, high-ranking Confederate officers played key roles, both substantive and symbolic, in the effort to make the New South a political and economic reality.[8]

In Grady's Georgia, the "Bourbon Triumvirate" of former Confederate governor Joseph E. Brown and former Confederate generals John B. Gordon and A. H. Colquitt had helped to overthrow Reconstruction in 1870–71, and for the next eighteen years, the three would dominate both the state's governorship and its seats in the United States Senate. As mainstays of the "Atlanta Ring," they consistently pursued both their personal economic and political interests and those of Georgia's capital city within the confines of the New South movement. Campaigning for the Senate in 1880, Brown declared, "Let us do all we can . . . to build up the manufacturing interests in Georgia and thus greatly augment her wealth by giving employment to her citizens . . . furnishing markets for their productions and sending those productions in a shape to be worth several times the amount that they are in the raw state when first produced." Heavily involved in railroad speculation, coal mining (in the cases of Brown and Gordon with convict labor), and other industrial and business ventures, this powerful trio typically allowed Grady to speak for them on New South issues, however. A similar pattern seemed to prevail throughout the region as the men who had brought Reconstruction to an end either joined or endorsed an aggregation of journalists, financiers, aspiring industrialists, and former Confederate leaders who embraced the ideal of a New South that would soon boast bustling factories and booming cities.[9]

By no means all ex-Confederates or other white southerners, from influential clergy to struggling farmers, embraced the New South identity. Some of its earliest and severest critics charged that it was actually motivated by the same "mammonism" and "money mania" that was the essence of Yankeeism. A former Confederate colonel, the Reverend Charles Colcock Jones, prayed that "this New South remain purged of all modern commercial methods" and "prove not the theatre of alienation and demoralizing speculation." Even theologian Robert Lewis Dabney, a qualified supporter of industrial development, warned his fellow southerners against believing that because "the North triumphed by its wealth . . . the surest way to retrieve your prosperity will be to BECOME LIKE YOUR CONQUERORS."[10]

Such concerns certainly seemed valid enough when New South proponents such as the editor of the *Vicksburg Herald* announced, "We are in favor of the South, from the Potomac to the Rio Grande, being thoroughly Yankeeized." Not to be outdone, Francis Dawson insisted that bringing in "about five hundred Yankees of the right stripe" would make Charleston "throb with vivid force." The legendary evangelist from Atlanta, the Reverend Sam Jones, rejoiced to see the South "completely transformed into a new 'Yankeedom,'" and observed that "the 'Yankees' are native southerners and not immigrants." Finally, as an ardent proponent of the Lost Cause, Edward Pollard had once condemned the North as "coarse and materialistic" and spurned the "coarse notion that the people should build up mills and factories." By the 1870s, however, even Pollard was exhorting fellow southerners to emulate the "superior thrift and enterprise of the North" and urging Yankee tourists to participate in the "social reconstruction" of Virginia by visiting one of its summer resorts.[11]

Despite their boosterist rhetoric, many influential New South spokesmen seemed hardly more interested than their Confederate predecessors in seeing their region "northernized" into an open, pluralistic society offering a variety of options for political expression or significant opportunities for widespread upward mobility, either economic or social. One of the geniuses of the New South's architects was their ability to present it as different things to different people, and they attracted a variety of followers with disparate and sometimes conflicting interpretations of their goals. Though he was sometimes invoked as an ideological ancestor by mid-twentieth-century southern white liberals, Henry Grady sounded more like Alexander Stephens affirming the Confederacy's commitment to keeping blacks subordinate "to the superior race" when he insisted that "the white race must dominate forever in the South." Grady also saw little need for anything beyond technical or vocational education for the white masses, championed one-party politics, downplayed both widespread farm poverty and the pitiful wages and deplorable working conditions that prevailed in southern factories, and even defended the use of convict laborers and the treatment that they received.[12]

For the most part, New South architects envisioned a society where conservative business, financial, and industrial interests controlled the cities. At the same time, despite some vague and unrealistic references to diversified small farming, large landholding interests would hold political sway in the countryside as the traditional social restraints of race, gender, and class remained firmly in place throughout the South. Intent on securing and preserving conservative, single-party Democratic dominance, New South advocates preached the politics of passivity rather than participation. "Activist politics," warned Grady, was anathema to "investors" and could result only in "such oppressive laws . . . that capital is kept away." Labor and agrarian organizers were condemned if necessary but ignored if possible. As the turbulent Populist political insurgency swept across the southern landscape, Georgia's Senator John B. Gordon found it "comforting, sustaining, and inspiring" to note that despite "industrial and social storms" raging in the North, "we of the South have been resting in peace, safety and serenity."[13]

Elsewhere, as Thomas W. Hanchett has shown, Charlotte's New South leaders congratulated themselves on a city that was industrializing without "the teeming immigrants, angry strikes and political upheavals" that plagued the North. In their view, the persistence of a rigid racial and class structure was both natural and divinely ordained. As the *Charlotte Chronicle* noted matter-of-factly, "Inequalities run all through the social fabric, irrespective of race or previous conditions. . . . There have always been and always will be social distinctions. . . . All will be ordered as Providence deems best and wisest." At the bottom of the New South order, black southerners were expected to labor in grateful, silent obedience to their white benefactors. The black man, wrote Watterson, could "do more good for his race by sobriety, industry and modesty than all his friends can do for him or his enemies against him." When

Watterson declared that "the ambition of the South is to out-Yankee the Yan-kee," he clearly referred to the manner in which the region should rebuild its economy as opposed to the way it would rebuild its society.[14]

Despite repeated statements for northern consumption that he favored full and immediate sectional reconciliation, Grady often played on anti-northern sentiments when speaking to the home folks. His famous story of a funeral in which the coffin was imported from Cincinnati and tombstone from Vermont, while the South furnished nothing but "the corpse and the hole in the ground" was appropriated from an antebellum orator's attempt to rally southerners against northern economic exploitation. In reality, the ultimate goal of many New South proponents was not just economic recovery but, as Gaston put it, "the South's dominance in the reunited nation." In this sense, the New South's pursuit of industry did in fact resemble what W. J. Cash called "a new charge at Gettysburg." Cash explained that what "the New South meant and boasted of was mainly a South which would be new in this: that it would be so rich and powerful that it might rest serene in its ancient positions, forever impregnable." In support of his contention, Cash quoted an 1880 editorial from the *Raleigh News and Observer*, arguing that "the South should . . . make money, build up its waste places, and thus force from the North that recognition of our worth and dignity of character to which the people will always be blind unless they can see it through the medium of material strength."[15]

Hoping not just to deflect the criticism coming from Lost Cause propo-nents but to redirect their zealotry and energy into the crusade for economic revitalization, New South advocates presented their program as the best means by which, short of restoring slavery, the social ideals of the Lost Cause might actually be secured. Far from repudiating the Lost Cause, the New South would make southern society essentially impervious to Yankee interference in the conduct of its affairs while forcing northern whites to acknowledge the just and honorable nature of the white South's position in 1861. Assuring white southerners that the New South would never surrender their birthright, Grady seldom passed up a chance to pay tribute to the "exquisite culture" of the Old South and insisted that "the civilization of the old slave regime in the South has not been surpassed, and perhaps will not be equaled, among men." He pledged always to honor its heroic defenders and hold sacred "the memory of the old regime, its tradition and its history." Fellow New South advocate Rich-ard Edmonds warned that it should never be said "that in the struggle for industrial advancement the South has lost aught of her virtues, domestic and public, aught of the manliness and self-reliance, aught of the charms of her women and the honor of her men which hallow the memory of the Old South." Grady and Edmonds found a valuable literary ally in writer Thomas Nelson Page, the exalter nonpareil of that old regime, who saw in the Old South "the purest sweetest life ever lived," one that "made men noble, gentle, and brave and women tender and pure."[16]

David Potter observed that the New South Creed's near seamless fusion of business boosterism and the Lost Cause made it difficult "to tell whether the Sons of Confederate Veterans would infiltrate the Chamber of Commerce" or vice versa, and by 1900 the United Confederate Veterans praised the former soldier for the "industrial victory by which he readjusted the labor system and created the industrial progress of the South." C. Vann Woodward suggested that the exaltation of the Old South and the Lost Cause was simply part of a propaganda blitz aimed at making the New South program more palatable by coating it with the "sweet syrup of romanticism." Paul Gaston put it less cynically when he observed that "under the circumstances," the New South effort to re-instill pride and self-confidence among white southerners involved "more than . . . building on the ashes. . . . [T]he ashes themselves had to be ennobled."[17]

In reality, the challenge facing New South leaders reflected not only the peculiarities of post-Reconstruction southern politics but also the broader requirements, already revealed in the effort to construct an antebellum southern nation, for building or remodeling national or cultural identities in general. As Eric Hobsbawm has explained, "History is the raw material for nationalist or ethnic or fundamentalist ideologies, as poppies are the material for heroin addiction. The past is an essential element, perhaps *the* essential element in these ideologies." Hobsbawm might have been referring specifically to the New South when he explained that "the past legitimizes" by giving "a more glorious background to a present that doesn't have much to show for itself," and especially when he added that "if there is no suitable past, it can always be invented."[18]

Woodward observed wryly that the Old South was the New South's most "significant invention." However, most of the fundamental elements of the Old South idyll had actually been laid down by the proslavery writers and orators in their idealized vision of what things had supposedly been like before the genteel old Cavaliers had begun to give way to Daniel Hundley's uncouth and totally mercenary "cotton snobs." The Civil War and Reconstruction not only provided the white South with its own distinctive experience, but it fast-forwarded the antebellum southern order through the process of aging and historical distancing. By the end of Reconstruction, what had simply been the South in 1860 had become the "Old South," frozen away in some distant corner of time and accessible only through the imagination.[19]

The unattainable perfection of the once-upon-a-time pastoral southern paradise of long ago was quickly and firmly fixed in the postbellum historical imaginations of many white southerners. By 1884 that novelist George W. Bagby could assert that "beyond question," antebellum Virginia had shone with "a beauty, a simplicity, a purity and uprightness, a cordial and lavish hospitality, warmth and grace . . . a charm that passes all language at my command." By the turn of the century the New South's financial leaders were assuring southerners and non-southerners alike that the antebellum South had been "the home of culture and refinement. With thousands of slaves to cultivate their broad acres, our people lived in ease and plenty."[20]

If it had little else, the white South had at least emerged from Reconstruction with a heroic "golden age" that was to become a vital component of its new regional identity. By assuring members of the group of their grand communal heritage, the golden age encouraged them to unite in order to replicate the achievements and regain the stature that their society had enjoyed in the past. As Anthony Smith has explained, "Memories of a golden age . . . proclaim an imminent status reversal: though at present 'we' are oppressed, shortly we shall be restored to our former glory."[21]

Those who rally support for their cause by invoking a heroic past do not necessarily wish to submit to its ideals so much as to recover its self-confidence and sense of destiny. As Smith noted, the fascination with Joan of Arc in nineteenth-century France did not stem from religious zeal but a desire to destroy the nation's enemies and ignite the spirit of its people. Although the tactics employed to achieve this kind of spiritual resurrection may actually seem quite at odds with the values and goals associated with the golden age, they can always be justified as mere means to a far greater end, so long as a sense of continuity with the glorious past is maintained.[22]

Accordingly, architects of the New South stressed its umbilical connection to the magnificence of the Old South and the heroism of the Lost Cause. Page insisted that the New South "was simply the Old South with its energies directed into new lines," Grady presented it as "the Old South under new conditions," and Edmonds called it an "evolution" and "a revival of the Old South." For others, the New South was really the "Renewed South," or "the old South asserting herself under a new dispensation."[23]

When he died two weeks after Jefferson Davis in 1889, Grady was compared not only to Davis but Jackson, Lee, and other Confederate heroes as "the knightly and chivalrous leader of the peaceful hosts of the New South." He would doubtless have been especially pleased with a eulogy offered by a Georgia editor who testified to his success in linking the New South to the Lost Cause and the leaders of the former to the leaders of the latter: "Mr. Grady, as the representative of what people are pleased to call the 'New South,' but which is the 'Old South' rehabilitated was . . . calculated to do for his country what Hill, Gordon, and other brilliant lights of the old *regime* could never have compassed."[24]

Within the New South Creed itself, the vital linkage between the past and present was embodied in a heroic portrait of the "Redeemers," who, while maintaining complete fidelity to the courageous and honorable traditions of the Lost Cause as practiced by their planter-aristocrat forebears, had first rescued the white South from the living hell of Reconstruction and then embraced the New South vision of industrial progress. From the Redeemer perspective, Goldfield wrote, "the best tribute" to the memory of the Old South and the heroes of the Lost Cause "was to build a new South: to beat the Yankees at their own game, to build factories and cities and not corrupt the morals of the people or upset the racial, gender, and social balances derived from the vanished civilization."[25]

The reference to those who overthrew Reconstruction as "Redeemers" was noteworthy in itself, for New South proponents hoped to be seen as the much anticipated messiahs who could lead their region out of despair and into salvation. Sensitive to clerical critics of New South materialism and hoping to tap into the same religious fervor that had surrounded the Confederate cause, they sought and won the endorsements of prominent clergymen such as Richmond minister Moses D. Hoge, who suggested that, thanks to the New South movement, the heroism and sacrifice of the Confederate veterans would someday be vindicated and the South would "stand before the world like the bronze Athena."[26]

Vanderbilt theologian Wilbur Fisk Tillet dismissed worries about a society corrupted by New South materialism, arguing in 1881 that "the South is morally better than before the War" and pointing out that white southerners now contributed "twice as much to benevolent objects" and built "neater and finer churches than they ever did." In his 1880 Thanksgiving sermon, the Reverend Atticus G. Haygood of Emory College thanked God for the material blessings of progress such as "mattresses, stoves, lamps and parlor organs" and credited the New South's emphasis on hard work and thrift for eradicating the sloth and dissolution that had afflicted some members of the antebellum elite. Evangelist Sam Jones praised the New South's commitment to progress and urged southerners to commit themselves to the "work, perseverance and suffering" necessary to achieve it. Released by Southern Methodist Publishing House, *The Law of Success* suggested that good Christians made good capitalists and vice versa by drawing on the experiences of a number of "self-made" southerners to emphasize "the commercial value of the Ten Commandments and a right-eous life."[27]

Far from a negative influence, Richard Edmonds insisted, "material pros-perity" was "an essential factor in ethical advancement." The New South's leaders were "really messengers preparing the way for religious advancement itself" and were resolved to "make 'Dixie' the Canaan of the new world." In addition to trumpeting exaggerated claims of New South progress in his *Manufacturer's Record*, Edmonds also published a pamphlet in 1890 proclaiming the New South's triumphant role in *The South's Redemption*.[28]

As the righteous high priest of the New South crusade, Henry Grady played the role of evangelist with gusto, urging white southerners to "consecrated service" as the "Great Physician" used the New South crusade to heal the re-gion. He also assured them that "the basis of the South's wealth and power . . . is laid by the hand of the Almighty God, and its prosperity has been estab-lished by divine law." With their faith and support, the New South would "thrill and swell with growth until it compasses the full measure of the destiny for which God intended it"; He would lead them "from one triumph to another" and ultimately, to "a glory unspeaking." Not surprisingly, at his death Grady was remembered as a gift of "the Providence of God," a "Moses" who "had sighted the promised land" and a Solomon who began building "a temple of prosperity for the South."[29]

The New South's evangelists preached a more worldly gospel of wealth and opportunity to northern journalists, businessmen, and financiers who found it difficult to resist the appeals of a once-wayward region now apparently com-mitted to rejoining the union and grateful for the opportunity to benefit from both the example and investment capital of the North. Like their predecessors of the early national era, when late-nineteenth-century northern capitalists looked southward, they saw a land ripe with exploitive promise. In an address to Yale alumni entitled "Go South, Young Man," Chauncey M. Depew pointed to Dixie's vast untapped forest and mineral resources and described it as "the Bonanza of the future." Elsewhere, according to the author of *How to Get Rich in the South*, the region was unrivaled in offering "tempting inducements to the capitalist for profitable investments."[30]

In case the South's abundant incentives, including "cheaper money, cheaper taxation, cheaper labor, cheaper coal, and cheaper power," failed to make them feel sufficiently welcome, Grady used his famous 1886 "New South" address at Delmonico's Restaurant in New York to assure northern investors that his region had "smoothed the path to southward, wiped out the place where Mason and Dixon's line used to be, and hung out our latchstring to you and yours." When he asked his listeners if "New England" would permit "the prejudice of war to remain in the hearts of the conquerors when it has died in the hearts of the conquered," he elicited a resounding chorus of "No's."[31]

The promise of untrammeled, even subsidized, exploitation of the New South's human and natural resources did nothing to dampen the spirit of reconciliation among northern investors, but many northern whites seemed just as enthralled with the New South's mythic vision of the Old South and the Lost Cause. New South spokesmen may not have actually invented this vision, but they adapted it so cleverly to their purpose and promulgated it so energetically and persuasively that it did, in a sense, become one of the region's most exportable commodities. In both North and South, writers like Thomas Nelson Page, who churned out treacly romantic portraits of the Old South, achieved what Francis Pendleton Gaines called a "complete conquest" in the 1880s when "the romancers of plantation life were allowed any measure of romantic abandon." In their vivid imaginations, "estates swelled in size and mansions grew proportionately great. Gentlemen were perfected in lovely grace, gay girls in loveliness, slaves in immeasurable devotion." By 1888 Albion Tourgeé could observe that "our literature has become not only distinctly Southern in type but distinctly Confederate in sympathy."[32]

A number of observers have attributed the national appeal of the romantic pre-bourgeois plantation ideal in both the antebellum and postbellum eras to what C. Vann Woodward called "the compensatory dream of aristocracy, the airs of grace and decorum left behind, yearned for but never realized." Seen in this light, here was the resurrected vision of a distinctly southern way of life that had been so seductively rendered by John Pendleton Kennedy and other writers of the 1830s. The idea of a society modeled on "Swallow Barn" surely offered a most admirable and appealing contrast to many northerners who, in the midst of an economic revolution, were troubled by ethnic and labor unrest and the rise of a business and industrial elite notably short on breeding, manners, idealism, or any other traits not directly relevant to making money. As David Blight put it, "an unheroic age could now escape to an alternative universe of gallant cavaliers and their trusted servants."[33]

Although it clearly provided a welcome escape from contemporary northern realities, part of the appeal of the Old South legend may actually have been
not its "otherness" but its quintessential Americanness, or at least its capacity
to convey a sense of what it would be like to achieve the ultimate and complete
fulfillment of the American dream. After all, antebellum southern planters
had been free to indulge their lust for wealth, power, and status in a setting
unmarred by the class conflict, greed, apprehension, and guilt, not to mention
the material as well as moral grime, that seemed to pervade the Gilded Age
North. The mythical planter-Cavalier faced none of these, but enjoyed the affection and respect of everyone, even those whose exploitation and subjugation underwrote his exalted lifestyle and position.

Meanwhile, the wealthy planter's legendary indifference to his account books
was not necessarily a sign of weakness but an indulgence much coveted by Gilded
Age northerners pursuing what Henry James called "the main American formula" by trying "to make so much money that you won't, that you don't 'mind,'
don't mind anything." As we have seen, large slaveholders were the richest class
of people in the nation by 1860. In *Swallow Barn*, Kennedy's narrator takes envious note of what Frank Meriwether has managed to acquire despite his laziness
and "thriftless hospitality." With tongue in cheek, the narrator reveals his own
modest estimate that he could be happy with no more than "a thousand acres of
good land, an old manor-house on a pleasant site, a hundred Negroes, a large
library, a host of friends, and a reserve of a few thousands a year in the stocks in
case of bad crops, and finally a house full of pretty, intelligent and docile children, with some few et ceteras not worth mentioning."[34]

Noting that the appeal of the Lost Cause to postbellum white southerners
was "buttressed by every man's dream of the good life," Rollin G. Osterweis
understood that "the willingness to perpetuate the Southern system, to help
keep Blacks in perpetual if not legal bondage, to resist stoutly all liberal efforts
at social reform . . . came not purely from a depraved lust for oppression or
innate bigotry; slavery, and afterwards, white supremacy, were the means of
achieving the leisure and enjoyments which a beneficent climate and bounte-
ous land made possible."[35]

In addition to selling this Dixiefied version of the American Dream, fiction writers, both North and South, saw in the sentiment for sectional reconciliation a
bull market for stories of intersectional romance and marriage. Regardless of

the author's regional origins, in the popular "reconciliation" or "reunion" novels of the 1870s and 1880s, the South was portrayed more in feminine than masculine terms. The standard formula for this genre was a tempestuous courtship between a fiery, unreconstructed southern belle and a solid, sophisticated northern man who ultimately tames and marries her (thereby subduing the South for the second time), often using his Yankee ingenuity and drive to restore the economic vitality of her family's crumbling plantation in the bargain.

Acutely sensitive to the northern literary market, Thomas Nelson Page understood that "the female rebel element . . . *will* not wound any one," and Nina Silber has observed that as a symbol of "proper, well-ordered and hierarchical gender relations," the intersectional marriage became "the metaphor for the reunited states. . . . By treating reunion mainly as an amorous endeavor," Silber added, the reconciliation novels also "contributed to the increasingly depoliticized assessment of the Civil War and its aftermath by hiding all political and sectional view points behind the rubric of romance and sentiment."[36]

Despite his personal reservations about New South materialism, Georgia writer Joel Chandler Harris lent his legendary portrayal of the former slave, "Uncle Remus," to the New South's mythology of both sectional and racial reconciliation. In "Uncle Remus as a Rebel," published originally in Henry Grady's *Atlanta Constitution* in 1877, Uncle Remus shoots and kills a Yankee sniper who is about to kill his master. However, when the story appeared in Harris's *Uncle Remus: His Songs and Sayings*, the nation's best-selling book in 1880, the old man only wounds the Yankee, and after helping to nurse him back to health, looks on happily as he marries "Miss Sally," his former master's sister. Uncle Remus remains a faithful and undemanding servant of his family, and when he is asked by an incredulous northerner how he could shoot a man who was fighting for his freedom, he explains that, owing to his dedication to his master, mistress, and "Miss Sally," he "jes disremembered all 'bout freedom en lammed aloose." The son born to Miss Sally and her Yankee husband ultimately becomes both the chief recipient of Uncle Remus's "Brer Rabbit" stories and a symbol of the fruits of the North-South reunion. Although the Uncle Remus tales helped to validate the region's racial order for several generations of southern white children, Harris's yarns suggested to white Americans at large that, in the words of David Blight, "their terrible war had nothing to do with race" and "never really needed to have happened."[37]

Offering up a steady diet of black characters who defended their former owners and often waxed nostalgic about their carefree days as slaves, writers like Harris and Thomas Nelson Page assuaged any lingering feelings of guilt among northern whites about their abandonment of Reconstruction or their ready reacceptance of southern whites into their good graces. This provided no comfort, of course, to southern blacks, who were largely reduced to invisibility save in the role of happy, loyal, and totally servile retainers who affirmed the wisdom of the New South's racial ethos.

The readiness of whites outside the South to embrace this stereotype of southern blacks was evident as early as 1876, when the Philadelphia Centennial Exposition presented "a band of old-time plantation darkies who will sing their quaint melodies and strum the banjo before visitors of every clime." At the World's Columbian Exposition in 1893, officials accepted the proposal of a southern white board member to offer an exhibit that would celebrate "the slave days of the republic" and present contemporary examples of the "ignorant contented darky" with two hand-picked "well-behaved . . . real colored folks."[38]

Noting the apparent nationwide groundswell of sympathy for the New South's version of slavery and the Civil War, Albion Tourgeé lamented the "tendency to forget altogether the fact that a war could not be waged for the preservation of the Union unless someone was responsible for the attempt to destroy it." In an effort to explain how so many northern leaders could so readily re-embrace their rebellious countrymen, Blight has argued that the "emancipationist" legacy of the Civil War was abandoned when southern white supremacists simply "locked arms" with those northern "reconciliationists" who for economic, political, or other reasons put restoring national unity ahead of insuring racial justice. Blight's explanation of the means by which white southerners who had lost the war seemed to win the peace has considerable merit. Still, the relative ease with which this was accomplished may say something about not only the persuasiveness of the New South appeal but the modest numbers and limited influence of those, other than African Americans, who had seen the Civil War as a crusade for emancipation and black uplift in the first place.[39]

The willingness of northern whites both to forgive the white South's racial sins and to forget those whom it had sinned against reflected not only disillusionment with the economically and politically disruptive social experimentation of congressional Reconstruction but also the ascendance of Social Darwinism whose proponents, like the New South's D. A. Tompkins, insisted that "survival of the fittest, is, has been, and will always be the law of progress." The obvious enthusiasm of southern whites for the Spanish American War and the ensuing strain of exercising dominion over the non-white inhabitants of territories acquired as a result of the war also encouraged greater empathy with the defenders of white supremecy in the South. With both racism and nativism rife throughout the land, a Lost Cause orator thought it a propitious time to dust off the Confederacy's paradoxical contention that the South had proven its Americanness by seceding from the United States. "The Southern people are the Americans of Americans," he declared, and Confederate veterans "are representatives of an American army—not an army of foreigners and blacks fighting for pay."[40]

The creation of any new group identity typically requires the "invention of tradition," which, according to Hobsbawm, is likely to occur wherever and whenever "a rapid transformation of society weakens or destroys the social patterns for which 'old' traditions had been designed." In many cases, invented traditions are the key to securing the emotional and political allegiance of the majority of the population at large. For the New South, this meant not only the celebration of a greatly embellished Old South but the almost ritualistic trotting out of the old captains of the Lost Cause to convey their blessings on the new captains of industry and commerce whenever the latter sought local financial and moral support for their ventures. In the New South, Gaston explained, "the romance of the past was used to underwrite the materialism of the present" because "the New South prophets were well aware that the blessing of a 'colonel' (if there were no generals handy) would do as much to float bonds and raise subscriptions as a dozen columns of optimistic statistics in the *Manufacturer's Record*."[41]

In *Colonel Carter of Cartersville*, a popular novel of the period, one character observes that "in a sagging market, the colonel would be better than a war boom." The colonel in question, "Colonel George Fairfax Carter, of Carter Hall, Cartersville, Virginia," is "frank, generous, tender-hearted . . . as simple as he is genuine . . . of good birth, and limited knowledge of the world and of men, proud of his ancestry, proud of himself, believing in states' rights, slavery and Confederacy." Cheerfully indifferent to the somber realities of his own depleted finances, Colonel Carter's antebellum mind-set seems to render him an unlikely candidate for economic success in the New South. Yet, his casual revelation that he has long known of what he has always deemed a worthless coal deposit on the Carter Hall estate leads to the purchase of said deposit by an English syndicate at a price that promises to restore him to financial security and material comfort. In the end, the dynamic developing New South not only saves the charming but economically clueless Old South but keeps its gracious and generous spirit alive.[42]

Here again, as Catherine W. Bishir explained, the linkage between antebellum planter aristocrats and the industrial capitalists of the postbellum era provided "a legitimizing continuum from the Old South to the New South." In

fact, the societal model advanced by the embellished and highly selective historical and literary portraiture of the Old South and the Lost Cause provided
a blueprint for the gender, class, and racial hierarchy envisioned in the New
South Creed. At the top of the pyramid, the planter represented both patriarchy and deference to upper-class white authority in general. Subservient to
him was the much-celebrated mistress of the plantation who had stepped forward to meet the challenges of war without ever straying from the feminine
ideal of dedication and obedience to one's husband. The totally virtuous, kind,
gentle, but quietly strong plantation mistress had shown her husband "the
utmost confidence in his manhood and valor" before and during the war and
had enjoyed in return "the devotion that one pays to the soul's idea of pure
womanliness."[43]

There were also tributes to the loyal and deferential enlisted men who had
served, suffered, and died for "their childhood homes, their firesides, the honor
of their ancestors, their loved ones, their own native lands." Contradicting many
wartime observers, New South orators praised the Confederate rank and file
for their strict discipline and respect for private property, drawing an implied
contrast with the labor agitators and agrarian insurgents of the 1880s and 1890s.
North Carolina industrialist Julian Carr seemed to anticipate the place of many
a former Confederate private in the New South order when he praised the
common soldier for permitting himself "for duty and for love to be made into
the cog of a wheel."[44]

Lost Cause orations also heaped praise on the dutiful slaves who had never
hesitated to follow their masters to war or to remain faithful to and protective
of their mistresses back home. The *Georgia Christian Index* even insisted that
the South had held out for four years only because the slaves had been "quite
as loyal to the Confederacy as their masters." This wishful contention ignored
not only widespread evidence of the wholesale flight of slaves to meet the union
advance but the eagerness of the former slaves to celebrate their freedom. As
early as January 1, 1864, blacks had taken to the streets in Norfolk, Virginia, to
observe the first anniversary of the Emancipation Proclamation. The following year, black Charlestonians had assembled for a celebratory parade on March
21, 1865, at the Citadel Green. (Ironically, the Citadel, a military college, had
been founded in the wake of the Denmark Vesey insurrection plot to protect
white Charlestonians from slave uprisings.) Schoolchildren carried banners
reading "We know no masters but ourselves" and sang "We'll hang Jeff Davis
on a sour apple tree." A group of young women rode in a wagon draped with
United States flags and dubbed the "car of liberty." Another wagon featuring a

mock slave auction was followed by a hearse with a sign reading "Slavery is dead." In later years, on the Fourth of July, blacks took over Charleston's Battery, which was otherwise unofficially off-limits to African Americans, for a day of celebrating with food, frolic, and inspirational songs and recitations by schoolchildren of the Emancipation Proclamation and excerpts from the antislavery oratory of Frederick Douglass.[45]

In Augusta, Georgia, African Americans were prohibited from entering the public cemetery to decorate the graves of Union soldiers in May 1865, but in the years immediately after Emancipation, the city's black residents nonetheless began to celebrate their freedom and the opportunity for racial advancement. Educator John Hope recalled seeing as a young boy a huge multitude massed around the Augusta city hall to hear an array of orators and to observe "military and civic organizations parading, each to the triumphant music of the bands." A crowd estimated in the thousands flocked into Augusta to celebrate July 4, 1865, as the Reverend James Lynch stood at a podium draped with the American flag and asked his audience to swear on Abraham Lincoln's grave to "maintain the honor of the starry standard . . . the liberty of all men forever and forever." Augusta's African American marches took on special significance as participants passed by former slave marketplaces and the city's monuments to the American Revolution, whose heritage Confederate orators had also sought to appropriate. Similar African American Independence Day celebrations were organized near Union Army posts in Kentucky in 1865. In Richmond, meanwhile, black citizens thronged the state capitol grounds to celebrate the Fourth of July, and after 1890 black militia units paraded by the imposing statue of Robert E. Lee on Monument Avenue.[46]

Through these celebrations, black southerners had shown, as Kathleen Clark has pointed out, that "whites did not have a monopoly over the public memory," and as a black orator in Texas said in 1896, by advancing a narrative of the past that held substance and meaning for them, they had offered "consolation to generations unborn." These ceremonies laid the groundwork for an alternative, African American version of southern identity, but although they were never abandoned altogether, as white harassment and the threat of bloodshed intensified following the collapse of Reconstruction, public celebrations of emancipation were scaled back and toned down considerably.[47]

Whites in Georgia eventually succeeded in banning black militia participation in African American parades, thereby denying blacks one source of potential protection from white violence. Black orators were obliged to offer more restrained and conciliatory rhetoric as atrocities such as the Atlanta riot of

1906 offered deadly proof of white resolve, and when John Hope came back to
Augusta as an adult, he saw immediately that celebrations of freedom and
black achievement had fallen on hard times. "On my return [I] found that vast
multitude of my boyhood years [had] shriveled into a church." The speaker,
meanwhile, avoided such terms as "emancipation, freedom, [or] liberty." Still,
even when reduced to individual observances, commemorations of the fight
for black freedom retained an enduring significance for African Americans.
Every May during her Chapel Hill girlhood, when Pauli Murray strode by graves
decorated with Confederate flags to plant "Old Glory" on the grave of her
grandfather, a Union veteran, she realized that "upon this lone flag I hung my
nativity and the right to claim my heritage."[48]

By the 1890s southern blacks and whites were clearly separated not only by
color but by sharply contrasting historical visions. As Joan Marie Johnston
observed, "One group celebrated the birthday of Lee, the other the life of
Douglass. One group read Thomas Nelson Page . . . but with tears in their eyes,
while the other read Dubois with determination. One group vilified Harriet
Beecher Stowe, and the other celebrated her birthday."[49]

The insistence of the New South's white leaders that their historical representations must prevail underscored not only the power of the past but also the
importance of that power, especially in a society whose identity is a work in
progress. As Blight put it, "those who can create the dominant historical narrative . . . will achieve political and cultural power." In the long run, the installa-
tion of the Old South–Lost Cause as the "dominant historical narrative" among
southern whites played a key role in achieving not just the New South objective of restoring white supremacy over blacks but of restoring the supremacy
of white elites over the entire society.[50]

The most significant political threat to this white elite came as the Farmer's
Alliance and Populist insurgents of the 1880s and 1890s demanded more progressive taxation, lower interest rates, and other government regulatory and
assistance measures designed to help the increasingly impoverished and dependent small farmers who were largely excluded from the New South narrative. In Georgia, New South leaders proved especially effective in fusing the
goals of white supremacy and industrial development with the ideals of the
Lost Cause and presenting themselves as the champions of all three. Faced

with a tentatively biracial Populist challenge, they invited the white "country people" to hear General John B. Gordon's legendary lecture on "the last days of the Confederacy." It may also be worth noting that groups such as the United Confederate Veterans and the United Daughters of the Confederacy emerged at or near the high tide of the Populist challenge to the New South identity.[51]

In reality, as Sarah H. Case has pointed out, "the families of many UDC members depended on the new economy to perpetuate their elite status." UDC membership rolls were full of wives and daughters of prominent New South industrialists, bankers, and businessmen. In Athens, Georgia, Mildred Rutherford, the niece of Confederate generals Howell and T. R. R. Cobb, achieved nationwide acclaim as historian general of the UDC, using her prolific writing and stirring oratory to propound the gospel of the Lost Cause and legitimize "secession, segregation and 'home rule.'" Rutherford's pride in the Old South blended seamlessly with her faith in the New, and she proved as adept as Henry Grady at rattling off a list of the region's industrial accomplishments and nearly as eloquent as Grady in touting its even greater economic potential.[52]

Throughout the South, white social and political elites used their power over how the past was both remembered and represented publicly to consolidate their power over the present and the future. A former Confederate officer descended from North Carolina's colonial pioneers and revolutionary leaders, Alfred Moore Waddell called in 1885 for publicly financed memorials to the state's white heroes. Waddell worked closely with many of the state's affluent white women in organizations like the North Carolina Monumental Association and the Ladies Memorial Association to assure the erection of monuments that would show the state's gratitude "to her heroic sons."[53]

Waddell and his female counterparts were more than mere harmless Lost Cause romantics, however. With the election of 1898 approaching, Waddell took to the stump to champion white supremacy. True to the Lost Cause ethos, he made no distinction between Revolutionary patriots and Confederate patriots. As their "sons" and "brothers," he vowed, "we ourselves are men who, inspired by these memories, intend to preserve at the cost of our lives, if necessary, the heritage that is ours." The key to preserving this heritage of white dominance was doing whatever was necessary to eliminate black voting and thus restore the Democratic party's political supremacy in the upcoming election. Noting the "intolerable conditions" in Wilmington, Waddell warned, "We are resolved to change them if we have to choke the current of the Cape Fear [River] with carcasses."[54]

Such bloodthirsty rhetoric might seem likely to offend the delicate sensibilities of the good ladies of the various monument and memorial associations, but Waddell's wealthy and superbly pedigreed cousin, Rebecca Cameron,
declared his tirade "the equal of Patrick Henry's famous oration." The speech
did her good "down to the ground," she confessed, because she and her friends
had been "amazed, confounded, and bitterly ashamed of the acquiescence and
quiescence of the men of North Carolina . . . and more than once have asked
wonderingly, Where are the white men and the shotguns?. . . It has reached the
point where bloodletting is needed for the health of the commonwealth, and
when the depletion commences, let it be thorough!"[55]

Cameron soon had her wish. The Democratic ticket won a major victory
on November 8, and two days later Waddell himself led a mob that destroyed
the local black newspaper and burned the building that it had occupied. The
violence escalated quickly as armed white men took to the streets, and at day's
end at least twenty blacks were dead and a number of both blacks and whites
had been wounded. Black and white Republican leaders were herded onto
northbound trains the very next day. As the celebrations of North Carolina's
Confederate and Revolutionary heritage continued apace, the Wilmington Race
Riot quickly became "the Revolution of '98," and it was woven seamlessly into
a historical tapestry touting the wisdom and heroism of the state's white elite
from the colonial era to the Civil War. North Carolina's Democratic upper
crust had secured their place in the New South order by celebrating and monumentalizing a storied Old South past.[56]

African Americans understood full well what monuments to the antebellum white régime were all about. When Charleston officials erected a statue of
proslavery champion John C. Calhoun, "blacks took that statue personally,"
Mamie Garvin Fields recalled. After all, "here was Calhoun looking you in the
face and telling you, 'Nigger, you may not be a slave but I'm back to see you
stay in your place.'" In response, Fields explained, "we used to carry something with us, if we knew we would be passing that way, in order to deface
that statute—scratch up the coat, break up the watch chain, try to knock off
the nose. . . . [C]hildren and adults beat up John C. Calhoun so badly that the
whites had to come back and put him way up high, so we couldn't get to him."[57]

Blacks in Charleston also knew that the fine houses south of Broad Street
with their two-story columns and great spreading piazzas were such powerful
symbols of a white family's historic prestige and influence that even the black
servants who worked in them sometimes saw themselves as "powers in the
community." As part of their effort to reaffirm the link between power in the

past and power in the present, across the South the resurgent white leadership also pushed for the revival of classical and colonial architectural styles in both public buildings and private homes both to affirm the contributions of their ancestors to the South's first "golden age" and to serve notice of their own determination to play a dominant role in constructing the second one. Bennehan Cameron, the only surviving son and principal heir of Paul Cameron, was not only a leading agriculturalist but was heavily involved in both banking and textiles and manufacturing. He was also a prime mover behind the great Seaboard Airline Railroad, which became one of the premier bragging points of New South boosters. Cameron had been active in the 1898 Democratic campaign, and in 1901 he and his wife, Sallie Mayo Cameron, the daughter of a prominent Virginia manufacturer, enlarged the Cameron family's Raleigh home, adding huge Ionic columns and porticos at each end so that it represented "a fine old colonial-type residence" that harkened back "to the days of large plantations and baronial rule." Catherine Bishir contended that, in this case, the South's upper-class whites had not so much invented tradition as arranged it to suit their ends. The New South entered the twentieth century bedecked in the grandiose architectural splendor meant to invoke the Old South Golden Age. Charles R. Wilson observed that this arranged tradition had "dictated . . . that the southern legend needed not only high cotton but high columns as well."[58]

The symbolism of invented or reconfigured traditions is both purposeful and pragmatic. This was obviously true of racial segregation, which not only represented a triumph for white supremacy but, as John Cell has made clear, was "nothing less than an organic component of the New South Creed." Legal segregation became one of the New South's invented traditions in response not just to the destruction of slavery but also to the expansion of the region's railroads and the accelerated movement of the population into the region's urban areas and industrial workplaces. All of these developments increased the likelihood that the two races would come in contact—and into conflict—without the controlling presence or influence of slavery. As racial tensions rose and violence flared, the wisdom of both the federal retreat from Reconstruction and the transfer of northern industrial capital to the South might well be called into question.[59]

Racial separation became a prominent theme in Henry Grady's speeches as early as 1883, and by 1885 he was insisting that the doctrine of segregation should apply "in every theatre," as well as in "railroads, schools, and elsewhere." In the long run, racial harmony and labor stability—and hence an attractive investment climate for northern capitalists—could be insured, argued Grady and his associates, only if the white South was allowed to handle the region's racial problems without fear of further interference from Washington. "Otherwise," Cell explained, "the tense divisiveness of the Reconstruction era might return."[60]

Grady and his colleagues blamed the unsettled racial conditions in the late-nineteenth-century South on the tragically misguided policies of Reconstruction. The image of that "tragic era" as a reckless social experiment that had visited untold injustice and suffering on the white South became as crucial an element of the New South version of southern history as the genteel Old South and the heroic Lost Cause. Both this highly critical vision of Reconstruction and the New South's racial ethic won widespread acceptance among whites outside the South as well, thanks in no small measure to the impassioned, racially charged novels of the Reverend Thomas Dixon. *The Clansman* was eventually adapted to the screen in D. W. Griffith's 1915 feature-length film *Birth of a Nation*, which became an extraordinarily influential popular sensation, searing horrific portraits of Reconstruction and frightening images of sexually savage black men in the minds of white audiences nationwide.[61]

Dixon's *The Leopard's Spots* revealed his conviction that resubjugating blacks was a prerequisite for southern industrial expansion. Dixon's hero, Charlie Gaston, visits the impressive complex of cotton mills owned by his prospective father-in-law, General Worth, who rebuilds his mills after the war. In rhetoric reminiscent of both Henry Grady and Booker T. Washington, the General advises both whites and blacks to put politics aside and "build up the waste places till our country is once more clothed in wealth and beauty" and urges Gaston and other "boys of brain and genius" to "quit throwing yourselves away in law and dirty politics and devote your powers to the South's development." Gaston replies that "the people of the South had to go into politics instead of business on account of the enfranchisement of the Negro. It was a matter of life and death." When the General reveals that "we don't allow a Negro to come inside the enclosure," Gaston responds, "Precisely so. You have prospered because you have got rid of the Negro."[62]

Dixon emphasized the restoration of white supremacy as a New South priority because he saw it as not only a social and political necessity but an economic one as well. So long as blacks could vote and openly challenge white authority, the South would be vulnerable to northern influence and interference. Yankee capital was invested in General Worth's mills, but the General, who epitomized the Old South's values of integrity and honor, was clearly in charge. (A close friend of North Carolina's planter-industrialist Camerons, Dixon built *The Clansman* around an aristocratic family of the same name, and when the novel was filmed as *Birth of a Nation*, much of the shooting was done at the Cameron family's plantation.) As Wayne Mixon has pointed out, in *The Clansman*, Phil Stoneman, who organizes a textile company, is northern-born, but "a naturalized southerner" who opposes Radical Reconstruction. In Dixon's *The Traitor*, John Graham, a former KKK leader, organizes a cotton mill overseen by a northern superintendent who has been "southernized" by his marriage to a southern woman. In all three cases, the mill owners seem less concerned about personal gain than regional recovery, suggesting that the New South could conquer the world of business and industry without abandoning the humane and nonacquisitive ideals of the Old.[63]

Henry Grady had insisted that if his fate was left "to those among whom his lot is cast ... the negro will find that his best friend is the southern democrat." What the New South's Democratic politicians actually sought, however, was the regional equivalent of white supremacist "home rule" in both social and political relations, the former through institutionalized racial separation and the latter through institutionalized denial of the vote to blacks. Disfranchise-ment quickly purged the electorate of almost all potential black voters and a great many lower-class white ones as well, thereby assuring the Democratic party's dominance and facilitating the invention of yet another New South tradition—one-party politics. Effectively insulated from lower-class insurgency, conservative white Democrats soon enjoyed a stranglehold on congressional, state, and local offices. As they returned to Washington year after year, the New South's democratic representatives eventually capitalized on their seniority in Congress to give white southerners a good measure of the political self-determination that New South advocates had sought.[64]

Although neither segregation nor disfranchisement did anything to stem a rising tide of racial violence, white orators and editors consistently reaffirmed Grady's insistence that "nowhere on earth is there kindlier feeling, closer sympathy or less friction between two classes of society than between the whites and blacks of the south today." Booker T. Washington had corresponded with Grady in 1887, and both had agreed that there should be "no hostility between the white and colored people in the South" because their interests were absolutely "identical." Still, public confirmation of the suitability and success of New South racial policies by an acknowledged black leader did not come until Washington delivered his famous "Atlanta Compromise" speech at the Cotton States Exposition in 1895.[65]

Intended as a showcase for New South progress, the exposition itself was a perfect setting for the New South's model black man who through determination, thrift, irreproachable public behavior, and not a little cunning had managed to pull himself "up from slavery" into a position of influence, prestige, and relative prosperity, all the while exhibiting the humility that the New South demanded in equal measure of all its black residents from the lowliest to the most accomplished. As Louis R. Harlan explained, New South proponents had been searching for "a black man who would symbolize that Reconstruction was over and one they could consider an ally against not only the old Yankee enemy but the Southern Populist and labor organizer."[66]

Such a symbol reassured not just southern whites who supported the status quo but also northern whites who saw the New South identity as a rationale for shifting their attentions away from the region's racial problems and focusing on its economic prospects. Counting on Washington's conservatism and conciliatory rhetoric, organizers gave him the chance to speak on the Exposition's opening day, and he more than met their expectations. Some black Atlantans boycotted the rigidly segregated affair, but Washington's earnest counsel that blacks must accept their initial status at the bottom of the socioeconomic ladder and, beyond that, acknowledge "the fact that the masses of us are to live by the production of our hands" was music to the ears of New South proponents. The same was true of his reassurance that "the wisest among my race understand that the agitation of questions of social equality is the extremest folly." The day after his speech, Washington urged the southern black man to stop "fretting and fussing over nonessentials" and "throw aside his vagaries and enter in and reap the harvest." If he did so, then out of the union of southern men, white and black, would rise "not only a new South but a new Negro." Nothing since Grady's "immortal [New South] speech," a New York journalist declared, had illustrated "so profoundly the spirit of the New South." Clark Howell, Grady's successor at the *Atlanta Constitution*, obviously agreed, describing Washington's address as "a full vindication" of his predecessor's gospel of racial harmony and economic interdependence.[67]

Not all of Washington's contemporaries, black or white, accepted his endorsement of the New South identity. Although the New South Creed quickly became the dominant ideology among late-nineteenth-century southern white political, economic, and intellectual leaders, its contradictions, inconsistencies, and inaccuracies were too blatant to escape challenge altogether. The first generation of postbellum southern white intellectuals generally saw economic growth as the answer to a multitude of the region's ills. Still, by no means all of them accepted its highly romanticized version of antebellum southern life, its hyperbole about the era of progress already at hand, or its definition of progress as solely a matter of factories and profits. In fact, as they challenged the New South Creed, these early critics raised important questions and suggested crucial themes that would ultimately engage many of the leading figures of the twentieth-century Southern Renaissance.

Walter Hines Page embraced the New South's goal of industrial progress but not its worship of the romantic and encumbering traditionalism of the Lost Cause. As a lifelong proponent of educational improvement, Page even urged the United Daughters of the Confederacy to think more about building schools than erecting monuments to the Confederate dead. Impatient with the New South's obsession with ancestor worship, he angrily suggested that his native North Carolina needed nothing quite so badly as a "few first class funerals." Page sounded remarkably like H. L. Mencken and his South-baiting minions of the 1920s when he described North Carolina as "the laughing stock among the states" and declared, "There is not a man whose residence is in the state who is recognized by the world as an authority on anything." Page also protested the constraints on free speech in the New South: "I must be offensive or I must be silent on our history, on the real condition of Southern people, on the Negro, on the church, on almost all subjects of serious concern."[68]

In a sense, as one scholar noted, Page believed in *a* "new" South but not necessarily *the* New South as articulated by Grady and his contemporaries. He soon grew skeptical of incessant, exaggerated claims of economic progress, and where Grady had already declared his New South a *fait accompli*, Page's new South "was not then a reality," but something he hoped "to see a new South evolve into in time and with effort and expenditure." Describing Page as "a more effective critic of Southern sloth, poverty, and intellectual and cultural sterility than any southerner of his generation," Fred Hobson explained that when Page "looked at Dixie, what he saw was a problem South, the same South that Howard W. Odum and the social scientists would see and seek to remake thirty or forty years later." Like many New South critics of his era, however, Page would wind up exerting most of his effort to remake the region from afar. Convinced that he would never make a dent in "the strong southern conservatism," he moved to New York in 1882, and in 1900 launched his own magazine, *The World's Work*. He continued to write critically about the South, but the tone of his essays and public addresses was generally less caustic than many of his earlier pieces, and his iconoclastic novel, *The Southerner*, was published initially under the pseudonym, "Nicholas Worth."[69]

Like most of his white contemporaries, Page saw the "Negro Problem" as essentially unsolvable and more of a problem for whites than for blacks. This was clearly not the case with Charles Chesnutt, who, as Wayne Mixon points out, criticized the New South movement "from the perspective of the man most neglected by it, the Negro." Chesnutt's short story "The March of Progress" posed the ironic and complex dilemma facing a black community preparing to appoint a teacher at the new grammar school. The choice comes down to a northern-born white woman, "Miss Noble," who has already given years of dedicated service in the black schools and community or one of her former pupils, "Mr. Williams," a bright young black man who has few career options in the rigidly discriminatory New South.[70]

Although grateful for Miss Noble's contributions, one of Mr. Williams's supporters insists that "the march of progress requires that we help ourselves," because despite the best efforts of blacks to educate their children, "the white people won't hire 'em as clerks in their sto's and factories an' mills an' we have no sto's or factories of our own." Lacking funds to educate their youths as doctors or lawyers and unable to elect them to office, blacks face the reality that about all these young black people could do was to "preach in our own pulpits and teach in our schools." Otherwise, "they'd have to go on waitin' on white folks, like their fo' fathers have done because they couldn't help it."[71]

Though he lived most of his adult life in Chicago, Chesnutt wrote as a southerner, and some of his concerns about the direction in which the New South was headed transcended racial lines. In fact, his final novel, *The Colonel's Dream*, devoted considerable attention to the South's overworked and exploited poor whites. In detailing the frustrated efforts of Colonel French, a chivalrous ex-Confederate who sought to blend the best of Old South ideals with the economic benefits of New South progress, Chesnutt exposed the conditions confronting many white workers in the New South. When Colonel French asks citizens about conditions in the local mill, a liveryman fairly explodes: "Talk about nigger slavery—the niggers never were worked like white women and children are in them mills. . . . When I look at them white gals that ought to be rosy-cheeked an' bright-eyed an' plump an' hearty an' happy, an' them po' little child'en that never get a chance to go fishin' or swimmin' or to learn anything, I allow I wouldn' mind if the durned old mill would catch fire an' burn down. They work children there from six years old up, an' half o 'em die of consumption before they're grown."[72]

Chestnutt's contemporary, T. Thomas Fortune, who had been born into slavery in Florida, rose to prominence as one of the leading black journalists of his day. His book, *Black and White: Land, Labor, and Politics in the South* (1884), registered his strong objections to the New South's racial injustices and assailed its cruel and exploitive capitalism in a sharp critique informed by the writings of both Henry George and Karl Marx. Likewise, in *The Souls of Black Folk*, W. E. B. DuBois also attacked the racial repression that made the New South nothing more than "an armed camp for intimidating black folk." In a frontal assault on the New South accomodationism of Booker T. Washington, DuBois decried the paucity of educational opportunities available to the "Talented Tenth" of southern blacks who would never be satisfied to "lay aside their yearning and contentedly become hewers of wood and drawers of water." He also warned that "no secure civilization can be built in the South with the Negro as an ignorant, turbulent proletariat." DuBois foresaw that "as the black third of the land grows in thrift and skill, unless skillfully guided in its larger philosophy, it must more and more brood over the real past and the creeping, crooked present, until it grasps a gospel of revolt and revenge and throws its new-found energies athwart the current of advance."[73]

Although he protested the exclusion of blacks from full and fruitful participation in southern affairs, DuBois sounded like some of his unreconstructed ex-Confederate contemporaries as he cautioned ambitious young blacks against being seduced by the New South's greed and materialism. The money-mad capital of the New South, Atlanta, reminded him of the mythical winged maiden, "Atalanta," who had vowed to "marry only him who out-raced her" but fell into the grasp of Hippomenes after tarrying too long over the golden apples he had laid in her path. Acknowledging that "work and wealth are the mighty levers to lift this old new land," DuBois worried nonetheless that young black southerners might be seduced by the "rising Mammonism of the re-born South" so that their strivings for justice, righteousness, and knowledge might "suddenly sink to a question of cash and a lust for gold."[74]

Author and essayist George Washington Cable shared DuBois's concern with the materialism, rapacity, and almost delusional boosterism that characterized the New South. Cable was also the most prominent of only a few of DuBois's late-nineteenth-century white contemporaries who challenged the Jim Crow system within the context of the New South identity. The son of a slaveholder and a Confederate veteran himself, he seemed an unlikely critic of southern racial practices, but in several novels and numerous speeches and essays, Cable attempted to call forth a "Silent South" of humane, fair-minded whites who would challenge the region's racial code and restore the civil rights of black southerners. Cable praised whites who expressed support "for the

New South of American ideas, including the idea of material development," but not so those who envisioned "a New South with no ideas except that of material development for aggrandizement of the few, and the holding of the whole negro race in the South to a servile public status, cost what it may to justice, wealth or morals."[75]

Seeing little evidence that racial progress was on the New South agenda, Cable offered some poetic mockery of Henry Grady's famous New South speech, which had essentially ignored the region's racial problems. Cable was quick to praise the eloquence of "Grady" but equally quick to point out that "on MEN'S EQUAL RIGHTS, The darkest of nights, Compared with him wouldn't seem shady." Across subsequent generations, southern liberals would repeatedly attempt to arouse and rally the potentially dominant "Silent South" of whites who, Cable believed, privately deplored the irrational, racist hysteria of the white masses and the demagogic politicians who so crudely but effectively manipulated their ignorance and prejudices.[76]

Not surprisingly, Grady and other white critics accused Cable of favoring "social intermingling of the races." Despite his denials, the furor over Cable's writings and utterances played no small part in his decision to relocate permanently to New England, where he became an early prototype of the southern expatriate writers of the mid-twentieth century, many of whom consistently echoed Cable's call for the South to rejoin the nation and the world at large: "When we have done so we shall know it by this . . . there will be no South. . . . We shall no more be Southerners than we shall be Northerners." Instead of the "New South," Cable explained, "what we want—what we ought to have in view—is the No South." Realizing that this term had an ominous ring, Cable conceded that the idea of a "No South" might sound like "annihilation," but foreshadowing latter-day southern liberals, he insisted, "It is the farthest from it. It is enlargement. It is growth. It is a higher life."[77]

In Cable's novel, *John March, Southerner*, mulatto politician Cornelius Legget asks that blacks be given their share of New South prosperity: "White man, ain't eveh goin' to lif hissef up by holdin' niggeh down." Richmond merchant and Confederate veteran Lewis Harvie Blair echoed these sentiments in *The Prosperity of the South Dependent on the Negro*, charging that efforts to hold down blacks were also holding down whites as well. "Like a malignant cancer which poisons the whole system," Blair argued, "this degradation seems to intensify all the other drawbacks under which we labor."[78]

Blair eventually reversed his position on white supremacy, but even as he had called for fairer treatment of blacks, he realized that his skepticism about

New South economic boosterism might be almost as controversial. The architects of the New South had embellished not just the past but the present as well. In fact, even as the region's first golden age was being celebrated, its second one was declared to be already at hand. The crusade for industrial development was hardly launched before its proponents were lustily, if implausibly, declaring victory. By 1886 Henry Grady was already insisting that "we are entering upon an almost ideal era of progress" and professing to see "a tidal wave of prosperity . . . rushing over this region." Blair noted sarcastically that according to what he read in the newspapers, "the South is enjoying a veritable deluge of prosperity . . . surpassing even the Eastern States" and transforming itself into a place "where poverty is unknown and where everybody is industriously and successfully laying up wealth." To Blair, it seemed that the South had only grown steadily poorer and weaker, but the New South's boosterism was so pervasive and intoxicating that "to doubt the current charming presentations of southern growth and prosperity is to bring down anathemas on one's head. What! The South not prosperous. Impossible they cry; and the individual who questions is an idiot."[79]

For those who cared to listen, of course, a much more subtle challenge to the prevailing gospel of wealth and progress might be heard in the plaintive strains of the blues wafting up from the region's cotton fields and lumber and levee camps. When a bluesman sang "Goin' no higher, Goin' no lower down. . . . Gonna stay right here, 'til they shut me down," he was expressing what Alan Lomax called "the bittersweet of modern alienation" inherent in the New South Creed's stifling negation of the full promise of emancipation.[80]

Likewise, despite the tireless efforts of New South propagandists like Grady to convince them that they were prosperous and happy, the suffering small and middling white farmers who joined the Farmer's Alliance and Populist movements of the 1880s and 1890s clearly knew better. The agrarian insurgents offered no comprehensive critique of the New South identity as such, but they exposed both the evils that were sustained by it and the assortment of bankers, merchants, businessmen, industrialists, politicians, and planters whose interests it served. Rejecting New South romanticism and propaganda, the Populists, as C. Vann Woodward observed, insisted on "speaking openly of class and sectional conflict" and linking politics to "questions of land, markets, wages, money, taxes, railroads." According to the New South formula for southern agriculture, Populist leader Thomas E. Watson told Georgia farmers in 1894, "You cultivate the crop with hard work, and the North and the East does the reaping." Not only did they flirt with the heretical doctrine of interracial co-operation, but the very existence of the Populists as an independent political entity threatened the sacred principle of white solidarity as well.[81]

A number of others also attacked the New South indirectly through their efforts to reform some of the obvious social abuses that it fostered. Both Georgia's Rebecca Latimer Felton and Alabama's Julia Tutwiler assailed the convict-lease system and the use of child labor. Children under sixteen (the majority of them under thirteen) accounted for 30 percent of the cotton mill workforce in 1900. In Alabama, where a few years earlier the legislature had repealed a statewide anti–child labor statute at the behest of a single textile industrialist, Episcopal minister Edgar Gardner Murphy drew condemnation as an opponent of progress in 1904 when he bemoaned the fact that the South's hopes for prosperity "seemed far too dependent on the labor of little children." Also a tireless crusader against child labor, Virginia minister Alexander J. McKelway insisted that those who called themselves "'the New South'" should simply be called "'the Mercenaries.'"[82]

For all of their sensitivity to the impact of the New South's economic and social defects on whites, however, many of its critics showed little sensitivity to its neglect and subjugation of blacks. This was certainly true of Murphy, who even championed black resettlement to Africa. In his later career, Populist leader Tom Watson became known as a vicious Negrophobe and an advocate of lynching.

No New South critic was a more dedicated proponent of white supremacy than Rebecca Latimer Felton, whose zeal to protect white women from black rapists led her to defend lynching as well. Felton's rabidity on this issue exploded as the first decade of the twentieth century brought more forceful criticism of racial conditions and the mistreatment of southern blacks. As professor of Latin at Emory College and the son-in-law of Emory's past president Bishop Warren A. Candler, Andrew Sledd seemed secure enough to speak his mind on practically any topic, but he ignited a firestorm in 1902 when he reacted to a recent lynching in Georgia with an angry article in the *Atlantic Monthly*. Describing the horrific spectacle in which a black man was burned to death—on the Sabbath, no less, and before a huge crowd—Sledd wrote that the object of such "savagery" was not to administer "justice" but to "teach the negro the lesson of abject and eternal servility, [and] burn into his quivering flesh the consciousness that he has not, cannot have, the rights of a free citizen or even of a fellow human creature." The South's greatest "difficulty," Sledd concluded, "is not with the negro but the white man."[83]

Such pronouncements were nothing short of heresy to Felton, who led the charge against Sledd, condemning the "rot" which he had "vomited" into *The Atlantic.* Sledd should be shipped North immediately, Felton insisted, "Pass him on! Keep him moving! He does not belong in this part of the country." Even the efforts of his prominent father-in-law to defend him were to no avail, and Sledd was soon forced to resign.[84]

The Sledd affair sent a shock wave through the South's intellectual and academic community, but it did not deter Trinity College professor John Spencer Bassett from speaking out on the race issue only a year later. Sounding a bit like Walter Hines Page, Bassett had described white southerners as "emotional, loyal, orthodox, religious—and that is a good thing; but we are not so thoughtful, rational, self-cultured as we might be." In an effort to rectify this, he had established the *South Atlantic Quarterly* in 1902, hoping to reach the admittedly limited "audience of serious minded people of the South." True to his word, Bassett was soon decrying the "reign of passion" created by the South's racist demagogues who had warped and corrupted its political system and "pauperized the intellects" of its leaders.[85]

Bassett's biggest bombshell came in October 1903 when he reiterated his criticism of race-baiting politicians and, anticipating the arguments of C. Vann Woodward some half-century later, charged that disfranchisement and racial repression were the means by which the Democratic party in the South sought to insure not just white supremacy but its own political dominance. In his most controversial assertion, however, Bassett lauded Booker T. Washington as "all in all, the greatest man, save General Lee, born in the South in a hundred years." He also predicted future racial conflict as blacks grew stronger and more resolved to claim their rights because "the 'place' of every man in our American life is such as his virtues and capacities may enable him to take. . . . Not even a black skin and a flat nose can justify caste in this country."[86]

Bassett's words elicited a predictably hostile reaction from many white North Carolinians, including editor Josephus Daniels of the *Raleigh News and Observer,* who asked if Bassett prayed "with his face toward Tuskegee." Somewhat surprisingly, Bassett weathered the affair (in the short term at least) with strong support from his colleagues and students at Trinity and with crucial backing from the North Carolina business community, especially James B. Duke, a generous benefactor and a trustee of Trinity, whose support for Bassett no doubt influenced many of Duke's business associates.[87]

The backing Bassett enjoyed seemed to vindicate those who had predicted that industrialization would foster greater intellectual tolerance in the region, but his survival was hardly a definitive or lasting triumph. He insisted in a subsequent interview that he had advocated "equality of opportunity" rather than "social equality," and though he spoke out on the race question on several other occasions, he never regained the intensity revealed in his most controversial piece. Finally, in 1906 Bassett reluctantly headed north to Smith College, following much the same pattern as other New South critics such as Walter Hines Page and George Washington Cable.[88]

New South dissenters fared so poorly within the region because, as transparent and contrived as it may seem in retrospect, the New South Creed painted an almost seamless and undeniably seductive mural in which a glorious past, a reassuring present, and a glittering future were fully integrated and virtually indistinguishable. The Old South/Lost Cause legend was the New South's emotional and psychological anchor, but where the antebellum Cavalier had been done in by forces beyond his control or even his comprehension, his New South descendants were firmly in command of their own destinies. As champions of past, present, and future, the New South's proponents were in an all but impregnable position while anyone who challenged them could readily be cast as the opponent of both progress, tradition, and, for good measure, the status quo as well. Despite their ultimate failure to deliver the surging prosperity they promised, by serving up a potent mixture of myths about the past, illusions about the present, and fantasies about the future, New South spokesmen succeeded in constructing a remarkably durable and resilient regional identity, one that helped, in Michael O'Brien's words, "to make permanent the very idea of a South."[89]

As he made his way north in 1906, Bassett had predicted that it would be "another generation" before the South would be "ready for the scholar or the writer of serious books." Owing in no small measure to the pervasive and enduring influence of the New South Creed, Bassett's assessment was not far off the mark. In fact, the struggle to unravel the tangle of myth and contradiction that lay within the heart of the New South Creed's "idea of a South" proved to be a central dynamic within the post–World War I Southern Renaissance.[90]

4

The Southern Renaissance and the Revolt against the New South Creed

DANIEL J. SINGAL has pointed to the pervasive influence of the New South Creed and its role in retarding the growth of intellectual modernism in the region. Because it was grounded so firmly and rigidly in a carefully constructed historical narrative, the weight of New South orthodoxy fell heavily on an emerging cadre of southern historians who faced especially strong pressure to fit their version of the region's past within the framework of the New South identity. To question the New South Creed's historical tenets "at any point," C. Vann Woodward explained, "was not only to make judgments about history, but to pass judgment on the legitimacy of the social order sustained by the assumptions questioned." Consequently, the early postbellum generations of southern historians were expected to occupy themselves with "vindicating, justifying, rationalizing, and often celebrating the present order," and as the outspoken John Spencer Basset pointed out in 1897, anyone who failed to do so faced "denunciation as a traitor and a mercenary defiler of his birthplace."[1]

E. Merton Coulter observed that in the wake of the Civil War, history had taken on for southern whites "a more practical character than had ever appeared before in all the annals of the South. It was the last stronghold of the South not for the defense of its nationality but for the protection of something more clear and sacred, its reputation." Such a defense was necessary, argued Alfred Moore Waddell, because in northern accounts of the war, white southerners had been "pilloried before the world as ignorant, barbarous, cruel traitors and rebels, who, without justification or excuse, sought to destroy the best government under the sun, and deluged a continent in blood." Yankee writers, Waddell charged, saw history as nothing more than "a child's box of

letters with which we can spell any word we please. We have only to select such
letters as we want, arrange them as we like, and say nothing about those which
do not suit our purpose."[2]

In reality, the same might be said of the architects of new or resurrected
group identities across the centuries and around the world, including Waddell
himself, as well as other proponents of the Lost Cause–New South Creed version of the southern past. Established in 1869, the Southern Historical Society,
consisting of "some of the most distinguished soldiers and civilians of the
Confederacy," had set out to collect historical documentation sufficient to provide "a complete arsenal from which the defenders of our cause may draw any
desired weapon." A mainstay in this group, Jefferson Davis was understandably intent on presenting the Confederacy and his leadership thereof in the
best possible light, even suggesting at one point that a splendid new device,
the phonograph, might be useful in recording eyewitness accounts that would
support this effort.[3]

Although it was dedicated ostensibly to preserving the records of the Confederacy and the southern war effort, the real goal of the Southern Historical
Society, as Richard D. Starnes concluded, was the "creation of a Confederate
historical memory" that would vindicate both the Confederate cause and those
who served it. In the very first article in the very first issue of the *Southern Historical Society Papers*, former Confederate congressman R. M. T. Hunter blamed
the Civil War squarely on the North, which had forced white southerners to
choose between war and economic, social, and political ruin. Ultimately, the
South had fallen because of the scarcity of munitions, supplies, and manpower.
Certainly, Hunter argued, "she yielded no superiority in valor and skill, but to
the mere avoirdupois of numbers."[4]

Former Confederate Robert L. Dabney believed that history should serve
not just as justification, but also as propaganda, designed to stir the emotions
of succeeding generations of white southerners and even secure the sympa-
thies of white northerners as well. What the South needed was "a book of 'Acts
and Monuments of Confederate Martyrs.'" Dabney even urged southern writers to emulate the successful psychological strategies employed by Harriet
Beecher Stowe in *Uncle Tom's Cabin* in order to "paint the picture skillfully of
Southern martyrdom under ruthless abolition outrages" and dramatize "helpless sufferings of *weakness* under the brute hand of merciless *power*."[5]

As Anne E. Marshall has shown, a similar strategy allowed Lost Cause propagandists in Kentucky to construct a Confederate identity for a state that had

never even left the Union. Editors of the *Southern Bivouac*, which was published by the Louisville chapter of the Southern Historical Society, argued that "the survivors of the lost cause . . . can least afford to be silent," and taking their own advice to heart, they presented both secession and southern white resistance to Reconstruction as "a desperate struggle with influences which threatened to destroy their civilization and reduce their country to barbarism." Meanwhile, cooperative writers like James Lane Allen and later Annie Fellows Johnston with her "Little Colonel" series served up a richly romantic fictional vision of a Kentucky peopled by genteel and kindly masters and happy and obedient slaves.[6]

By the end of the nineteenth century, groups like the United Confederate Veterans and the United Daughters of the Confederacy measured the "truth" of any historical account according to how well it squared with the basic tenets of the Lost Cause. This meant defending secession and the southern war effort, extolling Confederate valor and virtue, and condemning the foul and vindictive deeds of the black-hearted Yankee oppressors. Both organizations were vitally concerned about the kinds of history being taught both to children and to collegians as well. Recognizing the importance of keeping the Lost Cause alive in the minds of younger white southerners, Mary Singleton Slack reminded her UDC compatriots that "thought is power" and declared that the greatest monument the UDC could erect would be "a thought monument" in the "pulsing hearts and active brains" of the South's white youth. A UCV Historical Committee report in 1897 declared that "works in vindication of the course of the South before and during the civil war will be invaluable . . . but controversial literature is not history, and is out of place in political instruction."[7]

The kind of history that the UDC and UCV members sought was supplied in copious quantity by Thomas Nelson Page, who told students at Washington and Lee in 1887 that not only had the South led the move toward American independence and the fight to make it a reality, but once that fight was won, "it was . . . Southern intellect and Southern patriotism which created the federal constitution" and forged "one grand union of the republics known as the United States." Southern whites had remained fanatically loyal to this union until "the North abrogated the solemn compact which bound the two together." In the wake of its defeat, "under the euphemism of reconstruction," the white South, which had been both womb and cradle to the American republic itself, had been "dismembered, disfranchised, [and] denationalized" by the leaders of that same republic. Here again was the recurring image of white southerners who had been scorned and persecuted by their countrymen for nothing more than their devout adherence to the most fundamental tenets of Americanism.[8]

As historian general of the UDC from 1911 to 1916, Mildred Rutherford trumpeted the same message in her books and public addresses, many of them published with titles such as *The Old South: What Made It, What Destroyed It, What Has Replaced It* (1916). In addition to a vigorous affirmation of the South's constitutional right to secede, Rutherford offered venomous indictments of Radicals like Thaddeus Stevens, who, under the alleged influence of his black mistress, had tried to "humiliate" the white South. The Freedman's Bureau, meanwhile, had been created solely to "punish the South," as had the coercive and illegal Fourteenth and Fifteenth amendments. Thanks to writers and orators like Page and Rutherford, the image of white southerners being persecuted by the North for simply defending the American faith quickly became a firmly fixed element of southern white identity, and woe unto the historian who dared to suggest otherwise.[9]

Writing from the standpoint of a trained professional historian in 1904, Professor William E. Dodd, then of Randolph Macon College, complained that certain lines of investigation or argument were best avoided by historians of the South. For example, "to suggest that the revolt from the union in 1860 was not justified, was not led by the most lofty minded of statesmen, is to invite not only criticism but an enforced resignation." Standing ready to sustain this lamentable state of affairs were what Dodd called "our grand confederate camps" who feared that what they saw as "false history" might be "smuggled in from the North." Such organizations featured "history committees" dedicated to keeping the schools free of "any book or books that fail to fasten in the minds of our children a becoming pride in the deeds of their fathers and that fail to give a truthful recital of the principles for which the Confederate soldiers fought."[10]

Presuming in 1911 that the passage of a half century should surely have made it safe to practice some "calm history," University of Florida professor Enoch M. Banks quickly and painfully learned otherwise when he wrote an essay identifying slavery rather than state rights as the true cause of secession and concluded that in the grand sweep of things, "the North was relatively right, and the South was relatively wrong." Facing the full fury of the UDC, a flood of condemnations in the press for his "false and dangerous" opinions, and the threat that university funding might even be withheld, Banks was forced to resign from the Florida faculty.[11]

In 1913 the History Committee of the John Bell Hood Chapter of the United Confederate Veterans raised a howl of protest over the University of Texas's use of "[Edward] Channing's *Student's History* 'so called' *of the United States*," which they condemned for its "narrow, contracted, bigoted New England Stand Point." Writing to George W. Littlefield, a fellow Confederate veteran now a wealthy and influential banker, the History Committee of the Hood Chapter reminded him that "the insidious effort to prejudice the minds of the rising generation in our Southland against the action of their parents in the great war of the '60s has been going on for years." As a result, "the minds of the pupils in southern schools are being saturated with false statements concerning both cause and effect." Rejecting the premise that "in order to reach a right conclusion," students must be exposed to "the evil and insidious slander presented by an artful and cunning opponent," the UCV representatives found it "better to have no History [*sic*] taught than to listen to the untruth and sophistry of a book like Channing's *History* or others of its ilk."[12]

Clearly sympathetic to the UCV's concerns, Littlefield, a member of the University of Texas's Board of Regents, led a behind-the-scenes effort to force its history department to stop assigning two texts that Littlefield and his cohorts deemed too critical of the South. In the process, however, Eugene C. Barker, the enterprising history department head, convinced Littlefield that the University of Texas should establish an archival collection to support research by southern scholars who desired to write books more sympathetic to the white southerner's point of view. Littlefield agreed to fund such an effort, with the expectation that the archive would result in the publication of a "history of the United States with the plain facts concerning the South . . . fairly stated that the children of the South may be truthfully taught." (As we shall see, the Littlefield Fund eventually helped to provide funding for the multivolume "History of the South" series published by Louisiana State University Press.)[13]

Such sentiments notwithstanding, as the twentieth century began to unfold, a growing number of observers had begun to call for a more objective, scientific, and scholarly approach to the study of the South's past, and by 1913 six colleges and universities were actually offering courses in southern history. This number grew, according to one estimate, to "thirty or forty" by the 1920s.[14]

Intent on stressing continuity with the Old South, New South propagandists had danced around the delicate issue of slavery, paying tribute to the grace and gentility of the slaveholding class without addressing the devastating human and economic impact of the institution that supported them. As a more objective approach to southern history began to take shape, however, professional scholars began to acknowledge this contradiction. Like a number of the first generation of professionally trained southern historians, William P. Trent had studied at Johns Hopkins under Herbert Baxter Adams. The founder of the *Sewanee Review* at The University of the South in Sewanee, Tennessee, Trent complained that southerners "cannot be made to take interest in any thing which has not the popular 'New South' for its watch-cry, the obvious fact being forgotten that a scientific study of the 'Old South' would be the best of all proofs of a 'New South's' being really born." Trent's effort to foster a more objective approach to studying the Old South also amounted to what Bruce Clayton called a struggle to "wrest Southern History from the hands of the ex-Confederates and lady writers" and penetrate the exceedingly dense layer of mythology and romanticism that they and other postbellum writers and orators had so speedily and successfully laid down.[15]

Trent's controversial biography of antebellum romanticist writer-turned-polemicist William Gilmore Simms anticipated W. J. Cash's critique of an intellectually constricted Old South that offered only "a life that choked all thought and investigation" and "rendered originality scarcely possible except under the guise of eccentricity." He went on in *Southern Statesmen of the Old Regime* to attack no less a southern icon than John C. Calhoun, who "lacked the power of creative and truthful imagination," and to consign Jefferson Davis, with whom New South spokesmen like Henry Grady sought to associate themselves publicly, to a "place . . . with the failures of history." Trent remained fervently committed to the New South vision of the future, but his rejection of its uncritical view of the past led some trustees at Sewanee to brand him "a dangerous religious and political heretic" and some of his more pious colleagues to pray fervently for his "spiritual regeneration." Increasingly interested in literature (as opposed to history) and distressed that "shallow thinking on political matters, provincialism of taste and sentiments—ignorance and vanity are the dominant characteristics of our people," like others who had begged to differ with some aspect of the New South Creed, Trent finally headed north and accepted a position at Columbia University.[16]

Another critic of the slave regime, William E. Dodd, left Randolph Macon in Virginia and moved to the University of Chicago, where he established another outpost for southerners interested in studying southern history. An ardent Jeffersonian, Dodd blamed "the giant planter machine" for secession and the Civil War, which became the next stage in the process of democratic decline, a stage in which Jefferson Davis completed Calhoun's work by perverting "the old and radical democracy of Jefferson into armies contending upon the field of battle for ideals and purposes absolutely foreign to the mind of the great founder."[17]

By the turn of the century, white southerners were also venturing farther north to study with Columbia University professor William A. Dunning, who, though trained as a European historian, had become an acknowledged authority on the Civil War and southern history and a forthright critic of northern policies during Reconstruction. Generally intent on correcting what they believed was a prevailing northern bias in the study of southern history, Dunning's southern protégés produced a number of state-level studies of Reconstruction in the South. As Peter Novick observed, these southern scholars "saw themselves, and did their best to get their northern colleagues to see them, as wounded victims of northern calumnies and lies, which they were valiantly trying to correct. Any excesses or exaggerations in the performance of that task were only attempts to redress the balance." Northern historians generally acquiesced in this, Novick explained, lest they be seen as "'adding insult to injury.'"[18]

One of Dunning's star pupils was Georgia-born Ulrich B. Phillips, who, after leaving Columbia, moved on to the University of Wisconsin, where he became a colleague of Frederick Jackson Turner. Like Turner, Phillips acknowledged the role of the frontier environment in shaping southern life, but Philips also saw the plantation as a civilizing institution that counteracted some of the frontier's less positive influences. Unlike Trent and Dodd who condemned the old slave regime as wholly antithetical to the aim and purposes of the New South crusaders, Phillips sought in his writings to present a rational, documented portrait of the Old South as a genuine and worthy ancestor to the New.

Although he clung to the Cavalier myth of the planter's origins, Phillips rejected early New South writers' portrayals of antebellum slaveholders as improvident and impractical aristocrats with little taste for Yankee notions such as profits and efficiency. Phillips's disciplined, down-to-earth, and commonsensical slaveholder was a thoroughly engaged manager and businessman who "deliberately and constantly preferred the career of the useful captain of industry to the life of the idle rich." In his view, the Old South's slaveholding planters were an integral element of a less contradictory and more rational past for the New South. Although Phillips's work is remembered primarily for its racism and romanticism, his ideal slaveholder was neither soft-handed nor soft-headed, but a calculating, firm, hardworking capitalist—in short, the perfect ancestor for New South business and industrial leaders.[19]

Moreover, instead of decrying the paternalism of these planters, Phillips lauded it, for he believed that the skillful practice of paternalism was actually the key to a slaveholder's economic success, and like his contemporary Broadus Mitchell, he suggested that the South's twentieth-century capitalists could learn much about effective labor management from their planter predecessors. Finally, Phillips not only characterized antebellum planters as industrial employers worthy of emulation, but he also portrayed their slaves as a competent industrial workforce that, under the civilizing influence of the plantation and the skillful oversight of the planter, had not only shown loyalty and deference but had achieved significant productivity as well. Accordingly, in contrast to the complaints of many New South apologists, Phillips's perspective on the antebellum plantation suggested that the postbellum black population should be seen as a potential asset rather than a perennial burden.[20]

Although Phillips's later writing reveals a growing emotional susceptibility to the romantic Old South legend, the great body of his research lent scholarly credibility to the New South identity by setting the record straight about the antebellum planter and the plantation economy and doing so in a way that reaffirmed rather than challenged the claim of continuity between the Old South and the New. As Phillips's biographer John Herbert Roper concluded, "The story of his life and the study of his thought are informative, since this man spoke for many. Phillips *was* the New South even though he studied the Old South."[21]

The emergence of a more objective, scholarly approach to studying southern history led in the short run to a more critical, analytical perspective on the Old South, but the romance of the antebellum South and the Lost Cause was not the only emotional and ideological challenge confronting the region's professional historians. There was also the obligatory, uncritical optimism of the New South Creed with its insistence on miraculous achievement, thoroughgoing progress, and complete racial and class harmony. As Dodd observed, "According to Southern public opinion, the whole race question is finally settled, never to be opened again, and in matters further removed from the field of politics, such as literature and art, it is exceedingly dangerous to give voice to adverse criticism of the South's attainments in the South or of her present status." The preface to Phillip Alexander Bruce's *The Rise of the New South* praised the volume as "a vital narration of the progress of a mighty people, who, from adversity such as no other section of North America has ever experienced," had risen and "won the race with adverse fate and become the pride of the Union."[22]

Albert Bushnell Hart pointed in 1910 to "a fixed belief that the South is the most prosperous part of the country, which fits in with the conviction that it has long surpassed all other parts of the world in civilization, in military order, and in the power to rise out of the sufferings of a conquered people." The miracle of resurrection had been accomplished, and the day of redemption and vindication was finally at hand. As Paul Gaston summed it up, "The South depicted in most of these early histories rose from the extraordinary devastation of Reconstruction to a glorious plateau of achievement."[23]

In the hands of many writers, the story of the New South was every bit as romantic as that of the Old. In *The Rise of the Cotton Mills in the South*, Broadus Mitchell promised readers that his account was "not only an industrial chronicle, but a romance, a drama as well." Mitchell proved as good as his word, as he consistently presented the nineteenth-century southern cotton mill builders as philanthropists of the first order, "far-seeing, public-minded, generous natural leaders" whose motivation for building their mills stemmed as much from altruism as any other cause. True to the New South myth, Mitchell presented his mill builders as direct descendants of the antebellum Cavaliers who had brought their instinctive paternalism direct from the plantation to the factory.[24]

Although his celebratory treatment of the South's mill-building pioneers essentially followed the New South party line, Mitchell could not blind himself to the deplorable conditions in southern textile mills of the 1920s that seemed completely at odds with the aims and values of the early mill magnates. Condemning what he saw in the "Fleshpots in the South" (1927), he also offered a portrait of intergenerational decline and decay that would also become a familiar theme in the works of many of the literary figures of the Southern Renaissance. The "gentlemen" who had predominated among the philanthropic and paternalistic early mill builders had clearly given way to a cruder, brutally exploitive, crassly materialistic "second generation of manufacturers" who, in his view, were "not subject to the restraints of their fathers" and "not burdened with a sense of noblesse oblige. They are not aristocrats, but bourgeois. They are class-conscious and money-wise." Manipulating ministers, welfare agents, and school curricula, they had managed to make "their private interests appear as synonymous with the well-being of society."[25]

Like many New South advocates, Mitchell tried initially to condemn slavery as a curse on the South's economic aspirations without condemning those who owned slaves directly. In his later writings, however, he charged that the southern slavocracy had not only pursued a "wasteful, staple agriculture" and treated industry "with fear or contempt," but their "vaunted chivalry" was nothing but a "mockery." Sounding the same note that Walter Hines Page had articulated some years earlier and one that W. J. Cash would echo only a few years later, Mitchell argued that the old plantation regime had offered only a life of "stagnation" because it had "no music, no art but Georgian porticoes and beaten biscuit and scanty few men of letters." Mitchell committed the ultimate heresy by attacking the cult of the Lost Cause, even singling out the sainted Robert E. Lee, whose real legacy, he declared, was "poverty, race hatred, sterile fields, the childish and violent crowd gulled by the demagogue." For all his resistance to the romance of the Old South and the Lost Cause, however, Mitchell remained enthralled with the romance of the New, insisting that "Compared to the Old South of cotton, tobacco, rice and sugar," his beloved "New South of industry and commerce" was "a steel blade compared to a stone shard."[26]

As Singal concluded, the case of Mitchell revealed "the extraordinary power that could be wielded by the New South ideology over one of the most intelligent, learned and compassionate southerners of his era." Still, though he remained too emotionally entangled in its mythology to escape its spell entirely, Mitchell's struggle with the inconsistencies and contradictions of the New South Creed reflected the increasingly critical scrutiny that it had begun to attract in the wake of World War I.[27]

Ellen Glasgow and Frank L. Owsley were but two of the participant/observers who suggested that the intellectual outpouring of the postwar "Southern Renaissance" represented in large part "a revolt against the philosophy of the New South." DuBois, Cable, Bassett, and other early critics of the New South Creed had already raised a number of objections and concerns that would fuel critical discourse about the region for much of the twentieth century. This discourse took on a much greater sense of urgency, however, as developments of the war era affirmed that, in Richard King's words, "the cultural superstructure to which educated and 'enlightened' Southerners gave their allegiance and by which they understood themselves was out of phase with the reality of southern life."[28]

Paul Gaston has argued that because myths such as the New South Creed "create mental sets which do not ordinarily yield to intellectual attacks . . . they may be penetrated by rational analysis only as the consequence of dramatic, or even traumatic, alterations in the society whose essence they exist to portray." As a consequence, "the critique and dissipation of myths becomes possible only when tension between the mythic view and the reality it sustains snaps the viability of their relationship." By the 1920s tensions between the New South's myths and its realities seemed to be approaching the snapping point.[29]

Events such as the 1915 lynching near Atlanta of Leo Frank, a Jewish factory superintendent wrongly accused of murdering a female employee, as well as the resurgence of the Ku Klux Klan and the wave of post–World War I racial violence had helped to draw unprecedented attention to the South's enduring problems and deficiencies. In the wake of the war, a multitude of observers within the region and without began a critical reassessment of the New South version of the status quo below the Mason-Dixon line. Published in 1924, Frank Tannenbaum's *The Darker Phases of the South* only reaffirmed growing perceptions of southern benightedness. In the same year, expatriated former Alabama Populist William H. Skaggs stepped forward in *The Southern Oligarchy* to focus the attention of Americans at large on the plight of "the great mass of white and colored citizens of the Southern States, who are held in political subjection and economic serfdom." Meanwhile, Oswald Garrison Villard repeatedly deplored the barbarity of lynching in the pages of *The Nation*, while W. E. B. DuBois assailed southern racial customs in a variety of publications. Focusing on Georgia, the supposed exemplar of New South progress, DuBois argued that "Georgia connotes to most men national supremacy in cotton and lynching, Southern supremacy in finance and industry, and the Ku Klux Klan."[30]

DuBois was no tougher on Georgia than the Baltimore essayist, critic, and editor of the *American Mercury*, H. L. Mencken, who dismissed it as "at once the home of the cotton-mill sweater and of the most noisy and vapid sort of chamber of commerce, of the Methodist parson turned Savoranola and of the lynching bee." Meanwhile, the entire South, "for all the progress it babbles of," was "almost as sterile, artistically, intellectually, culturally as the Sahara Desert." George B. Tindall saw Mencken as the "guiding genius" behind the "neo-abolitionist myth of the savage South" who was "continually trying to nurture the critics and rebels of the New South."[31]

In reality, through his caricatured critiques of the contemporary scene, the acerbic Mencken seemed to be trying to goad white southerners into restoring the erudition and gentility that, so he believed, had characterized the South before the political and cultural ascent of the ignorant white masses in the late nineteenth and early twentieth centuries. Mencken's various attacks on southern cultural and intellectual backwardness won him a significant following among young southern journalists. Among them was North Carolina's Gerald W. Johnson, who saw the South as the "Congo," rather than the "Sahara" of the "Beaux Art" that Mencken described. In Mencken's *American Mercury*, Johnson assailed and spoofed the region in a variety of ways. In the aftermath of a successful tent revival, he found Raleigh, North Carolina, "so thoroughly sterilized morally that it is doubtful that liquor would have been sold to a justice of the Supreme Court, not to mention the parched drummers in the city's hotels." Johnson found both these frenzied religious rituals and the Ku Klux Klan flourishing in the South and the Midwest because "both sections are generally ill-provided with public amusements," and he worried that "impressionable children, caught in one of these orgies may never recover."[32]

Another caustic Mencken disciple, Grover Hall of the *Montgomery Advertiser*, sneered at the South's superabundant "hell-fire alarmists" and "clay-footed pulpiteers and their lay footmen—the deacons, stewards, and elders." Elsewhere, Nell Battle Lewis of the *Raleigh News and Observer* praised Mencken's critiques of the South as both "a heady stimulant" and "a powerful cathartic—an effective purgative for intellectual inertia and dry-rot complacency and asinine self-glorification and pathetic 'artistic' clap-trap!"[33]

Mencken had his black disciples as well, and in fact, he played a role in encouraging some of the key literary figures in the "Harlem Renaissance" that blossomed after World War I. Even as a nineteen-year-old, Richard Wright was both captivated by the way Mencken used words "as one would use a club" and stunned by the substance of what he wrote: "What amazed me was not what he said, but how on earth anybody had the courage to say it." By the time Wright discovered him, Mencken had already influenced many of the leading black intellectuals of the day. In 1918 James Weldon Johnson praised Mencken as "the cleverest writer in America today." Johnson certainly sounded like Mencken when he wrote, "One of the mysteries to us is, what is there to boast of in being a southerner. . . . Among so-called civilized white men the Southerner is the most backward, the most ignorant, the most uncivilized and the most barbarous in the world. His section is without scholarship, without art and without law and order; it is even without money except what it can borrow from the North."[34]

Generally, however, Mencken encouraged black writers to write with less anger and more detachment, from the perspective of one intrigued and amused rather than wounded by the white South's ignorance and insanity. He urged George Schuyler to craft a piece on "how the whites look to an intelligent Negro" and to do it "realistically and fearlessly." When Schuyler expressed a desire to write a spoof about the white man, an enthused Mencken responded, "Lay on. . . . I'd be delighted to see him dosed with the same kind of medicine that he has been giving Ethiop for so many years. Certainly he must be a ridiculous figure seen from without."[35]

From 1929 to 1953, Mencken published fifty-four articles by or about blacks in the *American Mercury*. One of these, "I Investigate Lynchings" by Walter White, chronicled the racist insanity and ignorance that White encountered as he conducted his research into lynching. "Nothing contributes so much to the continued life of the investigator of lynchings and his tranquil possession of all his limbs as the obtuseness of the lynchers themselves," he explained. Published a year earlier, even White's book *Rope and Faggot: The Study of Judge Lynch* was often less scientific and objective than satiric in the Menckenian fashion. Quoting Mencken frequently, White also echoed his contention that the white South was a pathology-ridden, sick society lacking anything approaching real civilization.[36]

Clearly, Mencken's thought, prose style, and words of advice and encouragement had a profound impact on a number of contributors to the Harlem Renaissance. On the other hand, these writers taught Mencken a thing or two as well. His initial version of his famous "Sahara of the Bozart" essay, which first appeared in the *New York Evening Mail* in 1917, had made no mention of African Americans. Between 1917 and 1920 when the final, full-blown essay appeared, however, James Weldon Johnson had taken issue with Mencken's insistence that the cultural sterility of the South was simply a reflection of the decline of the aristocracy and the rise of the region's poor whites: "We do not think that the destruction of the old Southern Civilization or any innate inferiority of the poor white trash is the reason; the real reason is that . . . [a]ll of the mental power of the white South is being used up in holding the Negro back, and that is the reason why it does not produce either great literature or great statesmen or great wealth. . . . On the other hand, the Negro is not using up any of his strength in trying to hold anybody back; he is using every ounce of it to move forward himself. His face is front and toward the light."[37]

Mencken surely read this piece, and he also corresponded with Johnson on numerous occasions between 1917 and 1920. At any rate, in his revised essay that appeared in 1920, Mencken noted, "It is not by accident that the negroes of the South are making faster progress, economically and culturally, than the masses of the whites. It is not by accident that the only visible aesthetic activity in the South is wholly in their hands. No southern composer has ever written music so good as that of half a dozen black composers who might be named.

Even in politics, the negro reveals a curious superiority. Despite the fact that the race question has been the main political concern of the southern whites for two generations, to the practical exclusion of everything else, they have contributed nothing to its discussion that has impressed the world so deeply and so favorably as three or four books by Southern negroes."[38]

Within five years after Mencken's essay appeared, contemporary observers were beginning to speak of the "renaissance" that was by then under way throughout southern thought and letters. The most notable explanation for the timing of this flurry of intellectual activity came from writer and critic Allen Tate, who argued that a post–World War I economic transformation in the South had ignited "a curious burst of intelligence that we get at the crossing of the ways, not unlike on an infinitesimal scale, the outburst of poetic genius at the end of the sixteenth century when commercial England had already begun to crush feudal England." Robert Penn Warren agreed that "after 1918, the modern industrial world, with its good and bad, hit the South" bringing a "cultural shock to a more or less closed and static society" comparable "to what happened on a bigger scale in the Italian Renaissance or Elizabethan England." As a result, Warren believed, "all sorts of ferments began" out of a "need to 'relive,' redefine life."[39]

Some skeptics have challenged attempts to link the Southern Renaissance to economic and social modernization by arguing that the really significant changes in the South's economy and society did not even begin until the New Deal and World War II era when the Renaissance was already well under way, if not actually on the wane. As Reinhard Bendix has pointed out, however, in many modernizing societies "changes in the social and political order were apparent before the full consequences of the industrial revolution were understood." At the very least, Richard King contended, many of the key participants in the Southern Renaissance clearly shared "a pervasive, subjective sense that *something* fundamental had changed in and about the South."[40]

Thomas Wolfe set his classic novel *Look Homeward, Angel* against the backdrop of Asheville's tumultuous emergence as a tourist mecca. His hometown's rapid growth brought prosperity to Wolfe's hard-charging, hard-bargaining mother but left Wolfe decrying the New South definition of "Progress" as "more Ford automobiles [and] more Rotary Clubs." He admonished his mother that "Greater Asheville" did not necessarily mean "100,000 by 1930" and insisted "we are not necessarily four times as civilized as our grandfathers because we go four times as fast in our automobiles" or "because our buildings are four times as tall." Ellen Glasgow seemed to agree, observing in 1928 the rising influence of "noise, numbers, size, quantity," and warning that "the modern South is in immediate peril less of revolution than of losing its individual soul in the national Babel."[41]

Though he often focused on the depravity of southern poor whites, Erskine Caldwell also presented them as victims trapped between an outmoded agricultural system and the brutal, depersonalized industrial system that had begun to supplant it. In Caldwell's *Tobacco Road*, Jeeter Lester struggles to grow just one more cotton crop on worn-out land and refuses to go into the mills, which he condemns as "no place for a man to be." Caldwell envisioned his next novel as a sympathetic treatment of tenant farmers and mill workers "and all those living somewhere between those two occupations," and in *God's Little Acre*, the virile mill worker, Will Thompson, presents a stark contrast to the pathetic Jeeter. Although Thompson announces that he is as strong as "God Almighty himself," when he leads his fellow strikers in an abortive takeover of a mill about to be reopened with replacement workers, he is shot dead in front of the looms that were so much a part of his life. Will's death exposes the crushing indomitability and heartlessness of the New South's industrial system and the plight of those who had exchanged the poverty and frustration of the farm for the brutality and exploitation of the mill.[42]

Although Alabama remained overwhelmingly rural and agricultural at the end of the 1920s, Clarence Cason reflected on "the changes which the inevitable industrial development is making on the social and economic landscape of Alabama." Cason recalled that "fifteen years ago in the town where I lived the important names were invariably those of families who had held their land for generations." It seemed to Cason, however, that "the moment that cotton as a commodity passed from the agricultural to the industrial stage, there were signs of unnaturalness and unfamiliarity on the part of the people." Noting the construction of a "$2,000,000 cotton mill" in his hometown, Cason worried that "our local grocery stores are in imminent danger of being supplanted by chain companies. . . . We shall have new professional men in the town; new doctors, new lawyers, new Ford dealers, new radio men, a new and expanded country club." Extrapolating from his community's experience, he concluded that across the South "the old order—which placed living before livelihood— is losing its social and economic grip in many sections of the South."[43]

Elsewhere, writing in 1933 from what appeared to the casual observer a still sleepy Oxford, Mississippi, William Faulkner bemoaned the passing of the traditional, communal South that he pronounced "old since dead" at the hands of "a thing known whimsically as the New South." This, he was quite certain, was "not the South" but "a land of immigrants" intent on rebuilding Dixie in the image of "the towns and cities in Kansas and Iowa and Illinois" complete with filling station attendants and waitresses saying "Oh yeah?" and speaking with "hard r's" and once quiet intersections that now boasted "changing red-and-green lights and savage and peremptory bells."[44]

In both their social commentary and their fiction, Wolfe, Glasgow, Caldwell, Faulkner, Cason, and a great many other southern writers of the post–World War I era seemed much like intellectuals who lived in other modernizing societies and, according to Robert A. Nisbet, "exhibit the same burning sense of society's sudden convulsive turn from a path it had followed for millennia." Bombarded with the New South's mythology of progress, but confronted everywhere with overwhelming contemporary evidence of their region's backwardness and decline, southern white intellectuals did in fact have much in common with their counterparts in other "developing" societies. Certainly, in the 1920s the South appeared to reach a point at which, as Dewey Grantham put it, "the earlier equilibrium between the forces of modernization and those of cultural tradition could no longer be sustained."[45]

Of all its "cultural traditions," except perhaps its tragic propensity for racial savagery, none brought more criticism and ridicule down on the white South than its apparently unshakable dedication to evangelical, fundamentalist Protestantism. The entire region was a "cesspool of Baptists, a miasma of Methodism," Mencken shrieked, overrun with "syphilitic evangelists" who cast their spell of "implacable fanaticism" over its "yowling yokels." In response, many of the South's white clergymen simply grew more vocal in their defense not only of their religious faith but of the South as the last remaining holdout against the incursions of modernism, Roman Catholicism, feminism, and other assorted un-American "isms" that had "despoiled the old patriotism and the old culture and political ideals" in the rest of the United States. As Tindall observed, "The logic was inescapable. The hope of the world is America, the hope of America is evangelical religion of the most orthodox type, the hope of the American church is the southern evangelical churches." As it had since the late antebellum era, the region's religious establishment clung defiantly to a vision of a Christian white South striving simultaneously to serve God and save the nation.[46]

Nothing so graphically illustrated the contrast between the self-image of white southerners as "defenders of the faith" and "'the most American' of all Americans" and the way they were perceived by many in the nation at large than the 1925 Scopes Trial, which focused on a Dayton, Tennessee, biology teacher's violation of the state's law against teaching Darwin's theory of evolution in the public schools. With Mencken as a merciless, mean-spirited commentator on the "gaping primates" who lived in and around Dayton and with the rest of America looking on, the trial became what Fred Hobson called "the event that most forcefully dramatized the struggle between Southern provincialism and the modern, secular world . . . the event that caused Southerners to face squarely the matter of the South and their own place in it."[47]

A determined proponent of southern progress, Vanderbilt professor Edwin Mims insisted in *The Advancing South* (1926) that the Scopes Trial was by no means representative of contemporary conditions in a region where "reactionary forces" actually found themselves besieged by a "rising tide of liberalism." Mims even foresaw a "not far off" time "when scholarship, literature and art shall flourish, and when all things that make for the intellectual and spiritual emancipation of man shall find their home under Southern skies."[48]

Hobson observed that Mims's book was "in most regards a romanticizing of the New South just as surely as Thomas Nelson Page's work was a romanticizing of the old," and predictably, a disgusted Mencken condemned Mims as "the worst sort of academic jackass." Ironically, however, some of Mims's sharpest critics proved to be a group of his colleagues and former students at Vanderbilt, including Allen Tate, who dismissed *The Advancing South* as "probably the worst book ever written on any subject." Prior to the Scopes Trial, Tate, John Crowe Ransom, and Donald Davidson had shown no particular inclination to challenge either the New South ideal of progress or the steady stream of criticism leveled by Mencken and his disciples. In fact, as the moving forces behind the literary magazine *The Fugitive*, they claimed to be fleeing the sentimental, romantic "high-caste Brahmins of the Old South" and even won praise as exemplars of the New South's enlightenment and progress. The *Nashville Tennessean* remarked, for example, that "*The Fugitive* is an advertising instrument for this city and this state, which reaches a public that could be reached in no other way and by no other means," and the publication actually received a subsidy from the Associated Retailers of Nashville.[49]

In the wake of the Scopes Trial, however, the "Fugitive Group" began to sense that their region's future as a distinctive culture was endangered not only by the efforts of Mencken and his disciples to showcase its backwardness, but by the earnest efforts of its own disciples of "progress." In 1927 Tate announced to Davidson that he would no longer attack the South in any fashion, "except in so far as it may be necessary to point out that the chief defect the Old South had was that it produced, through whatever cause, the New South." An enthusiastic Davidson replied, "You know that I'm with you on the anti-New South stuff. . . . I feel so strongly on these points that I can hardly trust myself to write."[50]

As New South advocates sought to beat the North at its own game by emulating and even surpassing its economic achievement, Ransom, Davidson, and Tate began to argue that the South's way of life was already superior to that of the North, and therefore, the effort to "northernize" the region would pull it down rather than lift it up. In 1930 Ransom, Davidson, and Tate joined forces with several of their current or former Vanderbilt colleagues, including historian Frank L. Owsley, English professor John Donald Wade, political scientist Herman C. Nixon, psychologist Lyle Lanier, recent Vanderbilt graduate and Tate protégé Robert Penn Warren, and novelist Stark Young to publish *I'll Take My Stand: The South and the Agrarian Tradition.* Identifying themselves collectively as "Twelve Southerners," the authors contributed essays that varied widely in subject matter, emphasis, and quality. In general, however, they offered consistently vague tributes to the virtues of "agrarian" life and moderate to severe critiques of "industrialism."[51]

In reality, most of the "Agrarians" who contributed to *I'll Take My Stand* were less intent on defending agrarianism or even deriding industrialism than on inciting their fellow white southerners to rise in revolt against what they saw as the ongoing New South effort to northernize their economy and society and thereby destroy their regional identity. Lifted from the lyrics of "Dixie," the title of the controversial volume came across as "fightin' words," but the cause at issue was not, as the subtitle suggested, preserving "the Agrarian tradition" so much as defending "a Southern way of life against what may be called the American or prevailing way."[52]

In essence, the Agrarians sought in their erudite but diffuse treatises to discredit the dynamic, appealing, economically and politically pragmatic New South doctrine by emphasizing the threat that it posed to southern cultural identity. "How far," asked Davidson in his introduction, "shall the South surrender its moral, social, and economic autonomy?" as he urged young southerners to "look very critically at the advantages of becoming a 'new South' which will be only an undistinguished replica of the usual industrial community."[53]

Twenty years after the publication of *I'll Take My Stand*, Frank Owsley compared the sentiments of the Agrarians to "the bitter resentment of backward peoples in the Orient against what they term . . . 'Yankee imperialism.'" Some thirty years after Owsley's observation, John Shelton Reed insisted, "If we ask what else the Agrarians had in common with those backward but anticolonial peoples in the Orient, if we examine *I'll Take My Stand* in the light of nationalist manifestoes from around the world, the similarities are obvious."[54]

Reed explained that

> when nationalists come from a nation that is economically "peripheral" in the world economy, one like the South of the 1920s that produced raw materials and supplied unskilled labor for a more "advanced" economy, they often adopt the same stance the Agrarians did, rejecting the western science and technology that, in any case, they do not have, and insisting that their very backwardness in "western" terms has preserved a spiritual and cultural superiority. From the nineteenth-century Slavophils, to the Hindu nationalists of early-twentieth-century India, to the apostles of negritude, today, it is easy to find cases of westernized intellectuals assuring the masses of peripheral nations of their superiority to those who dominate them economically and threaten to do so culturally.[55]

Reed's analysis suggested the words of Mohandas Gandhi, who, as he lamented the incursions of Western culture and technology into India, had insisted, "we consider our civilization to be far superior to yours."[56]

In constructing an alternative to the New South identity, the Agrarians had to create an alternative southern past as well. Like their New South adversaries, however, they were less interested in history as fact than history as propaganda. Davidson had hailed U. B. Phillips's *Life and Labor in the Old South* as a "direct answer" to a "southerner's prayer" and suggested recruiting Phillips for the symposium that led to *I'll Take My Stand*. Tate, however, probably came closer to revealing the Agrarians' true attitude toward the use of history when he explained that "A man like Phillips, good as he is in his line, must be used only as a document; he is limited to facts, while we wish to rise upon facts to salvation."[57]

In their historical treatments of the Old South, the essayists had ranged from the romantic, aristocratic vision of Stark Young to the equally romantic celebration of the yeomanry offered by Andrew Lytle. In general, the antebellum South evoked in the volume was a balanced, orderly society where the yeomanry lived in relatively cozy co-equilibrium with the planters. The casual reader might find it difficult to draw sharp distinctions between the historical portraiture of the Agrarians and that of the New South school, but where the latter presented the culture and traditions of the Old South as somehow adaptable to a dramatic reversal of the region's economic direction, most of the former took pains to stress its almost otherworldly incompatibility with both the values and practicalities of contemporary industrialism. All of the essayists stressed the South's distinctiveness, Ransom hailing it as "unique on this continent . . . a culture which was according to the European principles of culture" and Tate describing it as a "feudal society," explaining that, unlike New England, which "lived economically on the South and culturally on England," the Old South "could be ignorant of Europe because it *was* Europe."[58]

Although the New South historians were fully subscribed to the Lost Cause, they tried to use it to secure not just southern but northern white sympathy and support as well. In their depictions of the Civil War and its aftermath, however, the Agrarians were far more consistently and stridently sectional, denouncing the North's exploitation and oppression of the South. Though he was a professional historian, Frank Owsley's essay in *I'll Take My Stand* was from beginning to end little more than a bitterly angry diatribe against northern political, economic, and cultural imperialism. Owsley all but echoed historians Charles and Mary Beard's earlier argument that the Civil War had not resulted from North-South divisions over slavery but from the incompatibility of their respective economic systems. For Owsley, the war was an "irrepressible conflict" between "the industrial and commercial civilization of the North and the agrarian civilization of the South" caused not by the North's desire to free blacks from slavery but by its determination to enslave the white South through economic and political strangulation.[59]

The Beardian interpretation set well with a number of the Agrarians because it generally accorded with their rather half-formed portrait of southern white society as a mixture of the most admirable traits of both yeoman and planter, while like most of their essays, it largely sidestepped the question of slavery, and more broadly, that of race as well. There were exceptions, however. Several of the "Twelve Southerners" found Warren's essay in defense of segregation a bit too tepid for their tastes, and Warren's mentor, Tate, later made quite a production of refusing to have dinner in Nashville with black writers James Weldon Johnson and Langston Hughes. Nor was there any fancy racial footwork in Owsley's portrait of Reconstruction. "For ten years," he wrote, "the South, already ruined by the loss of nearly $2,000,000,000 invested in slaves, with its lands worthless, its cattle and stock gone, its houses burned, was turned over to the three millions of former slaves, some of whom could still remember the taste of human flesh and the bulk of them hardly three generations removed from cannibalism." Manipulated by "carpetbaggers and scalawags," the former slaves "continued the pillages of war, combing the South for anything left by the invading armies . . . dragooning the Southern population, and visiting upon them the ultimate humiliations."[60]

After white southerners had been "conquered by war and humiliated by peace," Owsley added, northern leaders then "commenced a second war of conquest," this one "to remake every Southern opinion, to impose the Northern way of life and thought upon the South . . . and set the rising and unborn generations upon stools of everlasting repentance." As victims of what amounted to "a war of intellectual and spiritual conquest," the captive minds of young southerners were forced "to accept the Northern version of history with all its condemnations and its carping criticisms of Southern institutions and life," including "the crying down and discrediting of anything agrarian as old-fashioned and backward." Consequently, Owsley argued, "the South needs orientation and direction in its thinking," beginning with its history—"the point where it was thrown from its balance"—so that the contemporary whites could know that "the things for which it stood were reasonable and sound" and "that for it, at least, the philosophy of the North is the religion of an alien God."[61]

The attempt by the "Twelve Southerners" to save the South from northernization by constructing an agrarian identity for their region was in no small sense a by-product of the modernization effort that they opposed so vehemently. Reinhard Bendix provided a useful comparative framework for understanding the historical setting from which the Agrarians emerged and, for that matter, the context in which the larger intellectual awakening of the Southern Renaissance began. Observing that in backward nations governments typically play a major role in instigating efforts to promote economic modernization, Bendix also cited the tendency of such nations to emphasize education in the hope of finding a shortcut to bridge the gap between themselves and more advanced societies.[62]

In the late nineteenth century, a number of prominent southern journalists and other observers had touted education as the key to economic progress. In the early twentieth century, progressive and business-progressive reformers had installed economic development as a legitimate responsibility of state government and had also advocated fundamental improvements in education. Although per capita spending per pupil was still barely half the national average in 1920, total expenditures for the public schools had increased by 630 percent in the southern states during the first two decades of the twentieth century. This trend continued throughout the 1920s, with eight southern states exceeding the national rate of increase in expenditures for schools and per pupil as well.

In higher education, the regional preeminence of the University of Virginia was threatened by the surging growth and rising prestige of the University of North Carolina, whose faculty grew from 78 in 1919 to 225 in 1930. Meanwhile, philanthropy fueled the rapid ascendance of Tulane, Vanderbilt, and Emory. Shortly before he died in 1925, James "Buck" Duke announced the last of his huge donations to Duke University (formerly Trinity College), urging officials to "Get the best executives and educators, no matter what they cost. . . . I want Duke to be a great national institution."[63]

Typically, such increased support for education both encourages and expands a society's intelligentsia and enhances its influence. This intelligentsia, in turn, generally participates in the initial efforts to free the society from its backwardness, but as time passes, some of its members may become critical of these efforts or even reject them altogether. The result can often be a schism between those who believe their country can benefit most by following the example of more ostensibly advanced societies and those who think it is better to emphasize and preserve the innate strengths of their own way of life. For the latter in general and certainly for the Agrarians in particular, education and travel have not only heightened their awareness of other cultures but also made them more conscious of their own and of their feelings of alienation from it. "Their experiences," Reed has observed, "have left them like beached fish aware of water for the first time." Cosmopolitan and erudite, these intellectuals typically feel so far removed from the masses of their contemporaries that their affirmation of cultural kinship must be "willed." As the beneficiaries of modernization, however, they also possess "the ideological vocabulary to interpret their alienation and to defend their culture," and ironically enough, as Reed notes, "modernization itself is what they protest."[64]

New South proponents sought to build an "imagined community" organized around an identifiable and appealing economic and political agenda. On the other hand, despite their cultural objections to the New South program, the Agrarians offered no practical alternatives other than a romanticized historical vision of the country life that Depression-era southerners were then fleeing by the thousands. Still, as southern cultural supremacists they persisted in attacking those who occupied themselves with documenting and publicizing the South's defects and working tirelessly to help the region "catch up" with the rest of the nation. One of the principal targets of the Agrarians (within the South, at least) was University of North Carolina sociologist Howard W. Odum, who led his "regionalist" disciples at Chapel Hill in unloosing an avalanche of statistics and social research data pointing to the need to modernize the South's economy and institutions through a scientific, planned effort to promote both industrial development and agricultural revitalization.

Odum actually shared many of the Agrarians' concerns about the cultural consequences of wholesale industrialization. Still, his insistence on a realistic appraisal of southern problems led him to see their treatises as fanciful at best, even as it also set him squarely at odds with "the gross spirit of materialism" and the self-serving optimism that characterized the New South Creed. Established in 1922, Odum's *Journal of Social Forces* became the principal outlet for serious discussions of the South's deficiencies and failures and the inadequacies of southern leadership and institutions. Odum boldly proclaimed that the South needed "criticism and severe criticism," and H. L. Mencken, who had certainly done his share of criticizing, cited Odum as the embodiment of "the new spirit of the region" and the key figure in getting the new movement toward serious self-criticism that lay behind the Southern Renaissance "in motion."[65]

The South was hardly lacking for critics in the 1920s, but one of the things that set Odum apart was the scholarly approach and sober tone of his writings, a tone that contrasted sharply with the caricature and superficial mockery favored by Mencken and his followers. As it evolved during the 1920s, Odum's approach also entailed not simply documenting the South's contemporary problems but searching for their roots in its past. Unlike Odum, many of the critical commentators on the South in the 1920s seemed too astonished by the ongoing panorama of ignorance and depravity that it presented to reflect seriously on the historical context from which this sorry state of affairs had evolved.

Mencken's contempt for the claims of New South progress was obvious enough, but he was at times an all but uncritical proponent of the legend of the Old South, at one point even bemoaning the "Calamity of Appomattox." In his view, the Civil War had destroyed "a civilization of manifold excellences . . . undoubtedly the best that These States have ever seen," and "the old aristocracy" had gone down "the red gullet of war," leaving "the poor white trash in the saddle." The South's biggest problem, Mencken wrote Odum in 1923, was the "solidification into custom and law of the ignorance and prejudice of a very low grade of Caucasians." Embracing what was at best only a simplistic and superficial historical perspective, Mencken saw the bourgeois, banal New South as simply the genteel, aristocratic Old South reduced to rubble and ruled by the rabble. For him, the period of southern history since Appomattox could be summed up succinctly: "It would be impossible in all history to match so complete a drying up of a civilization."[66]

When Mencken pointed to the Scopes Trial as evidence of this "drying up," however, the more historically knowledgeable Odum warned that he might be "over optimistic . . . about the old-time South." Odum's historical focus was apparent in his *American Epoch*, which appeared in 1930, within a month of *I'll Take My Stand*. *American Epoch* was a partly fictionalized history of Odum's own family over four generations. The two principal characters were based on Odum's grandfathers, and ironically, both the more economically and socially prominent "old Major" and the other solidly independent farmer, "Uncle John," would have been right at home in the Agrarian portrayal of the antebellum South. Despite its ambivalence and imprecision, *American Epoch* was an attempt to sketch out the social, economic, political, and cultural history of the nineteenth-century South, and it both anticipated and influenced the work of many later writers who provided a sharper focus on the ties between the South's past and present. In fact, Odum's approach suggested the direction taken by some of the best writers of the Southern Renaissance, including Odum protégés C. Vann Woodward and W. J. Cash, as well as William Faulkner, whom Odum praised for daring to ask whether the South might well have both a "barbaric past" and "a . . . cherished past."[67]

As Odum's colleague and protégé, Rupert B. Vance emphasized the importance of southern history even more strongly than Odum himself. Although he shared U. B. Phillips's respect for the influence of the frontier on southern history, Vance broke with Phillips on the interaction between plantation and frontier. Where Phillips cited the plantation's organization and the planters' gentility as countervailing influences against the otherwise unchecked individualism and rough-and-tumble folk culture spawned by the frontier, Vance saw the plantation retaining "many of the frontier traits" and passing them from the Old South to the New. (Odum had suggested almost the same thing when he noted "a sort of arrested frontier pattern of life" in the Southeast.) As Singal observed, "Almost everywhere he turned in surveying the modern South, Vance discovered that the basic patterns of the frontier still prevailed. The region continued to make its living by exploiting its natural resources heedlessly, applying little capital, skill or technology, with dramatically low levels of income and living standards the result."[68]

For all the environmental influences on the formation of southern white character, however, Vance understood that ultimately it had been "history, not geography" that had "made the solid South." More so even than Odum's, Vance's work was cited and quoted again and again by southern historians, and he frequently reviewed books for historical journals. He was known for his encyclopedic grasp of southern history, and he often held informal tutorials for graduate students at Chapel Hill. Though he had been trained as a sociologist, his reputation as a historian led the editors of the Louisiana State University Press's History of the South to invite him to write the volume slated to cover the period 1913 to 1945.[69]

For Vance and Odum, the fusion of history and sociology was a means of offering a sound scholarly rationale for socioeconomic and political reform. This commitment to activist scholarship was enormously appealing to the young C. Vann Woodward, a native Arkansan who had graduated from Emory University with a degree in philosophy and earned an M.A. in political science from Columbia. Woodward had known Rupert Vance since his youth when Woodward's family lived in Morrilton, Arkansas, Vance's hometown. Vance would exert a profound influence on Woodward, encouraging and challenging him as a graduate student at Chapel Hill and continuing to read and critique his work well into the 1950s.[70]

Moreover, Odum's parents were neighbors of Woodward's parents after the latter moved to Oxford, Georgia, and Odum proved instrumental in securing a Rockefeller Foundation Fellowship for the young man. Two years after his latest protégé's arrival in Chapel Hill, Odum was assuring friends at the Rockefeller Foundation that he and Vance were "talking with him [Woodward] to be sure he finishes his study and gets himself all ready to become one of the younger leaders of the South." As Woodward's biographer noted, for Odum, leading the South meant "changing the South" through "the steady application of research and teaching by activist academics committed to reform."[71]

By the time he arrived in Chapel Hill, the twenty-five-year-old Woodward's activist credentials were well established. He had already visited the Soviet Union twice, and as an English instructor at Georgia Tech, he had participated actively in the defense of black Communist Angelo Herndon, who was convicted in Atlanta in 1932 of inciting insurrection. During his stint at Columbia, Woodward had also formed friendships with African American poets J. Saunders Redding and Langston Hughes and other participants in the Harlem Renaissance.

Despite his admiration for Odum and Vance, Woodward came to the University of North Carolina in 1934 to pursue a Ph.D. in history, rather than sociology. He was motivated primarily by his desire to secure the financial support (in the form of the Rockefeller Fellowship) necessary to complete his partially written biography of Populist leader Thomas E. Watson, which would also serve as Woodward's dissertation. For all his excitement about being on the same campus with Odum and especially Vance, however, when Woodward began his tutelage under the southern historians at Chapel Hill, he was soon and sorely disappointed. Owing to the stifling influence of the New South Creed on any impulse toward historical objectivity or candor, as the 1930s began, the formal study of southern history remained what Richard King called largely "an exercise in hagiography . . . monumentalizing and devoted antiquarianism," and its "dominant mood" was "celebratory and/or defensive." Hence, Woodward quickly discerned that far from "making waves," the masters of southern history seemed "united not so much in their view of the past as in their dedication to the present order, the system founded on the ruins of Reconstruction called the New South."[72]

Not surprisingly, save for Alex M. Arnett's The Populist Movement in Georgia (1929), as of 1934 there had been little attention to the most outspoken political assailants of the New South identity, the Populists. In his 1986 memoir, Thinking Back, Woodward reflected that the Populists had been an almost ideal subject for a fledgling scholar who realized that "to attack the ramparts of the establishment in southern historiography head-on would obviously have been unwise. Especially so when its views commanded such universal popular support as they did in the 1930s. . . . What was needed was a subject in Southern history and a means of writing it that would expose what seemed to be the fallacies, omissions, and long silences that characterized the New South school."[73]

Populism had been an "embarrassment" to New South doctrines because it contradicted historians' "pet themes of white unity and black satisfaction." "Disrespectful Populist critics" had not only dared to challenge Henry Grady and other New South icons, but "the New South double-think of worshipping the symbols and myths of the Lost Cause and simultaneously serving the masters of the new plutocracy was too much for Populist critics. So was the reverence demanded for the Redeemers, the South's new rulers who overthrew and succeeded the Reconstruction regime."[74]

In reality, Woodward had come to Chapel Hill not to write a revisionist history of southern Populism but to tell the dramatic personal story of a single Populist, Tom Watson, who had been at his best in the 1890s with his passionate articulation of the plight of the South's small farmers and tenants of both races, apparently only to sink thereafter into a relentless and sometimes bloodthirsty persecution of blacks, Roman Catholics, and Jews. Still, Woodward explained, Watson's life not only presented "a fascinating story in itself, but it plunged the historian into all the dark, neglected, and forbidden corners of Southern life shunned by the New South school."[75]

As they appeared in *Tom Watson, Agrarian Rebel*, the Populists seemed more radical and better organized in the South than many had thought, and by emphasizing Watson's attempts to form a biracial political coalition, Woodward suggested that neither the Democratic party nor white unity and supremacy had always prevailed in post-Reconstruction politics. Anticipating one of the principal themes of his later study, *Origins of the New South*, Woodward also offered a distinctively unflattering portrait of the Redeemers, exposing their corruption and challenging their claims to descent from the old antebellum plantation order.[76]

Whether or not it was interpreted precisely as Woodward intended, the Watson biography brought its young author sufficient notice that he was selected over several of his influential senior faculty colleagues at the University of Florida to deliver the university's first Phi Beta Kappa address in December 1938. Woodward used this opportunity to move on to more contemporary concerns. Revealing the influence of Vance and Odum, he urged southerners to reject both the Agrarians' "never-never land of the past" and the New South school's "never-never land of the future" in favor of the candid assessments of the present offered by the Chapel Hill Regionalists who were trying to lead the South "down the hard narrow path of realism."[77]

As he moved down this path himself, Woodward soon encountered Herman Clarence Nixon. An Alabaman who had studied under William E. Dodd at the

University of Chicago, Nixon was known primarily as a political scientist rather than a historian, although he both wrote and taught history and also employed many of the techniques of sociological and economic analysis favored by Odum and Vance. Nixon had actually penned a relatively restrained critique of industrialism for *I'll Take My Stand*, conceding that "moderate" industrialization was inevitable because "the human civilization now based on Southern agriculture is in no little peril," but warning as well that "industrial civilization under the capitalistic system does not offer a satisfying substitute in human values." He was clearly less conservative than the other Agrarians from the start, however, and by the end of the 1930s, Nixon had associated himself not only with the general aims of Odum and the Regionalists but with a number of liberal organizations, including the Southern Conference for Human Welfare, in which he played a leading role.[78]

This shift to the left was apparent in what Woodward called the "Hillbilly Realism" of Nixon's *Forty Acres and Steel Mules*, which spurned both the "pessimistic romanticism" of the Agrarians and the "optimistic romanticism of the New South school." Nixon condemned the New South's reckless courtship of "carpetbaggers of industry" who would only pull the South deeper into a colonial economy. He also pointed out that the Old South had been a "golden age" for, at most, "a few thousand families, while slaves, 'poor whites,' yeomen farmers, and small slave owners constituted the millions of the population and furnished the concealed reality of Southern economy."[79]

Forty Acres and Steel Mules offered an altogether brilliant blend of history, economics, geography, and sociology as well. Nixon's description of the old slave society was more candid, concise, and sharply analytical than anything then in print. "After the Civil War," he went on to explain, "the typical method for the 'come-back' of old families as well as for the 'arrival' of new ones . . . was through a combination of farm holdings and rural merchandising. . . . 'Merchant and planter' became a rather common expression in the cotton belt after 1865 to denote a rural baron, or a Main Street man of influence and power." Anticipating Will Varner, the "chief man of the country," in William Faulkner's *The Hamlet*, Nixon noted that "such a leader's store and office might be considered as a little commercial capital, and if there was ever an 'economic man' in the flesh, he must have been a supply merchant in the cotton country with a crop lien to give him a business monopoly." Nixon's treatment of the postbellum South sharpened the critique of the region's Redeemer leadership that Woodward had offered in *Tom Watson* and foreshadowed the more direct attack that he would launch more than a decade later in *Origins of the New South*.[80]

By the end of the 1930s, Woodward and Nixon actually had some significant company in the historical revisionist camp. In their slender 1935 volume, *The South Looks at Its Past*, Benjamin B. Kendrick and Alex M. Arnett had noted that the deepening depression of the 1930s was fueling "a growing tendency to question the validity of some of the New South doctrines." This tendency was actually already in evidence even before the region's economy collapsed, but the self-evident suffering of the Depression along with the programmatic and research initiatives of the New Deal affirmed Kendrick and Arnett's insistence that "a sympathetic understanding of the present South is impossible without a frank recognition of the darker as well as the brighter past."[81]

Like the work of Woodward and Nixon, *The South Looks at Its Past* clearly reflected the influence of Odum. In fact, it was intended to serve as a historical preface to Odum's *Southern Regions*, a massive compilation of data documenting the South's deficiencies and suggesting how they might be addressed. By offering "an interpretive study of those phases of the South's past that seem most pertinent to a fresh orientation in this age of dilemmas," Kendrick and Arnett provided a decidedly Odumesque example of what one reviewer called "the value of the historical approach in affording insight into present social phenomena."[82]

As the 1930s unfolded, a handful of scholars, seeking insight into the racial system that was the most problematic of the contemporary South's "social phenomena," had begun to challenge one of the New South Creed's most fundamental and sensitive historical tenets, what Kenneth M. Stampp would later call "the tragic legend of Reconstruction." In 1935 W. E. B. DuBois charged in *Black Reconstruction* that prevailing negative interpretations of that period were the work of writers who were "passionate believers in the inferiority of the Negro," excessively sympathetic to southern whites, and less than straightforward in their representation and selection of evidence. DuBois correctly assailed the unfairness of the Black Codes and rejected the prevailing notion of black political domination during Reconstruction, but rather than his own research, he sometimes drew on the works of the scholars he criticized. A few years earlier, Francis Butler Simkins and Robert S. Woody had published a solidly documented and remarkably candid book on Reconstruction in South Carolina, criticizing that state's Black Code and offering a more balanced appraisal of the Republican governments as well as an especially provocative argument that, in the hands of both politicians and historians, the New South vision of Reconstruction might have done the state more harm than Reconstruction itself.[83]

In 1938 Simkins pointed out that by discrediting the period in which southern blacks had enjoyed their only opportunity for political participation, southern historians had played as crucial a role in excluding blacks from politics as had the South's white supremacist politicians. It was time, Simkins added for good measure, to rethink white assumptions about the innate inferiority of blacks and the "gloomy generalization" that blacks must continue to play their "present inferior role" within southern society. A year later, Howard K. Beale, who had served as Woodward's advisor at North Carolina, called for a "rewriting" of Reconstruction history and urged historians to cease paying tribute to the Redeemers who had "restored white supremacy."[84]

Despite the emergence of a critical revisionist minority inclined toward rethinking the past as a means of challenging the present, however, throughout the 1930s and for much of the following decades as well, the southern historical establishment remained fundamentally conservative and largely in alignment with the New South Creed's version of southern history. As a case in point, although the Southern Historical Association was formed in 1934 by professional historians in order to encourage "the study of history in the South, with particular emphasis on the history of the South," many of the SHA's founders and early leaders seemed more interested in defending the South's past than in analyzing it. [85]

The group's first president was E. Merton Coulter, whose inaugural presidential address rebuked white southerners for their failure to gather and preserve the records necessary to defend the South from its northern critics. Five years later, Frank L. Owsley used the presidential pulpit to blame the Civil War on the "egocentric sectionalism" of the North. Other early SHA presidents of the era blamed the contemporary South's multitude of problems on Reconstruction or the region's ongoing colonial exploitation by northern industrialists and financiers. In a summary of the first fifteen SHA presidential addresses, H. C. Nixon noted that, overall, they were marked by "a strong regional concern and consciousness in contrast to the strong note of philosophy or laws of history which runs through many of the presidential products of the AHA (American Historical Association)." Instead of the "sedate wine of philosophy," some of these "regional" addresses were "pretty well spiked with the hard liquor of polemics," while others were simply "polemics themselves." Nixon also found too much emphasis on sectionalism and "little recognition . . . of anything inherently wrong with the South, or anything to criticize except that the South has neglected its historical records and evidence with which to answer criticism."[86]

As he had begun his studies at Chapel Hill, Woodward had contrasted his own uninspiring impressions of the sorry state of southern historical scholarship ("no renaissance here, no rebirth of energy, no compelling new vision") with his excitement over the contemporary "explosion of creativity . . . in fiction, in poetry, in drama." Nor could he help noting that the writers in these fields were "writing about the same South historians were writing about and making the whole world of letters at home and abroad ring with their praise." More than that, for the most part, the leading literary contributors to the Southern Renaissance were creating such a stir by holding the New South's vision of a glorious past up for inspection against the glaring light of contemporary injustice, poverty, and depravity.[87]

Writing in 1938, Donald Davidson pointed out that every major literary or scholarly contribution of the last fifteen years had explored "the historian's question—what the South was?—and the related question—what the South is?" as part of an ongoing search for "Southern policies that will be well founded historically and at the same time applicable to the existing situation." Still largely in the grip of New South orthodoxy at that point, however, as a group, no segment of the white South's intellectual community seemed less inclined to make "the historian's question" part of a larger effort to understand the southern present than its historians themselves.[88]

5

Southern Writers and "The Impossible Load of the Past"

WITH THE WAR OF 1914–1918, Allen Tate observed, "the South re-entered the world—but gave a backward glance as it stepped over the border; that backward glance gave us the Southern renaiscence [*sic*], a literature conscious of the past in the present." In reality, although a new spirit of critical self-awareness had clearly emerged in the South during the first decade following the war, its initial focus had been largely contemporary. The actual "backward glance" that marked the full flowering of the literary phase of the Southern Renaissance came primarily in the 1930s when, in the absence of a critical historical tradition, southern writers began to ask how such an appealing and glorious past could have degenerated into such a dismal and defective present.[1]

"It is the historical perspective that renders this [the South's contemporary problems] the more tragic," Louis D. Rubin explained, identifying the dominant concern of an emerging generation of white southern writers in the 1930s when he noted, "The South has not always been this way; it has become this way. The image of the heroic past renders the distraught present so distasteful, just as it is this very same heroic past that has caused the present." The desire to unravel this contradiction that had confronted southern intellectuals since the antebellum era created what Rubin described as the distinctive "two-way pull, the past-and-present perspectives that existed simultaneously in the writers of the Southern Renaissance." As they struggled to sort out the myths and inconsistencies of the New South identity, the major literary figures of the Southern Renaissance also had little choice but to grapple with what Rubin called "the impossible load of the past." Coming to maturity in an age of such rapid change where old and new collided so frequently and often so violently, they acquired an almost unique "two-way vision" that, as Rubin explained, "translated what they saw in terms of what *had been* as well as what now was." More recently, Richard Gray has agreed that "it was the disorienting experience of social change in the present that eventually drove the writers of the southern 'renaissance' to an investigation of their past."[2]

A key figure in the Southern Renaissance in her own right, Ellen Glasgow cited a move to the middle ground between sentiment and skepticism about both the past and the future as the key to the emergence of a new and exciting body of southern literature. What distinguished this new generation of writers from their predecessors, Glasgow believed, was "a detached and steadfast point of view." She conceded that the culture of the Old South possessed "grace and beauty and the inspiration of gaiety" but insisted that it was "shallow-rooted at best, since, for all its charm and good will, the way of living depended not on its creative strength, but upon the enforced servitude of an alien race." For Glasgow, however, detachment from the fuzzy sentimentality of the Old South was ultimately no more crucial than detachment from the equally uncritical orthodoxy of the New South, "which has remained invulnerable alike to the written word and to the abstract idea." She had begun to exhibit this detachment herself even before World War I and well in advance of some of her contemporaries who continued to churn out what she called "a mournful literature of commemoration." What the South needed, she insisted, was "blood and irony," the former because southern culture had "strained too far away from its roots in the earth" and therefore "grown thin and pale" and content with mere imitation. Irony, meanwhile, was "an indispensable element of the critical vision" and the most reliable "antidote" to the "sentimental decay" that stifled southern creativity.[3]

There was blood and irony aplenty in what Glasgow offered her readers during the first decades of the twentieth century. Her father had been the manager of Richmond's Tredegar Iron Works, and she used her novels to criticize the intellectual stagnation bred by the Old South and the rampant New South acquisitiveness that seemed to marginalize any thought not calculated to produce immediate and substantial material gain. Much of Glasgow's writing appeared to anticipate the efforts of some of the later contributors to the Southern Renaissance to explore the contradictions both within and between the legends of the Old South and the New.

Published in 1909, Glasgow's *The Romance of a Plain Man* was set in the Richmond of the mid-1870s, "where the industrial ethos of the New South first took hold," but before "progress, more fatal than poverty, destroyed the lingering charm of the place." Glasgow's "plain man" is the upwardly mobile Ben Starr, "a common boy . . . determined that I would not be a common man," whose energy and ambition eventually win him a position as assistant to banker, industrialist, and railroad executive General George Bolingbroke. A quick learner, Ben achieves financial security as a bank president only to lose it when the bank collapses. Striving to restore his fortunes, he neglects his loving and uncomplaining wife. When she develops an illness requiring a move to California in search of a more suitable climate, however, Ben abandons his dream of succeeding the general as a railroad president in order to care for her. Meanwhile, it is the aristocratic Bolingbroke who has succumbed totally to the temptations of wealth and power to the exclusion of the opportunity for any meaningful love or pleasures apart from the fleeting satisfaction that his commercial conquests can afford.[4]

Glasgow welcomed the New South's promises of expanded opportunity for white southerners of humble origins like Ben Starr. Yet, she also feared the corruption and moral decay that might result from the New South's obsession with material gain. In telling the story of a "plain man," she explained, she had tried to convey "the picture of the changing world about him" and "the rapidly awakening tumult and confusion of the New South."[5]

Glasgow also revealed her misgivings about the New South in her novel *Virginia*, which was set in the Virginia of the 1880s, where "from the ashes of a vanquished idealism the spirit of commercial materialism was born." The personification of this New South materialist ethos was tobacco manufacturer and railroad builder Cyrus Treadwell. Bearing a certain resemblance to Glasgow's father, Cyrus was "at once the destroyer and the builder—the inexorable foe of the old feudal order and the beneficent source of the new industrialism." Meanwhile, the Old South found its embodiment in Miss Priscilla Batte, headmistress of a female academy and the daughter of a fallen Confederate general: "Today, at the beginning of the industrial awakening of the South, she (who was but the embodied spirit of her race) stood firmly rooted in all that was static, in all that was obsolete and outgrown, in the Virginia of the eighties." The ultimate provincial, Priscilla is utterly indisposed toward critical thinking and admires Cyrus without understanding the threat he poses to the antebellum ideals she claims to venerate. Actually, much as W. J. Cash would later argue, Priscilla and Cyrus—Old South and New—share a common suspicion of art and ideas. They also ignore the racial and other problems their society faces, choosing instead to worship "the illusion of success."[6]

The novel's protagonist, Virginia Pendleton, is a graduate of Miss Batte's academy who, like Glasgow's own "perfect mother," had been "educated according to the simple theory that the less a girl knew about life, the better prepared she would be to contend with it." As a result, she becomes a self-sacrificing wife and mother and perpetual victim who is "incapable of altering the design of her life." For all her good intentions, Virginia represents both the Old South's fading genteel tradition and the New South's anachronistic ideal of white womanhood, "condemned to stand alone because it had been forsaken by time."[7]

Like Glasgow, Atlanta novelist Frances Newman focused on the white South's stifling and destructive gender conventions within a broader critique of both the Old South and the New. Both of Newman's novels, *The Hardboiled Virgin* (1926) and *Dead Lovers Are Faithful Lovers* (1928), expose the paradoxical reality that while middle-class white southerners are smitten with the New South Creed's gospel of success, by clinging to the Old South legend of pedestalized femininity, they make success something that women can hope to experience only through their husbands.[8]

In *The Hardboiled Virgin*, Katharine Faraday's aspirations as a writer are at odds with her desire for social acceptance as a woman. Realizing that men find southern women charming if they embrace traditionalism but intelligent if they challenge it, she offers such observations as "there was a great deal to be said for the Old South, but not nearly so much as people had already said." In *Dead Lovers Are Faithful Lovers*, Newman mercilessly satirized the New South's worship of the Old South and the Lost Cause, ridiculing the pretensions of an aggressive, grasping New South Atlanta trying to effect the genteel air of Old South Charleston while straining to "grow as far as possible toward New York."[9]

In 1928, the year Newman died, Glasgow cited her as one of "a little band of writers" who had broken away from "a petrified past overgrown by a funereal tradition" to attempt "a re-valuation of both the past and the present, . . . subjecting the raw material of life to the fearless scrutiny and the spacious treatment of art." In Glasgow's estimation, instead of embracing the New South's ambition "not to be self-sufficing, but to be more Western than the West and more American than the whole of America," Newman and her contemporaries had recoiled from "the uniform concrete surface of an industrialized South," and "for the first time in its history," the region was producing "a literature of revolt."[10]

In 1943 when Glasgow got around to updating her listing of leading southern literary rebels, it included not only Thomas Wolfe and William Faulkner but, surprisingly to some, Margaret Mitchell as well. In their retrospective appraisals, most critics have been quick to see Mitchell's *Gone with the Wind* as, in Joel Williamson's words, simply another "hoop skirt [*sic*] story lamenting the loss of the grand Old South," but the phenomenally popular novel was actually more critical and complex than it appeared. As a young woman, Mitchell had rebelled personally against the New South's Victorian social and gender traditions, and she steadfastly disavowed any desire to write a novel in the romantic "Thomas Nelson Pagish" tradition. Her biographer, Darden Pyron, has even argued that she actually saw her book as "a revisionist history of the planter class before and after Appomattox." Writing to journalist Virginius Dabney, himself a debunker of the Old South myth, Mitchell complained that she had "been embarrassed on many occasions by finding myself included among writers who pictured the South as a land of white-columned mansions whose wealthy owners had thousands of slaves and drank thousands of juleps." "I certainly had no intention of writing about cavaliers," Mitchell insisted. "Practically all my characters, except the Virginia Wilkes, were of sturdy yeoman stock." Certainly, this was true of the semiliterate, short but swaggering, "loud mouthed and bull headed" Irishman Gerald O'Hara, who parlays his facility at poker and his "steady head for whiskey" into ownership of a run-down plantation and ultimately satisfies his "ruthless longing" for a respected place in planter society.[11]

If Mitchell's challenge to the Cavalier myth was largely lost in Hollywood's rush to romanticize the Old South, the film version of her novel was a bit truer to the more openly critical treatment of the New South embodied in Scarlett O'Hara's rise to postbellum prosperity. Gerald does not survive long after the war, but his stubbornness and spunk sustain Scarlett as she claws her way back to material comfort if not quite full-fledged social respectability. Meanwhile, the high-minded, aristocratic Wilkeses flounder and fail, especially the wonderfully grand but woefully inept Ashley, who clearly lacks the grit and gall that Scarlett possesses in abundance.

Amazed at the efforts of other white women of her class to retain their appreciation for the importance of being a "lady" in the face of the defeat and economic devastation of the war, Scarlett observes, "The silly fools don't seem to realize that you can't be a lady without money." Because she believes "money is the most important thing in the world," Scarlett determines to prove that she is "as capable as a man" by making "money for herself, as men made money." Her concern with feeling like "a lady" suggests that she is not much of a feminist. Still, in her desire to enjoy some of the perks of southern bellehood while breaking free of some its more restrictive appurtenances, she resembles the characters created by Mitchell's fellow Atlantan Frances Newman and by Ellen Glasgow as well. In any event, like the proponents of the New South, Scarlett sets out to beat the Yankees at their own game, realizing that in the rebuilding of Atlanta there was "still plenty of money to be made by anyone who isn't afraid to work—or to grab."[12]

Scarlett is afraid to do neither. Securing a loan from Rhett Butler, she buys a lumber mill and proceeds to lie, cheat, and just plain out-compete many of her male counterparts, brazenly associating with common laborers and other such rough company, and even employing convict labor and turning her head when her foreman abuses them. Soon the whole town is talking about her and the manner in which she is "conducting her affairs in a masculine way." Thus does Scarlett "unsex herself" in the eyes of the community by becoming not just a ruthless businesswoman but a successful one. Despite its generally dismissive treatment at the hands of historians, Willie Lee Rose noted *Gone with the Wind*'s almost Beardian economic realism and observed, as Mitchell herself acknowledged, that Scarlett's "sheer greed" and "shabby dealings in business" were "meant as a personal characterization of the city of Atlanta itself and, by extension, the New South." For Mitchell, the story of the New South lay not so much in Atlanta's rising from the ashes as in Scarlett's rising from the garden at Tara and heading off to Atlanta to make good on her vow never to be hungry again.[13]

Succumbing to the adulation of those who read her novel as a simple reaffirmation of the New South version of the Old South or saw the film version that largely transformed it into such, Mitchell toned down her complaints about misreadings and mischaracterizations and sometimes equivocated in public discussions of the meanings of her story and its characters. Still, there was certainly more to *Gone with the Wind* than met the casual eye, and its juxtaposition of economic and material progress with social and cultural decline was a common theme for many of the more critically acknowledged writers of the Southern Renaissance, including Wolfe and Faulkner.

Actually, Wolfe seemed at different stages in his life and career to embrace conflicting perspectives on the South's past, present, and future. In an early playwriting effort at the University of North Carolina, he told the story of Colonel Tasher Weldon, "a typical Southern aristocrat" who dotes on the good old days while his fortunes crumble around him. After his death, when the Colonel's old manor is torn down, his son Eugene and his fiancée, "glorious forerunners of the New South," make a fresh start determined to succeed where the old Colonel had not so much failed as not even tried.[14]

Wolfe soon abandoned this uncritical perspective as "naïve and simplistic." On a visit to his booming hometown of Asheville in 1922, he saw little but "greed, greed, greed—deliberate crafty and motivated. . . . The disgusting spectacle of thousands of industrious and accomplished liars, engaged in the mutual systematic pursuit of their profession." When he returned to his graduate studies at Harvard, Wolfe wrote a play, "Welcome to Our City," which satirized the shallow materialism that gripped the New South. In the play, one "Altamont" booster brags, "We have eight schools, one of which cost over a half a million dollars, six banks, nine big hotels, over two hundred inns and boarding houses, and twenty-three churches, one of which cost half a million, over four thousand private-owned motorcars and over sixty-three miles of paved streets within our city limits."[15]

Wolfe clearly identified himself with "a new generation of southerners who refuse to share in the beautiful but destructive conspiracy of silence of their fathers," and he even seemed to foreshadow later critics like Lillian Smith when he described a South tormented by a "bitter, wounded, twisted hurt with all its pain, its terror, its lacerated pride, its fear and cruelty, its sweltered secrecies, its explosive and insane desire." In his autobiographical novel *Look Homeward, Angel* (1929), Wolfe focused on the familiar Faulknerian theme of family and community deterioration in the New South. Eugene Gant's brother Luke "could sell anything because, in the jargon of salesmen, he could sell himself." Meanwhile his mother, Eliza, becomes so obsessed with real estate trading that she seems largely oblivious to her dying husband and her quarreling children and their incessant "ugly warfare of greed and hatred."[16]

In Wolfe's *You Can't Go Home Again* (1940), George Webber's Libya Hill is riding the crest of a pre-Crash speculative boom. His aunt's funeral is even disrupted by one of her elderly friends who finds it "too bad, too bad!" that what is "by rights . . . *building* property" has been wasted on a cemetery. In the town at large, George finds "the real estate men were everywhere. . . . Everyone was fair game for them, the lame, the halt and the blind."[17]

Actually, Wolfe often seemed equally contemptuous of the South's mythically glorious past and its sordid materialistic present. In *The Web and the Rock*, George Webber identifies "the curse of South Carolina and its 'Southness'—of always pretending you *used to be* so much, even though you are not now." Yet, in the same novel, the spiritual presence of the southern past is almost palpable. In Richmond for a football game on the eve of World War I, George and his friends are immediately transported a half century back in time: "They saw the state house and heard the guns. They knew that Grant was pounding at the gates of Richmond. They knew that Lee was digging in some twenty miles away at Petersburg. . . . They felt, they knew, they had their living hands and hearts upon the living presence of these things." Wolfe's later work tended to be less autobiographical and offer more of a historical dimension. "Chickamauga," one of his last stories, and in his view "one of the best stories I ever wrote," was based on an account of the famous Civil War battle related to him by his ninety-five-year-old great uncle.[18]

Anyone who wrote that "each moment is the fruit of forty thousand years . . . and every moment is a window on all time" clearly agreed with William Faulkner that "yesterday, today, and tomorrow are 'Is': Indivisible," but Wolfe never struggled with the "impossible load" of the past so dramatically or doggedly as Faulkner. When *Time* magazine ran a cover story in 1939 touting Faulkner as the "central figure in any investigation of Southern literary life," the writer seemed to see him as the somewhat indifferent heir to an aristocratic family tradition, living in a plantation setting and surrounded by his black retainers. Faulkner sometimes presented himself that way as well because ambivalence about both the Old South legend and the New South identity permeated both his personal and literary world.[19]

His great-grandfather, the "Old Colonel," William C. Falkner, a dashing Confederate Cavalier who eventually became an aspiring railroad entrepreneur, personified the New South legend. Yet, the declining family fortunes and so-so social credentials of the Old Colonel's great-grandson hardly put him on equal footing with his future in-laws, the Oldhams, whose status he envied and whose acceptance he craved. To that end, Faulkner overextended himself dramatically in 1930 to purchase "Rowan Oak," a once-grand, but then badly rundown, antebellum estate. His love of horseback riding (despite the frequent bruises to his body and his pride suggesting that he was not much good at it) took on especially interesting symbolic overtones as, late in life, he began to spend more time in Virginia and gained a measure of entrée into the fox hunting society of the Old Dominion. The social exclusivity of these outings contrasted sharply with the much more socially democratic Mississippi hunts that

Faulkner had both enjoyed and incorporated into some of his best fiction. In a famous photograph taken in 1960, Faulkner posed in formal hunting garb, clad in an elegant pink coat with a blue collar, wearing a top hat and holding a riding crop.[20]

Faulkner was also known, on occasion, to regale his new Virginia acquaintances with artfully embellished accounts of his ancestry. In essence, he indulged in a lifelong flirtation with the image of himself as an aristocrat and a country squire. Likewise, although he often expressed frustration with the restrictions imposed by the old paternalistic and patriarchal order in the South, his relationship with his family and his employees and servants at Rowan Oak and at his Greenfield Farm largely followed these traditional guidelines.

Karl F. Zender has noted that "just as Faulkner's Yoknapatawpha fiction arose in large measure out of his sense of nostalgia, so also did his style of life." In his "style of life" Faulkner embraced anachronism in a variety of ways, refusing to allow a radio at Rowan Oak until his daughter Jill was a teenager and concentrating on the sale and breeding of mules at his farm at a time when the mule was clearly beginning to pass from the scene in southern agriculture. (In order to raise mules, Faulkner was forced to buy a tractor.) In yet another and more painful irony, the price of retaining his country-squire lifestyle and meeting his family obligations was Faulkner's much-despised labor as a screenwriter in Hollywood, a setting that embodied for him the utter hollowness and shallowness of modern life at its very worst.[21]

Frederick R. Karl observed that although he struggled to conceal it, Faulkner actually yearned for "position and respectability" and "the accoutrements of the antebellum planter class," while seeking, in the grand manner of the old Cavalier, to act as though these things actually meant nothing to him. More than any of his literary contemporaries, Faulkner, as Karl notes, was "born into history—not only a community with values which he assimilated, but into a historical process he could both struggle against and assimilate."[22]

For Faulkner, historical and contemporary processes were virtually one and the same. Like the writers of the post–World War II boom in Spanish American literature, he lived in a setting where, as Lois Parkinson Zamora wrote, "belated and abrupt modernization . . . masked (and sometimes exacerbated) long histories of political and racial and economic inequity." Deborah N. Cohn explained that both Faulkner and his contemporaries of the Southern Renaissance and Spanish American writers of a later era chronicled the "rocky transition from an agrarian social system, as well as the changing sense of community that this process entails." Not surprisingly, many of the key writers of Spanish America's literary boom readily acknowledged the influence of Faulkner, who, Joel Williamson concluded, had been "born into and reared among an imperialized people. . . . In writing about their plight, he met the plight of the imperialized people of the world, the people whose land had been raped and labor taken to supply raw materials for the factories of the industrial powers."[23]

Despite their dissatisfaction with certain aspects of the status quo, intellectuals in "developing" regions are often ambivalent about sweeping, externally induced social and economic changes that may destroy some of the best of their society's traditions along with the worst. Forced to consider both its strengths and its weaknesses simultaneously, they often develop a somewhat schizophrenic, "love-hate" relationship with their native culture. In this sense, there is more than a passing resemblance between some writers of the Southern Renaissance and the characters of novelist Chinua Achebe, who are caught up in the cultural conflict triggered by the growing Westernization of African life. In fact, Faulkner and his literary contemporaries often seem much like the "been-to," a once-familiar character in West African fiction, so named because he has "been to the West." When the "been-to" returns, he suffers from "psychic division," torn between his admiration for the power and enlightenment of the West and his anxiety about the cultural upheaval that accompanies Western penetration into the world of his youth.[24]

There is more than a hint of this ambivalence in the novels of Thomas Wolfe, who insisted that he considered himself a southerner and the South his "home" but doubted that "any man who writes as I write, who has to write as I must write can live there and get his writing done." This sense of simultaneous attachment and alienation was much more intense and painful for Faulkner, and numerous commentators have speculated that Quentin Compson was actually speaking for the author in *Absalom, Absalom!* when he insisted fervently, but none too convincingly, "I don't hate it . . . I don't !" "I love it and hate it," Faulkner himself explained to a Japanese audience, "Some of the things I don't like at all, but I was born there and that's my home, and I will defend it even if I hate it." He captured this feeling best when he wrote in 1933 that he and other contemporary southern writers "seem to try in the simple furious breathing (or writing) span of the individual to draw a savage indictment of the contemporary scene or to escape from it into a make-believe region of swords and magnolias and mocking birds which perhaps never existed anywhere." Faulkner's ambivalence about the essence of southern identity was readily apparent in his writing. In fact, Walter Taylor has argued that "Faulkner's career . . . reveals an inner dynamic in which each work may be seen as part of a progressive effort to imagine what 'the South' might have been, or might have become, in both its benign and nightmarish aspects—and to imagine a series of protagonists who cope, or fail to cope, with it."[25]

In *Sartoris* (1929), Faulkner drew heavily on both personal feelings and family experiences to present the ineffectual struggle of a venerable southern family trying to cope with the realities of life in a rapidly changing post–World War I South. The novel focused on the inability of young Bayard Sartoris to adjust or reconnect (after losing his brother John in a plane crash in World War I) to his family's (or his region's) honorable aristocratic tradition and the role he is expected to play within that tradition. In fact, the grieving, self-obsessed, self-destructive Bayard actually has no clear notion even of what this tradition is or how it should be revived or replaced. More revealing still is the inability of his grandfather, a former Confederate officer who represents the Lost Cause ethos in which his grandson has been thoroughly immersed, to be of much assistance. In the end, young Bayard finally finds the death he craves, knowing that something has been lost but never understanding exactly what it is.[26]

Faulkner went on to explore in grimmer and more complex detail the decline of a family, society, and a tradition in *The Sound and the Fury* (1929), where the patricians-gone-to-seed Compsons have reached the point of seemingly irreversible degeneration and decay, and the entire clan is dwarfed in courage, wisdom, and integrity by their black servant, Dilsey. The promiscuous daughter Caddy is the ultimate lost soul, and the obsessive son Quentin outstrips even the self-destructive Bayard Sartoris on his way to his suicidal demise. Ultimately, the only sane surviving Compson is their cold-blooded, mercenary brother, Jason. Reduced to clerking in a hardware store and insisting, "I haven't got much pride, I can't afford it," Jason embodies the most sinister aspects of the materialistic and corrupt New South and actually bears no small resemblance to the Snopeses, whose sinister ascent Faulkner would soon begin to trace.[27]

A central tenet of the New South identity justified segregation and disfranchisement as the only means of preserving the sacred southern tradition of white racial purity that had prevailed under slavery. Charles Chesnutt and a host of other black writers had already suggested that this oft-preached principle was an oft-breached one as well. In *Light in August* (1932), Faulkner followed the lead of his black predecessors in presenting the tragic mulatto figure of Joe Christmas. Faulkner provided a twist on the mulatto who tries to deny his or her identity to "pass" for white, however. The light-skinned Christmas could have done this, but instead he challenges the New South identity's rigid insistence on racial separation by attempting to be both black and white.

Not only does Christmas, a "white nigger" as one character calls him, refuse to defend himself from the murderous butcher Percy Grimm, who castrates him as he lies mortally wounded, but as he dies he looks upon his assailants "with peaceful and unfathomable and unbearable eyes." The analogy to Christ on the cross is difficult to resist as the dying Christmas seems to surrender his life in order to show that only by admitting the reality and then accepting the consequences of being simultaneously black and white can the South atone for its racial sins. In this sense, Daniel Singal explained, Joe Christmas was subverting contemporary racial beliefs, much as Jesus Christ had done with the religious beliefs of his time.[28]

A few years later in *Absalom, Absalom!* (1936), Faulkner examined the antebellum roots of the white South's aristocratic tradition and in the process exposed the fundamental weaknesses that would make this tradition so susceptible to postbellum decay. In the chilling story of the rise and fall of the relentless single-minded parvenu Thomas Sutpen, Faulkner forced readers to consider the darker underpinnings of the Old South tradition. As a late-arriving but obsessively ambitious aspirant to the planter aristocracy, Sutpen tries in the space of a few decades to make up several generations of social distance separating him from families like the Sartorises. Thus, he disturbs his socially superior contemporaries by engaging before their eyes in the kind of ruthless and amoral behavior that was carefully concealed in the history of their own families' rise to prominence. If Sutpen seems decidedly "New South" in equating economic status with social status, he also poses the unsettling question of whether, as F. Garvin Davenport put it, "The Cavalier myth contributes to and encourages the very exploitation and crass worship of material goods which other Southern traditionalists claim that it opposes." Cumulatively, the rise of the local planter aristocracy may have taken more time, but who was to say that it had not entailed many individual acts of brutality, selfishness, insensitivity, and greed comparable to those that had fueled Sutpen's meteoric, though ill-fated, ascent?[29]

If he was concerned about the underpinnings and the unexplored inner reality of the South's aristocratic tradition, Faulkner was hardly enthusiastic about what he saw replacing it. In *The Hamlet* (1940), Faulkner began what would become the "Snopes Trilogy," in which he demonstrated his thorough understanding of the changing white social and economic hierarchy of the early twentieth-century South. *The Hamlet* introduced supply merchant Will

Varner, "the chief man of the country . . . and hence the fountain head if not of law at least of advice and suggestion to a countryside which would have repudiated the term constituency if they had ever heard it." The yeoman inhabitants of this countryside, meanwhile, were "Democrats, Protestants and prolific," who "supported their own churches and schools, married and committed infrequent adulteries and more frequent homicides among themselves and were their own courts, judges and executioners." Faulkner clarified the ostensibly relaxed (but actually delicate and complex) southern white social structure by explaining that these sturdy and independent folk who were Varner's unwitting constituency came to him, "not in the attitude of *What must I do* but *What do you think you would like for me to do if you was able to make me do it.*"[30]

The foregoing description accorded well with the interpretation of the southern white yeomanry offered by historians Frank and Harriet Owsley, whose findings were just beginning to appear when *The Hamlet* was published in 1940. Faulkner's portrait also fit his perception of the white residents of "Beat Two," the county supervisor district where his own Greenfield Farm lay. While working actively to manage the farm, Faulkner had told his mother, "These are my kind of people."[31]

In *The Hamlet,* Faulkner showed these common whites struggling with the disappearance of a frontier-bred, agrarian barter economy. Where once even the hardest bargains had been struck in informal, face-to-face negotiations, people and personalities now figured but little in the outcome of transactions governed by bloodless, unblinking calculations of profit and the stern realities of the market. Still convinced that the true measure of a man's worth was not just his wealth but the stock he placed in his honor or his reputation for courage, strength, and fealty to his word and his family and community obligations, the country folk are no match for the soulless machinations of Flem Snopes.

Though it is generally suggested that he was born a poor white, Flem's own origins remain alien and obscure. When asked where he comes from, his only reply is "West." His father, Ab, is said to be a barn burner, but the Snopes genealogy extends back no further than Ab, and although Flem seems to have an endless supply of cousins, the actual details of their specific kinship lines are never revealed. Meanwhile, he connives, swindles, and hard-bargains his way to a position of power and influence and becomes what Williamson called a "symbol for the corruption of community, clan and family in the modern world."[32]

Flem begins his ascent by capitalizing on his father's intimidating reputation as an arsonist to become a Will Varner tenant. Before long, he is a clerk in Varner's store and then becomes Varner's son-in-law after Will's voluptuous daughter, Eula, is impregnated by a local swain who summarily skedaddles. As what Singal called a "hayseed Horatio Alger," Flem feels no ties or obligation to the old ways, and he uses this freedom to exploit his neighbors, selling them unbroken Texas ponies (acquisitions that reassert their frontiersman masculinity) and conning them into buying the Old Frenchman's place by claiming to have searched it for gold himself after "salting" it with enough gold coins to convince them that treasure may be buried on the property.[33]

Richard Gray has pointed to the critical subtleties of this episode. The country folk who are hoodwinked by Flem are hardly nonacquisitive by nature, and they actually admire a slick trader. They are drawn into Flem's scheme by a belief in the legendary wealth of the past, but even as he exploits their desire to live off this wealth, Flem knows that the future is where the real money is, and he soon abandons Frenchman's Bend, heading off to Jefferson "in search of more property and profit, a theoretically endless chain of exchange stretching before him."[34]

Although the local folk share Flem's desire for prosperity, they are still encumbered by an attachment to the past with its myths of glory and bounty whereas Flem is immune to such distractions. Instead, as what Gray calls a "seamless capitalist," he relies on "logic: that unswerving ability to strip things down to their essentials." In this sense, Flem is all the more frightening because he is not necessarily so much more mercenary than those he dupes but simply more evolved, or, as Gray put it, "he is a little further down the path of history than they are."[35]

This evolutionary metaphor seems even more apt when we consider that the Snopeses are rising from the depths to fill the vacuum created by the destruction and decay of the old order that had traditionally held sway in Frenchman's Bend and throughout the South. Irving Howe drew a sharp distinction between Will Varner, whose rapacity was "relaxed" and "unsystematic," and the Snopeses—"bloodless and calculating" and "taut with purpose." Yet, for all these contrasts, Varner is savvy enough to recognize Flem's triumph as inevitable, and he accommodates himself to it nicely as the two sit "side by side in outrageous paradox" and Varner, "cheerful as a cricket," watches approvingly as Flem makes the Varner enterprises more efficient and profitable.[36]

Though he, too, is taken in by Flem's buried-treasure scam at the Old Frenchman's place, the exceedingly "pleasant, affable, courteous anecdotal, and impenetrable" sewing machine salesman V. K. Ratliffe otherwise maintains a wary distance from Flem and understands that the rise of the Snopeses represents the death knell for the way of life to which the majority of his countrymen remain so firmly attached. Ratliffe, himself, however, is no prisoner of the past. He can practice cash or barter economics equally well. As the Snopes trilogy proceeds in *The Town* (1957) and *The Mansion* (1959), Ratliffe will prove himself remarkably adaptive to modernization, giving up his wagon for a Model T, which he modifies into a truck from which he eventually sells not just sewing machines but radios and even televisions. Like Varner (and the South itself), he survives the changes that give rise to the Snopeses not by resisting but by making accommodations to them.[37]

Not long after *The Hamlet* appeared, Faulkner explained that all of his writing had dealt in one way or another with "the capacity to endure well grief and misfortune and then endure again, in terms of individuals who observed and adhered to them not for reward but for virtue's own sake, not even because they are admirable in themselves, but in order to live with oneself and die peacefully with oneself when the time comes." As Frederick Karl observed, Faulkner was not writing to effect the destruction or conversion of "liars and rogues" or "hypocrites and liars," but for "others, who say it is preferable to be Ratliff than Flem Snopes."[38]

Even as he was offering this uncharacteristically forthcoming insight into his motives as a writer, Faulkner was struggling to piece together *Go Down, Moses* (1942), a set of short stories that would chronicle one man's personal struggle to "live with himself and die peacefully with himself when the time comes." In the central story, "The Bear," Isaac McCaslin discovers at age sixteen that his grandfather, Carothers McCaslin, had fathered a daughter by a slave woman, Eunice, who subsequently committed suicide when she learned that this daughter, Tomasina ("Tomey"), was then pregnant with Carothers's child herself. Tomey died in childbirth, and Carothers's will left an unexplained legacy of $1,000 to his unacknowledged and incest-begotten son, known as "Tomey's Turl." This, a rueful Isaac reckons, "*was cheaper than saying My son to a nigger*."[39]

After Carothers's death, Isaac's father, "Buck," and his uncle, "Buddy," had tried to ameliorate some of the wrongs done to their father's slaves by moving out of the big plantation house into a one-room log cabin and allowing the slaves freedom of movement at night. They also began a process of manumission that amounted, Isaac thinks, to a "slow amortization" of the "general and condoned injustice" of slavery but not of "the specific tragedy [his grandfather's miscegenation and incest] which had not been condoned and could never be amortized."[40]

Hoping to distance himself from this monstrously evil family and regional legacy as well, Isaac repudiates the plantation that he has inherited through his father from his grandfather, in the process losing his wife and the opportunity to have heirs of his own. In making this sacrifice, Ike is following a boyhood lesson taught him by the half-Indian-half-black Sam Fathers, an old hunting guide who instills in him a vision of the woods and wilderness as a pastoral Eden rightly belonging to no one. Therefore, for him, possession and exploitation of the land become a primary source of human corruption. As Richard King has suggested, Ike's moral vision is grounded in an idyllic vision of a wilderness whose rapidly shrinking physical reality is testimony to its defenselessness against the very forces Ike seeks to turn back. Nonetheless, Ike insists, by virtue of repudiating his inheritance, "I am free" and explains further, "Sam Fathers set me free."[41]

Ike's sense of separation from his family's history of injustice proves fleeting at best. In "Delta Autumn," the concluding story in *Go Down, Moses*, the aged Uncle Ike returns for a final hunt in the Delta woods that have now been largely devoured by the timber companies and, like Ike, are living on borrowed time. While there, he is confronted by a young black woman who has given birth to the child of old Carothers McCaslin's descendant, Roth Edmonds, who, true to family form, has refused to acknowledge her. To make matters more complicated (and Faulkner's point more pointed), the woman is the greatgranddaughter of Tomey's Turl, the product of Ike's grandfather's incestuous relationship with his own daughter more than a century earlier. In the end, a frustrated Ike can only send the woman away, telling her, "I can do nothing for you! Can't nobody do nothing for you!" As this incident indicates all too well, his declaration of personal freedom from historical responsibility notwithstanding, Ike is no freer than any other southerner because, as he observes, "the whole South is cursed, and all of us who derive from it, whom it ever suckled, white and black both lie under the curse."[42]

King has characterized *Go Down, Moses* as the culminating expression of "Faulkner's exploration of historical consciousness," and Frederick Karl found it ironic that Faulkner's final, full-blown "historically conscious" novel centered around one man's foredoomed attempt to "throw off history." In reality, however, Ike McCaslin sought not so much to flee from history as to escape any personal accountability for it. Much the same was true of Jack Burden, the protagonist in Robert Penn Warren's *All the King's Men* (1946), who resists the "burden" of responsibility for his past. As James H. Justus observed, Warren's poems and novels presented history as an omnipresent and potentially devastating force and yet "the salvation of those persistent seekers of self-identity." Regardless of their virtues or vices, only those willing to do "combat with the past" could hope to achieve self-understanding and deal constructively with the future. The theme of romantic idealism and ambition corrupted by the sweep of history had marked both Warren's 1929 biography of John Brown and his first two novels, *Night Rider* (1937) and *At Heaven's Gate* (1943). *All the King's Men* revealed much more clearly, however, that he and Faulkner shared, in Warren's words, the belief that "the sense of the past and the sense of the present are somehow intertwined constantly."[43]

Although it chronicled the demise of neopopulist political dictator and Huey Long clone Willie Stark, Warren's novel was really the story of the narrator Burden's struggle to come to terms with his own identity and self. While serving as Stark's assistant, Burden, a Ph.D. student in history, ponders the implications of his dissertation research on his great-uncle Cass Mastern. His findings reveal that his otherwise virtuous ancestor's affair with the wife of a close friend had caused her husband's suicide and led her to sell away her devoted slave girl whose knowing gaze had become an excruciating reminder of her guilt. Wracked by guilt himself, Cass had freed his own slaves, and although he had joined the Confederate Army as an enlisted man, he had refused to fire a musket, asking, "How can I who have taken the life of my friend, take the life of an enemy, for I have used up my blood." Mortally wounded at Atlanta, Cass was buried in an unmarked grave.[44]

At first Burden struggles to grasp the meaning of this story, perhaps "because he was afraid to understand for what might be understood there was a reproach to him." The implications of Cass's actions become both clearer and more disquietingly personal when, acting on Stark's orders, Burden uncovers evidence of misconduct by Judge Irwin, one of Stark's political opponents who, it turns out, is also Jack's real father. Jack's revelation triggers an almost soap-opera-esque sequence in which Irwin commits suicide and the woman Jack loves, Anne Stanton (whose own father, a former governor, had covered up Irwin's crime), becomes the mistress of Willie Stark, thereby enraging her brother, Adam, who assassinates Stark but is also killed during the attack. At this point, Jack learns, as did Cass Mastern, that "the world is all of one piece

... like an enormous spider web and if you touch it, however lightly, at any point, the vibration ripples to the remotest perimeter." Here Warren echoes Wolfe's description of "each moment" as "the fruit of forty thousand years" and anticipates Faulkner's observation in *Intruder in the Dust* that "yesterday won't be over until tomorrow and tomorrow began ten thousand years ago." For Burden, reality "is not a function of the event as event but of the relationship of that event to past, and future, events." Once Jack understands that "history is blind, but man is not," recovering and acknowledging his own past allow him, like Cass, to accept responsibility for the hurt and harm he has caused. In the end, realizing that "if you could not accept the past and its burden, there was no future," he prepares to "go into the convulsion of the world, out of history into history and the awful responsibility of Time."[45]

Where Faulkner's characters were often called on, as he explained, to do their best against indomitable historical forces and "to endure grief and misfortune and misfortune and injustice and then endure them again," Warren's were assigned a bit more responsibility for their own fates and those of others. Though they were in a sense "doomed" by both their frailties and their virtues and good intentions (Burden is drawn to Stark initially because he believes his goals are worthy even if his tactics are not), they nonetheless lived "in the agony of will," as Warren wrote in *All the King's Men*. Still, Jack Burden's examination of history and its relationship to the present reveals the same search for self-definition and identity that had engaged Faulkner and so many of the major southern writers who had preceded and influenced Warren. As Justus put it, "The past for Warren must be understood for him to know himself."[46]

The same might have been said of Warren's African American literary contemporaries as well. Black writers of this period not only shared an identity shaped by the southern context of black experience, but recalling Richard Gray's observations about the white writers of the Southern Renaissance, they too responded to "the disorienting experience of social change in the present" by taking a closer look at the past. In fact, a number of the themes that would engage the leading white writers of the Southern Renaissance had already been raised by black writers during and even before the Harlem Renaissance that blossomed in the 1920s. Because it is so closely associated with black migration out of the South and with the flowering of black literary, musical, and artistic talent in the less constricted atmosphere of the urban North, the Harlem

Renaissance has generally been seen as a "northern" rather than "southern" phenomenon. Yet, in many key aspects, the Harlem Renaissance was simply a geographically detached—but no less real or important—part of the Southern Renaissance. Alain Locke suggested as much in 1927 when he argued, "If conditions in the South were more conducive to the development of negro culture without transplanting, the self-expression of the 'New Negro' would spring up just as one branch of the new literature of the South, and as one additional phase of its cultural awakening."[47]

Both the Harlem Renaissance and the Southern Renaissance emerged within a common context of economic and demographic change. Facing lynching, disfranchisement, and economic serfdom in the South and responding to critical labor shortages in northern industries during World War I, an estimated half million southern blacks left the region between 1916 and 1929 alone, and nearly a million more would follow over the next decade. A key participant himself, Sterling A. Brown summed up both the causes and the implications of the Harlem Renaissance when he noted, "The extensive migrations from the South, quickened by the devastations of the boll weevil, the growing resentment at injustice, and the demand of northern industries; the advance of the Negro in labor, wealth, and education; the World War with its new experiences in camp and battle; the Garvey movement with its exploitation of 'race,' all of these contributed to the growth of the 'New Negro.'"[48]

For Locke, the more urbane, accomplished, self-confident "New Negro" had emerged because "a railroad ticket and a suitcase, like a Baghdad carpet, transport[ed] the Negro peasant from the cotton field and farm to the heart of the most complex urban civilization." These incoming "peasants" may have found themselves suddenly awash in urban complexity, but the new arrivals were definitely more "in" than "of" it and not nearly so immediately "new" as Locke implied. Sociologist Charles S. Johnson's estimate that the typical Harlemite in 1925 was still about 60 percent "southern" was surely on the mark. Although many of these were fond of declaring that they would rather "be a lamp post in Harlem than the mayor of Atlanta," for some of the key writers of the Harlem Renaissance, the move to the North afforded not so much an opportunity to turn their backs on the South as to turn and take a "backward glance" of their own. Freed from its constant emotional pressures and stifling intellectual restraints and deprivation, they could now look with greater detachment at a society and culture that, for better or worse, had helped to make them who they were. Finally, much like the major white writers of their generation, their encounters with the North also clearly influenced their perceptions of the South.[49]

These similarities should not be surprising. When forced to confront the nature of their own feelings about the South (again, like many of the white writers of the Southern Renaissance), blacks in the region had historically presented what L. D. Reddick called "a study in attachment and alienation" alternately expressing their "love and hate" and finding themselves struggling with "a great and confusing frustration." John Hope Franklin's research on runaway slaves has revealed that "though blacks, with few exceptions, rejected slavery, they did not reject the land or the region." Celebrated fugitive slave Frederick Douglass said as much, predicting that if emancipation came, "you would see many old and familiar faces back again to [sic] the South." Douglass may have spoken not just for those who had fled slavery but also for many who had subsequently fled Jim Crow when he explained, "We want to live in the land of our birth and to lay our bones by the side of our fathers; nothing short of an intense love of personal freedom keeps us from the South."[50]

Although he wrote of its racial horrors, Langston Hughes also recalled in 1922 "the magnolia-scented South,/Beautiful like a woman, seductive as a dark-eyed whore" and lamented the fact that "I am who am black, would love her" and "give her many rare gifts," but "she spits in my face" and "turns her back on me." Surveying Hughes's short fiction, Robert Bone found a "deep affection for the rural South, despite the terror and brutality which all too often were visited upon him within its precincts."[51]

Bone's generalization hardly seemed to apply to Richard Wright's work, but even an embittered Wright's abused and oppressed black characters appreciated the sensory splendors of the South, the droning bees and hovering butterflies, "the sweet scent of honeysuckles," and "the long gladness of green cornfields in summer and the deep dream of sleepy grey skies in winter." Thadious Davis has suggested that, however unpleasant in many aspects, Wright's life in the South was the source of his "artistic imperative"; and Wright himself knew, as he had made his way north in 1927, that he was "not leaving the South to forget the South, but so that some day I might understand it." For all his feelings of hurt and estrangement, "deep down" he realized "that I could never really leave the South, for my feelings had already been formed by the South, for there had been slowly instilled into my personality and consciousness, black though I was, the culture of the South."[52]

Even as his anger leapt from the pages of his partly autobiographical novel, *Black Boy*, in 1945, Wright was insisting, "There is a great novel to be written about the Negro in the south . . . telling how they live and how they die, what they see and how they feel each day . . . telling of the quiet ritual of their lives." Much of Wright's life in the South had been consumed by his refusal to accept the "place" assigned to him by southern whites who claimed that they "knew niggers" but "had never known me—never known what I thought, what I felt." Like Wright, a number of black writers of the Harlem Renaissance era not only acknowledged that they had been shaped by their experiences in the South, but they also understood well in advance of William Faulkner's depiction of Joe Christmas in *Light in August* that, as Robert Penn Warren wrote, "the nigger is a creation of the white man." Accordingly, they determined to shove aside the simple, convenient stereotypes used to justify the New South's racial system in order to understand how the South had become a part of them and to show that they had been a part of it as well.[53]

DuBois had written in *The Souls of Black Folk* of the "double consciousness" or sense of "twoness—an American, a Negro"—that came with being black in the United States. The challenge facing every black person in America, he argued, was to move beyond "always looking at one's self through the eyes of others" in order "to attain self-conscious manhood, to merge his double self into a better and truer self." DuBois had anticipated the aim and focus of most of the key contributors to the Harlem Renaissance, but many of these contributors found their task even more challenging than he had suggested. The search for the essence of black identity, many of them realized, must proceed not on two fronts, but three, for its sources were not only African and American, but "southern" as well.[54]

Thadious Davis pointed in particular to the influence of James Weldon Johnson and Jean Toomer, who "announced and reiterated the importance of the South in all of its beauty, complexity and pain" and "understood that the South, whether treated directly or not, was essential to the formal or folk art that would emerge among black artists." Born into the black middle class in Jacksonville, Florida, Johnson was educated at Atlanta University and in 1898 became the first black admitted to the Florida bar since Reconstruction. He also held a consular post in Latin America and served the NAACP as a field secretary charged with organizing chapters in the South and West. His best-known work, *God's Trombones* (1927), celebrated the primitive beauty of "the old time 'Negro sermon'" in verse.[55]

Johnson's novel, *The Autobiography of an Ex-Coloured Man*, was published initially in 1912 and reissued to much acclaim in 1927. The son of a light-skinned black woman and a white man in Georgia, the novel's protagonist spends much of his life passing back and forth across the color line. After he is stirred by a black classmate's oratory, however, he begins "to form wild dreams of bringing glory and honour to the Negro race." Blessed with considerable musical talent, he eventually resolves to go back to the South where he can "drink in my inspiration firsthand" by immersing himself in black folk culture and integrating it into his classical compositions. He aborts this mission abruptly, however, when he sees a black man burned to death by a white mob and is overcome with "unbearable shame . . . at being identified with a people that could with impunity be treated worse than animals." This incident leads him not only to return to "passing" for white but to abandon his artistic dreams to pursue "a white man's success" which he reduces to one word: "money." Although he eventually returns to the North and prospers economically, he never frees himself of "a strange longing for his mother's people" in the South and elsewhere or the feeling of having "sold my birthright for a mess of pottage."[56]

Similar themes permeated Jean Toomer's *Cane*. Also of mixed racial lineage, Toomer was born in Washington, D.C., in 1894, the grandson of P. B. S. Pinchback, who had served as lieutenant governor of Louisiana during Reconstruction. The light-skinned Toomer's exploration of his "black" identity began in 1921 after he spent three months in Sparta, Georgia, as principal of a black school. This visit fueled Toomer's curiosity about his black heritage, which, he admitted in 1922, "has stimulated and fertilized whatever creative talent I may contain within me. A visit to Georgia last fall was the starting point of almost everything of worth that I have done." Toomer's brief stay in Georgia had led him to identify with southern black country folk or "peasants," as he often referred to them: "My seed was planted in the cane-and-cotton fields and in the souls of black and white people in the small southern town." Toomer's fixation on southern black life blossomed in *Cane*, published in 1923 and described by Louis Rubin as "the first fully mature work of the Southern Literary Renascence of the years after World War I."[57]

In *Cane*, Toomer offered a three-part exploration of the interaction of race, history, and regional environment in shaping and reshaping the identities of black Americans. The first part of *Cane* reveals southern black rural life through a series of poems and stories. Toomer's black women are more in touch with their own human instincts and desires than the male characters who pursue and seek to dominate them. He often presented his female characters as one with the natural environment: "Her skin is like dusk, when the sun goes down. . . . Her face pales until it is the color of the gray dust that dances with the cotton leaves. . . . Her breasts, firm and up-pointed like ripe acorns."[58]

The stories in this section are replete with sexual and racial tension, and in one, "Blood Burning Moon," a black man is burned to death after killing his black girlfriend's white lover in self-defense. One of *Cane*'s most effective poems, "Portrait in Georgia," describes a woman whose features also suggest elements of a lynching, from her hair "coiled like a lyncher's rope" to eyes like "fagots," to her skin "white as the ash of black flesh after flame." Toomer was also entranced by the simple beauty of black folksong, which he blended with the natural environment: "Their voices rise . . . the pine trees are guitars./Strumming, pine needles fall like sheets of rain."[59]

The second section of *Cane* offers stories set in the sterile, inauthentic urban complexity of Washington and Chicago and provides a stark contrast to the lush lyrical portraits of black southerners living close to the soil and in harmony with nature. In this section, Toomer's characters struggle to suppress their normal instincts and desires in the face of the strict and impersonal social conventions and demands of style, sophistication, and self-control that the urban environment seems to impose. In "Kabnis," the concluding segment of *Cane*, Toomer introduced Ralph Kabnis, an educated, northern-born black teacher, who moves to the South in search of his identity but finds he cannot truly relate to black southerners who have taught themselves to live, however grudgingly, within the region's racial limits. The cultural gap between him and the uneducated black masses is too great, and he cannot bring himself to show the deference toward whites that the principal of this school demands of his teachers.[60]

Throughout *Cane*, it is the less-educated, economically deprived blacks who seem happier and better adjusted. Even in the South, middle-class "town" blacks appear more frustrated and conflicted than their rural counterparts because they are further removed from both their African and rural southern roots. If Toomer meant to encourage American blacks to see the beauty and mystery of their African and southern heritage, he also realized that the destabilizing forces of modernization were making this increasingly difficult, pointing out that blacks who lived in the town of Sparta disdained the "rich and sad and joyous and beautiful" sounds of "folk-songs and spirituals" as "shouting" and preferred "victrolas and player-pianos." With its romantic vision of the southern black "peasantry" and its critical perspective on the cultural consequences of urbanization and urban migration, *Cane* actually seemed to foreshadow some of the essays in *I'll Take My Stand*, which would not appear until seven years later. In fact, although a staunch segregationist, Allen Tate, one of the most prominent contributors to *I'll Take My Stand*, actually sought to meet and encourage Toomer in 1923 and again in 1924.[61]

Thadious Davis noted that along with Johnson's *God's Trombones*, Toomer's *Cane* had set the stage for younger black writers like Zora Neale Hurston, Langston Hughes, and Sterling Brown, "whose works revalued a South that gave them the most vital materials for their art." "As southerners, either by actual place of birth or by their own identification with the South as the signal inspiration for their writing," Hurston, Hughes, and Brown also celebrated the poetic and metaphoric speech of the black masses, accepting them on their own terms instead of decrying their backwardness and exhorting them to emulate the "New Negro" ideal.[62]

Born around 1900 in the all-black town of Eatonville, Florida, Hurston focused primarily on the culture of uneducated rural southern blacks, leaving her readers to draw their own contrasts between the characters and scenes that she presented and the realities of modern urban life. A decidedly free spirit, she joined a traveling show at fourteen and then went on to study at Howard University under Alain Locke and later at Barnard College with Franz Boas. As an anthropologist, between 1927 and 1932 Hurston collected the folklore that went into *Mules and Men*, which in the spirit of Toomer and Johnson, documented and illustrated the vitality of southern black folk culture.

Hurston's superb grasp of black folklore and dialect also enriched her fiction and made her the most identifiably "southern" of all the Harlem Renaissance writers. As Hurston explained, "I was a Southerner, and had the map of Dixie on my tongue." Her mastery of the southern black folks' artful simile and colorful invective permeated her work, and although it occasionally seemed intrusive and overdone, it proved particularly helpful in her development and presentation of strong female characters.[63]

In Hurston's novel *Jonah's Gourd Vine*, a male character observes that "jus' cause women folks ain't got no big muscled arm and fists lack jugs, folks claims they's weak vessels, but dass uh lie. Dat piece uh red flannel she got hung tween her jaws is equal tuh all de fistes God ever made and man ever seen. Jes' take an ruin a man wid they tongue, and den dey kin hold it still and bruise 'im up jes es bad." Holding their tongues was not exactly the specialty of Hurston's heroines. In her autobiography, *Dust Tracks on a Road*, she presented "Big Sweet," who was a formidable physical as well as verbal presence, especially when she played the dozens with an outmatched man, "bringing him up to date on his ancestry, his looks, smell, gait, clothes and his route through hell in the hereafter."[64]

In Hurston's most successful novel, *Their Eyes Were Watching God* (1937), heroine Janie Crawford does not hold back when her second husband ridicules her abilities, age, and appearance: "You bigbellies round here and put out a lot of brag, but 'taint nothin' to it but you big voice. Humph! Talkin' bout *me* lookin' old! When you pull down yo' britches, you look lak de change uh life." Later recognized as "a bold feminist novel, the first to be explicitly so in the Afro-American tradition," *Their Eyes Were Watching God* tells of Janie's alternately joyful and tragic search for love, autonomy, and self-realization in a society and cultural environment where any one of the three was exceedingly difficult for a black woman to achieve. After two unfulfilling marriages, Janie meets "Tea Cake," a free-spirited younger man with whom she finds happiness and "a self crushing love." Janie's refusal to sink into self-pity even when she eventually loses Tea Cake mirrored Hurston's own feelings about "the sobbing school of Negrohood who hold that nature has somehow given them a low down dirty deal" and her belief that "bitterness is the underarm odor of wishful weakness . . . the graceless acknowledgement of defeat."[65]

Hurston's friend and fellow writer Langston Hughes was born in Joplin, Missouri, and raised in Lawrence, Kansas, but his maternal grandmother had been a free person of color in antebellum North Carolina, and his grandfather had been active in the Underground Railroad in Ohio. Hughes was, as Davis points out, "a Southerner twice removed from the South," but his "formative world" was peopled with southern black migrants to the Midwest, and he "understood that the folk of the South were crucial to the imaginative impulse of black writers attempting to define themselves and to declare their independence from restrictive literary traditions and expectations."[66]

Hughes was greatly impressed by Toomer's *Cane*, and he often drew on the blues and jazz to convey the richness and meaning of black culture in the rural South. He found the blues "sadder even than the spirituals because their sadness is not softened with tears but hardened with . . . the absurd incongruous laughter of a sadness without even a God to appeal to." Hughes saw music linking rural black life to the new urban milieu fed by the Great Migration, writing of "Barrel House: Chicago," where a black singer played "a song that once was sung beneath the sun/In lazy far-off sunny Southern days."[67]

Although Hughes clearly worried that black migrants to the North might turn their backs on the southern folk heritage, he fully understood their desire to escape the New South's racial atrocities and depredations. In June 1922 *Crisis* published Hughes's poem "The South" in which he portrayed "the lazy, laughing South, with blood on its mouth . . . scratching in the dead fire's ashes for a Negro's bones." In 1931, with the nation and the world abuzz over the infamous Scottsboro case in which nine young black men were falsely accused of rape, Hughes also penned "Christ in Alabama." Appearing in the radical literary magazine *CONTEMPO*, published in Chapel Hill, this explosive composition proclaimed "Christ is a nigger, beaten and black . . . most holy bastard, of the bleeding mouth, Nigger Christ. On the cross of the South." The poem appeared just as Hughes arrived in Chapel Hill for a speaking engagement, where some of his white hosts at the university were outraged and distressed by it, to say the least.[68]

Two weeks before Hughes's poem appeared, *CONTEMPO* had announced that "William Faulkner is at present the guest of the editors of *CONTEMPO*" and promised that "parts of Mr. Faulkner's next book, *Light in August*, will appear in CONTEMPO." In fact, Faulkner was carrying the unfinished manuscript for *Light in August* (with its focus on a mulatto "Christ") with him when he visited Chapel Hill. It is impossible to know whether Faulkner may have been influenced by Hughes's poem, but it seems likely that he at least saw it before it was published.[69]

Hughes also pursued the theme of the tragic mulatto in his poetry ("*I am your son, white man!* . . . A little yellow Bastard boy") and in his play, *Mulatto*, where Bert, a young black man, kills "Colonel Tom," the white father who refuses to acknowledge him, and then shoots himself rather than face a lynch mob. Grief-stricken, Cora, Bert's mother and Colonel Tom's mistress, muses, "White mens, and colored womens, bastard chilluns. . . . They de ways o' de South—mixtries, mixtries."[70]

Like Hughes, Sterling Brown also savored the richness of southern black culture and appreciated its resilience in the face of white oppression. Brown learned much about the South from his father, a former slave who became a distinguished minister, but he also observed it firsthand as a teacher and traveler in the region. As he traveled, Brown was struck by the rural black folk who responded to life in such a simple and unpretentious manner and were "left to their own resources to articulate the terms of their existence." "Southern Road," the title piece of Brown's first collection of poetry, reflected the sense of struggle and travail that was the lot of rural southern blacks in general. In this poem, a black chain gang sings a work song as they swing their hammers while working along a "Southern Road": "White man tells me—hunh—Damn yo soul; Got no need, bebby, to be tole." Brown praised blueswoman Gertrude "Ma" Rainey as a keeper of black identity, urging her to "sing yo' song . . . Git way inside us, Keep us strong." Like Hughes, he also chided the children of the

Great Migration for laughing when they heard the old folksongs "born of the travail of their sires. . . . Diamonds of song, deep buried beneath the torrid Dixie sun."[71]

Some black intellectuals objected to such sentimental portrayals of the primitive rural culture they blamed for holding the masses of their people back. Black writers who emphasized the richness and distinctiveness of southern black culture also faced charges of simply marketing an image of black exoticism and primitivism to white readers. (Ironically, contemporary writers like Erskine Caldwell, William Faulkner, and Thomas Wolfe were similarly attacked for showcasing southern white depravity to a leering audience of northern book buyers.)

Alain Locke drew heavily on the celebrated March 1925 "Harlem" issue of *Survey Graphic* in putting together the *New Negro* anthology later that year. As Mark Huddle has pointed out, however, intent on showcasing a more urbane and northernized black identity, Locke deleted Charles Johnson's observation that the typical resident of Harlem remained quite southern. He also omitted altogether Rudolph Fisher's "The South Lingers On," a short story composed of several vignettes of recent migrants whose encounters with cruelty, callousness, exploitation, and moral degradation among their own people in Harlem stir longings for their southern roots. Zora Neale Hurston drew especially heavy fire as New Negro proponents accused her of pandering to wealthy white patrons who gobbled up her characterizations of blacks as carefree, happy, uneducated, and altogether entertaining creatures. Reacting to *Their Eyes Were Watching God*, Locke urged her to stop creating "these pseudo-primitives whom the reading public still loves to laugh with, weep over, and envy." Richard Wright also criticized Hurston's novel as a sort of literary minstrel show, a work that amused white audiences by exploiting the quaintness of black life but offered "no theme, no message, no thought."[72]

In reality, it was a particular theme, message, or thought that these predominantly male critics were demanding. Other women writers of the Harlem Renaissance were generally less likely than Hurston to downplay the effects of white oppression. However, they won few friends in the patriarchal black literary establishment by focusing on the plight of black women who often played the traditionally male role of family provider while struggling as well to overcome both sexual and emotional abuse at the hands of men of both races.

Locke's proclamation that "the day of 'aunties,' 'uncles,' and 'mammies' is . . . gone" was surely news to women like "Mrs. Jackson," who, in Ramona Lowe's short story "The Woman in the Window," reluctantly agrees to dress in Aunt Jemima garb to promote the restaurant where she works because "a family that had to be supported . . . made duty triumph over pride."[73]

Some black activists argued that regardless of gender, black writers could better serve the interests of their race by focusing on the repression and injustice that whites visited upon African Americans or on the remarkable progress many members of the race had made in overcoming the hardships they faced. "I do not care a damn for any art that is not used for propaganda," W. E. B. DuBois insisted, and in his "Blueprint for Negro Writing," Richard Wright attacked black authors who had not "taken advantage of their unique minority position" to develop "the highest possible pitch of social consciousness." Finally, in July 1931 the editors of The Crisis called for "fiction which shows the possible if not actual triumph of good and true and beautiful things. . . . We are quite fed up with filth and defeatism."[74]

Like Zora Neale Hurston, Langston Hughes also faced charges of catering to the sensationalist tastes of whites and of betraying his race by presenting "lecherous, lust-reeking characters" in poems that were "unsanitary, insipid, and repulsing." Hughes spurned such critics as narrow-minded, nouveau riche blacks who were obsessed with whites' opinion of them and struggling with their own low self-esteem. These detractors, he thought, were wedded to the notion "that we should display our 'higher selves'—whatever they are" and failed to understand "that every 'ugly' poem I write is a protest against the ugliness it pictures."[75]

Many who objected to the works of writers like Hughes, Brown, and Hurston complained that white readers would take their poor, uneducated characters as "representative" of all blacks and therefore overlook the sophistication and accomplishments of the black middle and upper classes. As Ralph Ellison would put it some years later, if such critics had their way, "one would simply portray Negro experience and Negro personality as the exact opposite of any stereotype set up by prejudiced whites." To those who argued that black writers should write about "a better class" of blacks, Sterling Brown retorted, "According to this scale of values, a book about a Negro and a mule would be, because of the mule, a better book than one about a muleless Negro . . . and a book about a Negro and a Rolls Royce better than one about a Negro and a Ford. All that it seems our writers need to do to guarantee a perfect book and a deathless reputation, is to write about a Negro and an aeroplane." Here again, in their concerns about the identity-stifling potential of the prevailing urban-bourgeois vision of black progress, Brown and his like-minded contemporaries invited comparisons with the Nashville Agrarians who believed that the purest form of southern white identity could be found among those who lived on and from the land.[76]

As editor on "Negro Affairs" for the WPA's Federal Writers Project, Brown coordinated the collection of the narratives of former slaves and of documents relating to black history and culture. Although he valued the authenticity of black folk culture, he also appreciated its complexity, and he bristled at any-one, white and black, who wrote of "the Negro" as if all African Americans were the same or served up one-dimensional, romanticized portraits of south-ern blacks living in ignorant bliss. Though he was clearly sympathetic to Hurston's overall approach, he took exception to her *Mules and Men* because despite the "squalor, poverty, disease, violence, enforced ignorance and ex-ploitation that were central to their existence," Hurston's characters exhibited no "smoldering resentment," and she had made their lives seem "easygoing and carefree."[77]

If Brown had little patience with those who emphasized only those aspects of black culture that they chose to see, he was even less tolerant of whites who seemed oblivious to its very existence at all. In 1937 he protested the removal of black communities from the FWP's state guidebooks produced in the American Guides series: "This New South (or New Midwest or New North) . . . from which the Negro is an exile, not self-imposed in this case, is hardly recognizable. . . . But if our publications are to be true guides to American life, the Negro cannot be so completely relegated to the background. In a subse-quent essay Brown pointed to a recently published history of Georgia that an-nounced matter-of-factly that the "Anglo Saxon . . . race makes up nearly one hundred percent of the South's population" as evidence of segregation's effec-tiveness as "a denial of belonging." Here Brown was suggesting the anti–New South animus that drove so much of black writing about the South before, dur-ing, and after the Harlem Renaissance: the determined assertion of belonging.[78]

Clearly influenced by Brown, Ralph Ellison made this "denial of belonging" a central theme of his work. Like Brown, Hurston, Toomer, and others who preceded him, Ellison believed the heart and soul of African American iden-tity was rooted in the black folk culture of the rural South. He was born in the border state of Oklahoma, but he attended Tuskegee Institute for three years, and though he eventually left the South, he later insisted that "it has never left me, and the interests which I discovered there became my life." Ellison had grown up in Oklahoma City, but some of his classmates had left school each year to go into the countryside during cotton picking season, and he recalled, "those trips to the cotton patch seemed to me an enviable experience. . . . [I]t wasn't the hard work which they stressed but the communion, the playing, the eating, the dancing and the singing. And they brought back jokes, our Negro jokes—not those told about Negroes by whites—and they always returned with Negro folk stories which I'd never heard before and which couldn't be found in any books I know about. This was something to affirm and I felt there was a richness in it."[79]

Later, as he faced the full-blown realities of Alabama-style Jim Crow, Ellison would begin what his biographer Lawrence Jackson called, "a life-long intellectual grapple between the genius of authentic American black folk and the complex of American social institutions that drew on the same folk materials to enforce the myth of black inferiority." This paradox of black folk culture serving both as a reservoir of strength and inspiration for blacks and a source of demeaning myths and stereotypes that could be used against them by whites helped to explain the mixed response to Zora Neale Hurston's writing. Ellison also drew criticism from those who thought his emphasis on the vitality of the black folk tradition minimized the damaging effects of white oppression. As he explained, however, while folklore conveyed what blacks had found to be the natural "limits of the human condition," it did not represent surrender to the artificial limits imposed on blacks by whites but triumph over those restrictions through "the group's will to survive . . . those values by which the group lives and dies."[80]

Ellison presented southern black folk culture as a key element in African American identity in his 1944 short story, "Flying Home," which anticipated much of the later message of his novel *Invisible Man*. In this tale, "Todd," a black pilot stationed at a training base in Alabama, attempts too steep a climb. Before he can correct for it, a buzzard (symbolic of Jim Crow) strikes his propeller, and he is injured in an extremely rough return to earth. He is then discovered by "Jefferson," an old black man who sends his son for help.

Jefferson admits that he "Caint tell you how it felt to see somebody what look like me in an airplane," but he also shares a cautionary folk tale, ostensibly based on his own experience in heaven. As an angel, Jefferson discovers that he can fly with extraordinary strength and swiftness, but because he is reckless and refuses to accept the restraints imposed on other black angels, he is eventually evicted by a white Saint Peter, who tells him he is a "danger to the heavenly community." Before he exits the Pearly Gates, an angry Jefferson tells

Saint Peter and the white angels: "You got to admit just this: While I was up here I was the flyin'est son-of-a-bitch whatever hit heaven." Aching with ambition and desperate to win the approval of the white officers who seem determined to keep him and other black airmen out of combat, Todd is angered by this tale because it effectively reminds him, in Jefferson's words, "You black, son. . . . You have to come by the white folks, too." By way of illustrating the inclinations of whites to use black folk culture to buttress their racial stereotypes, it is worth noting that when Delta aristocrat William Alexander Percy heard a variant of Jefferson's story, he took it as evidence that only a people so childlike and simple as blacks "could be at ease in heaven, much less confident of it enough to attempt an aeroplane stunt there."[81]

Because of just such thinking, Ellison's own experience in the South forced him "to evaluate my own self-worth, and the narrow freedom in which it existed, against those who would destroy me," and in *Invisible Man* (1952), his unnamed protagonist is an ambitious young black man who encounters a series of demoralizing, frustrating, dignity-denying examples of his anonymity and insignificance in the eyes of the white world. The young man's grandparents are former slaves who had seemed to buy into Booker T. Washington's doctrine of humility and hard work and had raised their offspring to do the same. Consequently, he is stunned when his grandfather rages at him from his deathbed to "keep up the good fight. I never told you, but our life is a war and I have been a traitor all my born days, a spy in the enemy's country ever since I give up my gun back in Reconstruction. Live with your head in the lion's mouth . . . to overcome 'em with yeses, undermine 'em with grins, agree 'em to death and destruction, let 'em swoller you till they vomit or bust wide open."[82]

Though he is shaken by his grandfather's outburst, the young man nonetheless clings to his "belief in the rightness of things," even after he attends a white men's club smoker where he has been invited to recite his high school valedictory speech and receive a scholarship. Upon arrival, however, he is forced to box with other black boys and then further entertain his white onlookers by joining his fellow combatants in a scramble for coins on an electrified carpet. He is finally allowed to give his speech, in which he embraces what is obviously Washington's accommodationist philosophy, but he angers his white audience nonetheless by mistakenly substituting "social equality" for "social responsibility," and he is able to salvage the occasion (and his scholarship) only by explaining that he had been distracted by the need to swallow blood from a cut which he had suffered during the boxing match.[83]

Like Ellison, the young man goes on to a Tuskegee-like southern black college, still the true believer, accepting, as Ellison put it, "the definition of himself handed down by the white South and the paternalism of northern philanthropy." He reluctantly complies with the wishes of one of the school's wealthy white benefactors to be taken off the beaten path, only to discover that confronting the raw realities of the underside of southern lower-class black life is more than the white man can handle. As a result of his incident, he runs afoul of Dr. Bledsoe, the college's president. Bledsoe has attained his position by shrewdly manipulating the "*big* white folk" and dealing ruthlessly with those black people who dare to challenge him, and he warns the unnerved idealist, "I'll have every Negro in the county hanging on tree limbs by morning if it means staying where I am." Shaken, the young man then leaves for New York where he initially spurns the food, speech, and mannerisms that would reveal his southern roots. Here the novel is reminiscent not only of James Weldon Johnson's *Autobiography of an Ex-Colored Man* or Jean Toomer's *Cane*, but of the work of a number of Harlem Renaissance writers who emphasized the tensions between rural black culture and the more sophisticated and impersonal demeanor of blacks in the urban North. [84]

It is in the anonymity of a large northern city, however, that Ellison's protagonist finally realizes that he is what one critic described as "an invisible man in an impersonal society," and eventually, he actually rediscovers his southern identity "as a means of anchoring himself in his new environment." Several characters lead him to come to grips with the southern roots he has tried to suppress. Both the outrageously caricatured bluesman Peter Wheatstraw, "the Devil's son-in-law," and the blues-singing Mary Rambo, who nurses him back to health after an explosion in the paint factory where he works, remind him of the times he has heard the blues back home and suggest that both strength and identity can be drawn from the stress and suffering that southern life imposes on black people. The most tangible evidence of his recovery of his southern roots comes in his encounter with an old man selling "Car'lina" yams. Having just passed an advertisement for a skin-whitening ointment that urged would-be buyers to "win greater happiness with white complexion," he smells the baking yams and suffers "a stab of swift nostalgia" for his youth. He buys a yam and eats it on the street, finding the experience both "exhilarating" and liberating: "I no longer had to worry about what was proper. To hell with all that, and as sweet as the yam actually was, it became like nectar with the thought." Impulsively buying two more yams, he exults, "They're my birthmark. . . . I yam what I am."[85]

By the end of the novel, the young man comes to terms with his invisibility and realizes that "I am nobody but myself." He is no longer ashamed that his grandparents were slaves, "only ashamed of myself for having at one time been ashamed." He even thinks of returning to the South, "that heart of darkness across the Mason-Dixon line. . . . Sometimes I feel the need to reaffirm all of it, the whole unhappy territory and all things loved and unlovable in it, for all of it is part of me." Although he may remain invisible to others, the young man has gained what Theodore R. Hudson called "self-visibility," because he can now "see" his own "heritage . . . his humanistic, Afro-American, Southern folkness."[86]

Ellison met William Faulkner only once, suggesting to him that he considered himself one of the "children . . . that you have . . . all around now." He became much better acquainted with Robert Penn Warren, "one of the best Southerners," who struck him as "a man who's lived and thought his way free of a lot of irrational illusions." After measuring his mind against Warren's, however, Ellison confided to Albert Murray that "if Mose [Ellison] takes advantage of his own sense of reality, he doesn't have to step back for anybody." Like Warren's *All the King's Men, Invisible Man* appeared to have one foot still anchored in the Southern Renaissance and one advancing toward a future in which questions about identity and human responsibility might seem no more applicable to the South than to the rest of post–World War II America. As Robert W. Rudnicki has pointed out, both authors understood "that the modern person, black or white, suffers from an attenuation of direction and an absence of identity caused in part by our cultural amnesia of any meaningful sense of the past."[87]

Just as Warren's Jack Burden realizes that in their search for identity humans are not doomed by history but live in "the agony of will," Ellison later explained that his work "tries to reveal the extent to which each of us is responsible for his own fate." *Invisible Man*'s protagonist comes to understand that he is actually complicit in his own invisibility because he has denied his people's legitimate history and his own heritage to pursue an identity defined by others. Moreover, like Warren's Jack Burden, Ellison's character vows to come out of hiding because he realizes that "even an invisible man has a socially responsible role to play."[88]

In 1953 an edited volume of essays, *Southern Renascence: The Literature of the Modern South,* failed to mention a single black author. When the same editors produced a revised collection some eight years later, Ralph Ellison was the only black writer deemed worthy of serious discussion. Regardless of racial and other differences, however, those who devoted their talents and energies to reexamining the South during the period between the end of World War I and the beginnings of the civil rights movement had much in common. In an era of human displacement and upheaval, the contradictions of the present and the uncertainties of the future gave them a clearer appreciation both of the power of the past and of its importance to their sense of self, purpose, and perspective. Sterling Brown's "Memphis Blues" pointed to the destruction of ancient Memphis and raised the possibility of a similar fate for its namesake. Yet, Brown declared, "Memphis go, Memphis come back, Ain't no skin off de nigger's back. All dese cities, ashes, rust.... De win' sing sperrichals through der dus'." Such expressions of a human present rendered perpetually ephemeral by the inexorable processes of history abound not only in the blues but throughout the works of William Faulkner as well.[89]

Faulkner devoted most of his attention to white southerners' struggles to maintain a sense of cultural or moral identity in the face of forces beyond their control, while writers like Hughes, Hurston, Brown, and Ellison focused on a similar struggle involving those who, by virtue of their race, had been relegated to the margins of America's most marginalized society. Though Ellison remained a great admirer, when Faulkner urged blacks to adopt a more gradualist approach to racial equality, Ellison complained that Faulkner "should know very well that we're trying hard as hell to free ourselves; thoroughly and completely, so that when we get the crackers off our back we can discover what we really are and what we really wish to preserve out of the experience that made us."[90]

As Fred Hobson observed, during the heyday of the Southern Renaissance, "the southern writer, who in most cases had left home for a time, focused his eye on a changing South, an industrializing South, but looked as well at a South that was slipping away, and the result was a creative mixture of detachment and involvement—an escape from, then an attempt to return to the southern community." Whether they were challenging the New South Creed's insistence on a genteel and aristocratic white past or its "denial of belonging" to African Americans and their culture, regardless of color, many of the writers of the Southern Renaissance were clearly reexamining southern identity at a time when the South seemed destined to disappear before it became, for them, a South they fully understood.[91]

6

The Mind of the South

THE LITERARY AND SCHOLARLY PARTICIPANTS in the Southern Renaissance were not alone in their struggle to understand the relationship between past and present in a society that seemed to be hurtling irreversibly toward a showdown with the forces of change. As the region struggled to rise from the depths of the Great Depression only to teeter on the brink of World War II, other southerners poured out thoughtful and yet intensely personal, emotionally freighted impressions of the South as it had been, as it was now, and as they hoped or feared it might become.

In *God Shakes Creation*, a vivid account of Mississippi Delta life written in 1935, David L. Cohn could well have been describing an invasion by Faulkner's Snopeses as he bemoaned the influx of lower-income, hill-country whites into his beloved homeland. Cohn warned that the displacement of the old planter aristocracy meant "the whole character of this civilization will be completely altered; its racial and social habits changed; its pride trailed in the dust; its memories erased and its flickering dreams of a better way of life extinguished."[1]

The deterioration of the social order was an even more vital concern of Cohn's mentor and fellow Deltan William Alexander Percy, who complained a few years later in his *Lanterns on the Levee* that the "bottom rail" had moved to the top. His own aristocratic family and their peers had given way to the abhorrent common whites whom Percy dismissed as the kind of people who attend revival meetings "and fight and fornicate in the bushes afterwards." To Percy the defeat of his father, LeRoy, in the 1911 Mississippi senatorial primary at the hands of "redneck" champion James K. Vardaman symbolized the irreversible disintegration of a way of life he held dear. He freely, though not painlessly, admitted his own inferiority to his heroic Redeemer grandfather and namesake, William Alexander Percy, a towering spectral presence known, like Faulkner's great-grandfather or his fictional John Sartoris, as "the old Colonel." Comparing himself to his "dazzling" father, Percy also felt wholly inadequate and unworthy, and his memoir bore the subtitle "Recollections of a Planter's *Son*" (emphasis added) despite the fact that he was hardly less of a planter than his corporate lawyer father had been.[2]

In January 1942, ten months after his book appeared, Will Percy died. At the time, another white southerner, writing about the "Red Hills" of the Piedmont rather than the dark loam of the Delta, was working furiously to complete what he called "An Upcountry Memory." Ben Robertson's people were small farmers who persisted, despite all manner of discouragement, in growing cotton, which was "like some member of the family that the folks have had a lot of trouble with but in whom they still believe." They had also come through the Depression still clinging "to our original Confederate theory that the land and not the factory was the rock to build the state on." Robertson recognized the inevitability and necessity of industrialization, but his heart clearly ached for the "mill people," who had once been farmers "born to the wild wind and to the Southern fields and to warm dry sun." Now it seemed as if "they had been captured . . . imprisoned, that they had given up being free." Robertson had begun his memoir while home on furlough from his duties as a correspondent covering the war in Europe. Slightly more than a year after his book appeared, he died in a plane crash on his way to assume his duties as chief of the *New York Herald-Tribune*'s London Bureau.[3]

Another concerned southerner who would not live to see how fundamentally his region would change was Clarence Cason. A thirty-nine-year-old journalism professor at the University of Alabama, Cason joined both Percy and Faulkner in lamenting "the appearance of a moneyed class which bore no blood relationship to the plantation group destroyed by the Civil War." In fact, as he explained in his *90° in the Shade*, which appeared in 1935, Cason's own family had suffered a significant social and economic displacement and thus had fallen real-life victims to the Snopesism that Faulkner would soon be decrying in other but no uncertain terms.[4]

Noting the emotional stress of "maintaining a sense of superiority on the basis of a past which grew increasingly shadowy and uncertain," Cason still remembered his anxiety as a lad still in "short trousers" when he took his first train trip. Having been assured that the black train porters were always able to identify "nice people" (translation: upper-class whites), the young boy desperately sought some indication that his porter recognized "that I belonged to the 'nice people,'" because with traditional white status and class relations in disarray, "Negroes seemed to be the most reliable touchstone." Looking back, Cason realized that this ironic reversal of circumstances, wherein those who were losing their grip on the top rung of the social ladder sought affirmation from those stuck on the bottom rung, furnished "an accurate source picture of the complex texture of racial attitudes in the South."[5]

90° in the Shade was much more than an elegy for the toppled southern aristocracy, however. In fact, although Cason displayed what Fred Hobson called a veritable "rage for moderation," even the most casual reader sensed that Cason found "more to censure than to admire" in the South. Labeling the region's politics "Fascism: Southern Style," Cason observed that the South was actually "self-conscious enough and sufficiently insulated from the rest of the country to be thought of as a separate province." He also took note of the white South's sensitivity to any form of external criticism, its repression of internal dissent, and its general suspicion of new ideas, especially those that came from outside the region. Sounding much like Frank L. Owsley as well as a number of William A. Dunning's protégés at Columbia University and all but outlining the arguments soon to be made by W. J. Cash, he attributed the unyielding conformity of the South's intellectual environment in no small measure to the experience of Reconstruction. During these years, Cason argued, the white South had suffered "the unspeakably cruel and conscienceless reign of . . . a vengeance far more terrible and relentless than that inflicted upon any other conquered nation in modern times—one which makes the Treaty of Versailles appear sweet and Christian by comparison."[6]

Cason also stressed the impact of climate, the influence of blacks on whites, and the striking juxtaposition of hedonism and religiosity that marked the South's character and mind-set. Quoting contemporaries such as Rupert Vance and Erskine Caldwell, he even suggested that the South would profit from "a nice quiet revolution," though he quickly added that he envisioned not a "communistic" or even "Populist" uprising but rather a "revision of the region's implanted ideas" and a realistic acknowledgment and contemplation of the South's problems. Almost invoking Cable's "Silent South," he pinned his hope on "a redirection of the South's courage and audacity and a determination that the Southern conscience shall be accorded the reverence due a sacred thing." Despite his self-imposed restraint and his efforts to conclude his observations on a positive note, Cason apparently grew so distraught over the prospect of a hostile reaction to his book that he took his own life the day before it was scheduled to appear. Cason's suicide foreshadowed that of W. J. Cash in much the same way that Cason's book so clearly foreshadowed and obviously shaped Cash's better-known and more influential book as well.

Wilbur Joseph Cash was born in 1901 in Gaffney, South Carolina, where his father managed the company store at a cotton mill. Cash's strict Baptist parents were also literary disciples of the stridently racist Reverend Thomas Dixon, a native of nearby Boiling Springs, North Carolina, where the Cashes moved when their son was twelve. Needless to say, the community of whites in which he was reared was virtually awash in sectional resentment and the romance of the Lost Cause.[7]

Setting an imaginative scene that Faulkner would later describe as the fantasy of "every southern boy," Cash recalled that he and his white playmates had "learned to read on 'The Three Little Confederates,' . . . and ten thousand times, in our dreams, rammed home the flag in the cannon's mouth after the manner of the heroes of the Rev. Tom Dixon, ten thousand times stepped on the reeking slope at Gettysburg, and with our tremendous swords, and in defiance of chronology, then and there won the Civil War." Like many white youths of his generation, Cash had been mesmerized by *The Birth of a Nation*, and he recalled "watching the Rev. Tom Dixon's Ku Kluckers do execution of uppity coons and low-down carpetbaggers, and alternately bawling hysterically and shouting my fool head off." Cash's first biographer, Joseph L. Morrison, noted that his subsequent "self-education in college and after was devoted to unlearning virtually every tenet of 'Southern patriotism' that had been taught him in those early days of the century."[8]

A great deal of this "unlearning" took place at Wake Forest College, where, to his surprise, the rebellious, free-thinking young man quickly found a hero in the school's president, William Louis Poteat, whose professed belief in Darwin's theory of evolution had drawn fire from many of the state's clergymen. In his editorials for the school newspaper, the *Old Gold and Black*, Cash delighted in baiting Poteat's fundamentalist detractors, becoming what Bruce Clayton described as "a cotton-patch Mencken." Cash not only defended Mencken's description of the South as "a desert—a barren waste, so far as the development of culture and the nature of the beaux arts are concerned," but sounding much like Walter Hines Page many years before, he insisted that "North Carolina comes near being the dreariest spot in the whole blank stretch."[9]

After graduating from Wake Forest in 1922, Cash eventually gravitated toward a career in journalism, and in 1929 he published two articles in Mencken's *American Mercury*, ridiculing the racism, religious bigotry, and anti-intellectualism that permeated and constricted the "New South" in which he lived. The second, entitled "The Mind of the South," was essentially a prospectus for the book that Cash planned to write, and it amounted to a full-scale assault on the New South identity. For all its propagandizing, the New South he saw was little more than "a chicken-pox of factories on the Watch-Us-Grow maps." It might look new (if not pretty), but Cash detected behind all of this nascent industrial clutter and sprawl "the mind of the Old South . . . a mind, that is to say, of the soil rather than of the mills."[10]

For Cash, the New South's prophecies of "social, political, and intellectual progress, like the great Woof-Woof in Kansas, arise from nowhere . . . hung upon nothing—unless indeed, it be the Cabalistic imaginations of those occult professors who write books called The New South or The Rising South or The Advancing South." Cash's contempt for the unfettered optimism of Edwin Mims and his vision of the "advancing South" was obvious enough, and he feared that the New South would "merely repeat the dismal history of Yankeedom" by simply "exchanging the Confederate for that dreadful fellow, the go-getter . . . the Hon. John LaFarge Beauregard for George F. Babbitt."[11]

After Mencken sent publishers Alfred and Blanche Knopf a copy of Cash's "The Mind of the South" essay, they contacted Cash about acquiring his book manuscript. At one point, Cash considered sending Knopf a sample chapter in which he attacked the Agrarians' romanticized depictions of the Old South and mocked Edwin Mims for his similarly rose-colored portrait of the New. Twelve years later in the introduction to his long-delayed, painfully birthed book, Cash observed broadly that the South's "peculiar history" had not only set it apart from the "general American norm" but had also created the "fairly definite mental pattern associated with a fairly definite social pattern" among white southerners in general. Still, he cautioned readers, in order to understand fully how the white South had become "not quite a nation within a nation, but the next thing to it," it was necessary to disabuse one's self of "two correlated legends—those of the Old and the New Souths."[12]

In his 1929 essay, Cash had paid relatively little attention to the myth of the aristocratic Old South, dismissing it as simply more evidence of the white South's penchant for the fantastic and unreal and joking that in the southern white imagination "every farmhouse became a Big House, every farm a baronial estate, every master of scant red acres and a few mangy blacks a feudal lord." Shortly after his article appeared, however, Cash had written at length to Howard Odum outlining his proposed book. As Cash's mentor of sorts, Mencken had insisted that "in the great days of the South the line between the gentry and the poor whites was very sharply drawn," and in his letter to Odum, Cash referred to the Old South's "static and paternal order" with its "landowners on the one hand, and the slaves and poor whites on the other." In response, Odum had gently pointed to the relatively humble origins of many planter "aristocrats," who had actually begun their meteoric socioeconomic ascent in "log cabins in the pioneer wilderness" which were "enlarged and rebuilt and then entirely transcended by the big house." Even then, he observed, "many of the southerners who were reputed to have a plantation and leisure still ate dinner in their shirt-sleeves and washed on the back porch and let the chickens roost in the top of the trees in the yard."[13]

Cash confessed in response that he had "ploughed through all the histories I know," and save for U. B. Phillips's *Life and Labor in the Old South*, he had found little discussion of "the lack of distinct lines between classes in the Old South." Twelve years later, he had clearly taken Odum's advice to heart when he attacked the Cavalier legend with a vengeance, ridiculing the Old South fantasy as a "sort of stage piece out of the eighteenth century," replete with "gesturing gentlemen" and "lovely ladies" living in "Old World splendor and delicacy." Savaging the New South Creed's claims of a grand aristocratic past, Cash insisted that even the early Virginians "were not generally Cavaliers in their origin." Most were actually little more than "superior farmers," many of them barely literate and scarcely distinguishable from the frontiersmen who populated "the vast back country of the seaboard states."[14]

If the Old South had no imported aristocracy, Cash argued, neither did it have time to grow its own. After all, people did not simply "spring up to be aristocrats in a day." The entire span from the invention of the cotton gin to the Civil War had been less than seventy years, and many who as children "had heard the whoop of the Cherokee in the Carolina backwoods" were still around "to hear the guns at Vicksburg." In reality, the Old South had been no more than "a few steps removed from the frontier stage at the beginning of the Civil War." Cash's emphasis on the impact of the frontier on the temperament of southern whites doubtless reflected the influence of both Odum and Rupert Vance, who had argued that "while they were formative, the folkways of the South got the stamp of the frontier. From the frontier, part of the area passed to the plantation, but the plantation area retained many of the frontier traits."[15]

Rejecting Mencken's grandiose assessment of antebellum southern culture, Cash echoed his fellow North Carolinian, Walter Hines Page, asking, "What ideas did it generate? Who were its philosophers and artists?" and—perhaps the most penetrating question of all—"What was its attitude toward these philosophers and artists?" This intellectual torpor, Cash believed, could be traced not only to the generally modest social origins of white southerners at

large but also to a simple, uncomplex, unvarying human and natural environment of "wide fields and blue woods and flooding yellow sunlight. A world, in
fine, in which not a single factor operated to break up the old pattern of out-
door activity laid down on the frontier . . . a world in which horses, dogs, guns,
not books and ideas and art were his normal and absorbing interests." Cash's
argument here was hardly original either. More than a decade earlier, Ellen
Glasgow had observed that in the South, "soil, scenery, all the color and ani-
mation of the external world, tempted a convivial race to an endless festival of
the seasons." As a result, Glasgow explained, "Philosophy, like heresy, was either suspected or prohibited."[16]

As Cash saw it, the principal outlet for the cerebral energies of the frontier-
bred, antebellum elite was the regional passion of politics, rendered all the
more intense by the growing sectional crisis. Compared to the rough and tumble
of politics and the chance to be "a captain in the struggle against the Yankee,
. . . the pursuit of knowledge, the writing of books, the painting of pictures,
the life of the mind, seemed an anemic and despicable business, fit only for
eunuchs."[17]

If the members of the Old South's "ruling class" were not cultured and refined aristocrats, then who were they? "Manifestly, for the great part," Cash
insisted, they were "the strong, the pushing, the ambitious, among the old coon-
hunting population of the backcountry." He offered "a concrete case" in the
story of "the stout young Irishman," a character based loosely on Cash's great-
grandfather and one strikingly similar not only to Odum's "Uncle John" but to
Margaret Mitchell's Gerald O'Hara. Cash's Irishman had arrived with his bride
in the Carolina upcountry in 1800 and used his life savings of $20 to buy forty
acres of land, toiling round the clock with his wife's help to clear and plant
cotton on it. Bit by bit, he acquired slaves and more land until, at age fifty and
by then a magistrate, he built a true "'big house,'" crude and box-like but large
and fronted by huge columns so that when it was eventually painted white, it
stood out from the fields and pinewoods as a most "imposing" structure.
(Odum's description to Cash of the process whereby the "log house" was eventually "transcended by the big house" comes to mind here.) Finally, "as a crown
on his career," the old Irishman went to the legislature, where he "waxed innocently pompous, and, in short, became a really striking figure of a man." At his
death in 1854, his estate included 2,000 acres of land, more than a hundred
slaves, and four cotton gins, and, of course, the fledgling county-seat newspaper had eulogized him as "a gentleman of the old school" and "a noble specimen of the chivalry at its best."[18]

If the Irishman's ascent seemed miraculously rapid, Cash insisted that in areas like Mississippi "because of the almost unparalleled productivity of the soil" the same thing had actually happened "in accelerated tempo." Such an observation underscored the similarities between Cash's Irishman and Faulkner's parvenu planter Thomas Sutpen, although the latter met with a considerably less respectable end. Certainly, Sutpen, who had made his appearance in print some five years earlier, exemplified the would-be planter aristocrat who possessed an abundance of what Cash described as the "cunning . . . hoggery . . . callousness . . . brutal unscrupulousness and downright scoundrelism" that, like the Irishman's "industry and thrift," were also often rewarded on the antebellum South's plantation frontier.[19]

Cash believed that those who by virtue of their sloth, timidity, or simple hard luck did not rise to wealth on the plantation frontier constituted the remainder of white society. The best of the rest, so to speak, were the large number of landowning, but not slaveholding, white farmers who nonetheless enjoyed "a kind of curious half-thinking, half-shiftless prosperity—a thing of sagging rail fences, unpainted houses and crazy barns which yet bulged with corn." Cash's treatment of the common whites was remarkably similar to Faulkner's almost simultaneous depiction of them in *The Hamlet*, and his book appeared just as Frank and Harriet Owsley began to publish the results of their research on the antebellum white yeomanry that would eventually culminate in their *Plain Folk of the Old South* (1949). In general, the Owsleys found no evidence of antebellum class consciousness "in the Marxian sense," and they argued that such class lines as there were in the Old South were rendered all but imperceptible by ties of kinship, proximity, and an overall "sense of unity between plain folk and planters."[20]

Similarly, as Cash saw him, the po-white or "Cracker" was not really so different from his planter brethren as he seemed: "Catch Calhoun or Jeff Davis or Abe Lincoln (whose blood stemmed from the Carolina foothill country, remember) young enough, nurse him on 'bust head,' feed him hog and pone, give him twenty years of lolling—expose him to all the conditions to which the Cracker was exposed—and you have it exactly." Cash also emphasized the possible, even probable, kinship ties among white southerners of the highest and lowest station, pointing out that a well-established southern gentleman who identified a passing poor white as "my cousin Wash Venable," might not be speaking simply in jest.[21]

Cash occasionally lapsed into some of the romantic exaggeration that he so assiduously debunked in others. He insisted, for example, that owing to a frontier heritage that had been sustained and nurtured by a plantation society, from planter to plain folk, all southern white men were much inclined toward "bald, immediate assertion of the ego." This "chip-on-the-shoulder swagger and brag of a boy" had found "its ultimate incarnation" in the fierce, but undisciplined Confederate soldier, who was not really so much a soldier as a rabidly individualistic fighter governed by "the conviction . . . that nothing living could cross him and get away with it."[22]

If Cash's attack on the Old South myth sometimes seemed to substitute one romantic legend for another, there was nothing romantic about his effort to shatter the soothing New South illusions of unity, harmony, and restraint against the concrete realities of southern white schizophrenia, violence, and irrational excess. These pathologies, he insisted, were just as common among the New South's better-element whites as among their poor-white inferiors who bore most of the blame for the lynchings that had once been almost a daily reality of southern life. "I have myself," he revealed, "known university-bred men who confessed proudly to having helped to roast a Negro."[23]

New South apologists had bragged of a comprehensive unity of spirit and purpose among white southerners, but Cash understood that this unity was based on color rather than a common economic and political agenda. Whenever lower-class whites began to question whether upper-class whites truly had their best interests at heart, the New South's leadership had only to warn that such discordant and divisive suggestions threatened the racial solidarity that was absolutely essential to maintaining the supremacy of all whites over all blacks. In the mind of Cash's "common white," the "vastly ego-warming and ego-expanding distinction between the white man and the black" had "lifted" him to "a position comparable to that of, say, the Doric knight of ancient Sparta," making him "by extension a member of the dominant class."[24]

As Cash saw it and as proslavery propagandists had in fact articulated it, the "Proto-Dorian convention" assured the common whites that regardless of their material circumstances, they would never be at the bottom of the southern social pyramid so long as they refrained from undermining white supremacy by challenging their more prosperous but pragmatically folksy white superiors. (In the work of some later writers, Cash's Proto-Dorian convention effectively resurfaced as a form of whites-only "Herrenvolk democracy.") "The grand outcome," Cash wrote, with some exaggeration, was "the almost com-

plete disappearance of economic and social focus on the past of the masses"
who had marched unblinking behind their planter "captains" into a disastrous
conflict in 1861. Upon returning (if they did), they had proceeded to reject the
class-based entreaties of the Republicans, and after a brief flirtation, those of
the Populists as well. Even against the surging labor unrest of the 1920s, the
Proto-Dorian bond held, providing a major thread of continuity between the
New South and the Old.[25]

For Cash, no less than for his New South predecessors—or his white intellectual contemporaries, for that matter—"southerner" was a designation that
applied only to whites. Although he noted insightfully that "Negro entered
into white man as profoundly as white man entered into Negro—subtly influ-
encing every gesture, every word, every emotion and idea, every attitude," he
devoted relatively little attention to African Americans themselves. To his credit,
he clearly rejected the widely embraced U. B. Phillips/New South notion of
slavery as a "school for civilization" that, despite its regrettable aspects, had
actually elevated the fortunate African captives out of savagery. Cash saw slavery as an "inescapably brutal and ugly" system maintained by white force and
coercion rather than the affection and appreciative deference of the bondsman. Yet, though he was sympathetic to blacks as the victims of slavery and
lynching, he nonetheless depicted them as almost childlike creatures of "gran-
diloquent imagination, of facile emotion and, above everything else under
heaven, of enjoyment." He also embraced the prevailing white perception of
the sensuality and "easy complaisance" of black women. Deplore racial injustices as he might, Cash's characterizations of blacks as childish, carefree, and
sexually casual merely perpetuated the suffocating, emotionally destructive
Jim Crow–justifying stereotypes imposed by whites and enforced under what
Richard Wright had already described as "The Ethics of Living Jim Crow." Had
Cash encountered the somber and thoughtful Wright as a young man, he too
might well have wondered, as did one of Wright's white employers, "Why don't
you laugh and talk like other niggers?"[26]

Despite his own racial profiling, however, Cash understood that although
"the white South delighted to say and believe that it knew the black man through
and through . . . even the most unreflecting must sometimes feel in dealing
with him that they were looking at a blank wall, that behind the grinning face
a veil was drawn which no white man might certainly know he had penetrated."
Almost simultaneously, Delta patrician William Alexander Percy had admitted that despite their claims to have "an innate and miraculous understanding
of one another," blacks and whites in the South "understood one another not

at all." Cash's observation also anticipated Wright's insistence, a few years after *The Mind of the South* appeared, that although "the white South" repeatedly claimed that it "knew niggers," it had never "known" him. In sum, although Cash mischaracterized blacks in some important ways, he also recognized that in other important ways, he knew almost nothing about them.[27]

In recent years, Cash's perspective on gender has drawn almost as much criticism as his treatment of race. Yet, as a southern white man in 1941, he had shown uncommon discernment and candor when he suggested that the "downright gyneolatry" expressed in the antebellum gentry's rhetorical flourishes about the purity of southern womanhood was in fact emblematic of the impurity of southern manhood because it amounted to psychic compensation for the plantation mistress whose husband's sexual transgressions down in the slave quarters were not so discreet as they might have been. On the other hand, unlike some female contemporaries such as Ellen Glasgow, Lillian Smith, and Katharine Du Pre Lumpkin, Cash failed to explore the broader role of racial and gender stereotypes in sustaining patriarchy within the white South itself. Here his analysis could also have benefited from Smith's subsequent writings on the sexual anxieties of southern white men and other more recent studies of gender, both masculine and feminine.[28]

As Winthrop D. Jordan has shown, white men's fears of their sexual inadequacy compared to that of stereotypically well-endowed and virile black men dates back to earliest European contact with Africa. Other historians have shown that after the Civil War especially, southern white men felt their masculinity had been called into question on a number of fronts, not just by emancipation and black enfranchisement but by their own failures as providers that had toppled their families into tenancy and debt or forced them to leave the independence of the farm for the regimen of the textile mill. Protecting their wives and daughters from anything resembling black male sexual aggression was a last-ditch imperative if their personally and socially constructed masculinity was to be preserved. In addition to symbolizing the New South's ties to the old chivalric order, the pedestalized and protected purity of southern white womanhood was in some ways also a symbolic assertion of white southern manhood as well. Louis Rubin recalled that when a monument to the Civil War defenders of Charleston harbor was unveiled in 1932, it featured a woman, representing the city, under the protection of a muscular, shield-bearing war-

rior whose masculine endowments were so prominently displayed that officials later decided the addition of a cosmetic fig leaf was in order.[29]

Cash did understand, however, that the New South's sexual and racial fictions, double standards, and taboos were both formidable barriers to change
and critical elements of its identity. As its "shield-bearing Athena" and "the
mystic symbol of its nationality in the face of the foe," the white woman was
virtually synonymous "with the very notion of the South itself." Cash seemed
to go a bit overboard in suggesting that the "misty conviction" that they were
fighting for southern womanhood had actually propelled the "ranks of the
Confederacy" into battle, but in doing so, he nonetheless captured the extent
and intensity of this belief among many white southerners. As a teenaged girl
in Birmingham after World War I, Virginia Foster Durr had rebelled at being
forced to serve as an escort at reunions of elderly Confederate veterans who
invariably wanted to plant wet, whiskey- and tobacco-flavored kisses on the
young ladies. Still, when the standard retinue of politicians began their ora-
torical tributes to "pure white Southern womanhood," Durr confessed, "I believed it. I was pure white Southern womanhood and Southern men had died
for me. . . . I got to thinking that I was pretty hot stuff, to have the war fought
for me."[30]

This symbolic feminization of southern white identity helps to explain why
the experience of the white South during Reconstruction was easily likened to
rape. Cash sounded much like Cason or Thomas Dixon, not to mention Freud,
when he insisted that "for all the massacres, the pillage, and *the rapes* to which
they have so often been subjected," no other defeated nation "was ever *so point-
edly taken in the very core of its being* as was the South." [Emphasis added.]
Southern white womanhood and, by inference, the identity of the entire white
South seemed very much threatened by emancipated blacks who had been
emboldened during Reconstruction to believe that they could advance and
claim the fruits of freedom whenever and wherever they chose.[31]

"What [white] Southerners felt, therefore," Cash explained, "was that any
assertion of any kind on the part of the Negro constituted in a perfectly real
manner an attack on the Southern [white] woman." Thus, "Reconstruction
was a passage toward a condition for her as degrading, in their view, as rape
itself." After studying Indianola, Mississippi, at approximately the same time
that Cash was writing, John Dollard had concluded that "behind the actual or
posited desires of Negro men for white women is seen also the status motive,
the wish to advance in social rank, to be as good as anyone else, and to have
available what everyone else has." For Cash, the tragic result was the white

South's "rape complex," which justified violence against blacks regardless of whether there was evidence of actual sexual advances on the part of black males. The real motive for white aggression was the perception that a black man was making or was simply desirous of making a social, economic, or political gain at the expense of whites.[32]

Because the potential for black advancement was attributable to the Yankees and their meddling in southern racial affairs, as Cash put it, "to give the black man the works" was, in the minds of the white perpetrators, "just as effectively to strike Yankeedom." Nearly eighty years after the Confederacy was formed, southern white insistence that blacks live subordinate "to the superior race" remained the key element in the ongoing "conflict with the Yankee," which had established and continued to sustain the South "as an object of patriotism" among white southerners.[33]

Maintaining racial supremacy was clearly the paramount concern of southern whites, but the determination to resist "northern" ideas and practices (if not northern money) drew on a vision of the North as the imperialistic agent of the socially and morally corrosive forces of modernity. This perception had emerged during the antebellum era, and Cash observed that as the twentieth century began, an industrialized and urbanized "Yankeeland" had become "a chief protagonist, not of the machine alone, but of the modern intelligence as well." Led by a determined evangelical clergy, many white southerners made no more distinction among the terms "infidel, atheistic, and Yankeeizing" than they did among the names "Darwin, Huxley, Ben Butler, Sherman, Satan." By making the "modern mind" synonymous with the North and resistance to it a litmus test of "southern loyalties," they hoped to "quarantine it at the Potomac." Cash may have gotten a bit carried away here, but he was by no means the only commentator who has equated northernization with conformity to "the modern world."[34]

White southerners had rallied against the effort to northernize the South before and during the Civil War and showed, if anything, even greater solidarity in resisting the incursions of the North during Reconstruction and in rolling back its accomplishments thereafter. In Cash's view, even more than the reality of wartime defeat, the bitter experience of Reconstruction had left white southerners intent on restoring, insofar as possible, the world that the Yankee had destroyed. Paradoxically then, instead of reconstructing the white South's mind, the Yankees had unwittingly succeeded in making it "one of the least reconstructible ever developed."[35]

As Cash had explained in his 1929 letter to Howard Odum, what "in the old days" had been "*merely* a way of thinking" had become, "under the pressure of Reconstruction, a sort of fetish, a matter of patriotism and religion." Consequently, "the South distinctly holds today that there are definite southern ideas and ideals to desert which is to be a traitor and to expose one to general indignation. It [the white South] has been turned back on itself. And it is that fact more than anything else which makes it a distinct entity within the United States."[36]

In later years, Cash would draw criticism for embracing the prevailing mythology that Reconstruction had been a tragic and cruel mistake that brought terrible suffering on the white South, although in this regard he was hardly different from the overwhelming majority of his professional historian contemporaries. Certainly, for all his insensitivity to both the long- and short-term benefits that Reconstruction brought to southern blacks, Cash did not overstate its importance in creating what Richard King called "a collective psycho-cultural-entity—the South." Actually, he suggested some fruitful comparisons to the white South's reaction to Reconstruction: "Not Ireland nor Poland, not Finland nor Bohemia, not one of the countries which prove the truth that there is no more sure way to make a nation than the brutal oppression of an honorably defeated and disarmed people . . . ever developed so much of fear, of rage, of indignation and resentment, of self-consciousness and patriotic passion." After Reconstruction, this volatile emotional amalgam had simply hardened over more than a half-century of continuing resistance to northern influences of all sorts into what Cash called the "savage ideal," a rigid communal conformity of thought and rabid hostility to criticism or change that had effectively "paralyzed Southern culture at the root." In fact, Cash believed the savage ideal had been more firmly fixed in white southerners than in "any people since the decay of medieval feudalism and almost as truly as it is established today in Fascist Italy, in Nazi Germany, [or] in Soviet Russia."[37]

Cash's analogy was apt, and even if his version of the reality of Reconstruction was not, it certainly accorded with the view of the great majority of white southerners for whom it clearly served a unifying and sustaining mythic purpose as a crucial element of their identity. Cash perceived, as Bertram Wyatt-Brown observed, that "like the Celtic fringe of Great Britain, the former slave states were compelled to assume the peripheral, subordinate role assigned agrarian outlands in relation to rich metropolitan cities." In this sense the white South described by Cash may have developed something akin to what recent students of Islamic nationalism have described as a "counteracculturative" or "defensive" culture, fiercely resistant to Western political or cultural imperialism.[38]

If Cash saw little good in Radical Reconstruction, he also pointed out (as C. Vann Woodward would argue so effectively a decade later) that for all their supposed benevolence and foresight, the Redeemers and their New South descendants had done little to make things better. He understood as well that leaders of the New South sought to modernize the region's economy without sacrificing its identity or its autonomy not simply to achieve material prosperity but to win the recognition and respect that the North would be obliged to grant. Critics have scoffed at Cash's suggestion that careful listeners might hear the gallop of Jeb Stuart's cavalrymen behind the din of skyscraper construction in Piedmont towns "with no more need for them than a hog has for a morning coat," but during the 1950s southern newspaper accounts of Dixie governors' industrial recruitment trips to the Northeast still conjured visions of the fabled Jeb Stuart on one of his daring raids behind Union lines. As recently as 1998, when Charlotte's Nation's Bank merged with San Francisco's Bank of America and brought the new corporate headquarters to the Tarheel state, a North Carolina–based Nation's Bank official responded to a wave of criticism and condescension from the California media by asserting that the bank's move was motivated in part "to prove to the damn carpetbaggers that there was something intrinsically worthwhile about the South, and we didn't need to tolerate their looking down their noses at southerners."[39]

The notion that the Cavalier and Confederate myths of nobility and grandeur could find vindication in the New South campaign for economic advancement and triumph seemed to Cash nothing more than a manifestation of the hopelessly romantic white southerner's "histrionic urge to perform in splendor." Yet, in the skilled hands of the architects of the New South, these myths had served as the fundamental raw materials for the regional identity that, as he argued so persuasively, had turned southern white society into a virtual "nation-within-a-nation."[40]

For all his disdain for New South romanticism, Cash borrowed heavily from the writings of Broadus Mitchell when he noted the general benevolence of the original captains of the cotton-mill crusade, praising their paternalistic effort to create jobs and build schools for the region's pathetic and downtrodden poor whites. Although he lauded the intentions of the early mill builders, like Mitchell, Cash deplored the long-term results as the mills fell into the hands of a new generation of greedy owners who were responsible for the abysmal wages and deplorable working conditions that currently prevailed. As Bruce Clayton pointed out, Cash's portrait of the mill workers was "positively Dickensian": "A dead white skin, a sunken chest, and stooping shoulders. . . . Chinless faces, microcephalic foreheads, rabbit teeth, goggling dead-fish eyes, rickety limbs and stunted bodies abounded."[41]

In the final analysis, *The Mind of the South* was a powerful one-two punch at the very essence of the New South identity. Not only was there no grand aristocratic past that could be invoked whenever the region's critics or its self-evident ills became too unpleasant to bear or contemplate, but if the past looked far less rosy than many white southerners wanted desperately to believe, the myths of present-day progress and future prosperity were largely hollow and false as well. The *Atlantic Monthly* hailed Cash's book as "a literary and moral miracle," and despite its controversial thesis and content, reactions to *The Mind of the South* in the southern press were overwhelmingly positive as well. A reviewer for the *Houston Post* called the book a "magnificent study," while the *Baltimore Evening Sun* found it "persuasive" and "charming." In the *Birmingham Age Herald*, John Temple Graves praised Cash's "objectivity" and saluted his "extraordinary" accomplishment. Finally, in the *New Republic*, fellow southerner Gerald W. Johnson felt Cash had produced a better book than Rupert Vance's *Human Geography of the South* or even Howard Odum's *Southern Regions of the United States*.[42]

Certainly, scholarly reviewers seemed neither shocked nor offended by Cash's book. Historian Clement Eaton noted that Cash "discards the legend of the Old South" but added perceptively that "*The Mind of the South* is especially significant in its interpretation of the New South." In the end, Eaton saw Cash's work as "a brave and critical book about the South which deserves a wide circle of readers, including the effective political leaders of the day." C. Vann Woodward questioned what he saw as Cash's overemphasis on unity and continuity in the southern experience, but he conceded, nonetheless, that *The Mind of the South* offered both "brilliant analysis" and "penetrating observation," and he praised Cash's bold attack on "the most difficult and obscure problems of southern mentality."[43]

According to Daniel Singal, *The Mind of the South* "represented a complete reversal of the region's history once offered by the New South writers—it read like a compendium of those aspects of the South they had deliberately screened out." In Singal's view, its very publication symbolized "the triumph of Southern modernism," while the warm reception it received in the South attested to the "firm hold the modernist viewpoint had gained among the South's educated elite." Whether the triumph of modernism was as complete in 1941 as Singal believed, the relative absence of controversy surrounding Cash's book seems less remarkable when we consider that much of what he said about the South had actually been said before, and often more than once and in more than one way.[44]

For all his boldness and originality in some aspects, Cash was indebted not only to Mencken, Cason, and Odum but to numerous other New South critics who had preceded him in the late nineteenth and early twentieth centuries, including George Washington Cable and Charles W. Chesnutt, both of whom had recoiled from the New South's commercialism and acquisitiveness and challenged its racial underpinnings as well. After the turn of the century, Andrew Sledd and John Spencer Bassett had also called attention to the South's racial savagery, while Ellen Glasgow had emphasized the intellectual sterility of the Old South and the New South's struggle with the "sentimental infirmity" of the past and the blind "patriotic materialism" that marked both its present and its future. Cash's reference to the white South as "not quite a nation" clearly echoed writers like Frank Tannenbaum and William H. Skaggs. In fact, William J. Robertson, whose *The Changing South* was published in 1927, had already dubbed the region "a nation within a nation," and Clarence Cason, Allen Tate, and Carl Carmer had said much the same thing. Cash was similarly indebted not only to Odum but to historian William E. Dodd for his discussion of the humble origins of the antebellum planter class and to H. C. Nixon, who emphasized the "romanticism" of both New South boosters and Old South apologists, who were not infrequently the same people. His book also reflected the thinking of Rupert Vance and Gerald W. Johnson, who in 1929 had referred to the postbellum South as "to all intents and purposes a frontier."[45]

If much of what Cash wrote had been written or implied earlier by scholars and journalists, *The Mind of the South* also bore a strong resemblance to the work of the leading literary figures of the Southern Renaissance. As late as 1929 Cash was expressing doubts that the New South would generate "a broad culture and what they call a 'renaissance'—a flowering of the arts." Slightly more than a decade later, however, he saw a region astir with literary ferment, noting that "in 1939 the South actually produced more books of memorable importance than any other section of the country, until anybody who fired off a gun in the region was practically certain to kill an author."[46]

Cash's interest in the sudden outpouring of southern literature was more than casual. In fact, he actually yearned to be a part of it. Though he had never published any fiction or even submitted any to a publisher, he had insisted in a biographical sketch prepared for Knopf in 1936 that "I want above everything else to be a novelist." Subsequently, in his 1940 application for a Guggenheim fellowship, he described *The Mind of the South* as "'creative writing'" of a sort, although he insisted that he was "well aware of the difference between social analysis and fiction" and believed that he could "do the latter better than the former."[47]

In 1936 he had applied unsuccessfully for a Guggenheim fellowship, proposing to write a novel about "the Old South as it was." Cash proceeded in his application to quote from *The Mind of the South* manuscript the entire passage dealing with the "stout young Irishman" which he offered as "a sort of skeleton of the novel" in which he would spin the tale of "Angus Carrick, who ended his career as a 'major' in the Southern hierarchy." In telling this story he would also tell "in part or in whole" the story of Angus's children, "John, Bayles, Bogan, Bess, Laura, and Kathe," as well as that of his neighbors, "including particularly the Surrats, another plantation family, and the no-count Martins, a family of so-called 'white trash.'" (As Cash sketched it out, this story did not seem terribly far removed from Margaret Mitchell's *Gone with the Wind*, which had just appeared in print.) Shifting his focus to the New South in his successful Guggenheim application in 1940, he promised to tell the story of "Andrew Bates, born the son of a wealthy cotton mill family in Piedmont, North Carolina, in 1900, down until the outbreak of the second world war in 1939." Perhaps taking his cue from Howard Odum's *American Epoch*, Cash proposed that his novel would also incorporate the saga of Bates's father and grandfather into the story of the "rise of an industrial town in the South after the introduction of the idea of Progress after 1880."[48]

Despite his unfulfilled creative ambitions, everything Cash wrote about his literary and journalistic contemporaries could have been written about him as well, especially his praise for the realism and social relevance of their work. Although traces of the old sentimentality lingered, he felt these new writers showed a pronounced tendency in the other direction, as they rejected the "old imperative to use their writings as a vehicle for glorifying and defending Dixie" and seemed instead "to take more or less actively to hating and denouncing the South." Cash cited such examples as Faulkner, Wolfe, and Erskine Caldwell, and he, of course, could speak from personal experience when he noted that "baiting the South" in the pages of *The American Mercury* had once been "one of the favorite sports of young Southerners of literary and intellectual pretensions."[49]

In truth, however, Cash understood that the South's young writers actually hated the South "a good deal less than they said and thought," or at least theirs was "the exasperated hate of a lover who cannot persuade the object of his affections to his desire or, more accurately, as Narcissus, growing at length analytical, might have suddenly begun to hate his image reflected in the pool." Ironically, in what was perhaps the most perceptive initial review of *The Mind of the South*, David L. Cohn saw Cash as "a great despiser because he is a great adorer. And being such he lashes out in language which reveals not only his adoration of the South but his own essential southernness."[50]

Even at age thirty-nine, Cash admitted, "my blood still leaps to the playing of 'Dixie' and to such flourishing phrases as 'the sword of Lee,'" and he could also have been referring to himself as well when he wrote of his contemporaries that "Intense belief in and love for the southern legend had been bred into them as children and could not be bred out again simply by taking thought." Again describing himself as well, he observed that the "hate and anger against the South" sometimes exhibited by these new writers was in part "a sort of reverse embodiment of the old sentimentality itself."[51]

William Faulkner had observed several years earlier that southern writers "who write savagely and bitterly of the incest in clay-floored cabins are the most sentimental." Faulkner believed that the southern writer "unconsciously writes into every line and phrase his violent despairs and rages and frustrations or his violent prophesies of still more violent hopes. That cold intellect which can write with calm and complete detachment and gusto of its contemporary scene is not among us; I do not believe there lives the Southern writer who can say without lying that writing is any fun to him."[52]

A few years later Cash would confess to Alfred A. Knopf that every word in his long-awaited book had been "written in blood," explaining his difficulty in completing the manuscript by admitting that "I have never been able to approach the task of continuing it without extreme depression and dislike." Cash had characterized Faulkner in 1935 as one of those "disillusioned romantics at eternal war with themselves, the emotions ranged on one side and the intellect on the other." This description was, Cash's biographer Bruce Clayton observed, "a sentence that could also stand as a self-portrait." Many of Cash's insights were not original, nor were all his feelings about the South by any means peculiar to him. Yet it was not only his skill in synthesizing the views of the New South's other critics, but his own painfully intense personal struggle with its hopelessly entwined myths of past and present that established *The Mind of the South* as what Richard King called "a quintessential expression of the regional self-scrutiny which marked the Southern Renaissance."[53]

In the long run, however, Cash's book would become the most widely read and influential attempt to unravel the mystery of southern white identity because it linked the South's past not only to the uneasy present in which it first appeared in 1941 but to the violent, conflict-ridden future that its agonized author stopped just short of predicting in its final paragraph. Anticipating and even looking beyond American entry into the war in Europe, Cash warned that "in the coming days and probably soon," the white South's "capacity for adjustment" would be "tested far beyond what has been true in the past." As its "loyal son," he hoped that the region's virtues "would tower over and conquer its faults." Yet he clearly doubted that qualities such as loyalty, pride, bravery, honor, courage, and personal generosity stood much of a chance against the savage ideal, the darker and ultimately dominant side of the white southerner's mind manifested in traits such as "violence, intolerance, aversion and suspicion toward new ideas, . . . an incapacity for analysis, . . . an inclination to act from feeling rather than thought, . . . an exaggerated individualism and . . . too narrow concept of social responsibility."[54]

Cash's greatest single apprehension clearly lay not simply with southern white society's "attachment to fictions and false values" but its "too great attachment to racial values and . . . tendency to justify cruelty and injustice in the name of those values." Despite a decrease in racial violence after 1900, his repeated emphasis on continuity in the racial attitudes of white southerners left an indelible impression of contemporary white southerners who were still capable of inflicting the "most devilish and prolonged agonies" on black people at the slightest personal provocation or hint of a challenge to the Jim Crow order. Asked whether he expected the contemporary South's racial tensions to lead to further violence, Cash had replied, "Certainly, I do." Only his suicide less than five months after *The Mind of the South* appeared prevented him from seeing his worst fears realized. Ultimately, owing to the tragic events that Cash had so fearfully anticipated, his book would achieve its most profound impact, not as a cumulative example of the thoughtful "regional self-scrutiny" of the Southern Renaissance but as the enormously influential embodiment of the more emotional school of self-accusation and shame that would dominate writing about the South and perceptions of southern identity for at least a quarter century after World War II.[55]

7

The South of Guilt and Shame

Writing the closing lines of *The Mind of the South* "in the fateful year of 1940," W. J. Cash would "venture no definite prophecies," but he clearly sensed that America's inevitable conflict with fascism might set the stage for the South's own inevitable day of reckoning with the rest of America, and in fact, it did just that. George Orwell contended that "if the war didn't kill you, it was bound to start you thinking." In reality, many southerners, black and white, were already thinking, particularly about the South, well before World War II. The combination of "New Deal idealism" and the ascendant "critical realism" that marked much of southern thought during the 1930s had combined to produce what Ralph McGill described as a "mighty surge of discussion, debate, self-examination, confession and release."[1]

As he observed white-black interaction in Indianola, Mississippi, in 1935, John Dollard found local whites "sane and charming except on one point." That point was race, and it so dominated their thinking and overall behavior patterns that Dollard quickly developed a sense of "a white society with a psychotic spot, an irrational, heavily protected sore through which all manner of venomous hatreds and irrational lusts may pour." Most of the region's white writers, scholars, and journalists in the 1930s and early 1940s saw things differently. For them race was simply one strand in a complex, tightly woven tapestry of problems, and they seldom addressed it apart from economics, politics, culture, or class. Even leaders of liberal organizations like the Southern Conference for Human Welfare insisted that the "Southern Negro must be emancipated economically and politically before he can be emancipated socially." In 1942 liberal journalist Virginius Dabney typified what Morton Sosna called the "separate-but-equal liberalism" of enlightened white southerners when he called for fairer legal treatment and improved educational and economic opportunities for southern blacks, but all within the context of continuing segregation. Likewise, organized in 1944, the Southern Regional Council sought, through research and education, to, in Numan Bartley's words, "improve race relations within a segregated society."[2]

During World War II, however, the hypocrisy of tolerating a separate, racially repressive and thoroughly undemocratic regional subculture at home while sending American troops to prevent a totalitarian takeover in Europe and Asia had simply become too blatant to ignore. As John Egerton explained, "At a cost of a million casualties and tens of billions of dollars, the United States came to the aid of its allies and saved 'the free world' from an 'outlaw world' personified by Hitler and Mussolini and Tojo. And then, having done that, we had to face the question of whether all those things we were fighting for would be the birthright of whites only, or of all Americans."[3]

The ideological contradictions raised by the war were only magnified by the rise of the United States to free world leadership at the end of the conflict. In C. Vann Woodward's view, Cold War America "presented herself to the world as a model for how democracy, power, opulence, and virtue could be combined under one flag." The Jim Crow South was the principal blemish on this model, one that defied concealment as the United States and the Soviet Union vied for the affections and allegiance of Africa and other sectors of the non-white "developing world." Beginning with World War II, Sosna explained, "Southern liberalism received a rude jolt. At best, liberals had ignored segregation; at worst, they had defended it. But now whether they were committed to segregation or not, the issue was out in the open. To a nation fighting totalitarianism abroad, Jim Crow became an embarrassment."[4]

No southern liberal seemed more jolted than William Faulkner, whose *Go Down, Moses* had been in preparation as American involvement in the war in Europe grew ever more likely. In this novel, Faulkner had seemed less interested in the fundamental human struggle with moral complexity than in projecting what Richard Gray has called a more "declamatory" voice given to affirming "eternal truths." For example, apparently presuming to speak for God, Ike McCaslin excoriates white southerners who "can learn nothing save through suffering, remember nothing, save when underlined in blood" and insists that where "truth" is concerned, "You don't need to choose. The heart already knows . . . there is only one truth and it covers all things that touch the heart." Some critics have suggested that *Go Down, Moses* may have signaled Faulkner's grudging acceptance of the responsibility of educating his fellow white southerners not just to the error of their ways, but to the serious consequences of those erroneous ways for the nation at large.[5]

The war had clearly intensified the urgency of this message for Faulkner, whose unrealistic efforts to enlist in the military are well documented. In an oft-quoted letter to his stepson who was then in service, Faulkner seemed to echo Cash when he insisted, "A change will come out of this war," adding that "if the politicians and the people who run this country are not forced to make good the shibboleth they glibly talk about freedom, liberty, human rights, then you young men who lived through it will have wasted your precious time, and those who don't live through it will have died in vain." For himself, Faulkner could only hope that there would be "a part for me, who can't do anything but use words, in the rearranging of the house, so that all mankind can live in it."[6]

Faulkner's expressed desire to make mankind's house more livable reflected more than simple patriotic fervor, however. For all of the acclaim he would later receive, six years after he had appeared on the cover of *Time*, his reputation, his readership, and his royalty income remained surprisingly limited. In 1944 literary critic Malcolm Cowley matter-of-factly informed him that "in publishing circles your name is mud. They are all convinced that your books won't ever sell." Perhaps his greatest work, *Absalom, Absalom!*, returned only $3,037 in sales during its first four years in print (1936–1940). In part these figures reflected the difficulties of selling books during the Great Depression, but all of Faulkner's novels, save the somewhat lurid *Sanctuary*, were out of print by 1945. When he encouraged Cowley to undertake a comprehensive assessment of his work that would eventually lead to *The Portable Faulkner* (a volume that would soon boost Faulkner's reputation and appeal and set him on course toward the Nobel Prize), he explained that, "I have worked too hard . . . to leave no better mark on this our pointless chronicle than I seem to be about to leave."[7]

Faulkner certainly seemed to be trying to leave his "mark" as a moralist and social reformer in *Intruder in the Dust*, published in 1948. Yet, like many other white proponents of racial change in the postwar South, he recoiled from the prospect of immediate, federally mandated desegregation and insisted that changes in southern racial practices should be initiated by white southerners themselves. In *Intruder in the Dust*, an indomitable black man, Lucas Beauchamp, faces the prospect of having his part-white blood spilled for a murder he did not commit. Meanwhile, long-winded lawyer Gavin Stevens agonizes in the fashion of many flesh-and-blood white moderates of his day that the lynching which is almost certain to come will only strengthen the position of the South's condescending would-be saviors from without.

Educated at Harvard and Heidelberg, the bookish and cosmopolitan Stevens hardly fits Cash's stereotype of a volatile white southerner governed by emotion rather than reason, but he nonetheless manages to work himself into a decidedly Cashian lather on this issue. Offering the familiar portrait of white southerners as the quintessential Americans, Stevens insists they were "alone in the United States" as "a homogeneous people" in stark contrast to the population of the North, whose cities teem with "the coastal spew of Europe." Yet, during the "first" Reconstruction, the southern white had been "trampled for ten years on his face in the dust," and now his descendants faced a similar threat from "outlanders" who seemed to believe "that man's injustice to man can be abolished overnight by police." Stevens holds that in resisting northern encroachments on the racial status quo in the South, he and his like-minded counterparts are not opposing efforts to make "Sambo" free. Rather, simultaneously exhorting enlightened whites to right action and warning meddlesome northerners to stay out of the South's affairs, he argues that "the injustice is ours, the South's. We must expiate it and abolish it ourselves, alone and without help."[8]

In the end, Lucas is saved from lynching not by the garrulous Stevens but by the unlikely trio of Chick Mallison, Stevens's nephew and the young scion of an aristocratic white family; Alecksander, Chick's black contemporary; and Miss Habersham, a free-spirited white matron. Some readers saw this outcome as an expression of hope "that the South may yet extricate itself from the swamps of hatred and violence." One contemporary reviewer even announced that "never before has Faulkner been so explicit in presenting a solution to southern problems." Others read *Intruder in the Dust* quite differently. For Edmund Wilson, the novel seemed to represent "William Faulkner's Reply to the Civil Rights Program . . . a kind of counter blast to the anti-lynching bill and to the civil rights plank in the [1948] Democratic platform." Another reviewer noted *Intruder in the Dust*'s "distorted but nonetheless sentimental and romanticized expression of a familiar southern chauvinism" and even speculated that "the great Southern literary rebel and realist of the early 1930s" might become, "in his own paler and tortuous fashion, the Thomas Nelson Page of the 1940s."[9]

This projection was a tad far-fetched, but *Intruder in the Dust* did offer more than a whiff of the white southerner's almost instinctive resistance to northern intrusion that Cash had expounded upon so thoroughly. (At one point in the novel, Stevens becomes so overwrought that he even engages in a paranoid fantasy, a taunting match in which he invites a sneering northern liberal to "*come down here and look at us . . . before you make up your mind*" only to have his imaginary invitation elicit an imaginary rebuff: "*No thanks the smell is bad enough from here.*" [All italic in original text.]) Speaking through Stevens, Faulkner simultaneously encouraged white southerners to instigate gradual racial change themselves while resisting northern efforts to impose immediate equality on the South. Otherwise, the region would lose its "identity and its birthright." Malcolm Cowley suggested that *Intruder in the Dust* exposed the "dilemma of Southern nationalism" and especially the contradictions of even Faulkner's eloquently expressed and relatively enlightened viewpoint. "The tragedy of intelligent southerners like Faulkner," he wrote, "is that their two fundamental beliefs, in human equality and in southern independence, are now in violent conflict."[10]

Many reviewers also found the novel's story line erratic and murky. Wilson described *Intruder in the Dust* as one of the "more snarled-up of Faulkner's books," and subsequent critics generally agreed that it was a jumble of inconsistency and contradiction or, as Richard Gray put it, "a register of the confusion of the time when it was written and the man who wrote it." The race issue would continue to confuse and bedevil Faulkner until his death in 1962, as he continued to take positions that seemed alternately enlightened and reactionary, insisting that white southerners were "wrong and their position is untenable," but vowing at one point, apparently while intoxicated, to take up arms to defend Mississippi should Washington resort to military force to compel racial integration in his native state.[11]

Faulkner insisted that in *Intruder in the Dust* Gavin Stevens "was not talking for the author, but for the best type of liberal Southerners." Surely this description also applied to Greenville, Mississippi, newspaperman Hodding Carter, whose wartime service in Cairo as editor of the Middle East edition of *Stars and Stripes* allowed him to see firsthand how bitterly many Egyptians resented British colonial policies and racial presumptions. Carter's 1944 novel, *Winds of Fear*, told the story of a wounded white veteran, the son of the editor of the local newspaper, who returns to find his hometown gripped by the racial hysteria that leads ultimately to a lynching. Although Greenville had recorded no such lynching, Carter exploded in anger when a move to establish a monument to local veterans was derailed by whites who were opposed to listing black and white names together. "How in God's name," Carter asked, "can the Negroes be encouraged to be good citizens, to feel that they can get a fair break, to believe that here in the South they will some day win those things that are rightfully theirs—decent housing, better educational facilities, equal pay for equal work, a lifting of health standards, and all of the other milestones along an obstacle filled road—if we deny them so small a thing as joint service recognition?"[12]

Yet, despite the sense of urgency he conveyed in the immediate aftermath of the war, in his *Southern Legacy*, which appeared in 1950, Carter sometimes sounded remarkably like Gavin Stevens. Conceding that racism and Jim Crow had "infected the white South with a moral sickness," he nonetheless warned that "any abrupt federal effort to end segregation" would seriously undermine the "progressive adjustments between the races" that had come in recent years.[13]

Despite such claims by Carter and other white moderates, these "progressive adjustments" were not coming fast or frequently enough to silence a rising chorus of postwar criticism from without and, increasingly, within a region that was no longer simply the nation's "number one economic problem" but its most pressing moral one as well. Southern liberals of the 1930s and early 1940s may have stressed the economic interdependence of blacks and whites, but by 1944 Gunnar Myrdal's *American Dilemma* emphasized the competition and hostility that divided working-class whites and blacks. The "Negro problem" was no longer just a southern one but "a problem in the heart of the American," Myrdal insisted.[14]

Criticism from blacks within and outside the South also grew more forthright and pointed during the 1940s. NAACP membership increased nine-fold as the organization won crucial judicial victories such as the 1944 *Smith v. Allwright* decision striking down the white primary. University of North Carolina Press director William T. Couch was a leading separate-but-equal liberal, but when he asked Rayford W. Logan, a black historian, to compile a book of essays explaining *What the Negro Wants* (1944), he learned, to his amazement and dismay, that all fourteen essayists, even Frederick D. Patterson, the conservative president of Tuskegee, believed that "all negroes must condemn any form of segregation based on race, creed, or color." Couch went ahead with the publication of the book but felt compelled to add a disclaimer explaining that he was not in agreement with all the views expressed in it. Virginius Dabney was not surprised by his friend Couch's experience, explaining that recent events and trends had made him "realize all too vividly that the war and its slogans have roused in the breasts of our colored friends hopes, aspirations and desires which they formerly did not entertain, except in the rarest instances."[15]

During the war, many African Americans embraced the "Double-V" ideal of victory over fascism abroad and racism at home. Poet Langston Hughes was determined to link the fighting overseas to the struggle for racial justice in the United States. Hughes had exulted early in the war that "Pearl Harbor put Jim Crow on the run/That Crow can't fight for Democracy/And be the same old Crow he used to be." As segregation continued to flourish at home and in the armed services as well, however, a disappointed Hughes would ask, "Jim Crow Army and Navy, Too/Is Jim Crow freedom the best I can expect from you?"[16]

Ralph Ellison also took on the race question within the context of the war. In his brilliant 1944 short story, "In a Strange Country," Ellison related the experiences of "Mr. Parker," a black soldier who is assaulted by the first white American G.I. he encounters in Wales but enjoys hearty acceptance by the Welshmen he meets first at a pub and then at a choral concert at a private club where, ironically, the performers try to honor him by singing the "Star Spangled Banner."[17]

The irreverent novelist and folklorist Zora Neale Hurston had drawn consistent criticism from other black intellectuals for refusing to use her writings as a weapon in the struggle against racism and Jim Crow. Yet, in the original manuscript for her autobiographical *Dust Tracks on a Road*, she pointed out that "President Roosevelt could extend his four freedoms to some people right here in America. . . . I am not bitter, but I see what I see. . . . I will fight for my country, but I will not lie for her." Like several others, this passage was subsequently excised after Hurston's white editor deemed it "irrelevant." Elsewhere, Hurston noted Roosevelt's reference to the United States as "the arsenal of democracy" and wondered if she had heard him correctly. Perhaps he meant "arse-and-all" of democracy, she thought, since the United States was supporting the French in their effort to resubjugate the Indo-Chinese, suggesting that "the ass-and-all of democracy has shouldered the load of subjugating the dark world completely." Hurston also announced that she was "crazy for this democracy" and would "pitch headlong into the thing" if it were not for the numerous Jim Crow laws that confronted her at every turn.[18]

Although his Communist party membership eventually forced him to endorse the war effort after Hitler invaded the Soviet Union in 1941, Richard Wright insisted initially that the conflict was "not my people's War," pointing out that "the Negro's experience with past wars, his attitude toward the present one, his attitude of chronic distrust, constitute the most incisive and graphic refutation of every idealistic statement made by the war leaders as to the alleged democratic goal and aim of this war." Wright had solidified his literary reputation with his 1940 novel, *Native Son*, a challenging and deeply troubling story about the impact of racism and bigotry on the human spirit and aspirations, set not in the South, but the urban North. Having fled to this impersonal, destructive environment himself, Wright proceeded in 1945 to explain why in *Black Boy*, a loosely autobiographical account of his youth and adolescence in the Jim Crow South. As seen in *Black Boy*, Richard's childhood was a succession of traumatic, degrading, and brutal encounters not just with whites but with other blacks as well. He actually makes whites nervous by refusing to steal or to join in the carefree banter they saw as an indication that blacks were contented with their lot. Because he refuses to conform to any of the stereotypes that whites tried to impose on all African Americans, Richard cannot relate to the blacks who do succumb to white pressure to affirm these stereotypes. As a result, the young man lives in almost total emotional and intellectual isolation, presenting an enigmatic and discomfiting figure to blacks as well as whites. The environment in which he had grown up, Wright explained, was simply "too small to nourish human beings, especially Negro human beings," and he held nothing back in depicting its physical and emotional cruelty.[19]

As Michel Fabre explained, in *Black Boy* Wright had forced white readers "to consider the South from the black point of view." Not surprisingly, many of them rejected what they saw. Mississippi's race-baiting congressmen Theodore G. Bilbo and John Rankin denounced *Black Boy* as "a damnable lie from beginning to end" and the "dirtiest, filthiest, lousiest, most obscene piece of writing that I have ever seen in print," pointing out that "it comes from a Negro and you cannot expect any better from a person of this type." Some white liberals and a great many black leaders were also displeased with Wright's unflinching portrayal of the intellectual and emotional barrenness of black life in the South and his suggestion that there was little reason to think things were getting better. "A sorry slander of the Negroes generally," one reviewer called it, castigating Wright for "his total failure to see that the clock of history is moving ahead, not backward."[20]

Despite its mixed reception in some circles, however, perhaps nothing written or said by any African American since the publication of DuBois's *The Souls of Black Folk* in 1903 had succeeded in bringing as much national attention to the reality of racial persecution in the contemporary South. In June 1945 *Life* magazine featured it in a five-page spread illustrated by posed photographs depicting key scenes in the book. The *Life* article described Wright's account as "a bitter, true story of a Negro boy's struggles against the life imposed on his race in the South." It was "not only a brilliant autobiography but a powerful indictment of a caste system which is one of America's biggest problems."[21]

Black critics were not alone in their frontal assaults on the South's caste system. Katharine Du Pre Lumpkin was "reared in a home where the Confederacy is revered as a cause, holy and imperishable," and steeped from childhood not only in the emotion and romance of the Lost Cause, but the dogma of "white supremacy" and "keep them in their place." The primary agent of her education in the mores of white southernness was her father, William Lumpkin, a domineering embodiment of southern patriarchy. His influence over his daughter was such that many years later as she recounted an indelible childhood image of him brutally beating the family's black cook for her "impudence" toward Katharine's mother, she could bring herself to identify him only as "the master of the house." Only after her father's death would Lumpkin begin to express publicly her doubts about the gospel of race, region, and gender in which she had been so assiduously catechized and weigh what she had been taught against what she had actually observed and experienced on her own. Her family's move from Georgia to the Sand Hills of South Carolina had allowed her to see firsthand the poverty and perilous circumstances of the area's blacks. During the 1920s her involvement with the interracial activities of the YWCA left her convinced that race was "nonexistent, only a fiction, a myth, which white minds had created for reasons of their own" and that "wage earning whites and Negroes were, functionally speaking, not so unlike after all."[22]

In the wake of World War II, Lumpkin noted that the cumulative impact of Depression, war, agricultural mechanization, and industrial development was weakening the region's resistance to change: "I know the old life continues, but not serenely, not without a struggle to maintain its existence. . . . [T]he Southern people are pressing against the enclosing walls." No white southerner pressed harder than Lillian Smith. Her solidly middle-class origins made Smith seem an unlikely crusader against the status quo, but financial reverses had forced her father to move his family from their Jasper, Florida, home to their summer place near Clayton in the Georgia mountains. Smith attended nearby Piedmont College at Demorest for a year and studied music at the Peabody conservatory in Baltimore. She had envisioned a career as a concert pianist, but her father had established the Laurel Falls Camp for Girls in 1920, and five years later his failing health forced his daughter to become the camp's director. Through the camp, Smith met Paula Snelling, who would become her lifelong companion and co-founder and co-editor of a controversial literary magazine that began as *Pseudopodia* and became the *North Georgia Review* and later *South Today*.[23]

Smith's 1944 novel *Strange Fruit* was a searing story of miscegenation and murder that concluded with the lynching of an innocent young black man. It was condemned by Georgia governor Eugene Talmadge as "a literary corn cob" and banned in Boston, leading to a well-publicized censorship trial. Eventually translated into fifteen languages, the novel also became a Broadway play. Smith spared her readers no grisly details. After the lynching, an excited older white woman is obsessed with the smell of the victim's burning flesh, which she compares to barbecue. This passage is strikingly similar to one in an unpublished short story by Ralph Ellison—probably written about the same time that Smith was working on *Strange Fruit*. In Ellison's story, a young white boy witnessing a lynching insists, "I'll never forget it. Every time I eat barbecue I'll remember that nigger. His back was just like a barbecued hog."[24]

Smith clearly felt a certain kinship with contemporary black writers. She assured Richard Wright they shared similar views "about the responsibility of writers to their culture and its problems" and suggested that they collaborate to help other writers find ways "to do more creative thinking and writing about our cultural problems, and yet leave them free of any ideological ties." Aware of the difficulties of separating race from "other aspects" of southern "cultural personality," she observed in *Killers of the Dream*, published in 1949, that most southern white children lived what she called a "haunted childhood." In her own case, she wrote: "The mother who taught me tenderness and love and compassion taught me also the bleak ritual of keeping Negroes in their place. The father who rebuked me for an air of superiority toward schoolmates from the mill and rounded out his rebuke by reminding me that 'all men are brothers,' trained me in the steel-rigid decorums I must demand of every colored male. They who gravely taught me to split my body from my feelings and both from my 'soul' taught me also to split my conscience from my acts and Christianity from southern tradition."[25]

Killers of the Dream often drew comparisons with *The Mind of the South*. Smith expressed great personal empathy for W. J. Cash and pointed to his suicide as evidence that "writing about the South is a heartbreaking job for those of us who love it and yet see its self-destructiveness." Writing *Killers*, she confessed, had left her in an almost unshakable state of "anguish," and Smith knew from her own "painful experience how wounded one feels." Yet, although she praised Cash's work and admitted the two had "admired and respected" each other, Smith had found "no in-depth probing in that book" because Cash simply "wasn't capable of such, too sick himself, too involved with his own taboos to handle it the way I did."[26]

In Smith's view, racial, gender, and religious orthodoxy had sustained the South's stifling and emotionally destructive social order from one generation to another. Exploring the apparent contradiction between the white South's earnest professions of Christian faith and the horrible realities of its racial obsessions, she found it small wonder that "guilt" was "the biggest crop raised in Dixie, harvested each summer [during the traditional "revival" meetings] just before cotton is picked." Smith's analysis of the relationship between race and sex in the South went considerably beyond the one offered by Cash, who believed that the white South's "rape complex" simply reflected a symbolic amalgam of white female purity, white male power, and the very essence of southern white identity itself. Smith pushed the Freudian angle even further, suggesting that male sexual anxiety lay at the heart of the white man's impulse to lynch and torture black men. After the lynching in *Strange Fruit*, a poor white who lost both his legs in a sawmill accident finds his sexual potency restored by this brutal reassertion of white supremacy. In such circumstances, Smith explained, "the lynched Negro becomes *not an object that must die* but a receptacle for every man's dammed-up hate, and a receptacle for every man's forbidden sex feelings." The horrible fact that sometimes the "lynchers do cut off the genitals of the lynched and divide them into bits to be distributed as souvenirs is no more than a coda to this composition of hate and guilt and sex hunger and fear, created by our way of life in the South, and by our families and by our ideas of right and wrong."[27]

Even before *Killers of the Dream* appeared, Smith had insisted that southern white women had "never been as loyal to the ideology of race and segregation as have southern men." After all, they had also been segregated because the "secret enmity against women" had driven white men to imprison the white woman on a pedestal, "putting her always and forever in her 'place.'" Smith never wavered in her belief that the racist, sexist southern patriarchy had "long ago made Mom and her sex 'inferior' and stripped her of her economic and political and sexual rights." Still, she believed even those women who had challenged the racial/sexual status quo through organizations such as the Association of Southern Women to Prevent Lynching had too often made "no real attempt to change this way of life which they dimly realized had injured themselves and their children as much as it had injured Negroes."[28]

For the most part, southern white women went "compulsively about the training of their children as if it were a totalitarian discipline: imposing rigidities on spirit and mind." Such women, wrote Smith, "dared not question what had injured them so much. It was all wrapped up in one package: sex taboos, race segregation, 'the right to make money the way father made money,' the duty to go to church, the fear of new knowledge that would shake old beliefs, the splitting of ideals from actions—and you accepted it all as uncritically as the Communists accept their Stalin-stamped lives."[29]

Smith eventually concluded that Cash's *The Mind of the South* had been *Killers of the Dream*'s biggest competitor because white "moderates" who had been unable to handle her bold and blunt assertions had "grabbed" Cash's book and "hung on to keep from having to confront *Killers*." She had little use for these so-called moderates, describing them as the victims of "temporary moral and psychic paralysis" and insisting that "moderation never made a man or a nation great." Some leading southern moderates were equally critical of Smith. Neither Hodding Carter nor Ralph McGill had ever met her, but she complained that the former had ridiculed her as "a sex obsessed old spinster," while the latter had dismissed her as "a fanatic living on a mountain in sackcloth and ashes."[30]

Although Smith was convinced that her passion and candor had cost her the literary recognition she deserved, as the 1940s drew to a close, a great many more white southerners were willing to join her and Katharine Du Pre Lumpkin in taking a harder look at the schizoid realities of the "southern way of life." In the preface to *Southern Exposure*, Stetson Kennedy responded to the question of "Is the South insane?" with a "categorical 'yes,'" adding that "its insanity has affected the entire nation." Reflecting the growing emphasis on southern racial problems, Kennedy contended that "addicted as it is to protestations of Christianity and Americanism, the white South has long been suffering the mental torment of the damned, trying to rationalize the American doctrine of the brotherhood of man and the white supremacy." After so long a period of being "troubled in mind," the "white South" had now become both "the nation's economic problem No. 1." and its "pathological problem No. 1." as well.[31]

Echoing the apostles of secession of a century before, southern white leaders mounted their defense against the coming assault on their racial practices by invoking the doctrine of state sovereignty and casting themselves as the last lone defenders of the Constitution and the principles on which America had been founded. Yet, in his 1947 volume *Inside U.S.A.*, journalist John Gunther revealed that "once or twice" during his travels in the South he had felt he "wasn't in the United States at all." Evoking John Dollard's earlier comparison of southern whites to "the psychotics one sometimes meets in a mental hospital," Gunther described the South as "a land of paranoia, full of the mentally sick," most of them feeling "a deep necessity to hate something, if necessary themselves."[32]

By no means all such critical descriptions of a schizophrenic, religion- and race-obsessed white South came from outsiders. As Daniel Singal observed, southern writers and scholars actually led the way, carrying "the critical spirit to its logical extreme, until Americans living outside the region formed a picture of southern society as one immense Tobacco Road." In reality, however, as white southerners met the long-awaited assault on their racial system with a violent defiance that often seemed totally irrational, if not downright deranged, the South "of conflict and depravity" that was fast achieving "mythological status" belonged more to W. J. Cash than to Erskine Caldwell.[33]

Although Singal dubbed *The Mind of the South* "an instant classic," despite its positive reception among southern white intellectuals and a major advertising push by its publisher, sales of the initial print run of 2,500 were so sluggish that Alfred Knopf had felt some misgivings about a second printing. In May 1941 as he attempted to soothe the feelings of its emotionally fragile author, Knopf had suggested that sales of Cash's book had been so disappointing because "the very nature of its subject matter doesn't interest enough people." The full implications of Cash's devastating portrait of the damaged and dangerous southern white psyche might well have eluded a nation distracted by the growing certainty of global war, but Lillian Smith, who had in some ways probed that psyche even more deeply and painfully than Cash, sensed that attitudes had changed by the end of the 1940s. Despite her concerns about the book's limitations, Smith pressed Knopf to reissue *The Mind of the South*, arguing that when it had first appeared, "the country had not been aroused about the needs of the South, nor was there widespread curiosity about the needs of our people." Convinced that interest was "much greater" by 1949, she assured Knopf that Cash's book would now surely "gain the readers it deserves."[34]

Knopf was a bit slow to take Smith's advice, but her instincts proved sound. In its first thirteen years in print, *The Mind of the South* had sold only 8,000 copies in hardback. In its first paperback edition, which appeared in 1954, just before the *Brown* decision and the stormy reaction it elicited from white southerners, the book sold 59,000 copies over the next six years. The second paperback edition, issued in 1960, would push total sales of the paperbacks past the 100,000 mark by 1965.[35]

The 1960 paperback reissue elicited a single severely understated sentence in the *New York Times Book Review*: "The economic and social ferment of the war and post-war years has not dulled the incisiveness and cogency of this small-town newspaper editor's 1941 analysis and interpretation of the philosophy, temperament and mores prevalent South of the Mason-Dixon Line." As Jack Temple Kirby pointed out, "To a generation witnessing the Dixiecrat movement of 1948, the *Brown* school desegregation decision's aftermath, the Montgomery bus boycott, and the ensuing 'Negro revolt' in the South, Cash's South was more than adequate as an explanatory model. It was brilliant."[36]

As Kirby suggested, it was the actual behavior of so many white southerners during this period in combination with Cash's convenient and plausible explanation for that behavior that gave him such sudden and widespread credibility. Every day it seemed, southern whites were demonstrating their "too great attachment to racial values and . . . tendency to justify cruelty and injustice in the name of those values." The gruesome murder of young Emmett Till and the outrageous exoneration of his killers would have seemed entirely predictable to Cash. After all, in the South he had described, African Americans were little more than "open game," and white men known to have slain "five or eight or thirteen" blacks not only "walked about freely" but were regarded with ill-concealed "pride and admiration" by their peers.[37]

The events between the Till slaying in 1955 and the violent confrontation nearly a decade later on the Edmund Pettus Bridge in Selma effectively seared Cash's perception of southern white identity on the minds of at least a generation of observers outside the region. From the mob scenes of Little Rock, to the violent eruptions accompanying the Freedom Rides and the sit-ins, to the Meredith riot at Ole Miss, to the horror of Bull Connor's police dogs, firehoses, and the church bombings in Birmingham, to the atrocities of Freedom Summer, to the raw, billy-club brutality of the confrontation in Selma, every evening newscast seemed to offer another appalling reaffirmation of Cash's "savage ideal." Just as Cash had foreseen, the white South's "capacity for adjustment" was indeed being tested, and just as he had feared, it appeared to be failing the test.

In the publishing world, timing is everything, and the timing for *The Mind of the South*'s encore could hardly have been better. Bob Smith recalled, "In the fall of 1960 Cash's book blossomed on the reading lists in Harvard's Yard like some lush tropical growth. Everywhere the young in mind wanted to know about the South, and, of course, only Cash could tell it like it was. The book was instant revelation to a generation of yearlings who had never been south of the Jersey Turnpike," and many of them "swallowed it at an indigestible gulp like one of those dreadful purgatives of eighteenth-century medicine, sustained only by faith."[38]

Both for those who committed themselves to bringing racial change to a recalcitrant white South and for those who watched in horror from a distance, *The Mind of the South* soon became a handy one-volume troubleshooter's guide to the problem South. As Fred Hobson explained, by the 1960s it ranked as "a sort of southern testament, the first work on the South suggested to outsiders, the book Northern civil rights workers carried with them on their southern forays." And why not? As far as Edwin Yoder could see in 1965, "the essential behavior of the [white] South as Cash described it" had not "changed radically in the last quarter century" since his book was published.[39]

Perhaps observing the belated success that *The Mind of the South* had enjoyed in this environment, Alfred Knopf urged legendary Atlanta journalist Ralph McGill to write a similar book. Like Cash, McGill battled constant doubts before completing *The South and the Southerner* (1964), a book that many felt was the finest commentary on the South since the tortured North Carolinian had offered up his soul-wrenching masterpiece two decades earlier. Though he had consistently deplored the mistreatment and discrimination suffered by southern blacks, McGill had once warned that "anyone with an ounce of common sense must see . . . that separation of the two races must be maintained in the South." As time passed, however, he had grown increasingly aware of white southerners' "troubled conscience" over segregation.[40]

McGill reported on a visit with novelist Carson McCullers, who had remarked of white southerners, "There's a guilt in us—a seeking for something we had . . . and lost." There was obviously much to deplore and regret. Southern whites had done irreparable harm to generations of southern blacks and shamed and dishonored themselves in the process. "Southernism suddenly has become," McGill lamented, "the screaming, cursing mothers in New Orleans school troubles or the dynamiters of schools and churches."[41]

As sensitive as he was to both the anger and the guilt trapped within the southern white psyche, McGill's post in relatively tranquil Atlanta kept him off the front lines as the civil rights struggle reached its most violent phase. His book appeared before white hatred had exploded in its full, defiant fury in the face of Freedom Summer and the Selma March. In the wake of this conflagration, another lesser-known Atlanta journalist, Pat Watters, emerged as the quintessential journalistic representative of Fred Hobson's "shame-and-guilt" school of southern writing.

In *The South and the Nation*, Watters related an anecdote that seemed in its own way as cruel, shameful, and tragic as any of the bloody and brutal incidents that made headlines during the confrontational stages of the civil rights movement. A white teacher, considered "liberal" by the standards of her black belt community, had but one black student in her newly integrated second-grade class. As was her custom, on the last day of school, she had her class file by her desk for a hug and the requisite good-byes. "And do you know," she explained in a surprised tone, "that little colored boy came, too, holding his arms out to me like the rest. And I just had to push him away. All the other children were there watching. I just had to. Can you imagine him doing that?" Two years later, in *Down to Now*, Watters would almost echo Lillian Smith, asking, "How were we able to achieve such insensitivity, such cruelty, with never a pang of conscience?" His answer was, in part at least, "a compartmentalizing ability to shut out from consciousness the sad and the evil . . . to make unreal anything that we were unwilling to mention."[42]

Prior to World War II, no southern intellectuals had done less as a group to challenge white southerners in their conscience-soothing self-deception than the region's historians. The "History of the South" project had actually grown out of University of Texas benefactor George W. Littlefield's desire to see southern history presented in a more positive light. However, C. Vann Woodward had emerged in the 1930s as a path-breaking young scholar, and his selection in 1939 as the author of the post-Reconstruction volume in the new series helped to pave the way for a revolutionary new approach to writing southern history that would finally shatter the old New South school's historical orthodoxy by reading and interpreting the past so as to challenge rather than affirm the status quo.

When his *Origins of the New South* finally appeared in 1951, it amounted, so Woodward believed, to a sort of "historiographical black mass in the eyes of the believers." As his first heresy, Woodward attacked the "nostalgic vision" of a refined and genteel Old South, not, in Cashian terms, as a simple manifestation of the white southerner's penchant for romantic fantasy but as a deliberate fabrication of the architects of the New South Creed. Woodward also advanced what would become for many historians the book's boldest and most disputable contention when he argued that the Redeemers who engineered Reconstruction's demise were "'of middle class, industrial, capitalistic outlook with little but nominal connection with the old planter regime.'" This point was particularly crucial to Woodward's revisionist purpose, because it undermined the claims of the Redeemers and their New South descendants to ancestral legitimacy through their roots in the old cavalier order.[43]

After questioning the Redeemers' bloodlines, Woodward went on to assail their behavior, showing that their governments were neither more scrupulously honest nor more fiscally responsible than those of the Reconstruction era. Shamelessly insensitive to the exploitation of the South's human and natural resources, the Redeemers had willingly shackled the region with a colonial economy. They had also overseen the brutal repression of the South's black population and the wholesale relegation of its rural labor force of both races to the seemingly endless and hopeless cycle of tenancy, dependency, and debt that was the sharecropping and crop-lien system. Acutely sensitive to the symbolic as well as functional importance of the New South's invented traditions of Jim Crow and disfranchisement, Woodward also explained that "it took a lot of ritual and Jim Crow to bolster the creed of white supremacy in the bosom of a white man working for a black man's wages."[44]

Woodward felt that reviewers of *Tom Watson* had failed to acknowledge what he had thought were obvious continuities in plight and prospects between the "Okies and the Arkies" of the 1930s and the "rednecks, lintheads and Samboes" of the 1890s. In contrast, *Origins* all but defied readers to miss the connection between the contemporary South's multitude of problems and deficiencies and the racial, political, and economic transgressions of the Redeemers, whose political heirs continued to thwart the region's material and human development as the second half of the twentieth century began. Reviewer David Donald praised Woodward's "realistic reappraisal of basic social and economic forces in the South" and concluded that "today's Southern problem is the result of the historical processes which Professor Woodward so admirably analyzes." A decade after *Origins* first appeared, Woodward reiterated its message that "the modern South . . . is continuous in its economic, political and racial institutions with the order established in 1877."[45]

In *Origins*, Woodward succeeded, however belatedly, in transfusing the study of southern history with the same sense of the past as "always a part of the present, shaping, haunting, duplicating, reflecting it" that had energized and enriched the works of Wolfe, Faulkner, and Warren, the literary contemporaries he so admired. In fact, by the time it appeared in 1951, *Origins of the New South* represented something of a postscript, a second generation manifestation of the critical historical consciousness that had been so prominent in

southern literature when Woodward entered graduate school in the 1930s. It
also signaled that a new generation of southern historians was at last ready to
join the discussion that Donald Davidson had found well under way among
other scholars, writers, and journalists in the 1930s by focusing on the "strategic problem" of "how to arrive at southern policies that are historically sound
and at the same time applicable to the existing situation."[46]

Woodward continued to write provocatively, persuasively, and pragmatically about the relationship between the contemporary and the historical within
the southern experience. By 1952 he and his friend and fellow historian John
Hope Franklin were working as researchers and advisors for the NAACP's legal team preparing the case that would lead to the *Brown v. Board of Education*
desegregation ruling in 1954. In the wake of the decision, Woodward seized
the opportunity to provide southerners and Americans at large with a revised
view of the historical origins of segregation, because he felt that "the national
discussion over the questions of how deeply rooted, how ineradicable, and
how amenable to change the segregation practices really are is being conducted
against a background of faulty or inadequate historical information." Drawn
from a series of lectures delivered at the University of Virginia four months
after the initial *Brown* decree, *The Strange Career of Jim Crow* (1955) attacked
the fundamental historical premises used to justify the system of segregation.[47]

"The basic assumption" at the time, Woodward reflected, was that the South's
Jim Crow practices "were of quite ancient origin and that they were the inevitable consequence of the association between two races of markedly different
physical characteristics and cultural attainments." In the prevailing white mind
set in Jim Crow's New South, "Everyone was assured that this was the way
things had always been, that it was because of Southern folkways, that colored
people themselves preferred it that way, and anyway there was nothing that
could be done to change it." In *The Strange Career of Jim Crow*, however, Woodward maintained "first, that racial segregation in the South in the rigid and
universal form it had taken by 1954 did not appear with the end of slavery but
toward the end of the century and later; and second, that before it appeared in
this form there occurred an era of experiment and variety in race relations of
the South in which segregation was not the invariable rule."[48]

According to Richard King, Woodward "wanted to show that neither segregation nor disfranchisement was historically inevitable or part of a firmly established Southern tradition. Segregation had a relatively short history; and if
it had been consciously instituted (as it had), it could just as consciously be

abolished. . . . Thus Woodward's tract was clearly . . . an attempt to demytholo-
gize the existing social and legal institutions that regulated race relations." In
Woodward's view, the contemporary Jim Crow system was a product not of
culture but of codification, and having been created by statute, it might be
dismantled in the same fashion. In other words, laws or "stateways," Woodward argued, "did not always flow from customs or 'folkways.'" Sometimes the
reverse was true. This latter point was especially crucial, for it ran counter to
the thinking of those from white liberals to black conservatives to public
officials up to and including President Dwight D. Eisenhower, who had reiterated on several occasions his belief that "you cannot change people's hearts
merely by law."[49]

In contrast to the monolithically and irreversibly intransigent white South
that Cash had described (and that so many civil rights workers would soon
seem to be encountering), Woodward presented a society whose mores and
institutions, including its most sacred social premise, were anything but immutable. If he sought to rewrite the history of segregation in order to inspire
and encourage those working to bring about its demise, Woodward succeeded
admirably. Reviewing *Strange Career*, black historian Rayford W. Logan thought
that recent cracks in Jim Crow's armor might be attributable to "the relative
recency of many of the segregation laws" and that "additional breakdowns of
the barriers may be easier for the same reason." Meanwhile, black sociologist
E. Franklin Frazier thought Woodward had demonstrated that "the race problem was *made* and that men can *unmake* it, as they are attempting it today."[50]

In retrospect, the carefully selected evidence from five travelers' accounts
and two editorials that Woodward offered in support of his argument seems
much too thin and anecdotal to justify even a suggestion, much less a conclusion, about the origins of segregation. Yet *The Strange Career of Jim Crow* became an enormously influential book. The Reverend Martin Luther King, Jr.,
reportedly called it "the historical Bible of the Civil Rights movement," and as
a participant in the 1965 Selma voting rights march, Woodward even heard
his words quoted by King in front of the Alabama state capitol in Montgomery. Woodward's friend John Hope Franklin was also present on this occasion
and fittingly so; Franklin had been much more active than Woodward in as-
sisting Thurgood Marshall and the NAACP Legal Defense and Educational
Fund team in preparing the arguments that led to the *Brown* decision. He had
worked several days each week in the NAACP's New York offices during the
summer and fall of 1953, writing essays, coordinating research, and providing
historical background for the lawyers who were preparing their arguments.[51]

The contributions of both Franklin and Woodward to the effort to bring racial change to the South were clearly emblematic of an emergent trend toward
social activism in southern historical scholarship. In 1956 University of California historian Kenneth Stampp's *The Peculiar Institution* launched a frontal
assault on the widely accepted New South notion, as promulgated by U. B.
Phillips, that slavery had exerted a relatively benign, civilizing influence on the
slaves. In Stampp's view, slavery had been in no sense a blessing or even a
necessary evil but in all ways a curse for the South and all of its inhabitants.
The legacy of slavery was, therefore, as one reviewer suggested, "the bitter dissensions that are ripening today."[52]

Dissensions were considerably riper three years later when Stanley M.
Elkins's *Slavery* offered an even more devastating portrait of slavery and its
debilitating impact on the enslaved. In Elkins's view, slavery had stripped the
slaves of their cultural identities as Africans and reduced them to an emotionally infantilized, shuffling and shiftless "Sambo" in a process of personality
modification that he likened to what had seemed to happen to some Jewish
prisoners in Nazi concentration camps. Taken together, the Stampp and Elkins
volumes focused much broader scholarly and public attention on the plight of
the slaves and, by inference, their sorely disadvantaged descendants.[53]

With this growing awareness of the historical roots of black disadvantage,
however, loomed the specter of the still widely accepted view of Reconstruction as a woefully misguided previous attempt at federal intervention in the
South's racial affairs. Writing in 1957, Bernard A. Weisberger noted that the
school segregation conflict had "moved the race question into disturbing but
inescapable prominence," making it "more important than ever that progress
be made toward understanding the issues raised" in the old "Reconstruction
of 1867 to 1877." This made the failure of contemporary historians to undertake the rethinking of Reconstruction that had been suggested more than a
generation earlier by W. E. B. Dubois, Howard Beale, and Francis Butler Simkins
seem all the more puzzling to Weisberger. In the end, he could only attribute
the scarcity of revisionist scholarship on Reconstruction to the influence of
the "consensus" school of historians who, as the nation lay in the ideological
grip of the Cold War, showed a "marvelous ability to read unity, progress and
patriotism into every page of the American record."[54]

Even as Weisberger wrote, however, the challenge to consensus was well
under way. In 1961 John Hope Franklin attacked a host of misconceptions

about Reconstruction in his *Reconstruction: After the Civil War*, arguing, for example, that the extent of black political power during Reconstruction had been grossly exaggerated and that the average "Radical" or "carpetbag" regime usually lasted no more than five or six years. He also discovered much good in the Radical program (which he actually found more moderate than radical), and he likewise argued that black officeholders generally acquitted themselves quite well. Finally, hoping to dispel the deeply ingrained notion that Reconstruction governments were peculiarly corrupt, Franklin insisted that in that era "corruption was bisectional, bipartisan and biracial."[55]

Kenneth Stampp followed a similar approach in *The Era of Reconstruction, 1865–1872*, published in 1965. Determined to revise the traditional wisdom about Reconstruction, Stampp devoted his first chapter to toppling one of the historical pillars of the New South Creed that had become a national historical myth as well. Stampp's assault on the "tragic legend" that Reconstruction was a foolish and failed experiment in social engineering that had brought great hardship and persecution on southern whites was so straightforward and devastating that it appeared he had set out to dismantle the Reconstruction myth in much the same fashion as Cash had taken on the Old South myth. Noting the relevance of Stampp's work, one commentator found "compelling arguments that [the violent reaction to recent voting rights demonstrations in] Selma is the predictable heritage of a South that, though losing a war, at once conspired to evade the moral indemnity that was its toll." Even a conservative reviewer conceded that Stampp had effectively undermined the prevailing wisdom that federal action in behalf of black rights had failed during Reconstruction and therefore contemporary civil rights initiatives were foredoomed to fail as well.[56]

As the civil rights movement grew increasingly confrontational, many influential southern historians moved beyond relying on their scholarship to support the crusade for racial change and became active public participants in the crusade themselves. Clement Eaton of the University of Kentucky used his Southern Historical Association presidential address in 1961 to urge his colleagues to "stand with the future and not with the conservative past." "Although our association is not a reform or crusading organization," Eaton argued, "we do not go out of our province in taking a bold and courageous stand on the integration of the races in our educational system. . . . It should be a high honor for us to lead public opinion rather than tamely to follow it. We southern historians and teachers of history—I for one certainly—should hope not only to teach and write history but also to influence, even in a small degree, the course of its future history."[57]

Two years later, an even more direct call to activism came from University of Mississippi historian James W. Silver, who had emerged during the James Meredith crisis at Ole Miss as an embattled but pugnacious champion of integration and compliance with federal law. Silver took the podium in 1963 as president of the Southern Historical Association to discuss not the sins of the past but the sins of the present in "Mississippi: The Closed Society." The impassioned Silver sounded more like a crusader than a historian, pulling no punches in his attack on his state's politicians, its press, its university administrators, and its so-called "good men who to whatever degree had abandoned the feeling of accountability for conditions in Mississippi."[58]

Though he clearly shared the egalitarian ideals of activists like Silver, historian David Potter worried that many of his fellow academics were behaving "more as humanitarians than as historians." He cited both historian Frank E. Vandiver's assertion that Jefferson Davis would "certainly loathe" the contemporary reliance on the Confederate flag as a symbol of white supremacy and literary expert Louis D. Rubin's claim that, had he lived, Faulkner would have "stood quietly alongside of James Meredith" when he entered Old Miss in 1962. At best, both contentions were surely little more than wishful thinking. Faulkner, for example, had died only a few months before Meredith's tumultuous arrival in Oxford, and in the final years of his life he had grown increasingly detached from the South's racial problems. Such counterfactual examples suggested to Potter that many of his colleagues had become "much preoccupied with the present crisis in race relations, and seem, at the moment, more anxious to reform the South than they are to explain it."[59]

On the other hand, the architects of the New South identity had clearly understood the power of history and had used their own highly selective and carefully crafted version of the southern past quite effectively as a frontline defense against change for nearly three quarters of a century. With the South's day of reckoning finally at hand, however, its historical ramparts were beginning to crumble in the face of a withering assault by Potter's reform-minded colleagues who seemed "to regard history as a weapon in the ideological wars" and saw little reason to apologize for succumbing to the "liberal urge to find constructive meanings in the past for the affairs of the present."[60]

Prior to the civil rights movement, relatively few of the South's leading literary figures had spoken out personally against racial injustice in their region.

As late as 1959, Flannery O'Connor had refused to meet with African American writer James Baldwin in her native Georgia. "Might as well expect a mule to fly as me to meet James Baldwin in Georgia," she declared. "In New York it would be nice to meet him; here it would not," she explained. "I observe the traditions of the people I feed on—it's only fair." Elizabeth Spencer had grown up in an atmosphere of relative privilege and racial paternalism in the edge of the Mississippi Delta not far from where Emmett Till was murdered in 1955. Spencer broke with her father over his refusal to condemn the Till killing, however, and the following year her novel, *The Voice at the Back Door* (1956), highlighted the racial injustices so prevalent in Mississippi. Yet Spencer admitted that she had not written the book "to reform anybody but myself. . . . For I also had subscribed to the 'Southern Way of Life.'"[61]

Although she was not known for critical social commentary in her fiction, Spencer's fellow Mississippian, Eudora Welty, contributed to the explosion of shame and outrage after civil rights leader Medgar Evers was shot in Jackson, Mississippi, in August 1963. On hearing of the slaying, Welty suddenly realized, "Whoever the murderer is, I know him: not his identity but his coming about in time and place." Driven by "shock and revolt," at a single sitting Welty wrote a short story based on the slaying and told from the killer's perspective. Rushed into the next issue of the *New Yorker*, "Where Is the Voice Coming From?" proved so eerily similar to the emerging details of the shooting that the story had to be altered at the last minute so as to avoid prejudicing the case of Evers's accused slayer. In Welty's story, fed up with "Roland Summers" and his demands for racial equality, the killer lies in wait at Summers's house, noting resentfully that he lives on a paved street, has a well-watered lawn, and allows his wife "to leave the lights on all night." After shooting him in the back, the slayer explains to his dying victim, "There was one way left for me to be ahead of you and stay ahead of you and by Dad, I just taken it."[62]

Yet another Mississippi writer, Walker Percy, had observed as a youth the segregationist but compassionate paternalism of his cousin and adoptive father, William Alexander Percy. In the wake of the *Brown* decision and the emergence of the Citizens' Councils, however, Walker Percy realized that upper-class whites had failed to exercise the enlightened responsible leadership needed to defuse the South's racial crisis and stem the rising tide of violence and demagoguery in the region. Because of this failure, by 1965 Mississippi had become what Percy described as a "Fallen Paradise." He contrasted the heroism of Mississippians who fought to the death at Gettysburg with a state now "mainly renowned for murder, church burning, dynamiting, assassinations, night-riding, not to mention the lesser forms of terrorism." Percy observed that the students at Ole Miss had marked the Civil War centennial by following not the tolerant spirit of General Robert E. Lee but the reactionary rabble-rousing example of General Edwin Walker, who helped to incite them into "an assault of bullying, spitting, and obscenities" against James Meredith. Indeed, Percy noted, "The bravest Mississippians in recent years have not been Confederates or the sons of Confederates but rather two Negroes, James Meredith and Medgar Evers."[63]

Where Spencer, Welty, and Percy had simply moved from tacit acceptance to public criticism of segregation, in 1930 at age twenty-four, Robert Penn Warren had actually gone on record in its defense. "The Briar Patch" was a more than apt title for Warren's essay in I'll Take My Stand; for although he would go on to become an advocate of racial integration as well as the South's preeminent person of letters, he would spend not a little of the remainder of his long and distinguished career trying to explain, both to others and himself, why he had written this controversial piece. In the essay itself, Warren seemed to place no more historical responsibility for the South's racial woes on whites than blacks. Overlooking the fact that they had been brought to America against their will, he pointed out that blacks had resisted white efforts to repatriate them to Africa in the antebellum era and then behaved so badly in Reconstruction that they had lost the "confidence" of whites. In words reminiscent of Booker T. Washington, Warren endorsed vocational training for blacks but expressed wariness about too much emphasis on higher education until there was "a separate negro community or group . . . capable of absorbing and profiting from those members who have received these higher educations." He was especially critical of the educated "negro radical" who might insist that a black professional should have the right to stay in the same hotel as a white professional, even if he had access to a black hotel "as comfortable as the one from which he is turned away." Warren appealed to whites to show fairness and common sense, but his most straightforward response to the South's racial problems in 1929 had been to encourage "the Negro" to remain on the land where "he still chiefly belongs, by temperament and capacity," and to urge both black and northern white leaders otherwise to "let the negro sit beneath his own vine and fig tree."[64]

Though his essay had actually seemed too lukewarm in its advocacy of segregation to suit some of his more conservative fellow Agrarians, Warren's piece had certainly called for no sweeping alteration of the racial status quo in the South. He had admitted even before it appeared that it "doesn't fill me with pride," and that he only hoped it would prove "harmless." Suffice it to say, it did not, and Warren claimed subsequently that he never read the essay in print because he knew it would make him uncomfortable. In 1957 he conceded to Ralph Ellison that the piece had in fact been "a defense of segregation," but he argued that "there wasn't a power under heaven that could have changed segregation in 1929: the South wasn't ready for it, the North was not ready for it, the Negro wasn't."[65]

In keeping with his racially benign upbringing, Warren later insisted his "Briar Patch" essay had been "humane . . . very humane, self-consciously humane," envisioning "segregation in what I presumed to be its most human dimension," that practiced by his own family. He confessed, however, that he had always "uncomfortably suspected, despite the then prevailing attitude of the Supreme Court and of the overwhelming majority of the population of the United States, that no segregation was, in the end, humane," although "it never crossed my mind that anybody was capable of doing anything about it."[66]

Writing his piece as he completed his Rhodes Scholarship studies at Oxford, Warren had been out of the South for five years, and he had developed a vision of its "massive immobility." When he returned, however, the "unchangeable" had, in fact, begun to yield to the stresses of the Great Depression, whose desperate necessities had made the "inevitability" of change all too apparent. As the decade unfolded, Warren had slowly realized that "I could never again write the essay."[67]

In the wake of this realization, Ellison observed, each of Warren's written works seemed to mark "a redefinition of reality arrived at through a combat with the past." Race had not been a central concern in All the King's Men. Yet, amid the rapidly intensifying post–World War II pressures for racial reform in the South, the novel clearly could be read as a challenge to enlightened white southerners, Cable's heretofore "Silent" South, to step forward and accept responsibility for their region's history.[68]

Published originally in 1953, Warren's long poem Brother to Dragons again made acknowledging the past and one's responsibility for it the source of self-knowledge. Brother to Dragons was based on an actual incident in 1811 when Lilburne Lewis, a nephew of Thomas Jefferson, had brutally murdered and dismembered a slave. When a fictional Jefferson attempts to deny that Lilburne's atrocity was "possible even in the familial blood," he is accosted by the ghost of

Meriwether Lewis, Lilburne's cousin and Jefferson's kinsman as well, whom Jefferson had dispatched on the famed Lewis and Clark exploration of the Louisiana territory and later appointed territorial governor. Lewis had been driven to despair and ultimately to suicide by accusations of corruption while serving in that capacity, and with his head gaping from his self-inflicted wound, his spirit effectively tells Jefferson that he has been "murdered by your lie . . . that sent me forth in hope/To the wilderness—." Finally understanding that what Lilburne had done "in madness and exaltation," he simply had done in "vanity," Jefferson sounds like Jack Burden, acknowledging "that without the fact of the past, no matter/How terrible, we cannot dream the future." At the conclusion of the poem, the narrator, R. P. W., "a modern man," also evokes Burden as he pronounces himself "ready/To go into the world of action and liability."[69]

Ellison pointed to a "common element of personal confession" that made *Brother to Dragons* and Warren's next book, *Segregation: The Inner Conflict in the South*, seem like "two facets of a single work." In *Segregation*, Warren chronicled the traumatic and bitter "inner conflict" raging among white southerners as a group and within them as individuals. In a concluding interview "with myself," he affirmed his personal support for integration and suggested that the problem for southern whites was not learning to live with blacks but learning "to live with ourselves." If the white South could face up to "itself and its situation," he believed, it might achieve a certain "moral identity" sadly lacking in contemporary America and even provide a measure of leadership for the nation at large.[70]

Pursuing the central theme of his fiction and sounding much like his friend and colleague, C. Vann Woodward, Warren later suggested that a close inspection of their past might lead white southerners to discover heroic "ancestors who, were they alive, would not agree with the current heroes of Klan or [Citizens] Council, and would not be afraid to say so. That fact might even give the present-day Southerner the courage to say that he, too, disagrees. Discovering his past, the Southerner might find himself, and the courage to be himself."[71]

This was easier said than done, however, as Warren knew from personal experience. He admitted that when he had witnessed a white man beating a black teenager in Baton Rouge in 1939, he had initially been unable to act. Although he had finally moved to intervene after "a sudden access of shame," he had been "saved" by a bulky LSU football player who stopped the beating before Warren had to get involved. His problem, Warren explained, had not been "simple cowardice," but a "sudden, appalling sense of aloneness," a "paralyzing sense of being outside my own community."[72]

Such feelings of alienation were common among the southern white intellectuals who could no longer stomach the race-obsessed South of the 1950s and 1960s. As she fled her Mississippi home in 1955, with "parental abuse" ringing in her ears, Elizabeth Spencer realized "with a sick empty feeling there inside . . . *You don't belong down here anymore.*" Although Warren refused to apologize for being a southerner, after leaving LSU in 1942, he never again lived in the South. As he had headed down South to gather material for *Segregation*, he realized that "going back this time, like all other times was a necessary part of my life." Yet, as he turned north again, out of the South, he felt "the relief, the expanding vistas." This relief, he explained, is "the relief from responsibility . . . the flight from the reality you were born to." Slightly more than a decade later, another southern expatriate, Mississippi writer Willie Morris, confessed to similar feelings, asking in his memoir, *North toward Home*, "Why was it, in such moments just before I leave the South, did I always feel some easing of a great burden?"[73]

As Morris struggled with his feelings of regional and racial guilt, his friend and kindred spirit, Texan Larry L. King, came forth in 1971 with his own *Confessions of a White Racist*. Like Morris, King agonized over his own youthful insensitivity as well as the racial transgressions he had observed from his Texas childhood through his years as a congressional aide in Washington to his stint as a Nieman Fellow at Harvard. His evolving racial views estranged him from family and friends, but his time at Harvard ("that bastion of reason, that sunny intellectual garden in a mindless world of thorns," which he had presumed would be "the one place in America where racial bigotry was not visible") was, in some ways, even more traumatic. Racial animosities had flared often, even in Cambridge and among the Nieman Fellows, and he recalled a black visitor who asked, "God, . . . if Harvard professors and big time journalists are this goddamned bigoted, where's all the racial progress I read about in the *New York Times*?"[74]

King's disillusioning discovery of racism and hypocrisy alive and well in the ivy-draped environs of Harvard itself marked his book as a transitional work. One of the last examples of the "shame-and-guilt" indictments of region and self that had poured forth in a flood in the post–World War II years, it also foreshadowed the new challenges that southern white intellectuals of all sorts would confront as their region's problems and afflictions revealed themselves to be not just regional but national in scope.

8

No North, No South?

THE CRISIS OF SOUTHERN WHITE IDENTITY

As THE TWO COMMISERATED in 1965 about the white South's racial obsessions, Robert Penn Warren observed to Ralph Ellison that "A white Southerner feeling that his identity is involved may defend a lot of things in our package as being Southern, and one of those things is segregation." Ellison agreed and wished "that we could break this thing down so that it could be seen that desegregation isn't going to stop people from being Southern, that freedom for Negroes isn't going to destroy the main current of that way of life."[1]

The problem here, of course, was that so many white southerners had believed for so long that their racial system was in fact "the main current" of their "way of life." In 1861 Alexander Stephens had made dedication to white supremacy the cornerstone of Confederate distinctiveness, and seven years later Edward Pollard had cited the restoration of same as the key to regaining the Confederate cause. In the wake of Reconstruction, as Grace Elizabeth Hale observed, the ascendant culture of segregation had "made a new collective white identity across lines of gender and class and a new regional distinctiveness." By 1909 Edgar Gardner Murphy believed that southern politicians had created "an all absorbing autocracy of race" and "an absolute identification of the stronger race with the very being of the state." In 1928 historian U. B. Phillips had felt confident in concluding that for whites in the South the "common resolve, indomitably maintained," that the South "shall be and remain a white man's country" was both "the central theme of southern history" and "the cardinal test of a Southerner." On the eve of World War II, W. J. Cash had concurred that the regional and racial identities of white southerners were virtually indistinguishable, and twenty years later, observing the spectacle of rabid white resistance to integration in New Orleans, Walker Percy had realized that preserving "the 'Southern Way of Life'" actually meant "let's keep McDonough No. 6 segregated."[2]

In reality, segregation had become synonymous with southern identity not · only for those who defended the practice but for those who wanted to destroy it as well. As the veteran journalist Joseph B. Cumming, Jr., explained, most southern liberals of the civil rights era believed that "once segregation was lifted from the South as a burdensome dogma, then the South, for better or worse, would become Americanized." In fact, for a growing number of would-be reformers within the region, the need to destroy the Jim Crow system had actually become so urgent that questions of the overall fate of southern identity no longer seemed very important. Their emotional ties to southern people and places were still obvious enough, but they professed increasingly to welcome the destruction of this most problematic southern characteristic, even if it meant that the New South must, alas, give way to the No South. This seemed to be the sentiment of Arkansas journalist Harry S. Ashmore, who even penned an "Epitaph for Dixie" in 1957. For Ashmore, the South's peculiar identity derived primarily from its system of legalized racial segregation, which he saw beginning to crumble as the 1950s drew to a close, and despite the hastily erected legal and pseudo-legal barricades that characterized the era, he was confident that nothing could "turn back the forces that are reshaping the Southern region in the nation's image." Clearly welcoming this transformation, Ashmore insisted that "for better or worse, the South must now find its future in the national pattern."[3]

The architects of the original New South identity had not only promised to secure economic progress without sacrificing white supremacy, but they had also made segregation and disfranchisement a key element in their development strategy. In the wake of World War II, however, those who invoked the "New South" seemed to make little distinction between racial and economic change, and many saw the region's repressive and embarrassing Jim Crow system as a major impediment to its industrial progress. The stagnation that had descended on Ashmore's Little Rock in the wake of that city's integration crisis seemed to confirm this apprehension, and writing in 1960, economist William H. Nicholls warned that "the South can persist in its socially irresponsible doctrine of racism only at the ultimate cost of tearing its whole economy down."[4]

The race question, Nicholls believed, had "so shocked the Southern mind that it has been incapable of accepting social responsibility for the general welfare or of organizing common efforts for common benefit in other important directions as well." If the South's white leaders "could at last take . . . a fresh, honest and hardheaded look at the race problem, the gains which would accrue to the region would extend far beyond matters of race." On the other hand, Nicholls felt compelled to point out that if white southerners did choose "progress" over "tradition," then "many of those still strong qualities of mind and spirit which have made the South distinctive must largely disappear."[5]

In 1965 Mississippi's Frank E. Smith, a racial moderate who had essentially been gerrymandered out of his congressional seat, clearly spoke for many other members of the shame-and-guilt school of southern writing when he conceded that "in the mainstream of American life, much of the southern identity will be lost, but if 'Southern identity' is the price to be paid for removal of the racial scar which has been the mark of things southern, both the South and the country will have gained thereby." In a bold reiteration of George W. Cable's call for a wholly assimilated No South, Smith asked, "Why not plan and act on the principle that what is needed is not a New South but a South that is inextricably and indefinably a part of the United States?"[6]

Such a South had seemed a still-distant possibility in 1965, but a scant five years later, Joseph Cumming heard report after report of the relatively peaceful implementation of court-ordered busing across a region where segregation had been "defended as [a] sort of state religion, a 'way of life'" and concluded matter-of-factly that "the South is over. La commedia e finita!" For Cumming, the end of the South did not mean an end to its racial problems but rather that those problems were now simply no worse than, and even arguably not as bad as, those confronting a host of cities and communities above and beyond the Mason-Dixon line. Not everybody agreed with Cumming's assessment at the time, but twenty years later, Hodding Carter would base much of his argument for "the end of the South" on the reality that "segregation by law has been destroyed, and segregation is in fact no more peculiar to Jackson, Miss., than it is to Jackson, Mich."[7]

This turn of events was both noteworthy and ironic, because for most white southerners, the more than 150-year struggle to preserve white supremacy and to prevent any other meaningful alteration of the South's socioeconomic and political order as well had been waged not simply against abolitionists, the Union Army, Radical Republicans, civil rights marchers, or the federal government but against "the North." As Hale suggested, the postbellum association between southernness and "whiteness" had been "an identity to create and empower within an internal dynamic of white versus black and an external dialect of southern versus northern." Cash had clearly found it impossible in 1941 to separate southern whites' hostility to black progress from their feelings of anger and resentment toward the North. Four years later, Henry Miller concluded that the white South had "never recovered from its defeat at the hands of the North," and therefore it remained "solidly against the North in everything," waging "a hopeless fight, much like that of the Irish against England." Curtis Wilkie recalled that during his World War II–era childhood, he became aware not just of "Hitler, Tojo and Mussolini" but of "another more ancient enemy: Yankees. . . . Most of the South's hardships and indignities were blamed on Yankees." For Wilkie, "All Northerners were Yankees, and all Yankees were aliens, a threat to the Southern way of life. . . . This was not something taught in my home but learned by osmosis."[8]

When he was antagonized by a condescending Yankee, even the liberal humorist Roy Blount, Jr., was tempted to retort that the North was not "a place," but simply "a direction out of the South." In a similar but more serious vein, Faulkner's Charles Mallison also saw the North not as "a geographical place" so much as "an emotional idea, a condition of which he had fed from his mother's milk to be ever and constant on the alert not at all to fear and not actually anymore to hate but just—a little wearily sometimes and sometimes even with tongue in cheek—to defy."[9]

Spurning geographic coordinates, most white southerners saw what young Mallison called the "outland and circumscribing" North simply beginning wherever they believed that the South stopped, and therefore, effectively encompassing the rest of the nation. For John Egerton, "the North" consisted simply of "all of the non-Southern states," while for Curtis Wilkie, "Yankees meant anyone who lived north of Virginia." As a northern transplant to the region, Richard N. Current quickly discovered that in the minds of white southerners at large, "whether considered as a nation or as a notion, the North . . . consists of everything that is not southern. It is simply the rest of the country."[10]

Not only was the North every*where* the South was not, but in its relative affluence and presumed racial enlightenment, it had long seemed to be every*thing* the impoverished and backward South was not as well. As we know, the vision of the North as the essence of the nation and of the South as its antithesis had surfaced in the early national era and matured in the heat of antebellum sectional conflict. If the defeated southern states had emerged from the Civil War as a relatively cohesive "South," the triumphant North had simply affirmed its credentials as "America." After all, as early as the 1830s De Tocqueville had already seen the North providing "the common standard" for the entire nation. This had clearly been the goal of many influential Republicans who began their crusade to northernize the South before the Civil War and continued it through Reconstruction. In the wake of Reconstruction, Albion Tourgeé had described the North and the South as "two distinct, hostile and irreconcilable ideas," and though his experience in the South had taught him that it would not be "the work of a moment or a day," he was still clearly betting on the North when he predicted that "these two must always be in conflict until the one prevails and the other fails."[11]

In 1910 Harvard historian Albert Bushnell Hart observed that the North had long chosen "to consider itself the characteristic United States," while the South saw itself "set apart." In 1928 U. B. Phillips used a boatman's reference to the northern bank of the Ohio River (the unofficial boundary between North and South) as "the American shore" to suggest that the determination of white southerners to maintain white supremacy clearly distinguished their region from the rest of the country. Because "Americanizing" the aberrant South actually meant remaking it in the image of the North, most observers assumed that whenever Dixie finally met its demise as a distinctive region, the cause of death would be drowning in an American mainstream whose headwaters and currents were purely and exclusively northern in origin. Since the South's identity would have to be destroyed in order to save its soul, the healthier (read more "northernized") it became, the more frequently and fervently its obituaries were penned. A year before Ashmore's "Epitaph for Dixie," John T. Westbrook had already celebrated the "happy truth" that the South [had] lost its "regional integrity." Having grown "rich . . . , urban [and] industrialized," it was "no longer 'southern' but rather *northernized*, Europeanized, and cosmopolitan." [Emphasis added][12]

The white South's uncontrollable urge to self-obituarize actually became a steady source of supplementary income for a select squadron of the usual academic and journalistic suspects who convened with amazing frequency to deliver shamelessly recycled speeches at countless symposia dedicated to kissing southern distinctiveness good-bye one more time. This phenomenon had become so pronounced by 1972 that even as he proclaimed the South "over and done" and bade it "a final farewell" himself, Joseph Cumming noted that "the South seems to have an incurable impulse for bittersweet goodbyes to itself."[13]

However, even as the last rites were still being said in profusion for a South that had actually never looked better, it suddenly became apparent that the

North was no longer, and perhaps never had been, quite the picture of health it had always seemed. Both southern and northern liberals had presumed that the South could join the American mainstream only by emulating the North's racial model, but by the late 1960s angry and sometimes violent northern protests against open housing campaigns or school busing in the name of racial balance had made it all too apparent that white racism was hardly confined to white southerners. As Jack Kirby pointed out, the jarring television images of the South offered "by plump mothers abusing frightened little black children at school yards," suddenly gave way to the even more disconcerting spectacle "of plump Yankees behaving the same way." Likewise, George Wallace's impressive showings in presidential primaries well above the Mason-Dixon line led a veteran journalist to exclaim that Wallace had made a startling discovery: "they all hate black people. . . . They're all afraid, all of them. Great God! That's it! They're all Southern! The whole United States is *Southern!*" On other fronts, the military failure in Vietnam and the moral failure of Watergate also revealed some disturbing cracks in the North-derived American mystique of triumph and virtue. Southerners, as C. Vann Woodward had written in 1952, had long stood apart as the only Americans for whom history was not simply "something unpleasant that happens to other people." By the mid-1970s, however, history had clearly begun to catch up to the North as well.[14]

The South's long struggle to overtake the North economically was far from over, but by the 1970s the once dynamic northern Manufacturing Belt was suddenly hemorrhaging jobs as well as people with both flowing toward what Kevin Phillips described in 1969 as the warm, inviting "Sunbelt." Suddenly it seemed the process of regional convergence had become not just a story of southern progress but of northern decline as well. A *New York Times* report on one of the two "vanishing South" conferences held in 1972 concluded that "if a gathering . . . this week was any indication, Southern intellectuals have almost abandoned the North as a fit model for imitation in any field, from human rights to the building of cities."[15]

If anything, the North seemed to be imitating the South. As John Egerton observed in 1974: "Having failed for the first time to win at war, having found poverty and racism alive and menacing in its own house, the North has lately shown itself to be more and more like the South in the political, racial, social and religious inclinations of its collective majority." Woodward noted in 1965 that the South had long served the United States as "a moral lightning rod, a deflector of national guilt, a scapegoat for stricken conscience, much as the

Negro has served the white supremacist—as a floor under national self-esteem." In 1976 with Jimmy Carter's presidential campaign in full swing, Woodward offered a perceptive assessment of the reversal of regional fortunes that he had witnessed in the span of scarcely more than a decade. He pointed out that "northern cities burst into flame in the 1960s with insurrectionary violence surpassing any in the South" and that "it was northern schools that now had the most extreme segregation and displayed the most extreme reactions against integration." By the mid-1970s, Woodward observed, "passions had cooled on the racial front in the South," while "northern morale was further lowered by Vietnam and Watergate, devastating blows at the widely held myths of invincibility, success and innocence . . . myths [that] were never shared by the South anyway." The overall result, he noted, had been the " 'withering' of self-righteousness . . . along the Massachusetts-Michigan axis."[16]

Even liberal white southerners could not resist the temptation to revel in the astonishingly swift demise of their region's old tormentor and would-be conqueror, the omniscient, omnipotent, and omnipresent North. Although his 1971 memoir, *Confessions of a White Racist*, had been a self- and South-flagellating shame-and-guilt classic, a scant five years later Larry King was fairly bursting with tongue-in-cheek regional pride. Describing white southerners' reaction to Jimmy Carter's acceptance speech at the 1976 Democratic National Convention, King explained that "old Southern boys around the world, recognizing the nuances and shadings of home, lurched to their collective feet, spilling right smart amounts of bourbon and branch water over the rims of their gold goblets or jelly glasses, and with wet eyes blushingly proclaimed: 'We ain't *trash* no more.'"[17]

For King, Carter's anointment represented a victory for long-suffering white southerners over the "damnyankee peckerwoods" of the North who had been treating them like trash since "The War." King realized that Yankee disdain and derision would not go away, of course, "because y'all been conditioned to it just like the Russian's dawgs drooled at the ringing of bells." Having built up a good head of steam, he tweaked descendants of the old slave traders in Boston about the violence that had erupted around busing in that city. "Come on over here," King taunted for good measure, "and tell me about Bull Connor's police dogs and fire hoses in Birmingham, so I'll have a chance to drop it on you about the many race riots of 'Detroit City.'"[18]

It is worth noting that, from King's perspective, save for the symbolic importance of Carter's nomination, the South's triumph seemed not a matter of proving itself as good as the North, but of the North proving that it was no better than the South. Still, it seemed strange indeed that after nearly two hundred years of recurrent prophesies of the South's imminent death by northernization, southerners should be witness over the last quarter of the twentieth century to the decline, disintegration, and general demise of the North instead. It proved more striking still that without a starkly contrasting North to remind them constantly of what they were not and force them to defend and explain what they were, white southerners soon seemed hard-pressed to convince themselves, let alone others, that they remained distinct in any meaningful sense from other Americans.

Writing in 1971, Woodward had noted the long-standing "North-South polarity" and suggested that northerners and southerners had used each other "in the way Americans have historically used Europe—not only to define their identity and to say what they are *not*, but to escape in fantasy from what they *are*." In an insightful essay that appeared a year later, Sheldon Hackney seemed almost to echo W. J. Cash when he characterized the white South as a "counterculture" and described white southerners as "Americans who have taken on an additional identity through conflict with the North."[19]

More recently, James Peacock has noted the "oppositional" nature of southern identity and suggested that "it may not matter, even exist, until it is opposed." White southerners, Hackney observed, were "most likely to be most conscious of being southerners when they are defending their region against attack from outside forces," whether these took the form of abolitionists, the Union Army, carpetbaggers, civil rights activists, labor organizers, or "other by-products of modernity," such as fluoridation or daylight savings time, that had originated in or were associated with the North. Hackney's analysis points to some historic similarities between white southerners resisting northernization and cultural nationalists in other societies whose rejection of Westernization, or more accurately, Americanization, has also shaped their perceptions of themselves and their cultures.[20]

Southern whites had defined themselves not by their opposition to becoming more like the rest of America so much as by their refusal to accept the North as the emblem and arbiter of what that was supposed to mean. In 1972 John Shelton Reed's *The Enduring South* had identified a nasty little tangle of negative traits—such as provincialism, religious intolerance, and a proclivity for violence—as the cultural residue, by and large, of the white South's rabid

defense of segregation and its defiance of the North on a number of other
fronts as well. Reed noted that "if their culture serves Southerners, for better
or worse, in dealing with a hostile 'outside,' it will probably continue to serve
so long as the outside seems to be hostile." Still, he added prophetically, "The
traditional outside has been the North, and the occasion for sectional animos-
ity has usually been the South's racial institutions . . . : if the South's race relations improve or the North's deteriorate, white Southerners may yet realize
their ancient wish to be 'let alone.'"[21]

In scarcely more than a decade, all this had come to pass and then some.
When Reed updated *The Enduring South* in 1986, he found that "cultural
differences that were largely due to Southerners' lower incomes and educational levels, to their concentration in agricultural and low-level industrial
occupations—those differences already diminishing in the 1960s—were
smaller still in the 1980s," and a few had effectively "vanished altogether." Meanwhile, regional differences in tendencies toward localism and the acceptance
of violence were also converging. This convergence, however, was primarily
the result of the changes in non-southern attitudes that had emerged as the
late 1960s and 1970s confronted non-southerners with the unfamiliar experiences of frustration, embarrassment, and defeat. Thus, many northerners may
have taken on, as Reed put it, some of southerners' traditional "sense of the
intractability and perversity of the world," and the notion that it is "far safer to
be guarded in one's admiration and modest in one's expectations." (This might
help to explain why country music with its emphasis on human frailties and
limitations began to grow noticeably more popular throughout the nation
during the 1970s.) At the very least, the discovery and illumination of their
own racial and economic problems had rendered further finger pointing at
the South a risky business indeed for most northerners.[22]

Because of the South's long-standing role as "the binary opposite of the
North," Edward Ayers explained, the perceived disparities between the two had
been "transformed into traits that mark[ed] the very soul of the Southern
people." What then was the future of a distinctive southern identity now that
an overt defense of white supremacy was beyond the pale and empirically verifiable differences between white southerners and other Americans seemed so
drastically diminished?[23]

Actually, Reed had already suggested an answer to this question in *Southerners: The Social Psychology of Sectionalism* (1983). *Southerners* provided the
good news that economic progress, improvements in education, and the growing influence of the mass media had combined to erode the racism and

authoritarianism that had generally been associated with the most negative aspects of traditional southern white values. Reed appeared to abandon his old position entirely when he concluded, "Southernness as we have known it is almost over." Yet he made a crucial distinction between the familiar, rigidly traditionalist southern value orientation which (as he had already established) was in decline and a southern regional consciousness that he actually found on the rise, the latter boosted, ironically, by the same modernizing forces that seemed to be inflicting mortal wounds on southern traditionalism.[24]

Writing in 1956, C. Vann Woodward had described a rapidly urbanizing and industrializing South already caught up in a "Bulldozer Revolution," which he believed might well rob white southerners of "the very consciousness of a distinctive tradition along with the will to sustain it." In Reed's study, however, those most likely to identify themselves as southerners and to want others to see them that way as well were by and large the primary beneficiaries of the Bulldozer Revolution, the well-educated, well-read white urbanites who were also least likely to hold (or at least express openly) the racial, religious, and anti-intellectual values traditionally associated with southernness. This pattern seemed to hold throughout the 1990s as polls showed that a resident of the South who made more than $60,000 per year was nearly nine times more likely to retain his identification with the South than one who made less than $20,000.[25]

In other words, where Woodward had feared that it would render southern identity irrelevant, Reed found that, if anything, the Bulldozer Revolution had done just the opposite. By undermining some of the more negative traits commonly ascribed to white southerners, improvements in education and economic standing seemed simultaneously to make the more upwardly mobile among them seem less "southern" to others but much more aware of being southern themselves. Meanwhile, those whom economic progress had largely bypassed, the less affluent, less-educated whites, seemed less concerned about losing their regional identity, but more likely to cling to the prejudices and traditionalism that had so long defined that identity. Cash had linked southern white distinctiveness to resistance to change, and Woodward had also equated change with a loss of distinctiveness, but Reed crossed everybody up, suggesting that change might actually be sustaining southernness, or at least regional self-consciousness, among the better-educated, better-traveled, more-tolerant whites who were also those most committed to keeping a sense of southern identity alive.

Reed compared this group of white southerners to other American ethnic minorities who pull up short when they realize that their struggle for affluence and social acceptance may ultimately require them to sacrifice their cultural identities at the altar of assimilation. Hence, he contended, "it is those who are most modern in background and experience . . . who . . . are most likely to think in regional terms, to categorize themselves and others as 'Southerners and non-Southerners' and to believe that they know what that means." Upscale white southerners may have feared that their cherished fantasy of being "let alone" had been fulfilled at the expense of their regional identity, but it was by no means clear that they had retained a real sense of what southernness was all about after there was no more segregation to defend and no more North to defy.[26]

Writing in 1958, Woodward had warned that if "Southernism" became too closely associated with "a last ditch defense of segregation," it would be rejected by younger southerners. At the peak of the civil rights movement in 1965, he scoffed at the notion that because "the South's disputed 'distinctiveness' and Southern identity inhere essentially in retrograde racial policies and prejudices," destroying the region's repressive racial institutions would "cause southerners to lose their identity in a happily homogenized nation." In fact, both Woodward and David R. Goldfield went on to observe later that the civil rights movement had actually enabled southern whites to reconnect with their true identity by, as Woodward put it, moving "away from their [racial] obsessions and toward a recovery of their more genial culture." In reality, however, southern whites have found it no simple matter to reconstitute a kinder, gentler version of their identity from the rubble of the fortifications they had thrown up around the old Jim Crow system.[27]

In fact, the fundamentally negative and oppositional mind-set that had developed over nearly a century and a half of fighting to preserve white supremacy and repulse the forces of northernization in general had left southern whites ill prepared to construct a new, more affirmative identity for the post–North-South. The problem, as James McBride Dabbs posed it, was that "what a Southerner is and what he is supposed to do besides resist, nobody knows." Writing in the 1980s, Richard Current noted the continuing insistence of the proponents of southern distinctiveness on defining the South "in opposition to the North, even though there was no longer much of a contrast.

No North, no South. So one might predict," observed Current "but that would be to underestimate the power of the Southerners' imagination." In the long run, however, the process of reinventing their regional identity challenged even the fertile imaginations of white southerners. Once the "southern way of life" could no longer be grounded solely in segregation and white supremacy or fending off the meddlesome modernizing initiatives of the North in general, many white southerners were actually thrown into an identity crisis of sorts, and they began to search frantically for some tangible and demonstrative reaffirmation of their cultural distinctiveness.[28]

For many of them that search seemed to begin at the very end of the civil rights era with the cleverly commodified vision of southernness as it appeared in the comforting and aesthetically pleasing pages of *Southern Living* magazine. As the brainchild of the publishers of *The Progressive Farmer*, *Southern Living* both reflected and symbolized the emergence of an increasingly affluent white middle class and the shift of the region's white population from small town to suburb. In the February 1966 inaugural issue of *Southern Living*, editor-in-chief Eugene Butler explained that his magazine was aimed at "Southern and Southwestern urban and suburban families" in order to help them "live a more enjoyable life in the South by making better use of your growing incomes, your leisure and your mental and physical assets." Describing the South as a place "where emphasis is given to social, cultural, and recreational life," Butler promised that "month after month our new magazine will portray good Southern living ideas and qualities." As if to underscore this pledge, an advertisement next to Butler's piece offered a recipe for a "Frito Chili Pie," featuring Frito corn chips, canned chili, onions, and American cheese.[29]

Frito-chili pies were soon a thing of the past as *Southern Living*'s circulation skyrocketed to 500,000 by 1968 and 2.2 million by the early 1980s. By this time *Forbes* had already dubbed it the nation's most profitable magazine, and in 1985, ironically enough, it was gobbled up by New York–based Time, Inc. Adorning the coffee tables of at least one in four upper-middle-class white homes in the South, it became what Diane Roberts called "a cash cow for the media leviathan of corporate Yankeedom" because it had established itself, in John Shelton Reed's words, as "a sort of how-to-do-it manual in living the Southern good life." For example, the magazine informed new members of the region's "*haute bourgeois*" that snapdragons, okra, and butterbeans were out and azaleas—"always a feature of southern gardens"—and ham—"a traditional part of southern hospitality"—were in. Grits were still appropriate, though preferably only in casseroles laced with garlic and cheese. Moreover, it was now acceptable, even chic, to drink openly in social situations, provided, of course, one served or consumed only meticulously mixed Bloody Marys or top-shelf bourbons like Maker's Mark or "Gentleman Jack" (Daniel's).[30]

Nicholas Lemann observed that for affluent southern whites today, "the southern way of life" no longer means "white supremacy" but includes a list of essentials such as "the 'totally planned community' around a golf course, cheese grits and honey-baked ham at the pre-game brunch," and, of course, "a five-year subscription to *Southern Living*." Subscribers had every reason to feel good about their region, given the magazine's portrayal of it as what Sam Riley called "a relentlessly prosperous world of Derby Day brunches, cakes requiring twelve eggs, golf courses, and made-over gardens. . . .without memory of pellagra or racial unrest . . . .where none of the parents are divorced . . . burglary and street crime are unknown . . . few have Hatteras Yachts but one and all play golf and tennis at the club—and in the right outfits."[31]

Although the ease and affluence they represented were definitely contemporary, *Southern Living* offered more than a hint of the Old South romance, particularly in its "updated version of feminine graciousness à la Melanie Wilkes" and its more implicit portrayal of "self-assured, socially adept 'gentlemen' confidently surveying magnolia and crape myrtle from their piazzas, julep in hand." While the majority of the female devotees to *Southern Living* may have actually preferred Melanie to Scarlett, many of the males seemed disinclined to ape the wimpy and ineffectual Ashley Wilkes. Perhaps concerned that their Melanies might not tolerate a roguish Rhett Butler, many settled for simply becoming "bubbas." A common nickname that southern white girls applied to their younger brothers, "Bubba" became roughly synonymous with "good ol' boy," a drawling, disarming sort who actually thought much faster than he talked and was generally adept at seeming less competent or ambitious than he really was. In response to the burgeoning Bubba impulse, a new computer listserv called "Bubba-L" promised participants the opportunity to "swap anecdotes . . . discuss the proper plural of 'y'all, wax nostalgic about magnolias or most' all anything else that you feel like."[32]

The foregoing reference to "y'all" doubtless proved puzzling to native southerners who know quite well that "y'all" itself is plural, and it is employed in the singular only by those for whom it is a mere affectation. Seizing on the cultural resonance of this expression, the operators of "Southernness.com" called for the construction of a symbolic "Y'all Wall" along the Mason-Dixon line "to retard or halt the aggressive cultural globalization troops" who presumably planned to do to southern distinctiveness what Sherman did to Georgia. "Protest much," they admonished visitors to the web site, "Start a petition. Write a congressperson. Picket. Act now, y'all." Near the top of Southernness.com's list of "50 Ways Y'all Can Help Save the South" was a call to boycott any McDonald's restaurant that refused to use southern ingredients or inculcate southern-style manners among their employees.[33]

Quite coincidentally, of course, anyone who truly desired to save "the Southern life we love" was also urged to patronize a variety of establishments selling authentically southern products ranging from country ham to dog biscuits. Southernness.com's feature attraction, however, for those who wanted to be sure that they even smelled "southern" was "The Southern Fragrance Library," which included "Parfum Mist," the only world-class fragrance created to honor "The Southern Woman and her American South." This scent featured "alluring hyper-romantic floral with notes of jasmine and a base of amber" and customers were cautioned that it is "best worn by a woman beyond the early teen years." An even more compelling female fragrance was "Hidden Roses," which paid tribute to the "valiant Southern belles" who, as "union troops burned and ravaged grand Southern homes and gardens during the tragic days of the Civil War," managed to save "their cherished family roses." In addition to scents for babies, there was also "Southernness Gentleman 1768 Cologne," which "captures the great pleasures of the Southern out-of-doors . . . the classic fragrance with the celebrated Southern 'sense of place.'"[34]

Generally, the patrons of Southernness.com and Bubba-L were of the opinion that the newcomers flooding into the South from above the Mason-Dixon should opt to southernize themselves rather than persist in trying to northernize their new neighbors. (A popular bumper sticker even admonished, "We don't care how you did it in Ohio!") Sensing a niche market, southern booksellers soon served up a cornucopia of cutesy, one-sentence-per-page mini-books bearing titles such as *The Southerner's Instruction Book* and containing patently contrived pseudo-southernisms such as "Never drink the last diet Coke" and, worse yet, "Learn to say 'y'all' without feeling self-conscious."[35]

Transplanted Yankees who refused to assimilate were a pet peeve of Georgia-born humorist and thoroughly bourgeois "Bubba," Lewis Grizzard, who advised those who complained about the South's shortcomings relative to their former surroundings that "Delta is ready when you are." Conservative, and sometimes reactionary, Grizzard epitomized the ambivalence of many white southerners who have embraced the economic and material benefits that have come their way while remaining skeptical and sometimes resentful of some of the social and political changes that have accompanied these gains. He often celebrated the "rat killings" and other "redneck traditions" he had enjoyed as a youth, but the grown-up Grizzard was an excellent fit for John Shelton Reed's model of the regionally conscious, upwardly mobile white southerner.

Grizzard's small-town boyhood and adolescence in tiny Moreland, Georgia, provided him with a huge repertoire of stories about local characters, and his candid country-boy perspective shaped his reaction to all of his personal experiences as he became a national and international celebrity. In a hilarious story entitled "There Ain't No Toilet Paper in Russia," he described Peter the Great's palace as "fifteen times bigger than Opryland." Grizzard also confessed to having twice seen Pavarotti live—once in Paris and once in London—to having sat through at least the first act of "the Marriage of Figaro," and to visiting the Louvre. To compound matters, he owned two pairs of Gucci's, wore Geoffrey Beene cologne, and used the gun rack behind the seat of his truck to hold his golf clubs. Yet, although he had eaten caviar at Maxim's in Paris, Grizzard insisted that he liked pork barbecue much better.[36]

Some white males who found even the Bubba persona a bit too tame for their tastes actually began to identify themselves as "rednecks," a term historically synonymous with rural, lower-class whites who were aggressively ignorant, uncouth, and lawless and showed no particular ambition to be otherwise. During the civil rights era, "redneck" had become the nation's most acceptable ethnic slur, connoting the kind of southern white males who lynched blacks, slept with their sisters, and married their cousins. When they needed to unwind, rednecks generally ripped around in their gun-racked, jacked-up pickups, dipping snuff, chucking their empty beer cans out the window, and playing country music loud enough to wake the dead and deafen the living.

As the 1970s unfolded, however, in some circles at least, redneck ceased to be a term of opprobrium and began to convey a fierce and even admirable resistance to American mass society's insistence on conformity. In country music, for example, Johnny Russell's 1973 hit "Rednecks, White Socks, and Blue Ribbon Beer" ("We don't fit in with that white collar crowd, We're a little too noisy, a little too loud") opened the floodgates for Jerry Jeff Walker's "Redneck Mother" and David Allen Coe's "Long-Haired Redneck." Finally, even country music legend George Jones got into the act with his 1993 hit "High-Tech Redneck" and his subsequent "High-Tech Redneck Tour."[37]

As Jack Kirby explained, the appeal of the rednecks portrayed in these songs was strikingly "countercultural." Where middle- and upper-class white southerners once sought to distance themselves from their incorrigible white inferiors, in many cases their attitudes toward rednecks had now become not only less disdainful but downright envious. Asked by an astonishingly clueless V. S. Naipaul if rednecks were actually descendants of pioneers, a successful Mississippi businessman eagerly responded, "There's no question about it. They're descendants of pioneers. They're satisfied to live in those mobile homes. . . . They don't want to go to the damn country club and play golf. They ain't got fifteen damn cents, and they're just tickled to death. They don't like being told what to do. It's the independent spirit." Confessing the obvious, he added, "You know, I like those rednecks. They're so laid back. They don't give a shit."[38]

Explaining why white southerners were embracing a stereotype they had once so bitterly resented, sociologist Richard Peterson pointed out that "to call oneself a redneck is not so much to *be* a redneck by birth or occupational fate, but rather to identify with an anti-bourgeois attitude and lifestyle." This seemed to be the aim of a popular sweatshirt that not only identified its wearer as "Absolutely Proud to Be a Redneck" but explained, somewhat expansively for a sweatshirt: "This extremely proud group of Americans takes great pride in their laid back rural lifestyle. Dressed up in their baseball caps, flannels and bibs they cruise the dirt roads in their pickup trucks searching for a hoot 'n and holler'n good time down at the local water'n hole!" For a time at least, that watering hole might even have served "Redneck," a beer that promised "the Taste of America" and defined rednecks as "Good ol' boys n' gals who love cold beer, hot romance, fast cars, slow dancin', Bar-B-Q, long kisses, country music, pick-up trucks, good fishin', America, mom, apple pie and are proud to defend any of 'em." In addition to sweatshirts, beer, and bumper stickers, there was the "Redneck Briefcase," consisting of a pair of underwear with handles attached. "Redneck Pride" was the theme of Clemson, South Carolina's "Spittono" festival, which offered tobacco-spitting and beer-chugging contests that were in sharp contrast to Charleston's refined and sedate "Spoleto" arts festival.[39]

Meanwhile, young white southerners, especially collegians, embraced a host of "redneck chic" musical groups such as the Austin Lounge Lizards, whose gospel offering "Jesus Loves Me (But He Can't Stand You)" became an instant classic. In the music mecca of Athens, Georgia, there was Redneck Greece Deluxe, whose "Don't Let Another Penis Come Between Us" was a real crowd pleaser, but the hottest such group was clearly the aptly named Southern

Culture on the Skids, a Chapel Hill–based group that specialized in defiant, poor-but-proud anthems such as "Liquored Up and Lacquered Down" and "My House Has Wheels on It."[40]

If the foregoing evidence of newfound and widespread respectability for rednecks was not overpowering enough, there was the phenomenal success of comedian Jeff Foxworthy, who turned a long list of one-liners ("You may be a redneck if you've ever been too drunk to fish . . . you've ever worn camouflage pants to church, etc.") into a series of hot-selling comedy albums and network television series on both the ABC and NBC television networks. The broad national appeal of Foxworthy's redneck persona, like that of television shows such as *Roseanne* (featuring an amiably dysfunctional working-class family of confirmed ne'er do-wells), illustrated the likely outcome whenever mass marketers succeeded so well in commodifying an alternative, nonconformist countercultural lifestyle that it ceases to be any of the above.

Surely those white southerners most accurately described by the term "redneck" could take some heart in the radical overhaul of their image. On the other hand, it was obvious that many who were enthusiastically buying (both figuratively and literally) into the redneck craze were really the solidly middle-class folks who manicured the lawns and mangled the fairways of southern suburbia. There was no perceptible backlash, for example, when Foxworthy announced in 1995 that he was relocating from Beverly Hills to his native Atlanta, where he would move to a pretentious-sounding subdivision known as the "Country Club of the South." Elsewhere, Redneck Beer was the brainchild of Benson J. Fischer, a Washington, D.C., real estate broker who was also a co-founder of the "Yummy Yogurt" chain. Although touted as a moderately priced beer, Redneck was most readily found among the imports and designer beers at stores catering to those whose taste buds craved something a bit more up-scale than Milwaukee's Best, Busch, or the other bargain brews typically consumed by lower-income, working-class whites. Such evidence merely confirmed the growing perception that, having at last acquired the resources for full-scale participation in the national consumer culture, upwardly mobile southern whites were not only able but eager to consume their own regional identity as rapidly as commercial marketers could commodify it.[41]

The South's academic entrepreneurs were by no means reluctant to market southern identity as well. Veteran journalist Edwin M. Yoder, Jr., seemed to wax almost nostalgic in 1983 when he recalled that "the late 1950s and early 1960s—when so much of national importance was happening in and to the South—assured a cresting of interest in what it was like to be southern. We southerners were studied hard, everywhere, like savages brought in from a newly discovered continent in the Elizabethan Age." Twenty years later, however, Yoder sensed that in the nation at large the old fascination with what made white southerners tick had given way to "a mood of boredom and impatience" with "southern regionalism."[42]

Yoder may have been correct in his assessment of national attitudes, but despite—or, more likely, because of—growing statistical and anecdotal evidence of the South's assimilation into the American mainstream, interest in southern cultural identity soared on southern university campuses in the 1980s and 1990s. As one journalist noted, "Institutes, centers and programs for the study of the South are becoming as ubiquitous on Southern campuses as Wal-Marts are in Southern suburbia." Eric Bates of *Southern Exposure* magazine agreed that fascination with things southern is "the biggest craze since miniature golf."[43]

Fittingly enough, the leader among southern universities in this area was the University of Mississippi, which had established the Center for the Study of Southern Culture in 1979. By the 1990s Ole Miss had become what Peter Applebome called "Bubba Central," offering both undergraduate and graduate degrees in southern studies. The program's curriculum featured courses running the gamut from the predictable offerings in history and literature to those in music, art, folklore, and politics. Ole Miss may have been a leader in the study of southern culture, but it was hardly alone. The University of North Carolina at Chapel Hill had its Center for the Study of the American South and its ambitious journal *Southern Cultures*. At the University of Alabama, there was the Center for Southern History and Culture, while the University of South Carolina boasted the Institute for Southern Studies. Other schools offered Appalachian studies centers, and still others those focusing only on a particular state such as the Center for Arkansas Studies at the University of Arkansas at Little Rock.[44]

The southern studies boom on Dixie campuses reflected the concerns of many white southerners in the post–civil rights Sunbelt era who responded to the prospect of cultural homogenization by reasserting their regional identities and immersing themselves in what they saw as the South's culturally distinctive attributes. In fact, by the 1990s southern academics were also heavily involved in encouraging a greater popular appreciation of the richness and distinctiveness of southern culture. In 1989 the University of North Carolina Press published the *Encyclopedia of Southern Culture*. A valuable scholarly resource prepared at the University of Mississippi's Center for the Study of Southern Culture, the *Encyclopedia* pulled no punches in its depictions of racism, violence, and other darker aspects of the region's persona. Yet, it also seemed, in a sense, as one pundit described it, like "the intellectual equivalent of *Southern Living*." Though the massive volume appeared to great national and international fanfare and soon boasted sales totals well in excess of 100,000, the majority of these were to white southerners for whom it served as a sort of bible for the converted, an ideal coffee-table tome for those desiring to reaffirm their faith and be born again—perhaps in good Baptist fashion, again and again—in their own southernness.[45]

John Shelton Reed has suggested that for a southerner, reading the *Encyclopedia* might well be the "cultural equivalent of having your life pass before you as you're drowning—drowning in this case, in the American mainstream." Reed found it difficult to escape the "elegiac tone" and "sense of the old ways slipping away" that pervaded many of the *Encyclopedia*'s entries. In the foreword Alex Haley sketched a vivid portrait of a bygone South with "those elder southern men who 'jest set' on their favored chair or bench for hours" and "the elderly ladies, their hands deeply wrinkled from decades of quilting, canning, washing collective tons of clothing in black cast-iron pots." For Haley the *Encyclopedia of Southern Culture* was "the answer to a deep need that we resuscitate and keep alive and fresh the memories of those who are now bones and dust."[46]

By way of comparison, some observers have detected a similarly elegiac quality in another contemporary encyclopedic effort, *Les Lieux de memoire*, a massive seven-volume work, edited by Pierre Nora, aimed at exploring "France's memory of itself." Although the project was ostensibly a work of objective, scientific history, Nora seemed to suffer from what a critic called "nostalgie de Coeur, " and he even confessed to an overwhelming "sense that everything is over and done with, something long since begun is now complete." Like many of the contributors to the southern culture volume, a number of the essayists in *Les Lieux de memoire* clearly felt a strong attachment to a France beset by declining prestige, economic problems, internal dissent, and the perceived threat of American cultural imperialism. In this sense, as David Bell observed, the multivolume compendium was "something of a historical document itself," because it testified to "the present-day crisis in French national identity" in much the same way that the *Encyclopedia of Southern Culture* attested to the identity anxiety that gripped white southerners.[47]

The faster the region changed, it seemed, the more frenetic the effort to turn its identity into something permanent and immutable. In the wake of the *Encyclopedia of Southern Culture*, the Center for the Study of Southern Culture continued its effort to tap into the southern identity market with its *Southern Culture Catalog*, which sported a possum on its cover and listed a variety of items running the gamut from zydeco recordings to praying pigs videos. All of this seemed harmless enough to those who deemed it a high time to focus on some of the lighter, more lovable aspects of southern life. Yet, there was nonetheless a concern among some scholars that the "selling of southern culture" to a popular audience might be getting a bit out of hand. The Center for the Study of Southern Culture, for example, organized cruises down the Mississippi on the Delta Queen, featuring lectures and musical performances showcasing southern culture in an airy and upbeat fashion. Critics of such activities worried that blunt truth-telling and hard-nosed analysis of the South's past and present is giving way to a sort of "Hollywood" effect that leaves lynching, rape, and racial, sexual, and class exploitation on the cutting room floor while popular audiences are left to gorge themselves, as one journalist put it, on "big houses, Brunswick stew and banjo pickers."[48]

In August 1995, two days after the conclusion of its twenty-second annual conference on William Faulkner (which was itself marketed heavily to Faulkner aficionados outside the academic community), the University of Mississippi hosted the first "International Conference on Elvis Presley," whom Center for the Study of Southern Culture director William Ferris hailed as "the most important pop-culture figure of the twentieth century" and "a true modernist who eluded definitions like white or black, male or female." The other moving force behind the conference, English professor Vernon Chadwick, actually taught a course comparing some of the works of Herman Melville to some of the films of Elvis Presley, a course that students quickly dubbed "Melvis." The conference offered numerous surprises and innovations, including a performance by "El Vez," the "Mexican Elvis" (accompanied by his "Memphis Mariachis and the Beautiful Elvettes"), and a revelation by clergyman and folk artist Reverend Howard Finster (whose creations often featured a representation of Elvis) that he had once had a visitation from the dearly departed "King of Rock and Roll": "Several years after he died, Elvis Presley came to visit me in my garden. . . . I said, 'Elvis can you stay?' He said, 'Howard, I'm on a tight schedule,' and then he was gone."[49]

Of the estimated 200 or so in attendance at the conference, more than 100 were journalists, who at times gave the meeting the air of a "media circus." Undeterred by the criticism heaped on them for the nontraditional nature of their endeavors, conference organizers announced that the theme of next year's conference would be "Then Sings My Soul: Elvis and the Sacred South." Plans for that gathering included an all-night gospel sing and a concert by self-described "atomic-powered lesbian" "Elvis Herselvis," who with "the Straight White Males," was described as "one of the hottest new acts on the West Coast club scene."[50]

The controversy surrounding the first Elvis conference and the potential for more controversy over the second one led officials at both the Presley estate at Graceland in Memphis and the Tupelo, Mississippi, Convention and Visitors Bureau (Tupelo is Elvis's birthplace) to withdraw their support for the second meeting. Objecting to the inclusion of "quirky elements designed to get publicity," a Graceland spokesman complained that "by the time the media disseminates the information into sound bites and video bites, it looks like a freak show down there. . . . We're not comfortable being associated with it." No doubt reacting to these developments, Ole Miss provost Gerald Walton issued a memo shortly before the second conference announcing that the school would not host the affair in 1997, because "the university could spend its money and time and energy in more rewarding ways." The *Oxford Eagle*'s headlines on July 30, 1996, summed up developments succinctly but grimly: "Ole Miss Kills Elvis."[51]

The homicidal metaphors continued to fly when William Ferris lamented Elvisologist Vernon Chadwick's failure to receive tenure at Ole Miss, insisting that Chadwick had been "sacrificed on the cross of Elvis." The crucified Chadwick was soon resurrected, however, resurfacing in Memphis, where he continued to organize an annual conference on Elvis. The 1998 meeting was titled "Are You Lonesome Tonight? Elvis and the Dysfunctional Family" and featured speakers addressing topics such as "Elvis and Substance Abuse: Was It Inevitable?," "Redneck Diaspora: Surfing the South with Elvis," and "Philanthropy, Bipolarity, and Christmas at Graceland." "I like to call Elvis the canary in the mineshaft of the New South," explained Chadwick, who insisted that "Elvis can be a master key for the understanding of Southern culture" and maintained that not even William Faulkner could "tell you as much about the end of the twentieth century as Elvis can."[52]

As early as 1964, in a review of yet another volume produced by the era's countless symposia on the South's loss of distinctiveness, Edwin Yoder had evoked an image of cultural masturbation when he observed that as it became "increasingly homogenized with Main Street, U.S.A., Dixie gropes for and fondles its fading distinctions." Twenty years later, Yoder worried that what he now called the "southernizing enterprise" or "the Dixiefication of Dixie" had very nearly degenerated into little more than "obscurantism and self-caricature." No group of white southerners seemed to fit this description better than the members of the Southern League, which was organized in 1994 and eventually became the League of the South after baseball's Southern League threatened to sue rather than share its name. Dedicated to the defense of "the unique social, cultural and religious traditions of the Southern people," League spokesmen even touted the notion of giving secession another whirl and a bumper sticker urging, "If at first you don't secede, try, try again" seemed to carry their group's unofficial motto. The League's rhetoric was more than a little suggestive of the Nashville Agrarians, especially its pledge to prevent (presumably white) southern identity from disappearing under "the rising tide of secularization and crass commercialism that permeates contemporary Western culture and that works to undermine all of the institutions that are essential to a civil society."[53]

Not surprisingly, a key element of the league's strategy to revive a southern nationalist mentality was an effort to reenergize the old sense of grievance toward the arrogant and intrusive North. Materials on its web site condemned "Yankee-defined archetypes" of southerners, and league stalwarts even shunned the postal zip code that was actually "the Yankee occupation code." Revealing similar anti-northern sentiments, one neo-Confederate identified what he saw as the deplorable conditions in contemporary American society as "the fruit of Northern victory," insisting that "if something's fucked up, the North did it, not us." Tony Horwitz concluded in *Confederates in the Attic* that many white southerners who seemed to still be fighting the Civil War believed "it was the North—or Northern stereotypes—that still shadowed the South and kept the region down."[54]

Hoping to save future generations of white southerners from "cultural genocide," in 1996 the League of the South began an annual summer institute for high schoolers and collegians in order to inculcate in them a sense of regional pride and to "rectify among Southerners and others the one-sidedness of the Northern public-school view of Southern history." League officials conceded that most white southerners were probably more interested in a new bass boat than a new southern nation, but they dedicated themselves nonetheless to reminding "the Southern people . . . that they are a distinct people with a language, mores, and folkways that separate them from the rest of the world."[55]

The need for white southerners to reconfigure the identity of the post-North South affirmed that not only do identity groups tend to define themselves largely in contrast to other identity groups but when these contrasts begin to fade, as Anthony P. Cohen put it, these groups "exaggerate themselves and each other" and "write large" the "symbols" that "by their very nature . . . express contrast and distinction." Thus, no longer able or willing to defend the racial system that had once defined "the southern way of life" for them and many others, white southerners were caught up in what Freud might have called "the narcissism of small differences" as the demise of the idealized North as a steady source of "contrast and distinction" heightened their fears of cultural anonymity.[56]

Not everyone who lived in the region clearly preferred southernness to cultural anonymity, however. No white southerners displayed more ambivalence about their cultural identities than the movers and shakers of Atlanta. This much was glaringly apparent in the selection of "Whatizit," a computer-generated and wholly unendearing blue blob, as the official mascot of the Atlanta-based 1996 Olympic games. Described by one commentator as "a bad marriage of the Pillsbury doughboy and the ugliest California Raisin," Whatizit, a.k.a., "Izzy," met with "international derision," and among the locals the reception was even less cordial. Stunned proponents of the nondescript Izzy insisted that he or she (at birth the politically correct mascot was also "genderless") would grow on folks, but many in the multitude of detractors objected to Izzy primarily because his/her regionally neutral nerdiness seemed to reflect a desire to minimize public association of the Olympic host city with the South. Said one critic, "I don't get where he's coming from. I don't really see how it represents anything specific to Atlanta, to the South—the country, even. It ought to stand for something." Columnist Marilyn Geewax, a northern transplant to Atlanta, seemed to agree, noting that Atlanta was about to squander "a once-in-a-century opportunity to help reshape the image of the entire region."[57]

Atlanta's aspirations to regional anonymity had also surfaced during the effort to select a new slogan for the city before the Olympics came to town. The search produced a flood of suggestions from the Henry Gradyesque "Atlanta: From Ashes to Axis" to the more candid but less inspiring "Atlanta: Not Bad for Georgia" to the also accurate but decidedly unpoetic "Watch Atlanta Transmogrify." Many feared that this search for a slogan was likely to culminate in the verbal equivalent of the insipid Izzy, and the eventual winner,

"Atlanta: Come Celebrate Our Dream," was so slick, upbeat, and predictably generic that cynical observers suggested replacing it with "Atlanta: It's 'Atnalta' Spelled Backwards" or "Atlanta: Where the South Stops."[58]

The perception that many Atlantans would just as soon forget their geographic whereabouts even cost a local disk jockey his job in 2002, when his accent was deemed "too country" even for a country music station. "Moby," who had been a fixture in local radio for eleven years, was terminated, the station manager reportedly explained, because Moby's accent "didn't reflect the average Atlanta day." Regardless of whether, as one critic fumed, contemporary Atlanta actually represented "what a quarter million Confederate soldiers died to prevent," the city that had entered the twentieth century as a popular symbol of the dynamic but still familiar and distinctively "southern" New South departed it as a foreboding metaphor for what many feared was a rapidly northernizing, alien, and anonymous No South.[59]

9

"Successful, Optimistic, Prosperous, and Bland"

TELLING ABOUT THE NO SOUTH

As FRED HOBSON POINTED OUT, "Faulkner and the great fiction writers of the [Southern] Renaissance had written . . . with the assumption that the South was defeated, guilt-ridden, backward-looking, and tragic: much of the power of their fiction came from that assumption." Such a South had seemed very much alive (if not well) during the first two decades after World II as battalions of hostile whites rallied to the Citizen's Council, the Ku Klux Klan, and other less organized but no less menacing efforts to repulse northern "outside agitators" bent on destroying the "southern way of life." As the smoke from this battle began to clear, however, events and trends of the late 1960s and early 1970s signaled not only the decline of the economically and morally superior North, but the rise of a "suddenly virtuous" South, more intent on healing its wounds than picking at them, bustling with growth and brimming with hope rather than hatred. In the wake of this astonishing reversal of regional fortunes, instead of a society that had long seemed peculiarly and intractably "poor, violent, pessimistic, tragic, and mysterious," southern writers now confronted an abruptly transformed region that was "successful, optimistic, prosperous, and bland."[1]

The tendency to apologize for one's southernness "had become almost a regional personality trait, a distinctive manner of speech, of gesture, a habit of mind," C. Vann Woodward reflected in 1976. Now that "the incubus of the regional inferiority complex" had been removed, "a new personality" had emerged and, Woodward observed, "a welcome change it is if it can retain the humility without the inferiority." The absolute embodiment of this new southern "personality" seemed to be Democratic presidential nominee Jimmy Carter. Quietly confident but almost ostentatiously humble, deeply religious but free of the racial and ideological intolerance that had long constrained white southerners in national politics, the energetic, disciplined Carter was less like a stereotypical white southerner than what one biographer called a "Yankee from Georgia." Thus, he seemed an altogether appropriate personification of a nation finally poised for reunion a century after Reconstruction had expired.[2]

George B. Tindall had prophesied in 1973 that "reincarnated as the imperial Sun Belt," the South was "about to assume a new role—as arbiter of the national destiny," and Carter's candidacy inspired novelist Walker Percy to observe that "the North saved the union the first time" and to confess to being "slightly optimistic that the South will save it a second time." Vanderbilt University chancellor Alexander Heard went even further, predicting that the "third century of American independence" would be "distinguished by a South that would throw off the shackles of its inheritance" and become "a major locus of the nation's economic, social, and cultural strength." Many Americans now seemed eager to believe that southerners could show, as Paul Gaston put it, "how men may live harmoniously in a complex interracial, urban society." The region that had once been such a big part of the national problem now seemed poised to provide the solution, reincarnated as what Joseph Cumming called a "Good South" baptized by blood and fire, and ready to show a humbled North the way to simpler, more peaceful times.[3]

Amid such expressions of hope that the ascendant South might somehow help the dazed and confused North to recover its sense of direction and self-esteem, a larger, more-attractive-than-life vision of Dixie quickly took shape. *Saturday Review* marked the North's displacement as the embodiment of the national myth by proclaiming that the South, whose credentials as a legitimate part of America at all had so long been suspect, had not only been "accepted into the fraternity of states" but "its cities, its progressive leaders, and its vigor may well posture it as a foretaste of the New America."[4]

The not just economically vibrant but racially cleansed and thoroughly Americanized "No South" was apparently at hand in the mid-1970s, and the popular press bubbled over with an enthusiasm for sectional reunion not seen since the age of Henry Grady. Economic analysts now gleefully described what had once been the darkest and most dismal corner of the national economy as the brightest and most promising, and the *New York Times* gushed in 1976 that every southern city had its share of "transplanted Yankees" who had not only adopted the southern drawl but the region's favorite alcoholic concoction, "bourbon mixed with Coca-Cola." Meanwhile, native southerners had developed a taste for Scotch and were trying their luck at skiing on snow as well as water.[5]

Even Nashville got in on the act. In 1974 Tanya Tucker recorded a popular version of Bobby Braddock's "I Believe the South Is Gonna Rise Again (And Not the Way We Thought It Would Back Then)," a song reminiscent of the *New York Times* in its celebration of "sons and daughters of sharecroppers drinking Scotch and making business deals." Instead of sectional and racial differences, Braddock's tune stressed "brotherhood" and suggested that the South should simply "forget the bad and keep the good."[6]

Two years later, *Time* offered a notably upbeat report about the "reverse migration" of blacks to the South. The article was laced with testimonials from returnees who praised the region's relaxed pace of life and professed to feel more comfortable there than in the North, whose coldness and impersonality had helped to drive them back "home." In words that seemed reminiscent of Grady but with a meaning that clearly was not, one vowed, "The South is going to rise again, and I intend to be part of it." Much of the national media celebration of the South's resurrection focused on race, politics, or economics, but journalists also took a look at intangibles, such as southerners' historic insistence that "their region is kindlier, lovelier, and more conducive to the good life than any other patch of earth this side of paradise." Southerners displayed "an almost tactile empathy with the land," an intense "attachment to community" and an unfailing instinct for the "good manners" that were "a habit often neglected elsewhere in the U.S."[7]

As the foregoing suggests, not only did the nation elect a southern president, but many Americans also seemed to embrace the region's culture and mores during the decade. Country music achieved the long-sought crossover into the pop market so often that, for a while at least, Luckenbach, Texas, seemed almost as fascinating as New York, New York. And for an equally brief moment, Jimmy Carter appeared to represent a grown-up John-Boy Walton, whose television family challenged the disturbing poor-white portraiture of Erskine Caldwell by offering what Jack Kirby called "a small tractable world where place, people, and extended family ties are real."[8]

In addition to the question of how to explain this suddenly not just risen but redemptive South, southern writers also faced the question of why and for whom it should be explained. Certainly, with the North's long run as the essence of the American ideal apparently at an end, those outside the South were clearly in no position to demand any further explanations of southerners. The

North-South dynamic of conflict and tension had helped to shape the identities of generations of white southerners at large, but for the region's white writers the critical, condescending, and both despised and envied North had been even more vital, an alternately intimidating and energizing omnipresence that, as Louis Rubin noted, they had felt "all their lives."[9]

Eudora Welty recalled from her childhood the long drives to visit her parents' families in Ohio and West Virginia and remembered especially "crossing a line you couldn't see but knew was there, between the South and the North—you could draw a breath and feel the difference." Although he had done it many times, whenever Thomas Wolfe's George Webber entered the North, he invariably felt "a geographic division of spirit . . . a certain tightening in the throat . . . a feeling sharp and physical as hunger, deep and tightening as fear." William Faulkner revealed his lifelong perception of the North through his young character Charles Mallison's "childhood's picture" of a North lacking precise boundaries or coordinates but brimming with incredulous residents looking down on him and his from "their own rich teeming never-ravaged land" with an "almost helpless capacity and eagerness to believe anything about the South not even provided it be derogatory but merely bizarre enough and strange enough."[10]

This intensely curious, instinctively critical North had virtually demanded that southern white intellectuals, as Faulkner's Shreve McCannon put it, "tell about the South." Hobson concluded that the white southern writer's "rage to explain" had been stoked by the need to respond to "an enemy across the line issuing an indictment that had to be answered," but in the post-North era white writers were now compelled "neither to defend nor to attack the South with passion and intensity." "The old enemy is no longer there," Walker Percy observed in 1979, "or if he is, he is too busy with his own troubles. There is no one throwing punches and no one to counter punch. . . . [I]t does not now occur to the serious writer in the North to 'attack' the South or to a serious southern writer to defend the South."[11]

"Now that the virtues and faults of the South are the virtues and faults of the nation, no more and no less," Percy suggested, "the peculiar isolation and disabilities under which the South labored for so long and which served some southern writers so well . . . are . . . things of the past." In the absence of a critical and antagonistic North, southern white writers could no longer draw on what Hobson called the "acute self-consciousness" and the "intense awareness of *being* southern, as well as [their] preoccupation with old theories, old settings and truisms" that had long been central to their literary tradition. By way of illustration, Percy suggested an intriguing analogy between the South's contemporary white writers and a man who has suffered so long from a constant toothache that he has actually come to enjoy the pain in much the same fashion as "one probes an aching tooth with one's tongue." Upon discovering that his toothache is suddenly gone, after a brief period of exultation, the man finds that without the pain he has lost his sense of focus and fulfillment.[12]

No southern writer better illustrated Percy's point than Willie Morris, whose autobiographical *North toward Home* was, in Hobson's view, one of the last great works in the Faulknerian "love-hate" tradition in which the writer must "probe deeply and painfully his relationship to his homeland." Few southern writers of any era ever explored their relationships with the South more personally and painfully than Morris. However, unlike Faulkner and his contemporaries, writing in the post–Jim Crow era, he was driven less to tell about the South than to tell about himself as a southerner. Morris's writing about the South may be accurately described as "nostalgic," but not in the contemporary sense of nostalgia as a means of escaping the trials of the present by retreating into pleasurable recollections of the past. In fact, he was addicted to the past less as a source of painkillers than as a source of pain itself. Like the man pining for his lost toothache, he embraced nostalgia as the damaging, potentially destructive propensity for emotional self-flagellation that it was understood to be as far back as the seventeenth century, and it became, for him, a painful but necessary and even inspirational presence in his life as well as his work.

In *North toward Home* Morris revealed both the pain of his alienation as an adult from the brutal racism of his home state and his enduring guilt over his own cruelty to blacks as a youth in Yazoo City, Mississippi. He had hidden in ambush at age twelve and attacked a small black child toddling along behind his sister, and he recalled "for a while, I was happy with this act, and my head was strangely light and giddy. Then later, the more I thought about it coldly, I could hardly bear my secret shame." As he grew older, he had joined his adolescent peers in cruelly taunting and tricking black adults, cheerily participating in stunts such as driving close by black people seated on a concrete banister at the bus station and opening the car door, toppling them "backward off the banister like dominoes." Despite such behavior, he had taken it for granted that "even Negro adults I encountered alone and had never seen before would treat me with generosity and affection," because the conviction that blacks in Yazoo City were "ours to do with as we wished" like "some tangible possession" had been "rooted so deeply in me by the whole moral atmosphere of the place."[13]

At age seventeen Morris had been so comfortable with that moral atmosphere that "on any question pertaining to God or man" he would have "cast my morals on the results of common plebiscite of the white voters of Yazoo County." Born to middle-class parents, he dreamed of continuing emotional and physical comfort as a "member of Mississippi's educated landed gentry," married to a lovely Delta plantation belle and presiding over "boll weevils big enough to wear dog tags, pre-Earl Warren darkies, and the young squirearchy" from nearby plantations. Coupled with the disturbing reality of his youthful embrace of the perks of whiteness, however, were tender memories of the enveloping cocoon of confidence and security that his whiteness had afforded. Like much of his subsequent writing, *North toward Home* is awash with sentimental tales of Willie's boyhood adventures with his dog Skip and a variety of colorfully named childhood chums, his outrageous pranks on his slightly addled old-maid aunts, and his tender vignettes of his grandparents, Mamie and Percy. Yet, even as Morris grieved for the lost innocence of his youth he was haunted by his realization that this innocence had, in many ways, been underwritten by the monstrous evil of racial subjugation.[14]

When he wrote *North toward Home*, he was riding high as the thirty-three-year-old wunderkind editor of *Harper's* magazine during what were some of the most brilliant years in its storied history. This dazzling dreamlike existence would be shattered forever a few years later when a dispute with management led to Morris's resignation and retreat to Long Island, where he spent nearly a decade, writing an unsuccessful novel and a memoir about his friendship with writer James Jones. Even in the headiest of his New York days he had never escaped Mississippi's inexorable pull, and in 1980 after twenty years in self-imposed exile, he headed, as he later put it, "South toward Home" to become writer-in-residence at the University of Mississippi. With middle age setting in, he realized that he was returning "out of blood and belonging," and because it was "best to be getting on back before it is too late."[15]

During the two decades that Morris had been away, Mississippi had been marked by major changes, as evidenced by the election in 1979 of Democratic moderate William Winter to the governorship. There had been economic advances as well. The capital city of Jackson was now a sprawling, strip-malled monument to Sunbelt growth. Yet, for Morris, Mississippi remained a still complex and fascinating "blend of the relentless and the abiding." He settled into life at Ole Miss and in Oxford, where he quickly became a local celebrity and a bit of a character. Bringing in a host of renowned writers to speak at the university, Morris soon demonstrated that he could deliver on the literary names

he dropped. Meanwhile, his love of sports drew him to the playing fields of
Ole Miss, where he became a regular in the South end zone at Rebel football
games and a mainstay among the hecklers who sat in the third base stands at
baseball games.[16]

Ultimately, Morris's fascination with sports and his own emotional struggle
with Mississippi's racial heritage led him to chronicle *The Courting of Marcus
Dupree*. A phenomenal high-school running back, Dupree had been born in
Philadelphia, Mississippi, shortly before the slayings of three civil rights workers there in 1964. The subsequent investigation, cover-up, and travesty of justice that passed for a trial had branded Philadelphia as a racist hellhole, a vivid
reminder that Cash's South of bigotry, cruelty, and ignorance had not yet vanished from the face of the earth.

Seventeen years later Morris found a different Philadelphia, this one surprisingly united across racial lines in its pride in a wonderfully talented black
athlete. (One of Marcus's biggest fans was Cecil Price, Jr., the son of the deputy
sheriff who had been convicted of conspiracy in the 1964 murders.) A
countywide "Marcus Dupree Appreciation Day" was fully integrated and obviously a source of inspiration for the community, especially its black members. Given the reasons for his own decision to leave Mississippi, Morris was
also struck by the irony in the young Dupree's remarks as he departed to begin
his football career at the University of Oklahoma: "I wish I could stay in
Mississippi. I'd love to stay in Mississippi. Sometimes you just have to give
up the finer things in life to get what you want." Speaking from experience,
Morris replied, "Sometimes we have to leave home, Marcus, before we can
really come back."[17]

North toward Home surely ranks as one of the finest books ever written
about what it meant to be "southern." Yet, readers of this brilliant, impassioned
memoir could hardly escape a profound sense of *déjà vu* when they perused
Morris's subsequent efforts. These were also marked by his obsessive self-
identification with Mississippi and his near-masochistic insistence on not just
revisiting the most painful aspects of its collective past but on making them
part of his own personal past as well. He conveyed the same images and expressed the same sentiments repeatedly and often in practically the same words.
For example, in *Yazoo*, his chronicle of integration in his hometown, Morris
largely reprised the metaphoric irony of his conclusion in *North toward Home*,
recalling his family's history in Mississippi and admitting that "I, the inheritor
of all this, can hardly bear its burdens, am in misery with its past, and yearn
for 9:23 a.m. day after tomorrow when the plane will once again take me back

to the cultural capital, the Big Cave [his term for New York City], to its incho-
ate restlessness and security."[18]

Morris's most emotional expressions and experiences recurred throughout
his writing. In a 1981 *Life* magazine piece explaining his return to Mississippi,
he wrote, "Meanness is everywhere, but here the meanness and the desperation and the nobility have for me their own dramatic edge, for the fools are my
fools and the heroes are mine, too." More than a decade later these words would
resurface near the conclusion of his *New York Days*. Similarly, both the "hard
red earth" of Oxford and the cemetery in Yazoo City made him feel "as the
dispirited Roman legionnaire must have felt on re-entering his outpost . . .
after foraging the forlorn stretches of Gaul." Morris also retold the story of his
meeting with Richard Wright in Paris in 1957 several times. When he had
asked Wright if he would ever return to America, the embittered expatriate
had responded "No" because "I want my children to grow up as human beings." Thereafter, Morris recalled in both *North toward Home* and *The Courting of Marcus Dupree*, "a silence fell between us," that was respectively "like an
immense pain" or "old as time."[19]

Actually, Morris and Wright were more kindred spirits than either perhaps
realized. Describing *Black Boy* as "Richard Wright's Blues," Ralph Ellison might
have been referring to much of what Morris (whom Ellison also knew) wrote
as well when he defined the blues as "an impulse to keep the painful details
and episodes of a brutal experience alive in one's aching consciousness, to
finger the jagged grain. . . . As a form, the blues is an autobiographical chronicle
of personal catastrophe expressed lyrically."[20]

Like the blues, the corpus of Morris's writing on the South demonstrated
that nostalgia may reflect a need not to escape pain but to embrace it, to identify with it and through it. For him, as for Wright (or Faulkner or any number
of other southern writers, white or black, for that matter) the recurrent impulse to "finger the jagged grain" revealed an almost addictive dependence on
emotional distress as both a creative stimulant and a necessary source of identity. Morris conceded as much when, in the final chapter of *New York Days*, he
confessed the obvious: "The eternal juxtaposition of my state's hate and love,
the apposition of its severity and tenderness would forever baffle and enrage
me, but perhaps this is what I needed all along. Sometimes I cannot live with
its awesome emotional burdens, its terrible racist hazards and human neglects,
sometimes I can, but these forever drive me to words." The best and most
revealing of the words that Morris wrote about his identity as a southerner
reflected what his literary protégé Donna Tartt called a unique, "exquisitely

calibrated" awareness of "underground rivers of sorrow, constantly quaking beneath the rivers of everyday life," a sensitivity that made Morris "like a dog driven crazy by a whistle too high-pitched for the human ear." Although he was capable of extraordinary displays of hilarity and good humor, his vulnerability to feelings of sadness and loss explained why Morris returned regularly to visit the cemetery in Yazoo City where he had played as a child and where his parents were buried. Fittingly enough, at his death in 1999, the Yazoo City Cemetery became the final resting place for Willie Morris as well.[21]

Although the race issue had been the dominant concern of Morris and others of his school of southern writing, as the South's pursuit of industry grew ever more frenzied in the post–World War II decades, southern writers also remained deeply concerned about the cultural consequences of the region's economic modernization. The surging urbanization and industrialization of the post–World War II years had only heightened the anxieties of those who looked at a South supposedly enjoying unparalleled progress and actually saw a South on the verge of losing its identity.

Faulkner's fictional post–World War II town of Jefferson "awakened from its communal slumber into a rash of Rotary and Lions Clubs and Chambers of Commerce and City Beautifuls: a furious beating of hollow drums toward nowhere." Meanwhile, Jefferson's "old big decaying wooden houses" were rapidly giving way to "neat small new one-storey [sic] houses designed in Florida and California set with matching garages in their neat plots of clipped grass and tedious flowerbeds."[22]

Flannery O'Connor also witnessed the destabilizing and depersonalizing effects of industrialization and agricultural mechanization on the rural and small-town South. In "The Displaced Person," O'Connor told the story of a Polish immigrant, Mr. Guizac, who finds work as a hired hand on a run-down Georgia farm and revitalizes it through his energy, industriousness, and mechanical expertise. Yet, for all the economic benefits he brings, Guizac is also infected with alien values. His employer, Mrs. McIntyre, is impressed by his accomplishments and happy with the potential profits his efforts may reap for her, but she also worries that he is a stranger to the society and culture in which he lives. Her fears are confirmed when she learns that he plans to get a female cousin into the United States by betrothing her to a local black man, and in the story's startling conclusion, she looks on silently, offering no warning, as the unsuspecting Guizac is flattened by a runaway tractor.[23]

Robert Coles saw in O'Connor's story many of the concerns about economic modernization expressed by the Nashville Agrarians and other southern writers. His analysis also demonstrated the value of comparing a South in transition to other societies facing the challenge of Westernization. Coles described the ill-fated Guizac as "someone whose life has suffered at the hands of a 'civilization,' a modern industrialism, a Western, secular materialism gone viciously berserk—and now come South, full of promises, and ready to deliver immediate satisfactions: efficiency, reliability, productive mechanization, a kind of silent, impersonal competence and skill."[24]

By the time that "The Displaced Person" appeared, the Agrarians had long since scattered to the winds and southern leaders had become even more devout in their embrace of the gospel of industrial development as the key to regional salvation. Yet, the concerns they raised were clear enough in the work not only of O'Connor but of many other notable literary and journalistic figures in the post–World War II South. When Mississippi launched its "Balance Agriculture with Industry" program for industrial development in 1936, more than 60 percent of the state's labor force had worked in agriculture. This figure was less than 7 percent in 1970 when Eudora Welty published *Losing Battles*, a novel in which she explored the tensions between the simple country folk of Banner, Mississippi, and the resolute, aggressive schoolmarm and would-be modernizer Julia Mortimer, who took it upon herself to bring Mississippi into the twentieth century: "A state calling for improvement as loudly as ours? Mississippi standing at the foot of the ladder gives me that much more to work for."[25]

Despite her one-woman crusade to improve the state's ranking, the pupils who are receptive to Miss Julia, including a "Superior Court judge, the best eye, ear, nose, and throat specialist in Kansas City, and a history professor somewhere," wind up leaving not just Banner, but Mississippi altogether. For the most part, however, she simply finds herself fighting a "losing battle" when she prods the people of Banner to accept disruptions of their routines, their leisure pursuits, and, most important, their ties to each other, in the interest of the largely abstract and deferred gratification inherent in the "progress" of the entire society. Most of the people of Banner respond to her with a mixture of disdain and awe, and one recalls: "She had designs on everybody. She wanted a doctor and a lawyer and all else we might have to holler for some day, to come right out of Banner. . . . So she'd get behind some barefooted boy and push. . . . She put an end to good fishing."[26]

Miss Julia's refusal to leave the people of Banner alone is more complicated than it seems. First, she attempts to revise their attitudes toward nature itself, to make them less resigned to its vagaries and its destructive potential and to make them believe that, in many cases, they could actually change its course. Local legend has it that in the face of an impending flood, Miss Julia taught the children to swim rather than dismiss school. Likewise, in the midst of a cyclone, she has them brace themselves against the wall to hold the building together. She also urges them, to little avail, to plant better, scientifically improved seeds and fruit trees. One of her recalcitrant pupils concluded that Miss Julia believed "if she told people what they ought to know, and told 'em enough times, and finally beat it into their hides, they wouldn't forget it. Well, some of us still had her licked." In the end even the seemingly indomitable Miss Julia conceded as much: "All my life I've fought a hard war with ignorance. Except in those cases that you can count off on your fingers, I lost every battle."[27]

Suzanne Marrs identified an implicit agrarian perspective in several early Welty stories, such as "Death of a Traveling Salesman," "Flowers for Marjorie," "The Whistle," and "A Worn Path." In *Losing Battles*, Welty was ambivalent, still deeply sympathetic to the traditionalism of Banner's simple country folk, but also respectful of the values of the progressive Julia Mortimer. On the one hand, she admires the good intentions and courage of those who worked to make life in Mississippi better. Yet, though the inhabitants of Banner sometimes come through as silly and ignorant, Welty also seems to sense that their apparent complacence is really more like the contentment that comes from believing that they belong exactly where they are.[28]

Like Julia Mortimer, some southern intellectuals claimed that their long-sought goal of equality with the North was well worth the cultural costs. There were others, however, like Flannery O'Connor, who complained in 1957 that "the anguish that most of us have observed for some time now has been caused not by the fact that the South is alienated from the rest of the country, but by the fact that it is not alienated enough, that every day we are getting more and more like the rest of the country, that we are being forced out, not only of our many sins but of our few virtues."[29]

One of these virtues-in-jeopardy was the uncalculating, almost countercultural innocence that Welty seemed to capture in the people of Banner. Although some television shows like *The Waltons* and *The Andy Griffith Show* seemed to celebrate the simple honesty of southern country life, by the end of the 1970s on the phenomenally popular *Dallas*, J. R. Ewing and his good ol' boy compatriots robbed, swindled, and seduced at a pace that would have exhausted any northern robber baron of any era. Meanwhile Robert Altman's film *Nashville* used the suddenly ascendant country music scene to show post-

Watergate America that the plain folk on the bottom rung of society were every bit as corruptible and ruthlessly ambitious as the politicians up top.

Overall, John Egerton found it difficult to celebrate either the "Americanization of Dixie" or the "Southernization of America" because, taken together, they actually meant that "the South and the nation are not exchanging strengths as much as they are exchanging sins." Having made a name for himself primarily by showcasing the South's shortcomings before the rest of the nation, Georgia-bred journalist Marshall Frady was also singing a different tune by the mid-1970s as he recalled longingly a South that once seemed like "America's Corsica—an insular sun-glowered latitude of swooning sentiment and sudden guttural violence, always half adaze in the past." That imagery was fading rapidly, however, as Frady lamented a society suddenly grown "pastless, meaningless, and vague of identity." Here again was the specter of a No South where "the downtowns of Charlotte and Columbia and Jackson have become perfect reflections of Every City, and out beyond their perimeter expressways, barbecue patios and automatic lawn sprinklers are pushing out the possums and moonshine shanties in a combustion of suburbs indistinguishable from those of Pasadena or Minneapolis."[30]

Dismayed by the South's physical transformation, Frady was even more distressed by the "cultural lobotomy" evidenced by the disappearance of the "musky old demagogues" he had once so loved to pillory and even the "chigger bitten tabernacle evangelists" who had now given way to "manicured young bank accountants in horn-rim glasses" who were given to delivering weekly "Dale Carnegie devotionals and toneless litanies of upcoming softball games and men's waffle suppers." Instead of the "old fierce tragic theologies," the Sunbelt South could offer only the sort of superficial bumper-sticker sentiment observed in an affluent Atlanta suburb: "People of Distinction Prefer Jesus."[31]

Like Frady and his own father before him, Hodding Carter III had been an outspoken proponent of change in Mississippi and throughout the South. In 1990, however, he also suggested that in some important ways the South had changed too much as he offered his own decidedly wistful but more forthrightly definitive version of Ashmore's "Epitaph for Dixie." In pronouncing "The End of the South," Carter assured his readers that his was not "yet another fatuous proclamation of yet another New South." It was simply time, Carter insisted, to face the fact that "the South as South, a living, ever regenerating mythic land of distinctive personality is no more. . . . [T]he South that was is dead, and the South some had hoped would take its place never grew out of the cradle of old dreams. What is lurching into existence in the South is purely and contemporaneously mainstream American, for better or worse."[32]

Writers like Carter and Frady, whose unflattering portrayals of southern life had reflected their desire for change, now found themselves in a position akin to that of Julian, the overeducated ne'er-do-well liberal in O'Connor's "Everything that Rises Must Converge." An only son, Julian indulges in childish, vindictive fantasies about what will happen when his traditionalist mother has her first encounter with a black person on equal footing. Yet, when his mother suffers a stroke after being struck by a black woman—who sits near her on the bus and wears an identical hat, but is sullen and unlikable for all her equality—a tearful Julian embraces his mother and indicates that he would give anything to have her back just as she was, racism and traditionalism and all the rest.[33]

After visiting Samoa in 1936, William Alexander Percy had returned greatly troubled that a Western technological and cultural invasion was destroying the innocence and simplicity of Samoan life and fearing that economic modernization might have the same effect on his beloved Mississippi Delta. Years later, Will Percy's orphaned cousin and adopted son, Walker, would make the loss of individual and cultural identity a central concern of his writing. Foreshadowing a primary theme of his fiction, Percy suggested in 1957 that "perhaps the best imaginable society is not a countrywide Levittown in which everyone is a good liberal ashamed of his past, but a pluralistic society, rich in regional memories and usages." Although he hoped that the South's urban and industrial growth might actually facilitate desegregation efforts, he went against the grain of the contemporary liberal wisdom of the 1960s by arguing that not all the results of Americanizing or northernizing the South would be positive. "The sections are homogenized," he wrote in 1960. "Everybody watches the same television programs. In another hundred years, everybody will talk like Art Linkletter. The South has gotten rich and the North has gotten Negroes, and the Negro is treated badly in both places. The Northerners won and freed the slaves and now are fleeing to the suburbs to get away from them."[34]

Not only did Percy understand that the "southern" problem of racial prejudice and discrimination was really an "American" problem, but he recognized the "American" problem of alienation and disaffection with the shallowness and impersonality of modern life as a "southern" problem as well. Save for the improvements in its race relations, as a novelist, Percy found little reason to celebrate the changes he observed in the newly exuberant, self-congratulatory South. In his novel *The Last Gentleman* (1966), the partial amnesiac Will Barrett goes home to a South that is no longer grim and embattled but "happy, victorious, Christian, rich, patriotic, and Republican." Barrett has fallen in with the wealthy Vaught family, who own "Confederate Chevrolet," the second largest Chevy agency in the world, and reside in a purplish brick castle on a golf course. (Percy's family had lived in a house on a golf course in Birmingham before his own father committed suicide.) Barrett is overcome with depression at the "almost invincible happiness" he encounters at every turn: "The women were beautiful and charming. The men were healthy and successful and funny. . . . They had everything the North had and more. They had a history, they had a place redolent with memories, they had good conversation, they believed in God and defended the Constitution, and they were getting rich in the bargain. They had the best of victory and defeat. . . . Oh, they were formidable, born winners (How did they lose?)."[35]

In *Lanterns on the Levee*, Will Percy made it clear that the highlights of his life had been his service in World War I and his emergency leadership role during the great 1927 flood, and Walker recalled that his cousin was actually delighted by the news that the Japanese had attacked Pearl Harbor. Not only does Will Barrett have trouble being happy at the right times, but like Will Percy, he actually prefers a crisis or even a disaster to "everydayness." For Barrett, "It was not the prospect of the Last Day which depressed him but rather the prospect of living through an ordinary Wednesday morning." In Percy's *The Moviegoer* (1961), Binx Bolling awakens in the middle of the night "in the grip of everydayness. Everydayness is the enemy. . . . Perhaps there was a time when everydayness was not too strong and one could break its grip by brute strength. Now nothing breaks it—but disaster."[36]

In Percy's *Lancelot*, the deranged and violent protagonist Lance Lamar has grown so disgusted with all of modern America ("Which is worse, to die with T. S. Jackson at Chancellorsville or to live with Johnny Carson in Burbank?") that he plans to use Virginia as a base from which he can mount an effort to destroy and rebuild "both the defunct, befouled and collapsing North and the corrupt, thriving and Jesus hollering South." Though he clearly has little use for "the Northerner," who is "at heart a pornographer . . . an abstract mind with a genital attached," Lance holds special contempt for "the New Southerner" who "is Billy Graham on Sunday, and Richard Nixon the rest of the week."[37]

Percy had been optimistic about the South's future as he watched Jimmy Carter claim the presidency in 1976, but by the end of the 1970s he foresaw the region merely becoming part of "an LA-Dallas-Atlanta axis . . . an agribusiness-sports-vacation-retirement-show-biz culture with its spiritual center perhaps at Oral Roberts University." By 1981 he was describing the "terrible price we have to pay" for Sunbelt progress as "Losangelization. That's not good. The trick is, given the New South, which is not the South of Faulkner, not the South of Eudora, it is not the South of Flannery, it is the South of Interstate 12 and Highway 190. It is the South of Los Angeles. How to humanize that! How do you live with that? What I am trying to do is to figure out how a man can come to himself, living in a place like that."[38]

Percy's comments helped to frame the setting in which contemporary white southerners were struggling to redefine their regional identity and reestablish its distinctiveness. His concern with how one can "come to himself," not just in a New South about to or already become the No South but in the modern world in general had also been precisely the theme of Ralph Ellison's *Invisible Man*. Though many readers focused primarily on its racial implications, in one sense, Ellison's novel had simply told the story of modern America from the perspective of those most alienated from it and by it. At the very least, Ellison had suggested that the mass of white Americans might also be more anonymous and marginalized than they perceived when his narrator warns at the novel's conclusion, "Who knows but that, on the lower frequencies, I speak for you." Many white southerners caught up in the rapid economic and demographic changes of the post–World War II era surely shared the conviction of Ellison's protagonist that "to lose a sense of *where* you are implies the danger of losing a sense of *who* you are," and thus "to lose your direction is to lose your face." Although this problem of the loss of self and direction in modern society would become the central concern for Percy and a number of his literary disciples in the post-North South, as Robert W. Rudnicki has pointed out, Ellison was already "making the ontological connection between 'place' and 'face,' while Percy . . . was still learning his craft."[39]

Percy and Ellison clearly harbored similar views about "invisibility" and loss of individuality. In 1958 before he had published his first novel, Percy argued, "The dogfish, the tree, the seashell, the American Negro, the dream are rendered invisible by a shift of reality from concrete thing to theory. . . . As Kierkegaard said, 'Once a person is seen as a specimen of a race or species, at that very moment he ceases to be an individual.'" Still, despite their common concerns, Percy had no apparent contact with Ellison prior to 1967, nor does it appear that he had read any of Ellison's writings up to that point. However, after Ellison wrote with the news that Percy was to be honored at the National Institute of Arts and Letters annual awards ceremony in May of that year, Percy acquired an advance copy of a forthcoming *Harper's Magazine* interview with Ellison, which he scrutinized with great care, scrawling notes such as "What is he up to?" Of *Invisible Man*, he wondered, "To what extent is his invisibility a negro problem and to what extent universal?" Percy noted that Wright's *Black Boy* was about racial oppression, but he sensed that *Invisible Man* was not simply a "protest novel" or even "a Negro novel."[40]

Though he had publicly condemned racism and segregation, it was fair to say that up to 1967, at least, Percy himself had perceived blacks largely as somewhat distant victims of white oppression, and he had few personal contacts with black writers or intellectuals. After learning that they had read many of the same writers, Percy later confessed to Ellison's friend, writer Albert Murray, that "it's really hard for me to accept the fact that you and Ellison are for real." Impressed with the Ellison interview, in a letter to *Harper's* Percy suggested, "Maybe it is the likes of Ellison we've needed all along," a rather ironic observation given that Ellison had achieved literary prominence well before Percy and certainly well before Percy seemed to "discover" him. Even as he praised Ellison in *Harper's*, Percy offered a revealing racial dichotomy when he observed that perhaps "the American [read white] intellectual will not grow up until the Negro intellectual shows him how."[41]

Percy was struck by Ellison's determination to expose "inauthentic" identities, perhaps because in his then in-progress novel, *Love in the Ruins* (1971), Percy would introduce Colley Wilkes, "a super-Negro, a regular black Leonardo . . . electronic wizard, ornithologist; holds the Black Belt in Karate, does the crossword in the Sunday *Times*." A native of Dothan, Alabama, educated at Amherst and New York University, Wilkes strives to cover up his "Alabama Hambone" accent. He drives around in an orange Toyota, listening to "a Treasury of the World's Great Music, which has the good parts of a hundred famous symphonies, ballets and operas," and winds up diagnosed as "a self successfully playing at being a self that is not itself."[42]

Ellison may have been ahead of his time in foreshadowing Percy, but as the South "entered the mainstream of American life for perhaps the first time in 150 years," Percy's timing was perfect in reiterating Ellison's emphasis on the difficulties of remaining true to one's individual and cultural identity amid the turbulence and increasing superficiality of modern life. As Malcolm Jones summed it up, "In Percy's South, historical monuments and Hollywood fakery coexist cheerfully: Sunbelt newcomers pull on riding boots and take to drawling; the descendants of Civil War generals move to the suburbs and make fortunes converting slave quarters to $400,000 condos."[43]

In 1981 literary critic Cleanth Brooks named Walker Percy "our most acute commentator on the social life of the South during the last quarter of a century," and contemporary literary critics seem to agree that Percy was the post-Faulknerian South's most influential writer. This development is noteworthy, because Percy claimed that Faulkner "meant less to me than Camus" and denied that he had been shaped "by sitting on the porch listening to anybody tell stories about the South." Instead, Percy insisted, "My South was always the New South. My first memories are of the country club, of people playing golf."[44]

Ironically, the writer anointed by critics as the new standard bearer of the southern literary tradition had declared as early as 1971 that "the day of regional Southern writing is all gone. I think that people who try to write in that style are usually repeating a phased-out genre—or doing Faulkner badly." By 1979 Percy was suggesting that "what increasingly engages the southern novelist as much as his Connecticut counterpart are no longer Faulkner's Snopeses or O'Connor's Crackers or Wright's black underclass but their successful grandchildren who are going nuts in Atlanta condominiums."[45]

The emerging post-North generation of writers who followed Percy's lead seemed intent on exploring his contention that modern life subjects southerners, no less than their counterparts elsewhere in the nation and throughout the world, to what he called "deep dislocation in their lives that had nothing to do with poverty, ignorance, and discrimination." An excellent case in point was Percy's fellow Mississippian Richard Ford. When Ford returned to Mississippi after living outside the region for a while, he discovered that he could "live here and treat the South as if it were any place else in the United States" without falling under the spell of "'Southernness' with a capital 'S' and all of the baggage that goes with it."[46]

While living in Clarksdale in the heart of the Mississippi Delta (which Ford himself called "the South's South"), he wrote a novel set in New Jersey and a book of short stories about Montana. Ford's novel, *The Sportswriter*, won critical acclaim, but the protagonist, Frank Bascombe, though southern-born, seems wholly unsouthern, outwardly indifferent to the past and perhaps even more so to place. In fact, Frank seems to feel as much at home in one place as another. In *The Sportswriter*, while visiting Detroit he remembers reading "that with enough time American civilization will make the Midwest of any place, New York included."[47]

In *Independence Day*, Ford's Pulitzer Prize–winning sequel to *The Sports-writer*, Bascombe shows none of the southerner's traditionally profound attachment to the past. Frank insists, "I am a proponent of . . . forgetting. . . . [T]here is no hope unless we can forget." Fred Hobson has traced this assertion to Kierkgaard's admonition: "If a man cannot forget, he will never amount to much," which serves as the epigraph to Walker Percy's *The Last Gentleman*. Hobson may be correct that Frank Bascombe is far more "southern" a character than he seems at first glance, but Ford himself has insisted that he makes "a real distinction between literature and geography," noting, "In literature, the impulse towards regionalism is a bad one."[48]

A native Charlestonian and the great-great-granddaughter of the Confederate secretary of the treasury, Josephine Humphreys was well equipped personally to present the clash of culture and values that ensues when Old South meets No South. Set in the South Carolina Low Country, Humphreys's novels, *Dreams of Sleep* (1984) and *Rich in Love* (1987), present a second-generation Sun Belt where supermarkets have given way to super-supermarkets, and "the level of shopping" has become an index of "human trust in the future."[49]

One of Humphreys's characters, Alice Reese, asks, "Who can be sad in a supermarket, with all its proof of human omnipotence? . . . When you see such achievement, you must be hopeful; every box of quick grits, every can of cling peaches." Alice even fantasizes that "the store would be a good place to work in every day, clean and busy, filled with food." Likewise, Danny, one of her husband Will's closest friends, confesses: "I've spent the last two years in Hardee's." Of Arby's, Wendy's, Popeye's, and other fast-food emporiums, Danny concludes, "They're all good, all fine places, but in the end I went back to Hardee's. I feel at home there. They always take me in, give me a good hot meal, get me back on my feet. I appreciate that. You know?"[50]

Will Reese, meanwhile, is appalled by the apparent ease with which his friends and family have made themselves at home in this new, and to him, utterly foreign, Sunbelt South. His widowed and remarried mother is a relatively new but successful realtor, a latter day version of Thomas Wolfe's Eliza Gant with a license plate that reads "REALTY." To make matters worse, Duncan Nesmith, her new husband and Will's stepfather, is a land developer from Ohio, who tells him excitedly of his plans to develop a pirate-based theme park that, in contrast to Disney World, will be "much more low-key, more in tune with the environment and related to the historical traditions of the area." Will refuses to believe that any local investors are involved, insisting that the money behind this project is "money without a history. It's cut loose, and roams, raids us. Buys what of us it wants."[51]

In *Rich in Love* one of Humphreys's characters who lives in the nearby town of Mt. Pleasant, which has become part of Charleston's sprawl, compares her town to ancient Herculaneum, "engulfed not by mud, but by overflow from the city of Charleston." Writers, Humphreys believed, had a particular responsibility to prevent this sort of untrammeled development "because for us what's at stake is lifeblood." That lifeblood was "place," not the pristine wilderness that had long ago been destroyed, but now the town, the small-scale human setting "in which community itself is discernible."[52]

The diminished significance of place and community was also a common theme in the work of Bobbie Ann Mason, whose fiction has been classed as "K-Mart Realism" because it captures the worlds of rural working-class white southerners who are awash in contemporary pop culture and show little attachment to or respect for the past. One of her characters even insists, "The main thing you learn from history is that you can't learn from history." With the constant din of the television as a backdrop, many of Mason's people tell time according to whether they're watching the *Today Show* or *Charlie's Angels*. In "Airwaves," a young woman even declines her father's invitation to live with him after breaking up with her boyfriend, because "We don't like the same TV shows anymore." Mason's characters often find more pain than comfort in their families. If they do have a personal dream or ambition, those close to them refuse to share it. Although they are often unsure of what they actually want, they usually know that they like neither where they are, who they are, or who they are with.[53]

Perhaps no contemporary southern writer does a better job of presenting the interaction between an indigenous folk culture and the all-enveloping consumerist popular culture of the Sunbelt era than Lee Smith. Focusing primarily on female characters, she sees this interaction less in terms of conflict than adaptation to a world where encroaching modernity and the invasion of mass culture and its values are a reality that must somehow be accommodated. Smith's novel, *Oral History*, takes collegian Jennifer Cantrell back to her Appalachian roots as she visits Hoot Owl Holler to interview her relatives who generally prove to be anything but the uncomplicated, unspoiled mountain folk she envisions. Smith produces a wonderfully funny, heavily satirical conclusion in which Cousin Al (short for "Almarine") makes a killing in Amway and then builds a successful ski run before embarking on "his grandest plan yet": "Ghostland," a "wildly successful theme park and recreation area (campground, motel, olympic-size pool, waterslide, and gift shop) in Hoot Owl Holler . . . designed by a Nashville architect." Best of all, "smack in the middle of Ghostland, untouched," stands the old haunted family cabin for the benefit of visitors who have "paid the extra $4.50 to . . . see it with their own eyes when that rocking chair starts rocking and rocks like crazy the whole night long."[54]

We should note the similarities between Ghostland and the theme park proposed by Josephine Humphreys's Duncan Nesmith, who promises it will be "in tune with the environment and related to the historical traditions of the area." Nesmith's park is the brainchild of an Ohioan, however, while Ghostland is a southern invention. As Fred Hobson has observed, *Oral History* blends several cultures in "the worst possible manner" as "the indigenous folk culture turns into cheap imitation of itself for the sake of commercial mass culture," and hence, "what was once organic and natural becomes cheap and tawdry." Much the same could be said of Smith's later novel, *Saving Grace,* in which Gatlinburg, Tennessee, is like a much-expanded real-life version of Ghostland, complete with "Uncle Slidell's Christian Fun Golf" and "everything you can think of to do . . . , such as restaurants, shops, mountain crafts, chair lifts up the mountain, a giant needle, music, theaters, and souvenir shops and outlet stores and fudge factories and even a Ripley's Believe It or Not."[55]

While Smith, Mason, and Humphreys seemed to focus on whites who have already lost or are struggling to retain some sense of identity and belonging in the "successful, optimistic, prosperous and bland" No South, another group of talented writers presented the largely untold stories of whites living at the socioeconomic margins of contemporary southern life in a world that remained decidedly "poor, violent, pessimistic, tragic, and mysterious." Unlike Erskine Caldwell, who had formulated his vision of southern lower-class white life from a detached, if not distant, perspective, the new writers of "white trash" fiction could convey a sense of this culture from within.

Historically, designation as "white trash" carried not only economic implications but cultural and moral ones as well. Tim McLaurin observed that, depending on the branch of his family, his people were "known as either hardworking, God-fearing people or as bootleggers, whores, and delinquents," adding that, "by heredity, the McLaurin younguns . . . were in constant struggle between the pull of the pulpit and the jail house." Such judgments were primarily subjective, of course. As one of Larry Brown's characters explains, "Trash is always in the eye of the beholder. I know. There were probably some people who thought we were trash. I know there were people who looked down their noses at us because we were on welfare. That and my daddy being in the pen."[56]

In Dorothy Allison's semi-autobiographical *Bastard Out of Carolina*, the happiest day of Anney Boatwright's life might have been the one on which the Greenville County, South Carolina, courthouse burned and all of the official birth records with it, because the "Illegitimate" stamped on her daughter Ruth Anne's birth certificate might just as well have read "trash." As Ruth Anne, known to the family as "Bone," saw it, "Mama hated to be called trash. . . . [T]he stamp on that birth certificate burned her like the stamp she knew they'd tried to put on her."[57]

Rick Bragg's memoir, *All Over But the Shoutin'* (1997), described a poor-white childhood laced with fear, frustration, and deprivation, recalling the humiliation of having "people step away from you as you wait in line at the hamburger stand because you smell like sweat and fertilizer and diesel fuel." When Bragg heard he had won a Pulitzer Prize for journalism, he waited more than an hour to call his mother, fearful there had been some mistake because "it is a common condition of being poor white trash: you are always afraid that the good things in your life are temporary, that someone can take them away, because you have no power beyond your brute strength to stop them."[58]

Although, like Bragg, their characters often revealed a smoldering class resentment at the treatment they received from their socioeconomic superiors, the "white trash" writers did not flinch in their portrayals of the homicidal violence, physical, sexual, and emotional abuse, and other wounds that their characters inflicted on each other. Born in Bacon County, Georgia, Harry Crews came from a family of small landowning farmers struggling to hold on to their independence and keep from slipping into an even more precarious existence as tenants or sharecroppers. Recalling his parents' misfortunes and struggles, Crews explained that "the world that circumscribed the people I come from had so little margin for error, for bad luck, that when something went wrong, it almost always brought something else down with it. It was a world in which survival depended on raw courage, a courage born out of desperation and sustained by a lack of alternatives."[59]

While his family and their neighbors were bound by a common struggle, the impulse to survive or save one's own family sometimes overrode any sense of communal obligation. Scarcely a day after Crews's father was buried, one of his father's friends stole all his family's meat from the smokehouse. "Not many people may be able to understand that or sympathize with it, but I think I do," Crews explained. "It was a hard time in that land, and a lot of men did things for which they were ashamed and suffered all their lives. But they did them because of hunger and sickness and because they could not bear the sorry spectacle of their children dying from a lack of a doctor and their wives growing old before they were thirty."[60]

In his fiction Crews presented a southern poor-white netherworld inhabited by characters whose desperation, depravity, and grotesqueness went well beyond anything Erskine Caldwell had dared to offer. Crews's *A Feast of Snakes* emphasized the widening chasm between the caricatured, commodified representations of regional culture currently in fashion among upwardly mobile white southerners and the grim realities of life facing those for whom upward mobility did not exist. The novel is set in "Mystic," a small South Georgia town whose traditional rattlesnake roundup has exploded into a major tourist attraction. The protagonist, Joe Lon Mackey, is a former high school football star who was considerably more adept on the gridiron than in the classroom. Unable to pursue collegiate stardom, he descends into a miserable, hopeless existence, drinking incessantly and living in a mobile home with two smelly kids and a pitiful, long-suffering wife with rotten teeth. Joe Lon finally erupts in a murderous shooting spree and is thrown by an angry mob into a pit of writhing reptiles, rising to his feet for the final time with snakes hanging from his face.[61]

A former fireman in William Faulkner's hometown of Oxford, Mississippi, Larry Brown won critical acclaim for his stunningly realistic portrayals of poor-white life in the South, a life with which he, as the son of a tenant farmer, was intimately familiar. Unlike Faulkner's Snopeses, most of Brown's characters are not striving to join and then co-opt the middle class. Rather, they are either unable or disinclined to do anything other than stay put. In *Joe* (1991), Brown's Joe Ransom is a hardworking ex-con whose propensity for drunkenness and violence combine with his sense of class identity and honor to hold him firmly in place at the lower rungs of the socioeconomic ladder.[62]

Fleeing the father who had prostituted her younger sister and made sexual advances toward her as well, the title character in Brown's novel *Fay* walks away from her family, but not her identity. When a spoiled young rich woman from the Mississippi Delta calls her a "white trash piece of shit," Fay muses rather philosophically that "she never had been called a white trash piece of shit before, but she'd been called white trash." Innocent and shy, but quick to act on pure instinct, Fay leaves pain, suffering, and death in her wake, and despite the reader's hopes that she will be able to rise above her abusive, deprived upbringing and her own impulsive behavior, as the novel concludes, she is strolling through New Orleans's French Quarter, where she now works as a stripper.[63]

While most of Tim McLaurin's contemporaries focused on the durability of the white trash identity, his *Woodrow's Trumpet* chronicled the yuppiefication of North Carolina's "Research Triangle" area and the resultant trampling of southern rural culture by an influx of affluent, highly educated strangers who have no knowledge or understanding of the people and the values they are displacing. The novel's protagonist, Woodrow Bunce, lives in a small frame house on a five-acre tract in the middle of what was once his family's farmland but is now a Cape Cod–style residential development full of presumptuous and patronizing Yankee liberals. When Woodrow innocently transforms his place into a virtual monument to white trashiness, complete with an imported sand beach, palm trees, and plastic pink flamingoes, his neighbors drop their pretensions of tolerance and mobilize aggressively against this threat to their sensibilities as well as their property values. Violence ensues, including some vigilante-style class warfare, and tragedy is the ultimate result. As Erik Bledsoe points out, in *Woodrow's Trumpet*, McLaurin has inverted Faulkner's Snopes Trilogy by focusing on the threat to lower-class, rural southern culture posed by a bourgeois invasion.[64]

For all the physical and material comforts they enjoy, the characters created by writers like Walker Percy or Josephine Humphreys are often ill at ease because they have lost contact with the physical and human "place" that is such an important source of their identity. Yet, despite the tough times they have endured, writers like Crews, Allison, Brown, and McLaurin identify both themselves and their characters not just with the South as a place but with particular places within the South that shape and affirm them. Crews, for example, recalled with genuine affection the one-Saturday-a-month pilgrimages his family made to Alma, Georgia, where around the square, "the dusty air would be heavy with the pleasant smell of mule dung and mule sweat. . . . Farmers were everywhere in small groups, talking and chewing, and bonneted women stood together trading recipes and news of children." For Crews, the highlight of the trip to town was the chance to witness someone talking on a telephone, and he insisted, "No film or play I have ever watched since has been as wonderful as the telephones I watched as a boy in Alma, Georgia." Crews denied that he was "singing a sad song for the bad good old days, wishing he was back barefoot again traveling in wagons and struck dumb by the mystery of telephones. . . . What I am talking about here is a hard time in the shaping of the South, a necessary experience that made us the unique people we are."[65]

Few southerners experienced harder times than Allison's abused and neglected Bone Boatwright, who nonetheless sees Greenville, South Carolina, in

1955 as "the most beautiful place in the world." Bone remembers especially the weeping willows that "marched across the yard, following every warding stream and ditch, their long whiplike fronds making tents that sheltered sweet-smelling beds of clover." For all the trauma and tragedy he associated with his North Alabama childhood, Rick Bragg retained a strong sensory attachment to its sights, smells, and seasonal variation and took comfort in knowing that at the new place he bought for her, his long-suffering mother can "walk in the pines and smell the wood smoke and plant rose of Sharon on the chert-rock banks."[66]

Larry Brown thought that his strongest tie to Faulkner might be some of the people "who arrive out of that geography, out of that place where I live, that place where he lived. I think the landscape creates the people." "Sketched so vividly . . . you can all but mount it on your wall," as one reviewer put it, Brown's landscapes were often unattractive: "Tarpaper shacks and shabby mobile homes, actually no more than campers . . . yards full of junked autos and stacked firewood overgrown with weeds and pulpwood trucks with the windows smashed out and the rear ends jacked up and propped on oil drums." Unlike the shell-shocked yuppies of Percy or Ford, however, Brown's poor-white characters at least have access to more pristine natural settings: "a dirt road, its entrance overhung with great leaning trees and vines, the shade deep and strong like a darker world within the outer, a place of cane thickets and coon dens and the lairs of bobcats, where the sun at its highest cast no light over the rotted stumps and stagnant sloughs."[67]

Janisse Ray spent her "cracker childhood" living in a junkyard tucked into the South Georgia piney-woods. Although she concedes that many might find her part of the world unbearably hot and just as ugly, she admits that "the landscape I was born into, that owns my body" is also "scrawled on my bones, so that I carry the landscape inside me like an ache." In his memoir, *Keepers of the Moon*, McLaurin reveals that, for seven years, he has carried around a small bag of dirt from his family's homeplace, "a talisman that whispers to me the song of mourning doves, wind in longleaf pines, the low rumble of thunder from a summer storm that has recently passed and soaked the dry fields. I hope to waltz slowly to that tune the day I lift above this bright land."[68]

In *Woodrow's Trumpet*, McLaurin's Nadean Tucker, a black former prostitute, collects a pocketful of the rubble from her run-down homeplace and muses, "We don't tote home around with us and set it up like something out of a bag. Home stays in just two places—on the land where you were raised, and always, always in the back of your mind." For a black character to hold such a sentimental attitude toward the place where she spent her bitterly impoverished childhood may have struck some readers as unusual. As we shall see, however, in the wake of the civil rights movement, a hitherto muted or suppressed attachment to their southern roots led many African Americans in general and a number of African American writers in particular to acknowledge the South, for all its cruelties and unpleasantness, both as their "home" and a primary source of their identity.[69]

10

Blackness and Southernness

AFRICAN AMERICANS LOOK SOUTH TOWARD HOME

TWENTY-SEVEN YEARS AFTER HER ARRIVAL as one of the first two black students at the University of Georgia had helped trigger a riot, Charlayne Hunter-Gault came back to address the graduating class of 1988. Though not nearly so dramatic as her first appearance on campus, her return on this occasion was in some ways no less significant. She was speaking at commencement, but her remarks would have been equally appropriate for homecoming. Hunter-Gault established this theme at the outset, noting in language that contrasted starkly with the hateful rhetoric—"Two, four, six, eight, We don't want to integrate, Eight, six four, two, We don't want no jigaboo"—that had greeted her on her initial visit to the campus, that it was "good to be back home again. In a place that I have always thought of as 'our place.'" If, on the one hand, Hunter-Gault's remarks were remarkably gracious and even conciliatory, they were also noteworthy in the matter-of-factness with which she assured her mostly southern white listeners that the South was her home, too.[1]

When Hunter-Gault first arrived on the Georgia campus in 1961, Cash's *The Mind of the South* had recently surfaced in paperback and was just beginning to make its presence felt among students, scholars, and activists obsessed with the South's problems and determined to do something about them. Certainly, the mob violence that attended Hunter-Gault's enrollment at Georgia seemed merely to confirm Cash's distinctly unflattering portrait of an emotionally dysfunctional, race-obsessed white South. Had Cash not done himself in some twenty years earlier, he would not have been surprised that Hunter-Gault's presence at Georgia had set off a riot. Indeed, he would have expected no less. On the other hand, Cash would have been stunned that Hunter-Gault had not only survived but had then returned willingly to the university where she received a warm welcome from a predominantly white audience and actually claimed kinship with the sons and daughters of some of those who had once taunted and threatened her. Certainly, the only actors in the entire drama who would have been recognizable to him as southerners were those who had hurled rocks and racial epithets at her window on that evening in 1961.

Though sympathetic to southern blacks, Cash clearly had only whites in mind as he picked his way through the maze of contradiction, delusion, and irrationality that, for him at least, constituted the tortured southern psyche. In succeeding years, even more racially enlightened white observers followed Cash's exclusionary example by identifying southern whites as "southerners" and southern blacks as "blacks." Thus, black southerners were denied their regional identities not only by the antagonistic defenders of a southern racial system that rendered blacks virtually invisible, but even by their would-be liberators who wanted to destroy that system.

Focusing on the suffering and injustice imposed on African Americans by the Jim Crow South, external critics found it both easy and logical enough to conclude that the last thing any black person in the South would crave would be an identity as a southerner. When whites insisted that the blacks who sweated in their fields for starvation wages and bore the crushing burden of Jim Crow were satisfied and happy, many observers simply embraced the counter-fallacy that all southern blacks were hopelessly, totally, and eternally alienated from the place where they had seen so much injustice and hardship. Recognition of black southerners' ties to the South also ran counter to the emerging black-power/black-pride movements of the 1960s, which focused on the roots of black culture in the African homeland, rather than in the slave South where Africans had been dragged against their will and subjected to brutal, dehumanizing treatment at the hands of their white oppressors. As Ralph Ellison observed in 1965, "Love of the South is glamorized by the white Southerner; but the idea that a Negro may love the South is usually denied as an utterly outrageous idea."[2]

Viewed against this backdrop, perhaps no phenomenon of the post–civil rights era is more striking than the readiness, even eagerness, of African Americans both in the South and outside it to identify themselves unequivocally as southerners and claim the region as home. Survey data from the period 1964–1976 revealed significant changes in the sentiments of both southern and nonsouthern blacks who said they felt warmly disposed toward "southerners." In 1964, only 55 percent of southern black respondents expressed "warm" feelings toward southerners, as opposed to nearly 90 percent of the southern whites polled. By 1976, however, the proportion of southern blacks who expressed this warmth stood just below 80 percent and only slightly below the percentage of white southerners who felt this way. Analyzing these results, John Shelton Reed and Merle Black concluded that in 1964 "many Southern blacks may have been unclear about whether the category ["southerners"] was meant to include them and their black friends and neighbors. . . . By the 1970s, it appears, many southern blacks did understand themselves to be southerners, and they were not unhappy about it."[3]

Throughout the 1980s and 1990s, similar polls produced similar results, and by 2001 the percentage of blacks in the South who identified themselves as southerners was actually slightly higher than that for whites. Certainly, Peter Applebome was correct in 1994 when he wrote that "in a logical extension of the civil rights battles of the past, [blacks] are staking claim to their vision of the South—not as background figures on the mythic landscape of moonlight and magnolias, not as victims of oppression dragged here from Africa, but as southerners, with as much stake in the region as any Mississippi planter or Virginia farmer."[4]

The tendency to identify themselves as southerners and to want others to do the same seems to be reflected in regional demographic patterns as well. Although nearly 10 million blacks had left the South between 1910 and 1960, the reversal of this pattern that began in the 1970s continued throughout the 1980s and accelerated dramatically in the 1990s. During the last quarter of the twentieth century, the number of blacks entering the region exceeded the number leaving by more than 1.2 million. In the 1990s alone, the South's black population grew by nearly 3.6 million overall, nearly twice the rate of increase for the previous decade. Statistics showing that one of ten African Americans in the South in 2000 was a newcomer clearly reflected the dynamism of a South that led the nation in job production in the 1990s. Yet, the region's pull was more than economic. Harold Jackson, a Savannah native who left the South and eventually returned to Atlanta, insisted, "It's not just that the opportunities are here. It's that the opportunities to solve the problems that exist are here, too." Again and again, black returnees registered their surprise at the changes that had come in their absence. After forty-six years in California, Etta Willis came back to Mount Olive, Mississippi, in 1994 and quickly discovered "you don't have the racism here that you used to have." In fact, she admitted, "I have experienced less racism here than I did in San Francisco."[5]

Approximately 20 percent of the South's new black residents were college graduates (a figure above the average for the black population at large), and the growth of the region's black middle class was clearly an attraction for them.

Said one new resident of metropolitan Atlanta, "There are so many African Americans here who have made it or succeeded or gotten to that middle-class line. It's nice to see." The suburbanization of the black middle class helped to explain why segregation declined 10 percent faster in the metropolitan South than elsewhere in the United States during the 1990s, leaving the region with eight of the nation's ten least segregated metropolitan areas by 2000.[6]

The proportion of elected officials in the South who are black is also higher than in the nation at large. When, after growing up in segregated Savannah and spending time in the Northeast and Midwest, Orion Douglas returned to Brunswick, he won a judgeship in a county that was nearly 80 percent white. Douglas received his legal training in the North, but after seeing places like South Boston, Bedford-Stuyvesant, and East St. Louis, he realized "the South wasn't all that bad," and he returned to Georgia, "where I had a better chance of being who I could be. . . . I think I've done better here than I could have done anyplace else. . . . I actually love the South. I mean, after living in New England and the Midwest, this is it."[7]

As John Hope Franklin explained, "The South as a place is as attractive to blacks as it is to whites. . . . Blacks even when they left the South didn't stop having affection for it. They just couldn't make it there. Then they found the North had its problems, too; so you look for a place of real ease and contentment, where you could live as a civilized human being. That's the South. It's more congenial, the pace is better, the races get along better. It's a sense of place. It's home. In rare moments, it's something that blacks and whites have shared. The South in that sense rises above race." Veteran journalist Fred Powledge could not recall ever hearing a black person in the South object to being called a southerner. Writing in 1979, Powledge insisted, "Black people *are* Southerners. They are of and by and from and for the South at least as much as their white brethren, and many have repeatedly demonstrated . . . their love for and faith in the region."[8]

Not all black returnees were unequivocally upbeat about the South, but many of them spoke in terms of their spiritual ties to the region. Reflecting what L. D. Reddick called the black southerner's "inner conflict and outer ambivalence" about the South, Larry Conley first joked that he came back "just to get some decent barbecue," then confessed, "The truth is, I don't really know why I returned. The reasons, confusing and contradictory, are all wrapped up in that mixture of hope and despair I often feel for the South."[9]

In *Growing Up Black in Rural Mississippi*, Chalmers Archer recalled Holmes County and "how horribly and how wonderfully it treated me." As a youngster, Archer witnessed beatings and knew the grief caused by white violence firsthand. After a gang of whites threatened to kill him, his parents—in a move rendered deeply ironic by contemporary realities—had packed him off to Detroit for safekeeping. Yet, recalling his life in Holmes County, Archer remembered many more good things than bad in a childhood where hard work and ever-present racial anxieties were offset by a sense of belonging—to a family, to a community, and to a place. As he explained, "I have many good memories of my experiences growing up in Tchula. After all it was 'home.' And it's just human nature to want to look back kindly on a place of which you were once so much a part."[10]

Anthony Walton's father had insisted that leaving Mississippi for Chicago "was the best thing that ever happened to me." Yet, when Walton recalled his mother's perpetual homesickness and reflected on his childhood experiences in a Chicago area neighborhood full of fellow migrants from Mississippi, he remembered "the same church sermons and suppers, the same food as our families had in the South," all of them "quite different from that of the mainstream north." For Walton, Chicago had simply been "the northernmost county of Mississippi." After college, he lived in Rhode Island and New York City and "tried to *be* a northerner because this was what I thought it would take to make it." In the end, however, though a resident of the "resolutely Yankee" state of Maine, his "experience in the North" had taught him "that I am first and last a southerner, as I was raised to be." Though fully aware of the sacrifice and suffering that Mississippi had exacted from his forebears, after visiting the state and acquainting himself with the "ghosts and bones" of its historical landscape, Walton understood that rather than forget them, he must "embrace the ghosts and cradle the bones and call them my own."[11]

Walton seemed to confirm the judgment of African American literary scholar Thadious M. Davis, who observed that "while anthropologists and sociologists may see the increasingly frequent pattern of black return migration [to the South] as flight from the hardships of urban life, I would suggest that it is also a laying claim to a culture and to a region that, though fraught with pain and difficulty, provides a major grounding for identity." C. Vann Woodward agreed, noting black return migration to the South and concluding that "the attractions of the South for those returning were mainly old cultural constants . . . the values of place and past, the symbols and traditions of region rather than race."[12]

Ironically, black southerners often found it easier to come back to the South and feel at home than did their white contemporaries. When white expatriate James Morgan returned to his native state to interview actor and fellow Mississippian Morgan Freeman, who had recently forsaken Manhattan to live near Charleston in the edge of the Mississippi Delta, he was more than a little apprehensive because he expected Freeman to fit into "the angry black man box, the militant crusader container." He soon discovered, however, that Freeman "may feel more warmly about our home state than I do." When he learned of his visitor's apprehension, an amused Freeman assured him, "I really am a product of the South, easy-living, easy-going, quiet, gentle." Freeman seemed to see the South itself in much the same way: "that safe place, the womb of nativity. . . . [W]hatever I am I was nurtured there." A tour of his place was punctuated by frequent interruptions as Freeman pointed out the beauty of the countryside and exulted of the sweet-smelling honeysuckle: "You don't have to plant that. That just grows. That's Mississippi."[13]

Freeman's comments suggest that, like their white counterparts, black southerners defined their southernness primarily in terms of enduring attachments to community and place. David R. Goldfield noted that the civil rights movement went a long way toward removing "the public obsession with race" and thereby allowed white southerners "to regain contact with other cultural elements such as past, place and manners." In reality, Goldfield's observation was no less applicable to black southerners. Novelist Alice Walker explained that the history of her family, "like that of all black Southerners, is a history of dispossession" and that when she came of age in the early 1960s, she awoke "to the bitter knowledge that in order just to continue to love the land of my birth, I was expected to leave it." Describing the South of her birth as "a beloved but brutal place," Walker believed that "it is part of the black Southern sensibility that we treasure memories for such a long time, that is all of our homeland those of us who at one time or another were forced away from it have been allowed to have."[14]

This realization led Walker to recognize at once that the Reverend Martin Luther King, Jr., was "The One, The Hero, The Fearless Person for whom we had waited." Struck by King's serenity and courage, Walker knew immediately that she would resist the forces that sought to "disinherit" her and that she would "never be forced away from the land of my birth without a fight." In her 1972 tribute to King, she thanked him for leading this fight: "He gave us back our heritage. He gave us back our homeland, the bones and dust of our ancestors, who may now sleep within our caring *and* our hearing. . . . He gave us continuity of place, without which community is ephemeral. He gave us home." Morgan Freeman said much the same thing some thirty years later. Relishing the irony of the South's role as "the new comfort zone" for so many blacks, Freeman insisted, "If Dr. King were back and he were told that, I think he'd believe it. Of course he would. That's what he meant to happen, that the South would be a place that we don't have to run away from. As a matter of fact, we want to run home."[15]

King was not the only black southerner to lose his life in the struggle that reclaimed the South as home for black Americans. Yet, despite her husband's murder from ambush in 1963, Myrlie Evers insisted that "regardless of what happened in Medger's life, this was his state. There is a degree of anger but also a lot of love. . . . Mississippi is home. It always will be." Elsewhere, black poet and novelist Margaret Walker did not hesitate either in her writings or her conversations to assert that "Mississippi is the epicenter of my life" and that since childhood, she had "had the feel of the South in my blood."[16]

As the author of *Roots*, Alex Haley won fortune and acclaim by tracing his own family's historical and cultural ties to Africa, but he made it clear that his primary identity was derived from the South when he admitted, "I don't know anything I treasure more as a writer than being a Southerner." An enthusiastic supporter of the *Encyclopedia of Southern Culture*, in its foreword Haley not only waxed nostalgic about old men swapping stories and old women quilting, but paid tribute to those who had produced a volume dedicated "to presenting and distilling our southern distinctiveness."[17]

Haley's personal recollections of boyhood Saturdays in Henning, Tennessee, were remarkably similar to Harry Crews's memories of Saturdays in Alma, Georgia: "Saturdays were a big, big day for us. . . . Wagons, buggies, T-Models, A-Models—people bringing stuff from their farms to sell from the back of their wagons. . . . Around 10:30 in the morning the town square was one big, mingled aroma. Together with the noise of people talking and the cats and dogs, mules were stomping their feet and shuddering to make the flies get off for a moment. You'd smell watermelons cut open down the middle. . . . [Y]ou'd smell fried fish and then you'd smell fresh fish . . . celestial barbecue. . . . All these smells just came together—it just transported you. It was our circus, our carnival every Saturday."[18]

Commenting on the assumption that blacks would be hopelessly alienated from a setting where they had suffered so much, Ralph Ellison observed, "I suppose it is hard to contemplate an elasticity which allows us to survive the total efforts at brutalization during various periods and still to affirm the seasons, the landscape, the birds and so on." Charlayne Hunter-Gault called her 1992 memoir *In My Place* because it focused on her resolute decision to abandon the "place" to which the white South's insistence on caste conformity sought to confine her. In doing this, she also claimed her rightful "place" as an American judged by her talents rather than her race and as a southerner entitled by birth and struggle to claim the South as home. Hunter-Gault also found comfort and inspiration in a physical and sensory South that was her "place" as well. Attending summer school in a "hot sultry Athens," she received "an unexpected gift" when she encountered "the evocative sights, sounds and smells of my small-town childhood, the almost overpowering sweet smell of honeysuckle and banana shrub seducing buzzing bumblebees and yellow jackets; the screeching cries of crickets emanating from every shrub and bush; clouds of black starlings producing shadows wherever they flew over the dusty red clay haze. This was the part of the South that I loved, that made me happy to be a Southerner, that left me unaffected by the seamier side, which would deny I could have pride in anything but Aunt Jemima."[19]

Reflecting on her own youthful experiences in Tennessee, poet Nikki Giovanni realized that Knoxville was "a place where no matter what, I belong" and that in turn "Knoxville belongs to me." Determined that her son also "must know we come from somewhere. That we belong," Giovanni penned her autobiographical *Gemini* in which she reflected on her childhood in Knoxville and her grandparents' neighborhood, which had later been destroyed by urban renewal. Giovanni observed poetically that white biographers would "probably talk about my hard childhood/ and never understand that/ all the while I was quite happy." She addressed this concern in *Knoxville, Tennessee*, a beautifully illustrated children's book, which recalled the pleasures of fresh vegetables, barbecue, buttermilk, church socials, and mountain picnics with her grandmother.[20]

Maya Angelou also retained an intense connection with her grandmother's store in Stamps, Arkansas, a gathering place for black cotton pickers, who came in early, still sleepy, but expectant and hopeful, filling the lamp-lit store with "laughing, joking, boasting and bragging." By the end of the day, however, "the sounds of the new morning had been replaced with grumbles about cheating houses, weighted scales, snakes, skimpy cotton, and dusty rows. In cotton-picking time," recalled Angelou, "the late afternoons revealed the harshness of Black Southern life, which in the early morning had been softened by nature's blessing of grogginess, forgetfulness and the soft lamplight." Angelou felt a strong personal attachment to the South as both a place and a source of identity, however. "I do believe once a southerner, always a southerner," she confessed, explaining that the South was "so beautiful, you can understand why people were willing to fight and lose their lives for it. . . . I feel sympathy for black people who have no southern roots."[21]

Alice Walker also expressed regret for her "Northern brothers" who "have never experienced the magnificent quiet of a summer day when the heat is intense and one is so very thirsty, as one moves across the dusty cotton fields, that one learns forever that water is the essence of all life. In the cities, it cannot be so clear to one that he is a creature of the earth, feeling the soil between the toes, smelling the dust thrown up by the rain, loving the earth so much that one longs to taste it and sometimes does." John Oliver Killens found it ironic that the apostles of black nationalism in the 1960s and 1970s failed to understand the importance of the southern black experience rooted in "land, earth, soil, dirt. Black dirt: our own black dirt to dig black hands into, black Southern dirt to create upon, the good clean sweet loamy earth, to hold, to smell, to touch, to taste, to cultivate, to watch the good earth grow, harvest and prosper, to forge black and positive images."[22]

Such emotions seem strikingly reminiscent of the words of Harlem Renaissance writers like Jean Toomer, Langston Hughes, and Sterling Brown, all of whom alluded to the beauty and sensory pull of the South. Certainly, Walker's comments reflect the admiration for Zora Neale Hurston that led her to seek out Hurston's grave in an obscure, overgrown Florida cemetery and mark it with a headstone identifying the deceased as "Zora Neale Hurston: A Genius of the South." Hurston's perspective on southern black life had been too airy and upbeat for many black intellectuals of the Harlem Renaissance, but contemporary students of black culture (and southern culture in general) have praised Hurston for refusing to stress the total victimization of African Americans in the Jim Crow South. As Walker put it, Hurston's spirit and her work were distinguished by "racial health—a sense of black people as complete, complex, undiminished human beings."[23]

If, in the post–civil rights Sunbelt era, white writers seemed to shift their energies from the struggle with the South's backwardness to the struggle with its ostensible "progress," black writers could redirect their focus as well, following the example of Hurston by looking beyond the debilitating effects of slavery and Jim Crow. Instead, they emphasized the strength and determination of black southerners who had resisted these institutions and their potentially debilitating effects and in the process created their own sense of community, identity, and purpose.

Sounding much like Hurston, Raymond Andrews dedicated his novel *Appalachee Red* "to all those who ever picked a boll of cotton, pulled a peach or gone to town on a Saturday afternoon." When Andrews decided to become a novelist, he determined to write "books about what I knew best: small town and rural black folks in the South and their relationship to both the land and their white neighbors. . . . My American roots (like those of most Afro-Americans) are southern rural. This particular land and the individuals who have lived and died on it are what my books are about." *Appalachee Red* told the story of a young black man who returns to the small Georgia town where his father is the most prominent member of the local white community. Red effectively paralyzes the cruel and overbearing white sheriff who cannot bring himself to believe that this clever and audacious young man actually has black blood. As a result, Red runs his illegal liquor and gambling operations with apparent impunity, but when he shows up with a chauffeur and a "big new hardtop black Cadillac with its fishtails" and its "long, cloud-tickling radio aerial," he shakes the community "by the very roots, especially the white community, where the belief was deeply ingrained that any nigger, red or otherwise, with means enough to own, and gall enough to display, a car as big and expensive as a Cadillac posed a bigger threat to their existence than . . . than . . . Communism!!" Andrews succeeded in conveying the flavor of rural and small-town black life so well because his roots were in the village of Madison, Georgia, and despite leaving it in 1949, he maintained close ties there, insisting in 1988 that "I still care for Madison and its people because I have many memories of the place and to me it will always be home."[24]

No longer feeling such pressure to write anti–Jim Crow, "protest" fiction, black writers could also address issues like gender and other complexities, including tensions and conflicts within the black family and community. Born to a share-cropper family, Alice Walker grew up near Eatonton, Georgia, had studied at Spelman and Sarah Lawrence, and worked as a civil rights activist in Mississippi during the 1960s. Yet, Walker's fiction revealed her desire to look beyond (though certainly not ignore) white oppression and explore themes of community, identity, and gender in her writing. She found it regrettable that "even black critics have assumed that a book that deals with the relationship between members of a black family—or between a man and a woman—is less important than one that has white people as primary antagonists. The consequences of this are that many of our books by major writers (always male) tell us little about the culture, history, or future, imagination, fantasies, and so on, of black people, and a lot about isolated (often improbable) or limited encounters with a nonspecific white world."[25]

Walker's 1982 novel *The Color Purple* won the Pulitzer Prize and became a runaway best seller. In both the novel and the subsequent film adaptation, whites remain more of a secondary than a primary menace throughout. The most controversial aspect of Walker's story was the way the black male characters assert the masculinity that they must repress in the company of whites by brutalizing and exploiting black women. Raped by a man she believes is her father, Celie, the downtrodden protagonist, becomes a mother at the age of fourteen and is "given" by her "father" to "Mister," a widower, who further abuses and dominates her. When he brings his former lover, Shug Avery, into their home, however, what seems like Celie's ultimate humiliation actually marks the beginning of her liberation, as her emotional and physical relationship with Shug encourages her to resist Mister's tyranny. Celie, Shug, and Celie's stepdaughter-in-law, Sophia, present admirable examples of independence and determination, and by the novel's end a male-female rapprochement of sorts is effected, although on much more equal terms than those with which the novel began.[26]

The pressures to present a united front during the activist phase of the civil rights movement would have made a novel such as Walker's most unlikely during the 1960s, but *The Color Purple* represented a dramatic breakthrough in the treatment of southern black life by black writers themselves. It reflected not only the influences of the woman's liberation movement, but the accomplishments of a civil rights crusade that, whatever its shortcomings, had nonetheless given black writers the opportunity to treat their own culture and community with greater candor and critical insight.[27]

Like Walker, a number of women writers offered a decidedly more feminist perspective on southern black life. A victim of rape at age eleven, Endesha Ida Mae Holland was soon earning money as a prostitute, and by her account, it was her effort to offer her services to civil rights activist Bob Moses that led her into the SNCC office in Greenwood, Mississippi, and from there into the civil rights struggle itself. Describing the parameters of her life before the civil rights movement came to Greenwood, Holland admitted, "I had never read a book written by an African-American. I didn't know that black people could write books. I never knew that Blacks had done any great things. I was always conscious of my inferiority, and I always remembered my place—until the

Civil rights movement came to the town where I was born and grew up." Her involvement with the movement "turned my narrow space into a country bigger than I'd ever imagined," and by the end of the 1960s Holland was immersed in black studies, acquainting herself with the work of Richard Wright and learning that "it was okay to be black." Soon, as an aspiring playwright, she was using memory "to rescue and reconstruct—to search, document, and celebrate—my Mississippi Delta's community of Black people . . . and my community of black women in particular."[28]

Like many southern expatriates, white and black, Georgia writer Tina McElroy Ansa discovered "how southern I am" while living outside the region as she dreamed of "taking long car trips down red dirt roads that smelled rich and musty when a sudden cloudburst pounded them" or seeing "the figure of a farmer way off in the field and blow my horn and see him raise his arm in an anonymous greeting." In her fiction Ansa abandoned the standard, almost formulaic setting of a black family struggling against racism and poverty to write instead about middle-class blacks. She also took on the venerable stereotype of the black mother as the long-suffering, always-loving matriarch who holds the family together and inspires her children to build a better life for themselves. "I wanted to write about a mother who wasn't always there for her children, who wasn't always good," she explained. This she did in her novel *Ugly Ways*, which opens as the three Lovejoy sisters return for the funeral of their mother, Esther "Mudear" Lovejoy. The girls recall their mother as selfish and cold, more interested in her garden, her television, and her luxurious private bathroom than her daughters or her husband. Meanwhile, Mudear is not taking all this lying down. Her spirit sees and comments caustically on her daughters' "ugly ways" throughout the novel and, for good measure, dismisses their father as just like all men: "none of them worth the hard-on they think they got to offer you."[29]

Ansa also explored the strong black woman stereotype in *The Hand I Fan With*. The title recalls a once-common expression among southern blacks that refers to a person on whom one depends heavily. "She's the hand I fan with" aptly describes Lena McPherson, who is constantly absorbed in fixing other people's problems. In a stunning revelation, Lena's grandmother, whom she has always considered "the very essence of power and wisdom," returns as a ghost and confesses: "We think we know so much while we alive, Lena. Deciding stuff, fixing stuff, saving people, settling turbulence. Especially us black women. We think we can fix it all. And we don't know shit, baby."[30]

One of the most remarkable of the South's new African American writers was Dori Sanders, a self-described "tired old bee-stung woman," who grew peaches and produce and sold them from a roadside stand in rural York County, South Carolina. Sanders was one of ten children born to one of the earliest black landowning families in the area. *Clover*, her first novel, told the story of a ten-year-old black girl, whose father dies suddenly after marrying a white woman, leaving the little girl struggling to establish a relationship with her white stepmother. The novel's opening sentence is so classically southern that it might serve equally well as the first line of a country song: "They dressed me in white for my daddy's funeral."[31]

Sanders's second novel, *Her Own Place*, focuses on one woman's successful struggle to build a life for her and her children in the post–World War II South. Mae Lee Barnes's story is told in straightforward, sparse prose without the tension typical of Alice Walker's fiction, but the story is nonetheless richly evocative of southern life and the changes and continuities it has seen in the last half century. Mae remains as resolute and admirable as a woman and as a member of the middle class as she was when she was struggling to feed her five children and hold onto her land. As she gradually becomes a respected matron, she interacts with whites on an equal, if somewhat tentative, even experimental, basis, but after she has hosted a highly successful tea party for her white fellow hospital volunteers, Mae observes matter-of-factly: "They're no better than colored people. . . . And no worse."[32]

Mae's perspective seems in keeping with that of Ernest J. Gaines, whom Alice Walker praised for treating "whites and blacks exactly as he sees them and *knows* them instead of writing of one group as a vast malignant lump and of the other as a conglomerate of perfect virtues." Gaines left Louisiana as a child in 1948 to live with his mother and step-father in California in order to get the education "that they thought I rightly deserved." Even as a youth, Gaines noticed that the white southern novelists whose work he devoured seldom developed black characters beyond the stereotypical "mammy" or "wench" or "Tom" or "bad nigger." The same writers who could so effectively evoke the "odor of grass and trees after a summer rain" or make you see "better than if you were actually there, the red dust in Georgia or the black mud of Mississippi" presented blacks as either "children" or "seers," sometimes needing "to be saved," sometimes acting as "saviors" for someone else but "very seldom what the average being was."[33]

In his own writing Gaines sought not only to capture the sights, smells, sounds, and feel of rural Louisiana but to "see on paper those Louisiana black

children walking to school on cold days while yellow Louisiana busses passed
them by" or "black parents going to work before the sun came up and coming
back home to look after their children after the sun went down." Gaines pursued this goal in all his fiction, but nowhere more successfully than in his *Autobiography of Miss Jane Pittman* (1971). In this "folk autobiography," as she
called it, Gaines told the story of a 110-year-old woman who was born a slave
but lived to witness and participate in the civil rights movement's assault on
the white-supremacist institutions that had circumscribed her entire existence. Because she is respected by white and black, the ancient Miss Jane is an
inspiring symbol of unity for local blacks who remain determined to challenge the Jim Crow system in the fictional Louisiana town of Bayonne even
after Jimmy (their leader and Miss Jane's grandson) is killed by whites. Miss
Jane is in some ways comparable to Faulkner's Dilsey in *The Sound and the
Fury*, on whom all, black or white, depended and to whom all likewise accorded a large measure of respect. Yet, more than a narrator, more than a sur-
vivor, and more than a pillar of strength, she is an active, though sometimes
flawed, participant in 100 years of black life and struggle.[34]

Where the autobiography of Miss Jane Pittman concludes with a communal black awakening, Gaines's *A Gathering of Old Men* (1983) is more the story
of a masculine awakening, again set in Bayonne, Louisiana. It focuses on the
shooting of Beau Boutan, a racially abusive Cajun whose death seems certain
to lead to the lynching of the suspected killer, an old black man named Mathu.
The dignified and courageous Mathu seems in many ways a dead ringer for
Faulkner's Lucas Beauchamp. Moreover, as with Charles Mallison in *Intruder
in the Dust*, Mathu's would-be protector is a young member of the white planter
class, Candy Marshall. In Faulkner's work, however, the salvation of Lucas
Beauchamp is left almost solely in the hands of the white better element, while
in Gaines's story Mathu's black contemporaries, the "old men" who "gather,"
all attempt (as does Candy) to take responsibility for the killing of which he is
suspected. Likewise, despite their age, they also come armed, if not quite dangerous, anticipating a showdown with old "Fix" Boutan, Beau's father, who,
like his son, has a reputation for racial abuse.

Fix never shows, however, his spirit broken by the refusal of his other son,
Gil, to take part in killing Mathu. While the Boutan family seems to be disin-
tegrating, the group of old black men who have suffered together through so
much comes and stays together as they find the courage to stand united in
armed defiance. When a gun battle erupts with Beau's redneck friends who are

bent on revenge, Charlie, Beau's actual slayer who has fled but returns to take responsibility for his actions, tells one of the "old men," "Don't never be scared no more. . . . Life's so sweet when you know you ain't no more coward."[35]

Gaines also weaves another favorite theme of the Southern Renaissance into his story—the traumatic effects of economic "progress" on a paternalistic plantation society. Throughout the novel, both plantation owners and plantation workers show contempt for the tractors that have revolutionized life in this agricultural region and come between the people and the land. One of Gaines's characters recalls his brother's John Henry-esque race in his mule-drawn wagon against a tractor and the fatal beating he received for winning. Another sees the tractor as a threat to his heritage, warning that "one day that tractor was g'on come in there and plow up them graves, getting rid of all proof that we ever was" but vowing, "they ain't go'n do it while I'm still here."[36]

Like Raymond Andrews, Alice Walker, and Tina McElroy Ansa, Gaines had no objection to having his work identified with the South. Likewise, asked whether he objected to being labeled a "southern black writer," Randall Kenan also responded, "I was born in North Carolina and my skin is the color of coffee without cream. To me it's silly to assume that I can be anything other than a Southern, black writer." Dori Sanders was particularly forthright when she insisted, "I am a southern writer and felt in advance I'd be seen that way . . . such a richness of place! How could someone grow up in the South and not aspire to be a writer?"[37]

Sanders's comments were hardly surprising. Unlike many of their white counterparts struggling to come to grips with what they saw as a contemporary No South, as Frank Shelton suggested in 1994, southern black writers were still pursuing "the meaning of life . . . through forging a personal connection with Southern history." Dominated by "enslavement, prejudice and racism," this history gave them the strength derived from "a relationship with the land and a place in a community of people nurtured by a pastoral environment." In fact, by the 1990s Fred Hobson believed the black writer might actually be seen as "the quintessential Southern writer—with his emphasis on family and community, his essentially concrete vision, his feeling for place, his legacy of failure, poverty, defeat, and those other well-known qualities of the Southern experience, his immersion in history and what it produced." To Hobson, any writer with those qualities and that legacy would seem to be, in many respects, "the truest contemporary heir to the Southern literary tradition."[38]

The emergence of black writers as the most identifiably southern literary figures of the late twentieth century struck Hobson as "a final irony of Southern
history." In reality, however, other but related ironies lay close at hand. Although they have yet to achieve the level of anxiety shown by their white contemporaries, there is growing evidence that the generally improving
socioeconomic circumstances of black southerners may be causing them some
concern about a loss of group identity as well. Writing in 1970, when the
echoes of the civil rights crusade had scarcely died away, Alice Walker had
exulted that "what the black Southern writer inherits as a natural right is a
sense of community." The hard-won advances of the civil rights movement
allowed blacks to embrace the South as their homeland and celebrate and
examine their attachments to its people and places. For many black
southerners, however, the long-awaited, much-suffered-for destruction of
Jim Crow with its barriers to educational, social, and economic advancement actually seemed in the long run to lead to erosion of this cherished
sense of solidarity and belonging.[39]

As the last generation of black southerners who grew up under segregation
approached middle age, some were even expressing a decided sense of loss
when they reflected on their experiences in the Jim Crow South. Born and
raised in Glen Allan, Mississippi, and gone on to a successful business career,
Clifton Taulbert admitted, "Even though segregation was a painful reality for
us, there were some very good things that happened. Today I enjoy the broader
society in which I live, and I would never want to return to forced segregation,
but I also have a deeply-felt sense that important values were conveyed to me
in my colored childhood, values we're in danger of losing in our integrated
world. As a child I was not only protected, but also nourished, encouraged,
taught, and loved by people who, with no land, little money and few other
resources, displayed the strength of a love which knew no measure. I have come
to believe that this love is the true value, the legitimate measure of a people's
worth."[40]

Thirty years after the blood and terror of Freedom Summer, some black
southerners associated integration with a loss of "spiritual backbone" in the
black community. Reflecting on the support she had received from fellow participants in the civil rights movement, Linda Taylor remarked, "I could do
nothing *but* succeed because these people would not *let* me do anything else."
Recalling her experience at all-black Williston High School in Wilmington,
North Carolina, Linda Pearce recalled that "we were in a cocoon bathed in a
warm fluid, where we were expected to excel. . . . [A]nd then something called

desegregation punctured it. We went from our own land to being tourists in someone else's. It never did come together, and I think it's on the verge of falling apart altogether now."[41]

As an adolescent returned to New York in 1971 after a four-year stay in Charleston, Jacqueline Joan Johnson soon realized that she missed the South: "I was used to having a community and a presence in that community. I was watched by my elders and my peers and expected to be somebody." Betty Jo Hayes had similar feelings about her student experience at Tampa's all-black Middleton High, where "we were indeed a family. We were embraced by teachers, protected, taught everything that they thought we would need to get out there and improve the world as such. . . . We were a proud, proud, proud group; a proud group of kids." When integration came and Middleton was closed, Hayes recalled, it was "as if death had come to a community." Otis Anthony conceded that despite the best efforts of his excellent, nurturing teachers, scarce resources and inadequate facilities had diminished the quality of the education he received at Blake, Tampa's other historically black high school. Yet, as a student at the University of South Florida, he had penned a nostalgic poem stressing the need to "Remember how sweet and communal it was to be black, on black, in black, with black, around black, being black, such a delight. Remember how it was before desegregation."[42]

In black neighborhoods at large, with integration and expanded opportunities, residents moved up and out in increasing numbers, and once-thriving black enterprises struggled to remain competitive in an integrated marketplace. Returning to Clarksdale, Mississippi, after a thirty-year absence, Helen O'Neal-McCray was shocked by the boarded up black businesses and the signs of community and individual deterioration and decay: "Black people used to live all together, shacks and nice houses. . . . Now they're divided." In his elegant memoir, *Colored People*, Henry Louis Gates, Jr., told the story of his youth in the paper mill town of Piedmont, West Virginia, and conveyed his genuine sense of loss as "the last wave of the civil rights era finally came . . . crashing down on the colored world of Piedmont."[43]

In reality, the sense of lost community among many black southerners who had lived in the South before and after Jim Crow merely confirmed that black southerners had managed to retain a viable culture and a sense of their own worth in a society where color barriers had confronted them at every turn. By the end of the twentieth century, they seemed to reflect so wistfully on this accomplishment precisely because they felt increasingly hard pressed to sustain it in a post–Jim Crow era where color counts for less but, apparently, so do family, religion, community, and other affirmative institutions that had helped to unite them in the face of oppression and restriction. This reaction seems comparable in a sense to the way some residents of the former Soviet bloc now seem to regard their former existence, however restricted and austere, behind the iron curtain. One of the most successful films ever made in Germany, the award-winning "Goodbye Lenin," quickly attracted more than two million viewers by demonstrating that, prior to the collapse of the Berlin Wall, East Germans had maintained their own "very normal German world" despite the efforts of the communist leadership to regulate their lives and restrict their thoughts.[44]

Before integration there had been "vibrant black communities all over the South," Randall Kenan explained. The destruction of these communities was "a necessary evil," but by the end of the twentieth century, he saw black people "recognizing bit by bit how important these places were. In this time we hated them but we also idealize them because you had black doctors living next door to black postal workers and institutions like the church were very active and powerful. Now you have people coming back and recognizing that these communities served a purpose." Kenan grew up in the post–Jim Crow era in the small town of Chinquapin, North Carolina, "going to hog killings one minute and watching Star Trek the next," and his fiction captured the struggle of black and white southerners to adapt to the changes both in their own interactions and in the larger economic and cultural contexts of their lives. Chinquapin formed the basis for Kenan's fictional "Tim's Creek," North Carolina, his equivalent of Faulkner's Yoknapatawpha. His descriptions of the people and their natural environs were typically evocative, but his portrait of small-town southern life was by no means totally romantic. Neither his novel *A Visitation of Spirits* (1989) nor his short story collection *Let the Dead Bury Their Dead* (1992) shrank from the reality of religious, racial, or sexual intolerance. In *A Visitation of Spirits*, black teenager Horace Cross attempts to come to terms with his homosexuality in a religious and social context where exposure meant condemnation and ostracism. Kenan's story "The Foundations of the Earth" offered a poignant treatment of an elderly black woman's attempt to understand her deceased gay grandson by getting better acquainted with his white former lover. Despite their shortcomings, for Kenan and many others the southern communities of their youth represented their cultural roots, the places where both their regional and racial identities had been shaped. Kenan believed that, much like William Faulkner and Robert Penn Warren, southern black writers also walked "a fine line, something between revulsion and acceptance . . . so often reflecting about wanting to get out of the South, but at the same time knowing . . . that this is what sustains you, this is what makes you who you are."[45]

In Toni Morrison's *Beloved*, the young Denver asks her mother, Sethe, why she and the others who had fled "Sweet Home" (the plantation where they had been enslaved) continued to talk about it so much: "Looks like if it was so sweet you would have stayed." Sethe explains that "it's where we were. All together. Comes back whether we want it or not." Throughout Morrison's fiction, as her characters reflect on their experiences in the South, painful as they were, they recall feeling a strength and wholeness that was lost when they moved to the North.[46]

Ralph Ellison observed in 1965 that "in this country no one is free not to have a homeland." His homeland consisted of Abbeville, South Carolina, and Oklahoma City, and "that is enough for me," he announced, warning that "by raising the possibility of Africa as a 'homeland' we give Africa an importance on the symbolic level that it does not have in the actual thinking of people." Some thirty years later, Eddy Harris explained, "I did not travel across Africa to find my roots. I traveled South to find them. For the South, not Africa, is home to Black Americans and Black Americans as a race are essentially southerners." As Randall Kenan trekked across the nation gathering material for *Walking on Water* (1999), his survey of African American identity and attitudes at the millennium, he met black people in locales as far flung as Utah and Alaska who yearned for a South they had never seen or experienced. "Most African-Americans in this country can't trace their roots back to Africa," he concluded, "but they can certainly trace them back to Tennessee, Georgia, North Carolina, Mississippi, the Southern states."[47]

Some black intellectuals actually seemed to think that the South represented both a North American homeland and a cultural way station where blacks could best explore or at least *feel* their African connections. John Oliver Killens argued that "the people of the black South are much closer to their African roots, in its culture, its humanity, the beat and rhythms of its music, its concept of family, its dance, and its spirituality." Although she was born in Ohio, Toni Morrison consistently presented the South as a vital linkage to Africa and the bedrock, not just of black suffering and struggle, but of black identity as well. Morrison's characters, Deborah H. Barnes observed, "recognize the South as . . . the wellspring of their notions of identity, community, [and] nurturance."[48]

Morrison's concern that African Americans might reject or lose sight of the importance of their southern (and African) heritage and experience came through forcefully in *Song of Solomon*, which told the story of Macon Dead III, a.k.a. "Milkman," an immature, self-centered young man who is dispatched to the South for the first time by his father to search for some gold, which the father believes his sister may have stolen from him. Ultimately, Milkman Dead understands that he had been figuratively "dead" or at least bereft of identity until he came to the South and learned about his family's history and his ties to a southern black community that serves as his connection to Africa as well.

Milkman's nurturing aunt, Pilate, is strikingly "African" in appearance and demeanor and exudes the mysterious and supernatural sensitivity of an African conjure woman. With Pilate's help, he gradually unravels the legend of his great-grandfather, "Solomon," one of the legendary "Flying Africans," who, according to a pervasive black folk tale, simply took wing and flew back to Africa, leaving behind not only the chains of slavery, but a wife and twenty-one children. At first, Milkman is elated to know that his ancestor had freed himself from slavery and its burdens, but he eventually understands that accepting responsibility for one's actions and obligations as a member of a family or a community is more spiritually liberating than physical or emotional flight, and he realizes that Pilate, who has bound herself so tightly to her ancestry and heritage, could actually fly "without leaving the ground."[49]

Several critics have argued that Morrison's novels warn blacks against "disremembering" their southern roots. Patricia Yeager has suggested that Morrison and other African American women writers who were not born in the South nonetheless "needed to think about the South as a way to think about the meaning of being black and . . . needed to think about the meaning of being black as a way of thinking about the South." Though he, too, was born and raised elsewhere, Eddy Harris came down to see the region for himself because "only in the South could I discover where my beginnings as a Black American have gone. Without realizing it at the time, I was going home." Harris had always felt shame and resentment toward his great-great-grandfather, Joseph, for not rebelling against his enslavement. In Virginia, however, he discovers Joseph's manumission papers and reflects on the fact that his ancestor rose from slavery to establish a stagecoach line and acquire 325 acres of land and nearly $3,000 worth of additional property and thus left a substantial legacy for his descendants, none of which he could have done had he sacrificed his life in a futile rebellion against his owner.[50]

After touching Joseph's papers, Harris knows that he had "found my roots." Afterward, he recalls, "I went outside and leaned against a tree that Joseph might have leaned against. I lay on the southern grass. The wind caressed my cheek. I looked up at the cloudless sky and breathed in the cool moist air of afternoon. It smelled like home." Not only had Harris become much better reconciled to the South, he had also realized that his journey to "touch the soul of the South" has actually led him to the discovery of "my own black soul."[51]

Even for those who tried, separating the sources and symbols of their southernness from those of their blackness was no easy matter. Though he did not object to being seen as a Southern writer, Randall Kenan wondered whether "I am a writer of the South and about the South or a writer of blackness." By the 1990s Kenan's Chinquapin had been "yanked . . . into the heady whorl of the postmodern era." Porch-sitting had given way to HBO and Cinemax, church attendance had fallen off noticeably, and small farms were being gobbled up by large ones. In this evolving "postmodern present," he could go out and get real down-home barbecue or chitlins and return home to "watch BET, and check my e-mail after calling my friend in Japan." Still, Kenan feels a distinct sense of loss as he sees Chinquapin "becoming like the rest of America," because it has provided the formative frame of reference not only for his southernness but his blackness as well.[52]

Kenan associated his initial "vision of being black" with "the plain yet endless beauty of the lowlands of North Carolina" and "the men in coveralls, the women with snuff tucked deep in their bottom lip." In his early years, blackness had meant "a pointillism of culture" that included "collard greens. 'Amazing Grace, How Sweet the Sound.' Grits and tote. Quilts and pig's feet. Thundering preachers and prayer clothes. It was head rags and chitlins, 'Chain of Fools' and 'Swing Low Sweet Chariot.' Ultra-sheen, Afro-sheen, neck bones, cornrows." Many of what Kenan called "these signs and symbols" of blackness that were "the air I breathed, the water I drank, the ground upon which I walked" were also the signifiers of southernness for many whites and blacks as well.[53]

When Kenan heard his elderly kin tell stories of the many hardships and scattered joys of "'the old days'" in the South, he had "taken for granted that this tapestry, this ever-reaching-back fabric was what being black was all about." As an adult, however, he seemed to realize that the same figures from his family, school, and church experiences who taught him "those things that I had taken so for granted about being black" had shaped his southernness as well. Surveying the contemporary scene, Kenan suspected that the experiences of Chinquapin's black children are now little different from those of black children "in Seattle and Madison and Salt Lake City and New York." Not only was Chinquapin "becoming like the rest of America," but instead of being instilled by people like his father, his aunts, and uncles, and his teachers and pastor, blackness was now being "dictated by The Martin Lawrence Show and Moeshea and Snoop Doggy Dogg and Dr. Dre and *Vibe* magazine, and . . . Paramount." Sensing this, Kenan also knew that "what's true of African-American identity is true for southern identity. A lot of it is fragile and in danger, and a lot of it is so much a part of us that we don't even see it."[54]

The discovery of what Thadious Davis called "the regionality of the black self" was not confined to black intellectuals. As the twentieth century drew to a close, some African Americans who lived outside the South were clearly drawing on their southern roots to help them define their blackness. The romanticization of the "redneck" that captivated so many southern whites already seemed to have a counterpart among southern-born blacks in northern cities who actively flaunted their southern drawls, dialects, and dietary preferences. Some even proudly identified themselves as "bamas," formerly a stereotypical term of derision directed by northern blacks at any southern black who seemed "country" or "rank and unrepentant in his or her backwardness."[55]

In Washington, D.C., Jerry "The Bama" Washington hosted a weekly radio program known as *The Bama Hour*, which featured not only blues music but the earthy, homespun stories and ruminations of Washington himself. Although he was the adopted son of a Georgia railroad laborer and a domestic worker, Washington's down-home drawl and rustic wisdom masked his study at Morehouse, where he was a classmate of the Reverend Martin Luther King, Jr. His defiant embrace of the Bama stereotype achieved what one journalist called a "sly reverse chic" with a huge listening audience who seemed to see his show as the black equivalent of Midwestern humorist Garrison Keillor's Lake Wobegon. There was even talk of national syndication before Washington's death in 1994 from complications of diabetes brought on by his insistence on living out "the grits- and chitlins-eating, hard-drinking, woman-chasing, blues-playing deejay" persona he had created for himself.[56]

"Nap" Turner, a bluesman who became the new host of *The Bama Hour*, explained that Washington had "used the attitudes and language of that rural southern world and what he said ranked with Langston Hughes or James Weldon Johnson." Turner even introduced *Bama Hour* listeners to Hughes's Jesse B. Semple, a countrified character created by Hughes in 1943 for his columns in the *Chicago Defender*. Hughes stopped using Semple in 1960 amid protests that the "Simple" stories were conveying a less than positive image of blackness to a younger generation. Reading from Hughes's "Simple Stories," however, Turner insisted that despite his atrocious grammar and mangled syntax, Semple's candid observations ("Whiskey just naturally likes me but beer likes me better") offered important insights into the feelings of "the common man" about black life and "the whole human condition" during that era.[57]

Nationally syndicated radio personality Tom Joyner, a native of Tuskegee, Alabama, was also a self-described "bama." His "southern" style drew some complaints when he first began work as a disk jockey in Chicago in the late 1970s, but he soon achieved phenomenal popularity with his down-home approach and his emphasis on the southern roots of black music. Alluding to the "'Mo' Town" sound, Joyner insisted, "Detroit is nothing but Mississippi North."[58]

Perhaps even more surprising than the "bama" phenomenon was the interest of some more affluent African Americans in collecting "black memorabilia" such as black-face lawn jockeys, cookie jars, salt shakers, lamps, posters, advertisements featuring the stereotypical black mammy or "Little Black Sambo" or other such racist representations produced originally by and for whites. A collector himself, former civil rights activist and board chairman of the NAACP Julian Bond explained that "for others . . . these artifacts summon up yesterday's world, but in our hands and homes they . . . speak of triumph and overcoming, and inform us that despite what others thought and believed, we were never what they suggest." Other collectors reportedly included Oprah Winfrey, Bill Cosby, and Spike Lee, who used them to symbolize African American wealth in his film *Bamboozled*. Well-to-do Houstonian Richard Newman, who owned roughly 1,500 such items, conceded that others might find them "distasteful," but, he explained, "If you are somewhat sure of yourself, I think it is easier to take it in a historic context."[59]

Elsewhere, Sherman Evans and Angel Quintero, two young African American entrepreneurs in Charleston, sensed that there might be a market among more affluent young southerners of both races for another distasteful southern symbol taken out of historical context. Targeting the upscale clothing market featuring brands like Tommy Hilfiger and Polo, the two launched a bold new venture called "Nu South Apparel," featuring sportswear bearing a logo of a Confederate battle flag whose green stars and black cross presented the symbolic colors of the African liberation movement.

For African Americans, Evans explained, the Nu South flag amounted to taking "the opposition's worst image" and wearing it "with pride. By wearing it . . . you embrace it and make it mean something else." To many preaching and practicing capitalists of both races, the Nu South logo offered "a simple message of work, self-improvement, independence, and by using the Confederate flag, a complete rejection of the lingering rhetoric of victimization." Preaching and practicing historians might take a more skeptical view. Observing that southerners of both races have been "oppressed by the history of the South," Evans seemed to suggest that keeping that oppressive history alive could serve no constructive purpose in the lives of up-and-coming young southerners of either color. "What we were saying," Evans explained further, "was that all that talk about the past is just that. It's past." An early version of the Nu South T-shirt even contradicted a famous Faulknerian dictum with the matter-of-fact declaration, "The Past is the Past." Troubling as it might be to some, behind the Nu-South idea was the kind of self-confidence born of upward mobility that had also allowed southern whites to embrace the stereotyping inherent in the "Redneck" or "Bubba" personae.[60]

Not everyone was pleased by this apparent affinity of some African Americans for the scenes and symbols of the good old days when times were bad. Shocked to find such a lucrative market among "urban, economically privileged" blacks for memorabilia that they once condemned as racist and demeaning, Lynn Casmier-Pas charged that those who acquired such items were not only seeking "a fantasy of black community in the racism of historical icons" but trying to distance themselves from their less fortunate counterparts who were still experiencing racial discrimination on a daily and firsthand basis. Meanwhile, Adolph Reed, Jr., noted that the "nostalgic" narrative of segregation had gained "nearly universal status in black public discourse." However, Reed argued that the major contributors to the "burgeoning black memoir industry" seemed to share a middle-class upbringing as the children or wards of "community notables and elites" who were often able to insulate them from constant contact with the most brutal aspects of the Jim Crow system and assure that they were "nurtured and catered to" in their segregated upbringing.[61]

It was certainly true that more positive reflections on black life under Jim Crow tended to be associated with a family history of landholding or relative prominence in the community. Clifton Taulbert's imposing, Buddha-like great-grandfather, "Poppa," was a "well-known and respected Baptist preacher" who shielded him "from the harsher realities of our complex social environment." Likewise, Henry Louis Gates was one of the first black students to attend a previously all-white school; "from the first day of first grade," he had been "marked out to excel," owing in no small measure to the prominence of his mother's family, the Colemans, who were "a very big deal in Piedmont," so much so that they were "classed off, as the tradition says," and "didn't hang out with other colored people very much."[62]

While there are definite class implications attached to the celebration of what Reed called "a prelapsarian black communal order," the nature of those implications is less than clear. Nationally, the growth in the ratio between the mean income of the top 20 percent and bottom 20 percent of black families exceeded that for whites by 21 percent between 1966 and 2001. Did, as Reed suggested, the effort to construct a warm and fuzzy memory of an era when a common oppression had ostensibly rendered all blacks fundamentally equal feed a self-satisfaction born of having triumphed over adversities that had vanquished others? Here again, it seems more likely that the expression of a perhaps reassuringly unrequitable longing for a time when all who were "colored" were supposedly united in their inequality reflected not smugness but genuine feelings of guilt or regret over the increasing social and economic distance among African Americans.[63]

Expressions of nostalgia for black life in the Jim Crow era certainly ran contrary to the recollections of veterans of the civil rights movement like Anne Moody, whose *Coming of Age in Mississippi* (1968) recounted her own traumatic conflict-ridden experience as she worked so hard and risked so much to bring an end to segregation. Yet, those who voiced such sentiments yearned not for the days of racial separation but for what Walker called "the solidarity and sharing a modest existence can sometimes bring." Another African American observer drew a sharp distinction between "nostalgia for segregation itself" and hunger for "the sense of community cohesiveness that segregation inadvertently helped foster" before the expanded opportunities and choices in housing, jobs, and schools secured by the civil rights movement "tended to

separate us, particularly by class." Clearly, concern about the loss of racial cohesiveness had intensified as it became apparent that growing numbers of the
black migrants to the South were upper-middle-class professionals who settled
in racially diverse suburbs beyond the economic reach of most of their fellow
African Americans. Racism and racial tensions were hardly on the verge of
extinction, but in the suburban South emerging evidence of new affinities based
on class as well as race suggested further erosion of a sense of community
among southern blacks.[64]

Writer James Alan McPherson remembered that during his childhood in
Savannah, "enforced segregation" had at least helped to sustain "a cohesive
black community." As he pondered the growth of Atlanta and especially its
suburbs, however, McPherson sensed a definite "tension between the new and
the communal South." Recalling an incident that occurred at a time when black
children in Atlanta were falling victim to a serial killer, McPherson explained
that he found himself at a black church in the Atlanta suburbs carrying a suitcase and needing a ride to nearby East Point, only to find that "no one seemed
willing to offer a ride to a stranger with a suitcase." Finally, a black man who
was picking up his daughter at a Girl Scout meeting agreed to carry him in his
truck. McPherson appreciated the man's generosity but noted his obvious anxiety about picking up a stranger, even another black man: "He drove with one
hand, placing his other hand and arm around his daughter, drawing her close
to him and away from me. He drove on through those suburban streets in this
way, torn between a fading communal sense and a determination to protect
his daughter. . . . I wish spirits like his could be preserved in all the suburbs,
black and white and ethnically mixed, in the Becoming South."[65]

As a concerned Henry Louis Gates explained, "Precisely because of the gains
we made through the civil rights movement and affirmative action, we have
two distinct classes in black America, and unless we do something drastic,
never the twain will meet between those two classes. Martin Luther King didn't
die for that." Randall Kenan certainly seemed to be worrying about this when
he asked himself, "Did I, in my attempts to learn and to experience another
world, somehow lose, divest, mitigate or disavow who or what I was? Did I in
mingling and commingling with white folks, dilute or pollute or weaken my
legacy as a son of a son of a son of slaves stolen from Africa?"[66]

Elizabeth Fortson Arroyo expressed similar concerns about her southernness
as she sought to measure it against that of others. Educated at Harvard and
Columbia, Arroyo insisted, "I feel Southern the same way an Irish American
feels Irish. My roots are in the South, and Southern words and ways are a part

of me." Arroyo nonetheless termed herself an "asterisk southerner," because although "I take great pride in being a Southerner, I'm just not sure if I am one." Her parents were indisputably Southern, but because of her birth in Washington, D.C., and her lack of a pronounced accent, Arroyo could not help but worry, much like her upwardly mobile white contemporaries, "Is it enough to feel Southern, or must others around you (with shinier credentials) also take you to be so?" Although she was "concerned . . . that the very act of my self-analysis on this topic betrays me," Arroyo also took some comfort in Drew Faust's observation that "attempts at self-interpretation have become one of the region's most characteristic cultural products," and she posed a question appropriate for many contemporary southerners, white and black, when she asked, "What could be more Southern than to obsess about being Southern?"[67]

11

Divided by a Common Past

HISTORY AND IDENTITY IN THE CONTEMPORARY SOUTH

BY THE END OF THE TWENTIETH CENTURY, a common desire among both blacks and whites to reclaim their sense of regional identity seemed to have the potential to further racial reconciliation in the South. W. J. Cash had argued, "Negro entered into white man as profoundly as white man entered into Negro" in the South, and Ralph Ellison put it more succinctly when he insisted, shortly before his death in 1994, that "you can't be Southern without being black and you can't be a black Southerner without being white." Charlayne Hunter-Gault assured her largely white audience at the University of Georgia in 1988 that the South was the nation's only "true melting pot," insisting that regardless of race, southerners were "*sui generis* in the way we talk, our preference for fried food, and, above all, our manifest humility as we fulfill our hopes and dreams." "As we shared our destiny," she added, perhaps a bit wishfully, "we came to know each other in new aspects, and I believe we came to acknowledge and respect both each other's abilities and each other's ways of life."[1]

Neither slavery nor Jim Crow had been proven particularly effective barriers against cultural exchange across the color line, as anyone familiar with the South's linguistic, culinary, and musical history could readily attest. Clearly, the southerner's vaunted attachment to the land, locality, and family was at least as strong among blacks as whites. Only the second black scholar to preside over the Southern Historical Association, Jimmie L. Franklin argued in 1993 that "when we begin to test for the existence of common cultural values . . . we see reflected amid hardship and sorrow ingredients of southern life that often transcended race or ethnicity—matters of manners and morals, folk beliefs and foodways, blended musical forms, material culture and others."[2]

Everyday life also produced a great deal of anecdotal evidence that, as Elizabeth Fortson Arroyo observed, "white and black southerners find all kinds of shared cultural experiences." Arroyo recalled an incident in a South Carolina supermarket in which she and her mother encountered a white woman who was purchasing large quantities of sugar. "Now, I want y'all to know that I'm canning," the woman volunteered. "This isn't for the *other* stuff." Comprehending immediately, Arroyo's mother, whose family had actually been involved in both the production and consumption of moonshine, remarked with pleasure, "You'd have to be a southerner to understand that one."[3]

Contemporary survey data showed that southern blacks shared not only experiences and cultural understandings but many core values with southern whites. Nowhere was this more obvious than on issues of religion and morality, where black southerners did more than their share to sustain the South's reputation as the "Bible Belt." Polls consistently showed black southerners even more likely to attend church more than once a week than their white neighbors, to "say grace" before meals, or to describe themselves as total abstainers when asked about their drinking habits. Black southerners were also just about as likely as whites to feel that southerners were looked down upon by non-southerners and that books and magazines often gave an unduly negative image of their region.[4]

In addition to cross-racial cultural affinities, many commentators pointed to the importance of a common historical experience as well. Hunter-Gault emphasized the role of "our tumultuous history" in shaping all southerners into "a definable people," and in his 1993 presidential address to the Southern Historical Association, Franklin spoke of a "shared past between black and white southerners." In the same year, Alabama journalist Brandt Ayers also wrote of the "whole amazing pageant of southern history—the saga of migration from continent to continent and from farm to city, of wars waged and lost, of atrocities committed and borne, of loving and hating, of the long trek from poverty to better times—a journey that blacks and whites took together."[5]

Ayers failed to mention, however, that, for the most part, each group had made portions of this journey against its will. Blacks and whites had not only clashed frequently about the direction in which they were traveling, but in the main, they had also made the trip in accommodations and circumstances that were strikingly dissimilar. Writing in 1958, C. Vann Woodward identified "the unique historic experience" of southerners as "the basis for continuity of their heritage," but on that occasion he was referring only to whites. Woodward could certainly have had both black southerners and white southerners in mind when he pointed out that "Southern history, unlike American, includes large components of frustration, failure and defeat," but blacks and whites defined their frustrations, failure, and defeats so differently that one group's tragedy quite frequently represented the other's triumph. After all, the white South's defeat in the Civil War freed the black South from slavery. Both Reconstruction and its undoing by the Redeemers were similar examples of diametrically opposite goals and outcomes for whites and blacks. As a result, for all the inspirational rhetoric about the heritage they share, contemporary black and white southerners have been and remain a people more divided than united by their common past.[6]

Nowhere is this division more obvious than in the never-ending conflicts over the Confederate flag, Confederate monuments, and other symbolic reminders of slavery and segregation. In the last quarter of the nineteenth century, the construction of the New South identity had helped to fuse the cult of the Lost Cause with the move to overthrow Reconstruction and restore white supremacy. In Georgia, the 1879 state flag—based on the "Stars and Bars," the original Confederate national flag—had served notice that Reconstruction was over and that white Democrats were now once again in control in the state. Mississippi's Confederatized 1894 state flag (still flying in 2005) came on the heels of the 1890 constitution that disfranchised blacks and reminded whites that "Our South . . . fought for her rights under the Old Constitution." In Alabama, the adoption of a new state flag incorporating the original Confederate battle insignia, a red St. Andrews cross on a white field, came in 1895 as Democratic leaders invoked both the Lost Cause and white supremacy against the Populist political insurgents who were courting the state's white yeomanry and tenant farmers of both races.[7]

The Confederate flag's symbolic ties to the Jim Crow order quickly resurfaced in response to the growing pressures for racial reform in the post–World War II South. At the University of Mississippi, students displayed the flag much more prominently and emotionally after a campus delegation returned from the 1948 Dixiecrat Convention. Nowhere did the relationship between the Confederate flag and the defense of segregation seem clearer, however, than in Georgia, where the rabidly segregationist state legislature moved to make the more defiant, emotionally charged Confederate battle-flag insignia the centerpiece of the state flag in 1956.

Proponents insisted that this modification was meant simply to honor Confederate soldiers, but it came at a time of angry confrontation, when the state's white political leaders were flocking to the banner of massive resistance to the 1954 *Brown* decision and vowing last-ditch opposition to any and all desegregation efforts. Flag critics pointed out that the day before the state House of Representatives approved the flag-change bill, it had passed by a vote of 179–1 a so-called Interposition Resolution declaring the U.S. Supreme Court's school integration decrees "null, void and of no effect" in Georgia. Expressing similar sentiments, state representative Denmark Groover vowed that the new flag would "show that we in Georgia intend to uphold what we stood for, will stand for, and will fight for." Some four decades later, a former member of the legislature who had opposed adding the Confederate battle flag to the state banner remained absolutely convinced that the intent of the bill's supporters was to affirm their support for segregation. He offered an analogy that anyone familiar with the rural South could readily understand: "There was only one reason for putting that flag on there. Like the gun rack in the back of a pickup, it telegraphs a message." (The association of this new state flag with the "southern way of life" was pervasive indeed. As an elementary and high school student in the late 1950s and early 1960s, I recall that classroom films acquired from the Georgia State Department of Education began with a vivid shot of the state flag accompanied by an exceedingly robust rendition of "Dixie.")[8]

After the passions of the civil rights era had cooled somewhat, several individuals and groups launched assaults on the Georgia flag, the most notable coming in 1987 after a widely publicized incident in which white supremacists waving rebel flags attacked civil rights marchers in Forsyth County, Georgia. Finally, in a move that reflected the changes that had swept across Georgia's political landscape in the last three decades, Governor Zell Miller announced in May 1992 that he would support legislation to restore the pre-1956 flag. As a candidate for Congress, Miller had campaigned against the Civil Rights Act of 1964, but he now insisted, "What we fly today is not an enduring symbol of our heritage, but the fighting flag of those who wanted to preserve a segregated South in the face of the Civil Rights movement." Seeking legislative support, Miller acknowledged that such a move would require "sheer guts," but as the great grandson of a Confederate soldier wounded at both Chancellorsville and Gettysburg, Miller found the flag a blemish on the state's image, and he added, "Frankly, I do give a damn." Miller's move seemed bold indeed in light of polls consistently showing that as many as 60 percent of those questioned favored keeping the state's flag as it was. By January 1994 he had conceded defeat on the flag, but hard feelings on the issue contributed to a surprisingly close race in his bid for reelection that year, despite Miller's role in implementing Georgia's widely acclaimed HOPE Scholarship Program, which had won him bipartisan praise across the state and the nation.[9]

With its large population of blacks and non-native whites and its economic stake in projecting an image of enlightenment and harmony, the Atlanta area had provided the strongest support for removing the Confederate battle flag from the state's official banner. Atlantans who wanted to keep the flag feared that once it was gone the next step might be a sandblasting of Stone Mountain, especially after a black clergyman admitted that his dream is that someday folks will look up at the Confederate generals depicted in the world's largest stone carving and say, "Who are those Fellows?" Some observers saw the flag controversy pitting the "fergit" crowd (composed of black activists and a smattering of white liberals) against the "fergit, Hell" crowd (anchored by the Sons of Confederate Veterans and the United Daughters of the Confederacy). In reality, the dispute was hardly that simple. The UDC had actually opposed changing the flag in 1956, and though pro-flag partisans insisted that white southerners saw it as a memorial to their heroic Confederate forebears, a 1994 poll of 465 whites living in the South showed scarcely a third of them were aware of any such ancestry and half of them agreed either "strongly" or "somewhat" that the Civil War "doesn't mean much to me personally."[10]

Meanwhile, to make matters even more confusing, from Israel to Northern Ireland, individuals or groups seeking to defend or gain their independence often seemed drawn to the Confederate banner. John Reed told of a visitor from Tbilisi, in then-still Soviet Georgia, who clutched the Confederate flag and swore, without apparent ironic intent, "Some day this will fly in a free Georgia."[11]

In Europe as well as the United States, the Confederate flag also sent a strong countercultural message. Groups like bad-boy bikers, punk rockers, street gangs, skateboarders, and members in general of what Reed described as the "kick-ass, boogie-till-you-puke crowd" seemed to wear it simply as an act of rebellion against social conformity. "When I see the Confederate flag," a solidly middle-class white collegian told Reed, "I think of a pickup truck with a gun rack and a bumper sticker that says I DON'T BRAKE FOR SMALL ANIMALS." In a real sense, the Rebel flag had become a signifier not just of racial but of class differences as well, and not simply the economic distance between white and blue collar but the emotional distance between believing the system is there for you and believing that it is there for everybody but you. Democratic presidential hopeful Howard Dean found little appreciation for the complexity of southern white attitudes toward the flag when he suggested in November 2003 that "white folks in the South who drive pickup trucks with Confederate flag decals on the back ought to be voting with us, and not [Republicans], because their kids don't have health insurance either, and their kids need better schools too." Dean's opponents ignored the self-evident political wisdom in his remarks in their rush to condemn him for expressing empathy for anyone who would be associated with "one of the most divisive, hurtful symbols in American history."[12]

Tony Horwitz showed more understanding as he watched a group of angry Todd County, Kentucky, white women protesting efforts to remove a pair of flag-waving rebels from the local high school logo. Sensing that their anger went well beyond "the rebel flag's historic symbolism," Horwitz observed, "The banner seemed . . . to have floated free from its moorings in time and place and become a generalized 'Fuck You,' a middle finger raised with ulceric fury in the face of blacks, school officials, authority in general—anyone or anything that could shoulder some blame for these women's difficult lives."[13]

Horwitz observed this scene in the wake of the slaying of Michael Westerman, a young white man shot by a young black man who was angered by the Confederate flag flying from Westerman's truck. In reality, Westerman may have flown the flag not so much out of pride in his southern heritage as out of pride in his new pickup. As his young widow explained, "He'd do anything to make his truck look sharp. The truck's red. The flag's red. They match." Her revelation that Westerman "wasn't into the Confederate history" counted little to the Sons of Confederate Veterans, however, who quickly provided an iron cross marker for his grave and proclaimed him a "martyr . . . simply one more casualty in a long line of Confederate dead in over one hundred thirty years of continuous hostility towards us and our people."[14]

Westerman's somewhat suspect credentials as a fallen Confederate patriot were also of little concern to an orator at a Confederate Flag Day rally who laid his slaying directly at the feet of "the goose-stepping storm troopers of the political correctness movement," singling out for special condemnation "the NAACP, the Queer Nation and others [who] have been fomenting hatred against the honorable culture of the South." As Horwitz observed, "the speeches weren't really about the South and Westerman had metamorphosed again, from a Confederate martyr into a front-line soldier in a contemporary culture war."[15]

Further evidence that the flag itself had become what Horwitz described as a sort of all-purpose "talisman against mainstream culture" came in 1996 when an Alabama state senator sought a law *requiring* that the Confederate flag fly over the state's capitol, arguing that the flag symbolized not white supremacy but "less government, less taxes, and the right of a people to govern themselves." In February 1997 a conservative spokesman even described the flag dispute in South Carolina in terms of a conflict over "Eurocentric principles," explaining that with "the heritage of European people . . . under siege worldwide[,] [t]he South is the last semblance of resistance to one world order."

This mingling of Confederate symbolism with widespread complaints about unwarranted interference by meddlesome "big government" could produce some intriguing juxtapositions. Despite its close association with the swastika and neo-Nazism, at a rally in support of an Alabama judge who insisted on defying a federal edict against displaying the Ten Commandments in his courtroom, the flag of the Confederacy waved alongside the flag of Israel.[16]

Clearly, the meaning of any flag may be largely a matter of its context. As a young girl in North Carolina, Pauli Murray was already cynical about the meaning of the United States flag for African Americans, but she nonetheless found special comfort on Decoration Day or Memorial Day in placing it on the grave of her grandfather, a Union veteran. To Murray, installing "this solitary American flag just outside the iron fence that separated it from the Confederate banners waving on the other side was an act of hunger and defiance. It tied me and my family to something bigger than the Rebel atmosphere in which we found ourselves . . . and it helped to negate in my mind the symbols of inferiority and apartness." Many years later, responding to the Confederate imagery he encountered throughout the contemporary South, Eddy Harris mused, "Symbols are indivisible. . . . If it's mine, it can't be yours." Bitter and frustrated, he demanded of a white southerner, "How do you expect a black person to feel . . . in a society that so blatantly reminds him how emotionally tied his government still is to a system that fought to keep his ancestors in slavery?" As Harris saw it, the white southerners who supported the flag seemed to be saying: "We don't care if our symbols are hateful to you and upset you or remind you of our inhuman treatment toward you. We don't care because these are sources of our pride and we do not concern ourselves with your pride. These are our symbols and not yours. And you do not share in what is ours."[17]

Columbia, South Carolina, attorney Carl B. Grant explained, "The flag embraces and perpetuates the ideology of white supremacy. . . . That flag tells me that, because of the color of my skin, I am considered a second-class citizen." Responding to the suggestions of a pro-flag partisan that "black people aren't really Southerners," Atlanta journalist John Head declared, "The South is my home. . . . I am a Southerner." Head simply refused "to allow others to say what that means," and he declined as well to "accept the Confederacy as the South at its best" or to "accept the Confederate battle flag as an emblem in which all Georgians can take pride." Black Mississippian Rip Daniels explained why the Confederate flag was so divisive quite nicely when he served notice that "you leave me no choice but to be your enemy as long as you wave a battle flag. If it is your heritage, then it is my heritage to resist it with every fiber of my being."[18]

Southern whites who disputed the flag's racist implications could not deny that it had been adopted for symbolic purposes by a host of racist hate groups from the KKK to the American Nazis to the Skinheads who regularly engaged nationwide in acts of racial as well as religious and ethnic bigotry. Writing in 1961, Walker Percy lamented that a once-venerable symbol had already been tarnished and trivialized by the segregationist demagogues who preached the gospel of massive resistance to desegregation: "When Lee and the Army of Northern Virginia laid down the Confederate flag in 1865, no flag had ever been defended by better men. But when the same flag is picked up by men like Ross Barnett and Jimmy Davis, nothing remains but to make panties and pillowcases with it." Percy's close friend and fellow writer Shelby Foote agreed, condemning the Ku Klux Klan as "the scum who have degraded the Confederate flag, converted it from a symbol of honor into a banner of shame, covered it with obscenities like a roadhouse men's room wall."[19]

Foote was revulsed by the contemporary company it was keeping, and he grew emotional when the flag was attacked. "I'm for the Confederate flag always and forever," he insisted. "Many among the finest people this country has produced have died in that war. To take and call it a symbol of evil is a misrepresentation." Although he grew up in a Mississippi home where his liberal parents actually flew the United States flag in defiance of their neighbors who were flying the Confederate flag, Hodding Carter III also confessed that the Rebel flag "still grabs me." To Carter, the flag "stands for bravery and doomed hopes and battlefield triumphs and the shared past of our forefathers. . . . [I]t touches me at a level too deep for intellectualization and stirs me in ways the national anthem does not. I can buy the bravery and the sorrow without once embracing the cause." Despite its associations with slavery, for Carter, as for many other white southerners, the Confederate flag loomed as the symbol of an older, but affirmative past that he and many other white southerners could (and very much needed to) embrace with passion and pride. Unfortunately, for many others, white and black, it also symbolized a more recent past, which Carter himself conceded, was little more than "a wretched record of racial murders, political demagogues, separate rest rooms and school closings."[20]

Regardless of whether at one point the Confederate flag could be seen as the symbol of an honorable but distant past, because of its subsequent associations, as one commentator explained, many black southerners now see it "much the way Jews see the Nazi swastika: a symbol not only of repression but of violence, torture, dehumanization and death." Not only do the two often show up in the same places in this country, but the Confederate flag has actually become a swastika substitute among neo-Nazis and Skinheads in Germany, where the swastika is banned by law. In fact, the swastika's long and ultimately tragic history has much to say to defenders of the Confederate flag. According to one expert, the term swastika itself derives from the Sanskrit "svastika," meaning "well being" and "good fortune." From its apparent origins in India and Central Asia around 3000 B.C., the swastika spread throughout the world as a symbol with decidedly positive connotations. Followers of Buddha thought it represented his footprint, and swastika murals even adorned synagogues from Palestine to Connecticut. Since it was claimed by the Nazis in the 1920s, however, in the Western world the swastika has symbolized nothing but hatred, racism, and cruelty. Efforts by groups such as "Friends of the Swastika" to "detoxify" and "resanctify" it notwithstanding, its fifty centuries as an emblem of well-being and good fortune now count for little against less than one century's association with the horrors of the Holocaust and the brutality of the Third Reich.[21]

The taint of racism rendered the Confederate flag so controversial that it even made waves in the once ideologically inert world of bass fishing. The cover of the April 1997 *Sports Afield* magazine featured a Confederate flag on which largemouth bass with their large mouths opened wide replaced the stars, and an article in the magazine explained that the popularity of bass fishing made the South the "confederacy of bass." Those who held the flag in reverence seemed to view the cover as a desecration of their cherished symbol, while admirers of the bass who held the flag in low esteem objected to what they saw as a desecration of their favorite game fish.[22]

Though the flag's defenders remained numerous and vocal, as the twentieth century drew to a close, its high-profile association with racist hate groups and the omnipresent reality of its divisiveness and disruptive potential were beginning to make even some of its most ardent proponents ask whether the costs of defending it had grown too high. Former Ole Miss chancellor Gerald Turner once observed that "if this university's not southern, it's not anything." Having already struggled with little success for more than a decade to dissociate their school from the Confederate flag, however, in 1997 Ole Miss officials finally retained a public relations firm to help them decide if jettisoning some other Old South/Lost Cause symbols, such as the athletic teams' (some of which, like basketball and football, were predominantly black) "Rebel" nickname and "Colonel Reb" mascot, might expedite both an anticipated $200-million fund-raising campaign and the university's efforts to gain a Phi Beta Kappa chapter. Though this move came at the behest of the new chancellor, Robert Khayat, a former football hero with impeccable Ole Miss credentials, critics immediately set up a howl about the school's apparent willingness to, as one reporter put it, trash its symbols "for prestige." Hoping to further deemphasize Ole Miss's Confederate connotations, officials had floated the idea of making the 2003 football season Colonel Reb's last, but alumni and student objections apparently won the controversial mascot a reprieve.[23]

In 1963 a defiant George Wallace had ordered the Confederate flag flown from the Alabama state capitol as he looked toward a confrontation with Attorney General Robert F. Kennedy over the integration of the University of Alabama. In 1988 several black legislators were arrested after an unsuccessful attempt to remove it physically. It was taken down temporarily during renovations on the capitol in 1992, and the following year four black lawmakers won a court judgment for its removal based on an old statute stipulating that only the state flag and the United States flag were to be flown above the capitol building. Republican governor Guy Hunt had vowed to restore the flag, but when Hunt was removed from office for misconduct, his Democratic successor, James E. Folsom, announced that he would not reopen the matter. In response, outraged members of the League of the South rallied in 2000 for a "Southern Independence Day Celebration" on the day before the thirty-fifth anniversary of the historic and bloody Selma voting-rights march. Demanding that the flag be restored to the capitol dome, league president Michael Hill alluded to the Reverend Martin Luther King, Jr.'s famous speech as he told chanting, flag-waving protestors, "We have a dream, too. . . . we are not going to allow anyone to take our symbols, demonize them and tell our children that their ancestors were traitors. . . . [O]ur symbols are not going away."[24]

The Confederate flag had been placed atop the South Carolina state capitol in 1962, ostensibly to commemorate the Civil War Centennial. In response to mounting objections, South Carolina attorney general Travis Medlock ruled in 1993 that there was no legal requirement to keep it flying in that particular location. Three years and numerous marches and protests later, outraged flag supporters invoked Neville Chamberlain's ill-fated bargain with Hitler at Munich when Republican governor David Beasley proposed that the flag be taken down from the capitol dome and placed in a Confederate memorial on the state-house grounds. After opposing any effort to move the flag during his 1994 campaign, Beasley stunned advocates and opponents alike by calling on South Carolinians to "compromise on the Confederate flag, and

teach our children that we can live together." Beasley's flip-flop on the flag
came after a raft of church burnings and other ugly racial incidents had marred
his state's image. Black leaders who had long objected to the flag were now
joined by business and development leaders who feared the controversy could
derail their highly effective industrial development effort, which had recently
brought, among others, a huge BMW assembly plant to the Palmetto State.
"The Confederate flag did not burn those churches," one of Beasley's many
vociferous critics pointed out, but Beasley countered that a flag "should be a
symbol of *all* the people" and asked, "Do we want our children debating this
in 10 years?"[25]

Beasley faced a veritable firestorm of denunciation, but he also drew support from a number of prominent conservative South Carolinians, most notably the venerable Senator J. Strom Thurmond, who had campaigned for the
White House under the Confederate banner as the Dixiecrat presidential nominee in 1948. In words that had the ring of Appomattox about them, Thurmond
conceded that the presence of the battle flag over the capitol "has moved past
its intended purpose of paying tribute to those who served South Carolina
during the Civil War."[26]

Thurmond's support notwithstanding, Beasley promised in his 1998 reelection campaign to discontinue efforts to remove the flag. He was nonetheless defeated by Democrat Jim Hodges, who also pledged not to revisit the
issue if he was elected. The controversy refused to go away, however, and on
July 15, 1999, the National NAACP convention approved a resolution calling
for a tourism boycott of South Carolina. During the next nine months, the
state was thrust squarely into the national and international spotlight. Republican presidential aspirants George W. Bush and John McCain danced around
the issue, but at a rally of flag supporters in Columbia, Republican state Senator Arthur Ravenel referred to the NAACP as "the National Association for
Retarded People." On January 17, 2000, nearly 50,000 people marked the Martin Luther King, Jr., holiday (not officially observed in South Carolina until
2001) by marching on the statehouse and calling for the flag's removal. National Democratic leaders denounced the flag, and a number of prominent
individuals and organizations did likewise, including the National Collegiate
Athletic Association, which threatened to keep certain NCAA-sanctioned sport-
ing events out of South Carolina if the flag was not removed.[27]

Tourism officials put the state's losses to the boycott in the neighborhood
of $20 million, and business leaders continued to pressure the legislature. Fi-
nally, in May 2000 the lawmakers acquiesced, passing a compromise measure

that moved the flag to a Confederate monument on the statehouse grounds. When Governor Hodges signed the bill to move the flag, he proclaimed that "today, the debate over the Confederate flag above the capitol passes into South Carolina history." Hodges surely should have known better. Like most compromises, the flag move left both sides dissatisfied. Not only did the NAACP reject the new flag arrangement as "insulting" and vow to continue its boycott, but a 10 percent drop off in white support played a key role in Hodges's failure to win reelection in 2002.[28]

In Georgia, meanwhile, an October 2000 poll had suggested that support for retaining the current state flag had fallen to 49 percent, with more than three in four African Americans, one in four white Democrats, and almost one in five white Republicans favoring a change. When the 2001 legislative session opened, facing the threat by black leaders of an economic boycott "100 times worse than South Carolina," Governor Roy Barnes moved quickly and quietly to defuse the crisis. Although as a legislator he had voted against observance of the Martin Luther King, Jr., holiday in Georgia, after meeting in secret with business, religious, and educational leaders for two weeks, Barnes introduced a new state flag that carried only a miniaturized version of the old flag as one of five previous state flags commemorated on the new banner. "The Confederacy is part of our history, but it's not two-thirds of our history," Barnes argued, referring to the Confederate flag's dominant place on the old 1956 flag. He also warned that continuing divisions over the state flag threatened to "erode four decades of economic progress" and to jeopardize Georgia's position as the South's economic leader. Former legislator Denmark Groover, who had sponsored the legislation that put the Saint Andrew's cross emblem on the state banner in 1956, backed Barnes by urging his old colleagues to "end this cauldron of discord that adversely affects our lives and the future of our children and grandchildren."[29]

Supporters of the old flag howled in protest at what they saw as the highjacking of their heritage by a group of powerful politicians and business leaders who had capitulated to the "economic terrorism" of a threatened NAACP boycott. Their demands for a statewide popular referendum on the issue went unheeded, however, and Barnes signed the new flag bill into law only a few hours after its final approval by the state senate on January 31, 2001. Almost immediately, the Georgia governor became the target of constant taunts and harassment by angry "flaggers" demanding a statewide popular vote on restoring the 1956 flag. In 2002, gubernatorial challenger Sonny Perdue's promise to hold such a referendum helped him to become Georgia's

first Republican governor in 130 years, making Barnes the third southern governor defeated for reelection after supporting a move to dissociate his state
from the Confederate flag.[30]

Perdue's exceptionally strong showing among rural whites upset about the
flag doubtless contributed significantly to his election, but his campaign promise began to haunt him as soon as the votes were counted. By reopening the
flag brouhaha, he had put himself squarely between the powerful business interests whose concerns for the state's image had led them to back Barnes's flag
switch and the angry flag partisans who claimed credit for Perdue's election
and promised him the same fate as Barnes should he renege on his pledge.

Predictably, Perdue's politically calculated call for a referendum on restoring the controversial 1956 flag in the interest of "healing" the wounds left by
the long flag battle simply reopened them, triggering numerous bitter, racially
tinged public confrontations and legislative votes divided sharply along racial
lines. When their political leaders finally realized that the state could stand no
more of Perdue's brand of healing, Georgians wound up with yet another state
flag, their third in two years, this one based on the original, pre-1956 model
derived from the design of the first official flag of the Confederacy. Voters
expressed a three to one preference for this latest banner over the Barnes flag
in a March 2, 2004, referendum, and its proponents imprudently announced
that "the flag debate is now a chapter in our history." The very next day an
angry group of flaggers gathered in front of the state capitol to voice their
displeasure that, contrary to Perdue's promise, the old massive-resistance-era
Rebel battle-flag design had not been an option on the ballot. Reviving the
rhetoric of the Lost Cause, a spokesman for the group declared, "We will keep
our anger alive. We shall be grim and unconvinced and wear our bitterness
like a medal." As for the elected officials who had blocked a vote on the 1956
flag, he warned, "We the flaggers are coming for you."[31]

In the meantime, in a Mississippi referendum held in April 2001, roughly
two-thirds of the voters had rejected a proposal for a new state flag bearing no
Confederate implication. This outcome surprised no one. When a gubernatorial commission held public hearings on a new flag, the sessions had often
been confrontational and vitriolic, and polls consistently showed defenders of
the current flag outnumbering the proponents of a new one by two to one,
with opinion breaking even more sharply along racial lines than it had appeared to in Georgia. Concerned about their state's image in the eyes of potential industrial investors, Mississippi's economic leadership had endorsed a
new flag, but the Magnolia state's business elite clearly lacked the influence

wielded by their counterparts in Georgia. NAACP officials responded to the outcome of the Mississippi referendum by calling for an economic boycott of the state and vowing to continue to challenge the constitutionality of the state's 110-year-old flag.[32]

The South's divisions over its history and the way it was represented were by no means confined to the Confederate flag. Throughout the region, black activists also demanded the removal of monuments or other symbolic reminders of the Confederacy. Nowhere in the South is the Confederacy more thoroughly iconized than in Richmond, Virginia, the former Confederate capital. Dubbed "Via Dolorosa" for southern nostalgics, the city's Monument Avenue boasts a mile-long tribute to the giants of the Confederacy, featuring statues of Jefferson Davis, Robert E. Lee, Stonewall Jackson, and numerous others. Another likeness of Lee stands in front of the Virginia capitol building in Richmond. In 1995 whites mounted an unsuccessful effort to keep a statue of Richmond native and African American tennis star Arthur Ashe off Monument Avenue. Many whites also grew indignant when a black city council member compared Lee to Nazi leaders and threatened a boycott if his portrait was not removed from an exhibition of paintings of prominent Virginians in his inner city district.[33]

Some whites even expressed outrage in 2003 when advertising executive Robert Kline, who had once helped raise the money for the Museum of the Confederacy, commissioned a statue of Abraham Lincoln with his son Tad, commemorating Lincoln's April 4, 1865, visit to Richmond. Although Kline's monument was slated for the National Park Service Visitor Center rather than a site in the city itself, it set off a firestorm of denunciations, threats, petitions, and angry e-mails. Some of the incensed even sent viruses to Kline's computers, and a Sons of Confederate Veterans leader condemned both Kline and Lincoln, whom he described as "this country's most notorious war criminal . . . this Marxist . . . this monster directly responsible for the killing of 620,000 Americans."[34]

Elsewhere in the South, African American leaders called for the renaming of public streets, parks, buildings, and schools commemorating Confederate leaders or prominent slaveholders. In Louisiana, critics charged that the majority black School Board of Orleans Parish had gone too far, however, when it voted unanimously to change the name of George Washington Elementary School to Dr. Charles Richard Drew Elementary in honor of a black surgeon known for his research on the preservation of plasma. Earlier, the board had adopted a policy forbidding the naming of schools for "former slave owners" and had changed the names of twenty-one other schools. Nearly half of New Orleans's public schools had originally borne the name of slaveholders, and journalist Brent Staples pointed out that "those who want the old names expunged argue that all slave masters were equally and irreparably evil and deserve neither forgiveness nor any place at all in the public esteem." Others contended that Washington's contributions as "the father of our country" far outweighed the fact that he had held slaves. Here again was the paradox. Blacks and whites had a common past, but they often interpreted it differently or refused to share or accept each other's version of that past. "This isn't our history" was a common assertion coming from both sides of the color line.[35]

For many black southerners, the widespread assault on Confederate icons and symbols went hand in hand with the creation, preservation, or renovation of a new set of icons and monuments memorializing the crusade to free the South from the racial system constructed on the ruins of the Confederate legacy. By 1996 the cities and towns of the old Confederacy accounted for 77 percent of the nation's streets named in honor of Dr. Martin Luther King, Jr. Meanwhile, from the Civil Rights Memorial in Montgomery to the Civil Rights Museum in Memphis, stirring memories of the campaign for racial equality drew black tourists and visitors in huge numbers. Many of these also visited historic landmarks of the movement, including the Edmund Pettus Bridge in Selma and the Sixteenth Street Baptist Church in Birmingham.[36]

When Birmingham eventually established a $12-million Civil Rights Institute and a relandscaped Kelly Ingram Park, where demonstrators once confronted Bull Connor's police dogs and fire hoses, speakers at the dedication ceremonies revealed the importance of a heroic monumentalized past to black southerners. One orator proclaimed, "This park is the Jerusalem of the Civil Rights movement . . . the mecca of the Civil Rights movement, the Iwo Jima of the Civil Rights movement."[37]

Though the move to establish civil rights memorials was not as confrontational as the fights over the Confederate flag, it nonetheless revealed the differing attitudes of black and white southerners toward different parts of their past. Many black southerners saw the civil rights movement as perhaps their finest historical hour and therefore sought to enshrine and memorialize it. On the other hand, as Hodding Carter observed in 1990, "Most older white South-erners overtly or passively supported massive resistance in the '50s and '60s." It was hardly surprising, therefore, that whites sometimes opposed or showed little enthusiasm for the establishment of civil rights memorials. The debate over turning Birmingham's old black business area into a "Civil Rights Dis-trict" revealed these racial divisions. Whenever whites told him, "We ought to forget that stuff," explained the city's white former mayor David Vann, "I told them the best way to forget it is to declare it history and put it in a museum."[38]

Forgetting history appeared to be precisely what some officials of the 1996 Olympic Games in Atlanta had in mind when they sent clear signals to local historical organizations and historical sites that the darker aspects of the South's past should be deemphasized. Prohibited from marching in a parade in nearby Roswell, Sons of Confederate Veterans members went to court to win the right to march, although the term "antebellum" was deleted from the official name of the event. Elsewhere, though normally in great demand during the summer months, Civil War reenactors were given the cold shoulder around Olympic Atlanta, while some publicists for local historical attractions sought to deemphasize slavery as a part of their story.[39]

At many historical sites across the South, the very existence of slavery had been obscured and even obliterated. At one point, a Georgetown, South Caro-lina, museum reportedly sought to educate visitors on the rice culture of the Low Country without mentioning slavery. At a restored antebellum mansion near Nashville when a young black couple asked, "Where were the slave quar-ters?" a noticeably discomfited white guide explained, "They were in the back, where the parking lot is now . . . but that's all been paved over now."[40]

At times, demands for the inclusion of slavery in historical treatments seemed a bit extreme. In 2004 black critics attacked the popular Civil War–era movie *Cold Mountain* for its failure to confront the issue, despite the fact that the novel on which it was based was, as Henry Louis Gates observed, "essen-tially a love story between two white people who live in a rural area where slavery was not a fundamental aspect of the economy." Although he under-stood the criticism, Gates added, "It's a mistake to think that most white people in the South had slaves. They didn't."[41]

As the twentieth century drew to a close, there was some evidence that white southerners were ready to acknowledge the racial crimes and abuses of the past. In 1994 the Florida legislature appropriated $2.1 million in compensa-tion for the survivors of the 1923 massacre in which six blacks were killed after whites went on a rampage in the small town of Rosewood. Two years later, the

city of Tulsa, Oklahoma, provided a memorial to the victims of that city's infamous 1921 riot. In 1998 black and white citizens of Wilmington, North Carolina, gathered to commemorate the centennial of the bloody riot that
accompanied the "Revolution of '98" campaign to overthrow Republican rule
and disfranchise blacks. Finally, in 2004 a marker was erected to identify
Scottsboro, Alabama, as the site of the internationally infamous trial of nine
young black men falsely accused of the rape of two white women in 1931.[42]

Even as some black southerners complained that their suffering and persecution had been excluded from the written and re-created past fashioned by
whites, others actually objected to classroom and other public portrayals and
discussions of slavery, lynchings, and the other brutalities and humiliations
that their ancestors had suffered at the hands of whites. In 1994, for example,
officials at Colonial Williamsburg who had come under fire for portraying a
racially sanitized version of life in Colonial Virginia staged a mock slave auction aimed at demonstrating the brutality of the peculiar institution as it was
practiced in and around Williamsburg. Rather than praise, however, the presentation drew loud and sustained protests from the NAACP and other black
spokespersons who claimed that black southerners did not want to see this
aspect of their past "rehashed again." Explained Dr. Milton A. Reid, a black
minister from Norfolk, "This is 1994. . . . As far as we have come, to go back to
this for entertainment is despicable and disgusting. This is the kind of anguish
we need not display." The mock auction had been planned by African American interpreters at Williamsburg, but two protestors disrupted it by standing
in the midst of the presentation, which also sparked a brief scuffle between six
protestors singing "We Shall Overcome" and costumed employees of
Williamsburg who tried to prevent them from interrupting the performance.[43]

Similar concerns also arose in Natchitoches, Louisiana. Efforts to stage a
dramatization of the slave experience disturbed not only local whites but many
blacks as well, including a park employee who complained, "I don't want to
hear about my people being beaten and raped. . . . Let it go." Such disputes
were by no means peculiar to the Old Confederacy. In December 1995 in response to complaints by black library employees who found it offensive, the
Library of Congress canceled an exhibit depicting slave life on southern plantations before it even opened.[44]

Spanning more than a decade, the campaign to erect a monument to African Americans in Savannah also revealed divisions among blacks about the relative emphasis that should be placed on black suffering and victimization as opposed to black achievement in the face of adversity. Many proponents of the monument, featuring a black family with broken shackles at their feet, wanted to include a quotation from poet Maya Angelou that referred to slaves lying "back to belly in the holds of the slave ships in each others excrement and urine together" often dying, "our lifeless bodies thrown overboard together." Mayor Floyd Adams, Jr., also an African American, objected to the inscription as divisive and declared, "If it's not positive, I'd rather see no inscription." Supporters of Angelou's inscription attacked Adams in an angry, profanity-laced meeting, one of them describing him as a "weak-kneed Negro, still enslaved, 400 years behind the times." On the other hand, arguing that Angelou's message about "suffering and togetherness" should give way to one emphasizing black strength and heroism, African American writer Pearl Duncan passed on the apparently telepathic intelligence that "our ancestors want to be remembered as heroes." Angelou finally ended the dispute by adding a more positive concluding statement: "Today, we are standing up together, with faith and even some joy."[45]

There could be little doubt that the recovery of an affirmative black past was crucial to making the South seem more comfortable and hospitable to African Americans. The Eddy Harris who had been so angered and repulsed by the Confederate symbolism he had encountered throughout the South was also an Eddy Harris who had been ashamed that his ancestors had not rebelled openly against their enslavement. However, as he rode out of Richmond, finally appreciating what his former slave great-great-great grandfather had endured and accomplished, Harris found that "along Monument Avenue the statues of Lee and Stuart and Jefferson Davis do not seem so chilly as before, not so frightening in their symbolism, for now I have a symbol of my own."[46]

As Harris's experience suggests, a truly appropriate representation of the southern black experience must incorporate not only tributes to those who overcame, but reminders of what they had to overcome as well. A promising step in this direction was a monument on the grounds of the South Carolina state capitol, featuring twelve bronze panels tracing the African American odyssey from enslavement through the struggle for freedom to the crusade for equality and culminating in a celebration of the achievements of black South Carolinians.[47]

The complexity of this monument to black South Carolinians and the sensitivity among many African Americans about the portrayal of their past only hints at the enormity of the challenge of creating a symbolic representation that simultaneously incorporates the historical experiences and perspectives of both black and white southerners. Any such candid and comprehensive representation is still likely to face opposition from members of both races, and anything less is a fatally compromised attempt to represent southern identity.

It is also worth noting that South Carolina's African American memorial sits some fifty yards from a statue of Confederate General Wade Hampton and within sight of the Confederate flag that was displaced from its perch atop the statehouse. As he reported from the steps of the state capitol in Montgomery on the observance of Jefferson Davis's birthday, a Scottish journalist captured the inseparability of black and white historical symbolism within the southern experience. Describing a profusion of Confederate flags sufficient "to fill the battlefield at Gettysburg," he noted that the celebration took place "on the very steps" where Davis was sworn in as president of the Confederacy and on "the same spot where George Wallace gave his infamous 'segregation now, segregation tomorrow, segregation forever' speech." Only through an appreciation of the more than a century's worth of symbolic continuity represented by those capitol steps could one grasp fully the importance of what had also happened hardly a stone's throw away at the Dexter Avenue Baptist Church, whose young pastor, Dr. Martin Luther King, Jr., had helped to organize the Montgomery bus boycott that marked the beginning of the protest phase of the civil rights movement. In Atlanta the Dr. Martin Luther King, Jr., Center for Social Change and the Confederate carving on nearby Stone Mountain remain two of the city's top tourist attractions, and the Stone Mountain Park's evening laser show has, on occasion, even superimposed King's image over the likenesses of General Lee and others.[48]

Elsewhere, controversy erupted over the positioning in the Maryland state capitol of a statue of civil rights pioneer and Supreme Court justice Thurgood Marshall near one of another Supreme Court justice, Roger B. Taney, whose infamous Dred Scott opinion gratuitously decreed that "the Negro has no rights that the white man is bound to respect." One might well argue that, rather than being demeaned, Justice Marshall's accomplishments are rendered all the more impressive by the placement of his statue near Taney's, but the larger point is that such starkly contrasting symbolic juxtapositions are inevitable in a society where two groups have experienced a common past in very different ways and now view it from very different perspectives.[49]

An editorial writer for the *Greensboro News and Record* was quite likely correct when he observed, "Our black citizens will inevitably have different perceptions of Robert E. Lee, Stonewall Jackson and Jefferson Davis from those held by whites." On the other hand, "whites will hold less sacred memories of Frederick Douglass, W. E. B. Dubois and Malcolm X. We can't repeal history, and it's hard for a person brought up to view it from one perspective to switch abruptly to the opposite perspective." Therefore, he concluded, "It's unlikely in our lifetimes or the lifetimes of our children that the South will become the kind of melting pot that allows all its citizens to adopt a common view of its racial past."[50]

Whether the myth-encrusted memorials to the Lost Cause can ever coexist peacefully with the proliferating shrines to the vindicated, if not totally fulfilled, cause of civil rights is impossible to predict, but the preoccupation of so many contemporary southerners with monuments and symbols confirms their involvement in what Eric Hobsbawm calls the "politics of identity" through which "groups of people today . . . try to find some certainty in a shaken and uncertain world." There is no doubt that removing the Confederate flag and other "offensive historical monuments" has created what W. Fitzhugh Brundage called "a less alienating" historical landscape for black southerners. The importance of such victories should not be minimized. On the other hand, neither should it be exaggerated. The always emotional politics of historical symbolism has often seemed to derail progress toward greater interracial cooperation and understanding. In the old civil rights battleground of Selma, Alabama, the election in 2000 of an African American, James Perkins, Jr., as mayor seemed to suggest the city was about to break free of its old racial animosities. However, a heated conflict over the placement of a bust of controversial Confederate general Nathan Bedford Forrest on city property quickly threatened to thwart Perkins's efforts to promote racial healing in his community. Opponents of the monument staged a mock trial of Forrest in protest, and some criticized Perkins's efforts to forge a compromise solution. Although the matter was eventually put to rest, temporarily at least, by moving the monument to a less conspicuous location, there was little doubt that the controversy had sapped much of the early momentum that Perkins had hoped to generate.[51]

Meanwhile, some wondered how well the politicization of historical symbols served the interests of lower-income black southerners for whom other more urgent and substantive day-to-day needs doubtless took precedence over concerns about Confederate flags or memorials. Berndt Ostendorf's assertion that "Cultural identity . . . is the privilege of the socially secure" may be a little extreme, but there is no question that expressions of concern with identity intensify as socioeconomic status rises. As historian Dan Carter pointed out, "Symbols never fed children . . . you can be obsessed in the struggle over symbolic issues as a way of avoiding hard issues." On the eve of the 2001 referendum on a new state flag, a black Mississippian explained, "It don't bother me either way it goes. . . . Money's my problem. As far as the flag and that kind of s—, I don't care. I can't live off a flag." [52]

In the midst of a severe fiscal crisis in March 2003, as Georgians watched their legislature spend an entire session arguing about the state flag, nearly 70 percent of those polled thought the flag debate was either a negative or divisive influence or simply a waste of time. Even a self-described "born-and-bred Georgia Rebel," eighty-year-old Frank Hyde, worried about "dividing the races" and pointed to Georgia's need for better roads, schools, and teachers: "we need money to be spent on something besides changing the color of a flag. It's the silliest thing I've ever heard of." Veteran civil rights activist and former Atlanta mayor Andrew Young had announced in 2001 that he didn't "give a damn" about the state flag and urged lawmakers to concentrate on more fundamental policy concerns. On the eve of the state's 2004 referendum, Young ignored the compromise Perdue flag's ties to the Confederacy and urged Georgians to vote for it in order to "put the flag issue to rest" and avoid "another round of bad publicity for our state."[53]

It should be not be surprising that Young's message was circulated throughout the state by the Georgia Chamber of Commerce. In their moves against the Confederate flag, black leaders have often found unexpected support among conservative white business and industrial development leaders who hoped to avoid the economic losses that continuing agitation or a full-scale NAACP boycott might mean. A similar strategy had helped to bring relatively peaceful desegregation of public schools in cities like Atlanta and Charlotte some two generations before, suggesting that the politics of black and white may be set aside, at least temporarily, in favor of the politics of green. The Nissan Corporation, which had recently announced plans to build a huge assembly plant in

Mississippi, had no comment on the 2001 flag referendum, describing it as a "state issue." An industrial-location expert foresaw no real problem in recruiting new plants to the state in the wake of the overwhelming vote to keep the Confederatized state flag flying "unless Jesse Jackson says he's going to put pickets in every Nissan dealership." Clearly, we should not lose sight of the fact that the politics of green responds to boycotts and protests (or to warnings thereof) primarily because they threaten profits or the social stability requisite to profits. The president of the metro Atlanta Chamber of Commerce even alluded to the Georgia state flag as "the brand name of Atlanta and Georgia," while representatives of the Mississippi Economic Council characterized its call for a new state banner as simply "a pocketbook issue" and "a strategic business decision."[54]

Follow-up research from the civil rights era suggests that despite their role in defusing racial confrontations, once stability was restored, many of the economic movers and shakers who had proclaimed themselves "Too Busy to Hate" were soon too busy to care, at least about further racial progress after the initial, often merely token, desegregation had been accomplished. Concerned about their state or community's loss of investment or tourism dollars, economic and fiscal conservatives are more likely to call for removal of controversial historical symbols or even to support the construction of civil rights museums or memorials (which, after all, might attract tourists) than to acknowledge the need for additional or continuing federal, state, or local action in behalf of the disadvantaged.[55]

If the struggles over history as symbolic memory affirmed once again that the politics of the past is always part of the politics of the present, the same was no less true of history as written narrative. In the 1950s historians such as Kenneth Stampp and Stanley Elkins had confronted complacent, self-deluded whites with the reality of slavery in all its brutality and the long-term disadvantages it and a century's worth of subsequent discrimination had inflicted on African Americans. Although Stampp and Elkins had helped to focus white attention on the victimization of African Americans, as more blacks flooded into the streets to demonstrate that they would be victimized no longer, they also sought a more aggressive and resolute historical ancestry. Referring to Elkins's infantilized slave personality type, David Brion Davis observed that no one seemed to want "Sambo for a grandfather."[56]

This became quite clear in 1965 when Daniel Patrick Moynihan drew heavily on Elkins's work in his *The Negro Family in America: The Case for National Action*, arguing that the problems of blacks in America's inner cities were a reflection of the deterioration of the black family "that had begun as a result of enslavement." "It was by destroying the Negro family," Moynihan concluded, "that white America broke the will of the Negro people," leaving "a tangle of pathology" as its tragic legacy. Moynihan's analysis was coupled with a call for a massive aid program along the lines of a "Marshall Plan" for African Americans, but its focus on black people as historically damaged goods outraged leaders of the emerging "Black Power" movement, which emphasized racial strength and pride. This controversy, as Kenneth Lynn has noted, brought a dramatic change to "the tenor of slave scholarship."[57]

Determined to stress the capacity of the slaves to endure their ordeal without suffering permanent psychological or cultural damage, historian John W. Blassingame argued in 1972 for the existence of a tightly knit "slave community" that functioned as a sort of emotionally compensatory and culturally sustaining extended family. Blassingame pointed out that by concentrating on planters' records and correspondence while essentially ignoring the historical testimony provided by slaves (who outnumbered slaveholders by ten to one), scholars had "been listening to only one side of a complicated debate." As a result, they had painted a "distorted" portrait of the plantation as "an all-powerful, monolithic institution which strips the slave of any meaningful and distinctive culture, family life, religion, or manhood."[58]

Agreeing that "almost all historians have presented the black slaves as dehumanized victims, without culture, history, community, change or development," George P. Rawick charged that to assume the slave was a total victim was "at its heart elitist and untenable." In the hundreds of interviews of former slaves conducted during the New Deal by the Works Progress Administration, Rawick saw the story of a slave community that was continually "making itself." Within this community, he insisted, "the patterns of communication set up by the daily and nightly exchanges of conversation, social activities, and fellowship were the most significant events that happened to the slave."[59]

Slaves may have labored from dawn to dusk for the master, Rawick argued, but they were by no means "totally dominated." Indeed, "they found ways of alleviating the worst of the system and at times of dominating the masters. They built their own community out of materials taken from the African past and the American present, with the values and memories of Africa giving meaning and direction to the new creation. They lived and loved from sundown to sunup." Thomas Webber even referred to "the paradox of the 'free slave,'" arguing that the residents of the black "quarter community" had "successfully protected their psychological freedom and celebrated their human dignity." Certainly, the independent, dignified, resourceful slaves depicted by Blassingame, Rawick, Webber, and others seemed very much the plausible ancestors of those who had so recently braved death threats, beatings, police dogs, and fire hoses in order to claim their civil and political rights. Other historians soon followed with studies of other topics and other eras, arguing that blacks had played the primary role in making their own histories and cultural identities.[60]

For all such scholarly efforts, however, the most far-reaching and influential challenge to the stereotype of black southerners as little more than helpless victims of white oppression came from Tennessee-born writer Alex Haley, whose Pulitzer Prize–winning *Roots: The Saga of an American Family* ostensibly told the story of his own family's odyssey from enslavement in eighteenth-century Gambia to post-emancipation settlement in Tennessee. *Roots* appeared in print just in time for the U.S. bicentennial observance in 1976 and sold 1.5 million copies in eighteen months. It also ran as a twelve-hour television miniseries in late January 1977. *Gone with the Wind* had drawn a record viewing audience estimated at 65 percent of the market when it made its television debut a few months earlier, but *Roots* attracted an even larger following. A. C. Nielsen reported that 130 million people watched at least part of the eight-night miniseries and estimated the market share for the final episode at 75 percent. Needless to say, *Roots* had an enormous impact on racial attitudes. By making all of his black characters seem either sympathetic or heroic, Haley's saga fueled black pride, and black infants were soon being christened with the names of his characters such as "Kunta Kinte'" and "Kizzie."[61]

Meanwhile, Haley's idealized portrait of African culture and his uncompromising treatment of the horror of slavery presented even the most resistant white viewers with, as Jack Kirby observed, the popular perception of *Gone with the Wind* "turned inside out." Comparisons to *Uncle Tom's Cabin* were also appropriate, although in this case, as critic Leslie Fielder pointed out, it was a black author who had succeeded "in modifying the mythology of Black-White relations for the majority audience." Moreover, where Uncle Tom stood by his principles and suffered a martyr's death for it, Haley's family had done the same and not only survived but prospered. A major part of its appeal, Willie Lee Rose has suggested, lay in the fact that *Roots* was a "success story."[62]

Researchers quickly found major factual errors and many unsubstantiated claims in that story, however, and Haley was hit with charges of both plagiarism and fraud. In response, he characterized *Roots* as a work of "faction," which blended fact and fiction but maintained "symbolic accuracy" and presented "spiritual truth." Critics also charged that Haley had made the village from which his ancestor was taken seem like a Gambian Club Med, and in truth, life in the pastoral paradise that was Africa in Haley's story was in many ways simply evocative of the "golden age" so commonly constructed by identity builders, including those who had shaped and propagated the legend of the Old South. "I, we, need a place called Eden. My people need a Pilgrim's Rock," he explained. Haley's identification of this hunger for an identity, even one based on feeling as much as fact, helped to explain why, despite the controversy that swirled about the book, *Roots* was so readily incorporated into the curricula of many of the Black Studies programs that were emerging in the late 1970s.[63]

New South historians had clearly ignored mountains of evidence to the contrary when they portrayed slavery as a benign and civilizing institution. Some historians of slavery in the 1970s also seemed to use their sources rather selectively in making their case for a viable black communal response to slavery. Intent on showing the slave conjurer as an influential agent of resistance to white authority, Blassingame argued that "sometimes the charms the slaves obtained from the conjurers bolstered their courage and caused them to defy their masters." As a case in point he cited an incident in the published narrative of former slave Henry Bibb. After the roots and powders he had secured from a conjurer appeared to save him from a flogging, Bibb wrote, "I had . . . great faith in conjuration and witchcraft." When his master came to punish him for a subsequent offense, Bibb "did not believe that he could do it, while I had this root and dust; and as he approached me, I commenced talking saucy to him." Leaving the reader to infer that this act of defiance was successful, Blassingame ignored the remainder of Bibb's account of the affair, which ended abruptly when his angry master grabbed "a handful of switches and punished me severely," forcefully convincing Bibb that there was "no virtue" in the conjurer's potions. Perhaps in the interest of depicting a tightly knit slave community, Blassingame also indicated that the conjurer "gave" his roots and powders to Bibb, when in fact the poor slave was forced to pay for them. He also failed to note that immediately after reporting this incident, Bibb recounted a later one in which he was again swindled by another slave "who professed to understand all about conjuration."[64]

By emphasizing the horror and cruelty of slavery, historians like Stampp and Elkins had helped to provide a crucial historical rationale for the crusade against Jim Crow. In the long run, however, their emphasis on the horrors of slavery had also fueled a perception that the slaves themselves had been little more than the voiceless and volitionless objects of white exploitation and abuse. If a new generation of professional historians who emerged in the 1970s clearly saw a legitimate need as scholars to offer a correction to this view, there can be little doubt that they also acted, at least in part, in response to the perceived desire of contemporary African Americans for a more affirmative and inspiring past. However, at a time when the political proclivities of white Americans were swinging decidedly to the right, the pronounced shift of historical attention toward black agency invariably meant less emphasis on black victimization, the premise that had been crucial to the hard won socioeconomic, political, and programmatic gains of the civil rights era.

Herbert Gutman had made no secret of his determination to refute the Moynihan Report's conclusion about the destructive impact of slavery on the black family in *The Black Family in Slavery and Freedom, 1770–1925*. Yet, in his strenuous effort to emphasize the strength of the black family and black culture, as David Brion Davis put it, Gutman seemed to come close to suggesting that slavery "really did not matter." Kenneth Lynn agreed, observing that "the culturally undamaged blacks" depicted by some of the anti-Moynihan historians seemed uncomfortably reminiscent of the stereotypical "carefree darkies" who once populated the historical and literary landscapes of New South writers.[65]

While acknowledging the important contributions of historians such as George Rawick, John Blassingame, and others, Peter Kolchin observed, "Eager to rebut images of slave passivity and docility, many of these historians have elevated the slave community to an all-embracing agency that gave order to the slaves' lives, expressed their deepest aspirations, and prevented their complete victimization." In the process, so Kolchin believed, "they have also come dangerously close to replacing a mythical world in which the slaves were objects of total control with an equally mythical world in which slaves were hardly slaves at all."[66]

In response to this trend, Bertram Wyatt-Brown argued, "We cannot continue expatiating on the riches of black culture without examining the social and psychological tensions that slavery entailed." Clarence Walker has also challenged the notion that white oppression was neutralized by a slave community, arguing that "community formed in response to oppression does not

automatically become the constructive community these historians assume."
More recently, in *Them Dark Days: Slavery in the American Rice Swamps*, William Dusinberre contended that "slavery was even more horrific . . . than is
generally acknowledged" and urged historians who "celebrate the strength of
the slaves' cultural defenses against their oppressors" to take care to set their
arguments "against the dark background of the slaves' lives."[67]

Although it is altogether reasonable to presume that professionally trained
historians would recognize the horrors of slavery as a given, such a presumption may be less warranted where college freshmen are concerned. The influence of scholarship stressing black community and agency under slavery is
readily apparent in contemporary collegiate United States history textbooks.
Surveying eight popular texts available in 1998, Kolchin noted that none of
them incorporated "recent suggestions that revisionists of the 1970s may have
exaggerated the cohesion of the slave community—if, indeed there was such a
thing as 'the' slave community—and the resemblance between slave families
and those of middle-class whites."[68]

In some texts, the brutality and potentially damaging effects of slavery were
allotted significantly less space and emphasis than that accorded discussions
of the slave community, slave culture, and, despite their relative rarity, slave
revolts. The result is a sometimes ambiguous or even contradictory message
about the slave experience. Students might read on page 87 that "to be a slave
meant that someone else possessed your body and could command your daily
activities," only to learn on page 307 that "slaves were well known for controlling the pace of work, reporting their tools broken or 'lost' when they were
forced to work too fast or too long." Another text announced that "*a number*
of slaves participated in revolts, showing their willingness to risk their lives in
a desperate bid for liberation," only to caution just a few sentences later that
"*only a tiny fraction* of all slaves ever took part in organized acts of violent
resistance against white power." [Emphasis added in both cases.] Although the
authors conceded that "slavery was, of course, often a demoralizing and brutalizing experience," their extensive discussion of its impact on the slaves themselves repeatedly stressed the "heroic effort to endure slavery without
surrendering to it" and suggested that "the inner world that the slaves made
for themselves gave them the spiritual strength to thwart their masters' efforts
to take over their hearts and minds."[69]

It is certainly important for students to understand that, brutal as it was,
slavery did not destroy the spirit, determination, and self-respect of African
Americans. Yet, it is striking nonetheless to find some collegiate textbooks of-

fering such relatively brief and matter-of-fact treatments of the damaging aspects of slavery at a time when the embattled defenders of race-based collegiate admissions (and affirmative action in general) still rested so much of
their political, if not legal, case on the historical logic of the much-maligned
Moynihan Report with its emphasis on the debilitating legacy of slavery. In
recent years, a growing number of black leaders have expressed support for a
program of reparations to compensate African Americans for the enduring
negative legacy of their ancestors' enslavement. Legal scholar Charles Ogletree's
description of reparations as "a full recognition and a remedy of how slavery
stigmatized, raped, murdered and exploited millions of Africans through no
fault of their own" also seems reminiscent of Moynihan's call for a domestic
"Marshall Plan" aimed at repairing some of the damage done to blacks by
"three centuries of injustice."[70]

The continuing need to educate whites about the raw realities of slavery has
been underscored in recent years by several incidents that might well have
transpired 150 years ago. In South Carolina, staunch Confederate flag defender
and Columbia barbeque impresario Maurice Bessinger faced a grocery-store
boycott of his famous sauce in the wake of reports that he was selling a booklet
in his restaurant that offered the "biblical view of slavery" and claimed that
many slaves had actually "blessed the Lord" for their good fortune in being
taken out of Africa. Surely, the author of the pamphlet concluded, there was
no merit in the arguments of those who would "load you up with guilt and say
you need to make reparations for what your forefathers did." Elsewhere, Alabama lawmaker Charles Davidson also offered a biblical defense of slavery,
maintaining that slaves were generally well treated and contending that "The
incidence of abuse, rape, broken homes and murder are 100 times greater,
today, in the housing projects than they ever were on the slave plantations in
the Old South."[71]

George Rawick had insisted in 1968 that "unless we find the real historical
roots of the Black Power movement, we are faced with a situation unparalleled
in world history: a massive revolutionary movement which comes from nowhere and is born fully grown." By 1983 this "massive revolutionary movement"
demanding historical explication had not been much in evidence for a long time,
but in that year the NAACP, which had also been party to the assault on the
Moynihan Report, placed "the precipitous decline of the Black family" at the
top of its list of concerns, and its president Eleanor Holmes Norton blamed
the backlash against Moynihan for "driving the issue from the public agenda
and delaying for a generation the search for workable solutions."[72]

Twenty years later, activist and educator Lenora Fulani charged that "efforts to solve the problems of undereducation in our communities with nationalist politics devastated our community and miseducated us." These frustrations seemed to be directed at those who had reasoned that, if by means of a creative cultural response, their slave ancestors had managed so successfully to resist the potentially damaging effects of slavery, then inhabitants of the nation's black ghettoes must be doing the same in response to continuing white repression. Hence, instead of pathological and dysfunctional, their behavior might be seen as an adaptive, culturally legitimate response to the racial persecution that had driven them there in the first place. In the final analysis, despite its corrective value for scholars and its emotional appeal for many African Americans, as Peter Novick put it, "the new black historiography of the seventies" may have also helped, however inadvertently, "to divert attention from the urgent needs of the constituency which those who produced it were dedicated to serving."

The foregoing surely suggests that, no matter how laudable their intentions, when historians are drawn into the politics of identity, they may unwittingly cease to be scholars who simply try to make the past speak to the present and become ventriloquists who are intent on making it say what they think their audience wants to hear. In doing so, they run the risk both of misrepresenting the past and of confusing what their readers *want* to hear with what they may actually *need* to hear. Nor should they forget that their version of the past will speak not just to their own present but to a future whose needs they surely cannot know.

The ramifications of history as identity politics may not only spill over into traditional policy debates about who gets what and how much, but as the suffering inflicted by contemporary conflicts over the historical origins of cultural and ethnic animosities elsewhere in the world all too vividly attests, the emotionalized representations of the past that often sustain the politics of identity can have brutal, even deadly, consequences. In the South and elsewhere, ongoing controversies over the symbols and meaning of the past surely reaffirm history as the indispensable base tissue, the virtual DNA-equivalent from which a sense of group distinctiveness must be teased and nurtured. As Eric Hobsbawm notes, however, once it is caught up in the process of identity-building, history as fact or scholarly interpretation may soon give way to history as "myth and invention."[73]

Weary of constant, potentially volatile confrontations over historical interpretations and symbols, some southerners might be tempted to think that a little less attention to the more problematic aspects of their history would not be such a bad thing. After all, Ernest Renan once suggested that "the essence of a nation is that its people have much in common and have forgotten much." In the long run, however, decisions about what to forget are simply the flipside of those about what to, as David Blight has put it, "remember big," and therefore they are no less likely to be divisive or to distort the past according to the wishes of the most powerful members of the group.[74]

The human rights track records of nations or ethnocultural groups whose leaders have succeeded in unifying them around what is effectively a false or skewed version of their history are truly appalling. Certainly, the abuses of history that were so integral to constructing the New South identity also bear considerable responsibility for its tragically enduring socioeconomic and political legacy, aptly summarized by Woodward as "caste, paternalism and segregation" and "juleps for the few and pellagra for the crew." At the end of the nineteenth century, the New South Creed had promised white southerners a bright and appealing future, but its actual legitimacy rested on a carefully fabricated version of southern history. At the beginning of the twenty-first century, the bitter fruits of this manipulated, misshapen past remain a formidable obstacle to the creation of yet another regional identity to which all southerners, white and black alike, may legitimately subscribe.[75]

12

The South and the Politics of Identity

SATURDAY REVIEW's 1976 DESCRIPTION of the South as "the New America" had seemed to suggest not only that the region's long run as the nation's "other" had finally come to an end but that a once ostracized Dixie might now actually show a stricken and uncertain nation how to rise above its divisions and doubts. Within a decade, however, many liberal observers were blaming the South's strong and still strengthening influence on national affairs for the emergence of what struck them as a very different "New America," this one rigidly conservative and at times even reactionary, its racism and intolerance, social indifference, and sometimes, its downright meanness, almost palpable.

In reality, of course, the fast-evaporating vision of the South as national redeemer and reconciler had been little more than wishful thinking in the first place. Although southern white leaders had been stressing the South's fundamental Americanness since the secession crisis, they had spoken not of a "new" inclusive, empathetic, ultra-tolerant America but an older one defined by uncritical adherence to political and moral absolutes and social laissez-faire. John Egerton had warned in 1974 that neither the South nor the nation were benefiting from the "Americanization of Dixie" or the "Southernization of America" so much as they were simply "sharing and spreading the worst in each other while the best languishes and withers."[1]

After the passage of the Civil Rights Act of 1964, the Republican party's racially based "Southern Strategy" of courting southern whites disaffected by Democratic civil rights initiatives proved so successful that even native son Jimmy Carter fell short of capturing a majority of southern white voters in 1976. In 1980 white southerners joined the overwhelming majority of white voters throughout the nation in an emphatic rejection of the luckless and uninspiring Carter's message of reconciliation in favor of the politics of polarization as preached and then practiced by both Ronald Reagan and his successor George H. W. Bush.

Reagan's pet story about a black "welfare queen" who supposedly raked in $150,000 a year would have done any southern segregationist demagogue proud. His attitude toward civil rights was clear enough when he opened his 1980 campaign in Neshoba County, Mississippi, site of the 1964 slayings of three civil rights workers, and neither mentioned the tragedy nor hailed the improvement in race relations in the years since it occurred. Instead, in language Mississippians had not heard since the massive resistance era, Reagan defiantly proclaimed his belief in "states' rights" and promised to "restore to states and local governments the powers that properly belong to them." As president, his indifference to the nation's widening economic disparities and his insensitivity to its pressing social problems evoked images of a Redeemer South governed by Woodward's julep-sipping few who showed little regard for the plight of the pellagra-ridden crew.[2]

Noting how effectively Jesse Helms had manipulated the "minority quota" issue in his 1990 North Carolina senatorial victory over black challenger Harvey Gantt, Edwin Yoder concluded that "the invidious use of race consciousness to undermine interest politics is alive and well." While it appeared at first glance that Helms had simply trotted out Cash's old Proto-Dorian convention in order to save his political neck, Yoder pointed out that this tactic—once the subterfuge of choice among southern Democrats—had now "gone national" and in fact had "taken on a certain shoddy respectability" among national Republican party leaders. The manipulation of the Willie Horton episode by Bush supporters in the 1988 campaign, Bush's veto of the Civil Rights Act of 1990, and his injection of the minority quota controversy into the 1990 congressional election seemed to confirm Yoder's assessment.[3]

The South remained a citadel of political conservatism by anybody's standard, but in reality, the GOP's presidential successes in the 1980s were so sweeping and national in scope that the Republicans could have claimed the White House in each election without carrying a single southern state. This seemed to count for little, however, as liberal journalists and pundits of all sorts seized on Egerton's "Southernization of America" as a convenient explanation/excuse for the sharply rightward shift in American politics and social attitudes. Southern white migrants to the North were singled out as the carriers of a contagion of grassroots racism, angry and intolerant religious fundamentalism, and the violent and misogynistic impulses that dominated country music. (The nationwide popularity of Merle Haggard's stridently authoritarian and super-patriotic "Okie from Muskogee" led some liberal commentators to proclaim it the unofficial anthem of the crusade to southernize America.)

Meanwhile, Texas oil money had ostensibly funded the reactionary religious and political programming that suffused the airwaves with latter-day right-wing mega-broadcasters like Rush Limbaugh and Pat Robertson. Not one to shy away from generalizations, James N. Gregory concluded, "Country music, the Wallace campaigns, and other southern-origin symbols were part of a multidimensional exchange that remade American patterns of class, race, and region in the middle decades of the 20th century."[4]

Having demonstrated his ability to tap into a northern white backlash against the civil rights movement, George Wallace was assigned major responsibility for racializing Republican politics, when, in fact, the Republicans had simply used him as a model in order to become more effective in what they were already trying to do. Some even blamed Wallace's relentless skewering of academic "pointy heads" who couldn't "park their bicycles straight" for Republican anti-intellectualism as practiced later by Dan Quayle and a host of others. Citing the 1994 conservative Republican "Contract with America" as primarily an expression of the "enduring values of an entire region," Alan Draper insisted that "where the South once obstructed liberalism from within the Democratic party, it does so today as the conservative vanguard of a resurgent Republican party." To Draper, the contemporary southern Republican leaders in Congress were "nothing more than 'Dixiecrats in drag.'"[5]

Senate majority leader Trent Lott of Mississippi seemed to affirm Draper's appraisal when he suggested in 2002 that the United States would have been better off had former segregationist Dixiecrat presidential candidate Strom Thurmond been elected in 1948. At the very least, Lott's remarks reinforced the enduring perception that the Republican party's manipulation of racial prejudice was orchestrated by and exclusively for white southerners. GOP leaders did little to discourage that view as they moved quickly to oust Lott, acting as if they had no idea how he became the party's most powerful senator in the first place. Some Republican leaders claimed that the handling of the Lott affair demonstrated their sincerity in trying to win over more African American voters. Others revealed privately that they had actually been more concerned that Lott's apparent nostalgia for blatantly segregationist politics had offended northern white suburban voters, a goodly share of whom, it might be noted, lived in all-white neighborhoods, relaxed at all-white clubs, and sent their children to what were effectively all-white schools.[6]

In reality, the insistence on associating the South with color-coded, reactionary politics was in itself racially exclusionary, for it overlooked the African

Americans in the South who consistently voted Democratic in overwhelming percentages as well as the fact that the South led the nation in black elected officials, including the sixteen southern black Democrats in Congress as of 2004. It also took no account of the South's new identity as African Americans' favorite place to live and work. Nor did it seem to matter that the only successful Democratic presidential candidates since 1964 were white southerners who had received overwhelming support from black voters.

None of this is to ague that white southerners had exactly become paragons of racial liberalism. For example, a 1999 poll showed that 56 percent of the southern whites surveyed were unequivocal supporters of integration as compared with 71 percent of the white respondents outside the South, and a 2003 survey revealed that only 59 percent of southern whites found interracial dating acceptable while 78 percent of non-southern whites said they were not troubled by it. On the other hand, while the 57 percent of whites in the South who thought the nation had "gone too far" in pushing civil rights was up slightly from the 55 percent who had registered this response in 1988, the percentage of non-southern whites who agreed on this point had risen from 43 to 49 over the same period. Likewise, while the proportion of whites outside the South who believed that instances of racial discrimination were rare remained almost constant at just below 30 percent, the percentage of southern whites who shared this opinion had fallen from 47 to 37 percent. Moreover, where only one-fifth of the blacks polled, both North and South, believed discrimination against members of their race was rare in 1988, by 2003 nearly a third of the southern black sample offered this response, while the reaction from non-southern blacks remained effectively the same. If occasional suggestions that the South now boasted the nation's best race relations were clearly wishful or speculative at best, it was nonetheless difficult to see how the region could be blamed for fostering racial polarization beyond its boundaries when in many categories related to racial tolerance or perceptions thereof, it was trending more positively, or at least less negatively, than the rest of the country.[7]

As often as not, the fifty-year retrospectives on the *Brown* decision that ran in major newspapers in May 2004 focused on the difficulties of achieving and maintaining racial integration in cities outside the South. Still, many Americans continued to project racist behavior anywhere in the nation into a southern context. Whenever a Yankee encountered racial problems in his own backyard, C. Vann Woodward complained, he blamed "the effort to Southernize the North." Like other shocked northern officials responding to racially motivated violence against blacks in their states or communities, a stunned New York mayor Ed Koch reacted angrily to the racially motivated 1986 beating death of a young black man in Howard Beach, Queens, by insisting that one would normally "expect this kind of thing to happen in the Deep South." Twelve years later when an unarmed and apparently unconscious black girl in Riverside, California, was shot twenty-seven times by police, a family friend expressed his disgust by commenting that "this might as well be Mississippi." Such responses meant, as Larry J. Griffin explained, that "regardless of where these racial horrors actually happened, they . . . should really have happened only in the Deep South." So long as white southerners are seen as "the 'real,' the 'main,' perhaps even the exclusive source of racial barbarism," Griffin added, "then America is permitted to distance itself from its racial problem, to localize and thereby regionally contain it . . . in the South." Peter Applebome agreed that "when the rest of the nation sees racism, it looks at the South and particularly its past and proclaims, in effect: We have met the enemy and it is them."[8]

In his thoughtful and sensitive 1995 book, *Dixie Rising*, Applebome found much to admire in "the South where I've lived half my life, where my kids were born, where I'd just as soon stay, the South that feels like home." He presented many examples of the fabled southern hospitality, humility, and openness, personified by a delightfully accommodating group of gentlemen who demonstrated the efficacy and entertainment value of do-it-yourself dentistry by relying on a pair of pliers as the extractor and a case of Budweiser as the anesthetic. In the end, however, even Applebome seemed to echo Egerton in suggesting that the South's vices had proven far more exportable than its virtues, and he left the definite impression that in areas such as politics, social responsibility, and tolerance of racial, ethnic, and sexual diversity, a rising Dixie was shaping "American values, politics and culture" in a decidedly negative way. At the end of the twentieth century, British scholar Helen Taylor detected a widespread belief in America that "divisions along race and class lines, conservative social and racial agendas, segregated schooling, unions in retreat, and an enthusiasm for country music are all national phenomena that reflect the power and influence of the South on national culture." Three years later, writer Joshua Zeitz observed that this influence was far greater than it had been "at any time since a Virginian was given command of the Continental Army." Like Taylor, Zeitz pointed to the explosive growth of evangelical Protestantism outside the

South as well as the national popularity of country music and NASCAR en route to what seemed to him an inescapable conclusion: "Southern culture has become American culture."[9]

American culture has always been more southern than many contemporary liberals are willing to admit, but the national embrace of so many of the activities and traits once deemed distinctly southern raises questions about how much longer they can be legitimately identified with the South. Since country music's emergence into commercial viability in the 1920s, its performers and promoters have pursued a "crossover" into the larger national popular music market. The broad appeal of artists like Johnny Cash, Willie Nelson, and Waylon Jennings in the late 1960s and 1970s finally cleared a crossover path that has steadily grown wider in the ensuing decades. In fact, it is now a two-way street with pop music stars like Jimmy Buffett and Kid Rock making successful forays into the country market. Along with the success of more pop-oriented country artists like Garth Brooks and Shania Twain, such developments have sparked periodic complaints from so-called purists that country music is no longer "country."

Such protests are hardly new. Patsy Cline, who is now viewed as the all-time classic female country singer, was actually part of the 1960s "country pop" movement whose slick orchestral arrangements and smoothed-out sound was seen by many as a commercialized sellout of the raw and gritty soul of country music. In any event, while its performers and song settings remain predominantly southern, country is America's single most broadly popular musical form. It accounts for nearly twice as many broadcast formats as talk radio, its nearest competitor, and an estimated 56 percent of its fans live outside the South.[10]

On a smaller scale, the recent history of the blues affords a comparable example of expanded popularity at the price of diminished distinctiveness. African American migration from the South took the blues northward and urbanward, where it was amplified and generally adapted to more sophisticated black city dwellers, eventually begetting rhythm and blues, which in turn begat Motown and Soul. Still, the original blues style never approached mainstream white acceptance until the 1990s when a Grammy-winning reissue of Robert Johnson's recordings sparked an explosion of interest across the color line. Promoters moved quickly to tap into this relatively affluent urban white market for the blues, establishing clubs like the multicity "House of Blues" chain, which soon faced charges of presenting only a watered-down version of the music while attempting "a major ripoff of African-American culture."[11]

A similar story unfolds with NASCAR. From its origins as a simple matter of southern whites risking their red necks roaring around red-clay ovals, stock-car racing has become the nation's second most popular spectator sport, claiming an estimated 35 million fans by 2004. NBC suspended its coverage of the 2002 Winter Olympics in order to televise the Daytona 500, and the typical television audience for a NASCAR event reached 9 million in 2003. With 60 percent of its fan base outside the South, NASCAR's racing circuit now includes thirty-eight states. Its executives have also shifted some of the bigger races from the sleepy southern towns that had hosted them for years to major media markets like Chicago and Los Angeles, which is now the home of what was once the fabled Darlington (S.C.) 500. As a Fox broadcasting executive explained, "As NASCAR grows, it has to cut some umbilical ties with the area that gave the sport birth."[12]

Although 42 percent of NASCAR fans are female and it boasts a solid and still growing national fan base among men earning more than $75,000 a year, in the 2004 election the term "NASCAR Dad" clearly implied a macho, socially and politically conservative working-class white man, southern in outlook if not in heritage and hell-bent on returning George W. Bush to office. Noting the continuing inclination to blame white southerners for the apparent metastasization of their values throughout the American body politic, Michael O'Brien has pointed out that it is hardly as if southern whites suddenly showed up "on the doorstep of American culture" saying "I'm here. Move over. Imitate me." "If their culture is expansive," O'Brien observed, "it is little they planned and something most of them have not noticed. This is not the stuff of which hegemony is made."[13]

With the nation at large still providing such a voracious export market for "southern" vices, continued insistence on pasting regional labels on national traits seems not only hypocritical but disingenuous. Some forty years ago, Howard Zinn observed that it was much less troubling to see the "American dilemma" as "the gap between an American dream and Southern reality" than to acknowledge it as the discrepancy between the "American dream and national reality." More recently, David Jansson seemed to concur, noting that "in constructing the image of the South as the American region uniquely beset with its associated array of flaws, the national identity is wiped clean of these unfortunate traits so that the presence of poverty, racism, etc., throughout the rest of the country is not considered evidence of the 'Americanness' of these characteristics, but rather is seen as anomalous, aberrational and ironic."[14]

Paradoxically, one of the reasons the South was seen as "anomalous " or "aberrational" by others was actually the long-standing determination of so many southerners to show their "Americanness" through ostentatious professions of patriotism and an aggressive "my country right or wrong" attitude that had typically translated into historically high levels of military participation and enthusiasm for military action. A nationwide poll released in October 2002 showed that nearly two-thirds of southerners favored an invasion of Iraq, as opposed to scarcely half of Americans in general. Even as the war grew more problematic and controversial, white southerners continued to provide the strongest support for the Bush administration's actions. Willingness to use force was nothing new to people who lived in what remained the nation's most violent region, and all the old Confederate states showed homicide rates that put them in the top twenty nationwide in 2002. On the other hand, George W. Bush's ties to Christian conservatives also played especially well in a region increasingly dotted with megachurches boasting memberships in the thousands and caught up in movements to restore school prayer and require the display of the Ten Commandments in public buildings.[15]

Premised on the religious fundamentalism and evangelical fervor of lower-class southern whites, derisive references to the South as the so-called Bible Belt largely ignored the strong spiritual attachments and stern fidelity to biblical doctrine that characterized perhaps an even greater majority of southern blacks. For example, when queried about their attitudes toward gay marriage in 1999, 58 percent of black southerners expressed their opposition, a figure roughly equivalent to that registered by white southerners but more than 10 percent higher than that for African Americans outside the South. Although Bush received only 11 percent of the black vote nationwide in the 2004 election, this figure was up from 8 percent in 2000. His opposition to gay marriage and his emphasis on conservative Christian values clearly paid off in his home state of Texas where he more than tripled his previous percentage among African Americans, and in Florida, where he nearly doubled it, as well as in Georgia and North Carolina where his black support grew by more than 50 percent. Yet such complexities simply did not register on the radar screens of many frustrated northeastern liberals who seemed to look at the thirty-one "red" states (three of which touched the Canadian border) that went for Bush and see only what the angry (but amusing) architects of *www.fuckthesouth.com*

described as the "liberal-bashing, . . . confederate-flag-waving, holier-than-thou, hypocritical bullshit" they had long considered the exclusive province of white southerners.[16]

Edward Ayers has pointed to the continuing inclination of some Americans to "exoticize" the South by "totaliz[ing]" some of its perceived features or traits, some good but mostly bad, into both the essence and extent of its identity. Citing "a troubled history of race relations" and "a national or regional tendency towards provincialism and caricature of the *other*" [Emphasis added], a Chicago marketing firm hired by The University of the South at Sewanee, Tennessee, pointed out in January 2004 that "the South, to which Sewanee is intimately linked because of history, location, and name, can prompt negative associations for prospective students." In response, officials announced the school would henceforth be known as "Sewanee: The University of the South." Elsewhere in the academic world, John Jett complained in 2004 that when he told his fellow students at Stanford that he was from Georgia, "a subtle change overtakes them as if I'd forgotten to put on my pants." Jett recalled a recent lecture in which the professor's matter-of-fact remark "that America would probably be better off without the South" had drawn approving chuckles from many of his classmates.[17]

Howard Zinn had caused more than a few raised eyebrows when he contended in 1964 that "those very qualities long attributed to the South as special possessions are, in truth, American qualities" and explained that "the nation reacts emotionally to the South precisely because it subconsciously recognizes itself there." Zinn's argument that the South could be "marvelously useful, as a mirror in which the nation can see its blemishes magnified," was understandably hard to swallow in the immediate aftermath of Oxford, Birmingham, and the bloodshed of Freedom Summer. Four decades later, although evidence of the Americanness of the South's imperfections is far more difficult to ignore, many non-southerners continue to see the region as a mirror image not in the sense of an accurate reflection of national realities, but as a total and exact reversal of America's fundamental ideals and expectations. Although he was exploring "Why America Still Needs the South" in the year 2000, Larry Griffin evoked recurrent depictions of the South as the nation's antithesis stretching back to the early national era; he explained that "when one understands the South as a negation of America . . . one is also likely to understand more deeply what America is, and what it is (or ought to be), in particular, is the opposite of the South."[18]

On the other hand, although the vision of the South as "a negation of America" may have been northern in origin, not only was it grounded in considerable historical substance, but it clearly owed much of its longevity to recurring examples and reminders of the sometimes savage, often sordid, conduct of white southerners themselves. By way of example, not long after Senator Strom Thurmond's death in 2003, Essie Mae Washington-Williams, a retired African American schoolteacher in California, revealed that the former Dixiecrat standard-bearer was her father. Even as he was vowing publicly in 1948 that "all the bayonets in the Army cannot force the Negro into our homes, our schools, our churches and our places of recreation," Thurmond was privately helping to support the daughter he had fathered at age twenty-two with his family's sixteen-year-old maid. In 2004 Alabama voters rejected by a slim margin an amendment to the state constitution that would have nullified a segregation-era amendment declaring that Alabama's children had no constitutional right to an education at public expense. Opponents of the measure insisted that they were motivated not by race but by the fear that it would encourage judges to mandate increased spending on schools; this position, however, did not seem particularly mitigating in light of Alabama's dead last standing in most national rankings of public educational support and achievement.[19]

The efforts of southern intellectuals to depict and analyze such behavior has also fed the enduring perception of southern otherness. A sense of the South as a counterpoint to the rest of America had permeated the work of southern writers of fiction and social analysis and commentary throughout the nineteenth century and for over half of the twentieth. Personified in the novels of Erskine Caldwell, William Faulkner, and Richard Wright, the plays of Tennessee Williams, and the scholarly tomes of Howard Odum and Rupert Vance, it had found perhaps its most definitive statement in the tortured ruminations of W. J. Cash. David Jansson pointed out that Cash's picture of the white South as "violent, intolerant, racist, xenophobic, simpleminded, hedonistic, cruel and unjust, irrational, unrealistic, poor, lazy, [and] immobile" was the equivalent of the negative for a snapshot of an American society that saw itself as "peaceful, tolerant, enlightened, cosmopolitan, ingenious, moral, just, rational, pragmatic, prosperous, energetic [and] mobile." With the strength of America's association with these latter traits dependent in part on the strength of the

South's association with the former, the South as portrayed by Cash and other southern writers became not only a perfect "foil for the construction of a privileged national identity," but the most convenient and logical suspect whenever the nation as a whole failed to live up to its lofty ideals.[20]

"It is great to be at home in a region, even this one," Flannery O'Connor had quipped in 1959, but in the globalized world of the millennium, southerners were hardly alone in their insistence on attaching themselves to some sort of distinctive group identity, even a still somewhat dubious one. Although the South had a clear head start, regional studies centers were sprouting throughout the United States from Maine to Arizona. In fact, a 2004 New England poll showed that a whopping 87 percent of those contacted wanted to be identified as New Englanders, compared to the 74 percent of the respondents to a similar poll in the South who wanted to be known as southerners. Likewise, in every region scholars were caught up in collecting, cataloguing, and emphasizing their distinctive cultural artifacts and traits in encyclopedias focused on New England, the West, the Mid-West, Appalachia, the Great Plains, and, of course, that most frightfully neglected of all regions, New York City.[21]

The South was not even unique within the United States in its ethnic divisions over which aspects of its regional culture should be preserved or emphasized. On the same day in February 1998 that the *New York Times* carried a story about a dispute in New Orleans over schools named for slaveholders, it also ran a lengthy piece about a controversial statue in New Mexico of Spanish conquistador Don Juan de Onate. In the midst of the observance of the establishment of the first Spanish settlement in the American West, a group of Native American activists used an electric saw to remove the right foot of the statue. This was an act of symbolic retribution for an atrocity that, according to an enduring legend, had occurred in 1599 when Onate punished the conquered Acoma Pueblo by ordering his men to chop off the feet of twenty-four of the tribe's warriors. This incident was but one of a number in which Hispanics and Native Americans clashed over representations of their identities within the history and culture of the Southwest.[22]

In the world at large, the South's divisions over regional and cultural identity seem even less peculiar. In fact, the rapid increase in contemporary global awareness confirms the prescience of C. Vann Woodward's observation that it is not the South's history of conflict, poverty, and defeat, but the North's heralded story of harmony, affluence, and accomplishment that stands out as distinctive or exceptional. To Europeans, Helen Taylor observed, the South "seems to share a troubled and profound burden of history; a confused but lasting caste and class system; ethnic and racial conflicts that have lasted for centuries; the experience of having a war fought (and lost) on its own land"; and finally, "a resistance to Yankee (indeed, twentieth-century) progressivism, progress, and efficiency." Michael O'Brien, who grew up in Plymouth, England, which had been "flattened by the Luftwaffe," explained that "war, failure, prejudice, these are European things. Europeans can see themselves in southern writing and history. . . . By contrast, Europeans can find much in the history of the North that is a puzzle, for having such peace, such success, such want of incident."[23]

William Faulkner's famous observation that "the past is never dead, it's not even past" was even more relevant to Europe than to the South. White southerners who are still fighting the Civil War hardly seem unusual to people in Ireland who speak of "King Billy's" great victory on "the green, grassy slopes of the Boyne" in 1690 as if it happened last week, and Serbs who are clearly still deeply embittered by the outcome of the Battle of Kosovo in 1389 could surely teach the "fergit hell" crowd of southern whites a thing or two about holding grudges. Italy's North-South antagonisms are much sharper than they are here, and pro-secession groups like our League of the South seem a little less unusual in a country where it is actually disgruntled northerners who have been threatening to break away. Expressing their defiance of the North, some in southern Italy even sport Confederate flag bumper stickers and wave the banner at soccer games. When Don H. Doyle asked if the people of the Italian South knew what the flag meant, a professor from the University of Naples assured him, "Oh, yes, we know what it means. . . . [W]e too are a defeated people. Once we were a rich and independent country, and they came from the North and conquered us and took our wealth and power away to Rome."[24]

Regional distinctions still matter throughout Europe, and while many in this country claim that the South is now indistinguishable from the rest of the United States, from their more detached perspective, Europeans can still see the differences, and these differences are precisely what makes the South so fascinating to many of them. Both the inexorable process of globalization and the ongoing efforts of the European Union to shape Europe into what is effectively a single nation (and, some think, a single culture as well) make the South's long-standing resistance to total immersion in the American mainstream seem not just relevant but in many ways admirable.

This identification with the American South has led a group of European scholars to organize the Southern Studies Forum, which convenes biannually to discuss various aspects of southern literature, history, and culture. At their 1991 meeting in Bonn, two Danes talked about antebellum southern literature and a Dutchman about Mark Twain. An Austrian focused on Walker Percy; an Englishman, a Frenchman, and a German tackled Faulkner; and another German discussed Thomas Jefferson. The theme for the 2003 meeting of the Southern Studies Forum in Thessaloniki, Greece, was "Southern Ethnicities." There were also a number of other European conferences dealing with the South. In a single academic year, one might hear Eudora Welty dissected in Dijon, discuss "Images of the South" in Seville, consider "Configuration of Race in the South" in Cambridge, or ponder contemporary southern literature in Reykjavik.

International interest in the South is hardly confined to Europe, of course. Southerners struggling to deny their past or throw off its burdens have nothing on the Japanese. Readers in Japan were among Faulkner's earliest devotees, and his popularity there is said to be second only to Shakespeare's. During a year teaching at Chiba University near Tokyo, southern literature specialist Anne Goodwyn Jones immediately saw parallels:

> Like Atlanta, but so much more recently, Japan's old cities were burned and flattened. . . . The stories of ordinary people's experiences of war and poverty that I had inherited from a privileged white Southern family and an American popular culture—burying the silver, living in slave quarters, eating weeds, drinking parched corn coffee, wearing feedsacks or draperies—were more than matched by the stories I read and heard about in Japan, of people whose lives burned up, of hunger that bent and shortened a generation's bones."[25]

An international perspective also suggests that the contemporary determination to reclaim or reconstruct a distinctive southern identity arose in response to the same kinds of homogenizing pressures generated by an emergent global mass culture that have triggered similar reactions throughout the world. Complaints that America had succumbed to a southern cultural invasion sounded doubly ironic in the world at large, where the dissolution of international barriers to trade and travel and the wonders of satellite and cyberspace communication threatened to create not just a global mainstream but an all-enveloping cultural tidal wave apparently driven in large measure by American tastes, styles, and preferences. This trend elicited a strong reaction from those who feared that their nation's cultural identity would soon be on the endangered species list. Noting a distinct southern parallel to this hostile response to "cultural modernization with a heavy American accent," Richard H. King observed that "left-wing French intellectuals bellyaching about the American cultural invasion sound like nothing so much as conservative Agrarians taking their stand."[26]

We have seen some notable examples of the commodification and marketing of southern identity, but the phenomenon is hardly confined to the South. Ironically, the ascendant global economy that has helped to plunge so much of humanity into a panic by threatening to take away our identities is now proceeding to sell them back to us. Despite the anti-establishment rhetoric of many of its proponents, as David Rieff has shown, multiculturalism has been an absolute boon to international capitalism. Although the concept of a distinctive identity seems exclusionary by definition, from the commercial standpoint, the more claimants and aspirants to a particular identity and the more intense their attachment to it the better. In such an environment, nations and products become almost indistinguishable. For example, Tetley Tea ads urge Jewish Americans to "Think Yiddish, but Drink British."[27]

The most challenging aspect of this process, a Malaysian marketing expert noted, was "how to put national character in a product without trivializing either the product or the character." As he stressed his nation's qualifications for independence, one writer to the *Glasgow Herald* insisted, "In marketing terms, Scotland could be one of the strongest brand names in the world." To many Americans, however, Scotland had become synonymous with the handsome actor Mel Gibson, who was raised in Australia but starred as Scottish national hero William Wallace in the stirring cinematic epic *Braveheart*. Inspired by the film, Scottish Americans hailed the observance of "National Tartan Day," a commemoration contrived by Mississippi Senator Trent Lott with the apparent approval of Scottish political leaders. Meanwhile, the mega-marketing of St. Patrick's Day had caused so many Americans to feel "Irish" that Dublin's tourism officials actually visited New York City to get some pointers on how to transform what had been a relatively low-key religious observance on the Emerald Isle itself into an opportunity for Irish American tourists to get in touch with their real or imagined Irish roots.[28]

As a matter of fact, southernness is a big hit in the international identity market as well. "Mississippi Mud" is manufactured in Germany for a company based in Scotland and touted throughout Europe as an "American" breakfast spread. Elsewhere, London offers many opportunities for fine southern dining, including a restaurant called Arkansas Barbeque and a huge cantina, "The Texas Embassy," just off Trafalgar Square. Texas is marketable as both West and South, of course, and on a Saturday night in 2002 the Italian town of Bellagio turned out in force for a "Texas Party," where a Gucci-scooting good time was had by all. Meanwhile, just across Lake Como at Tremezzo, dancers moved to a different but still decidedly southern beat at the "Jook Joint Café."[29]

All of this may seem no more serious than going to a costume party dressed as Gomer Pyle or Scarlett O'Hara. The problem here is that complex and often unwieldy identities are being reduced to trendy and attractive lifestyles which, if not exactly up for grabs, are certainly up for sale. If one identity is disappointing or grows boring, it is simply time to go shopping for another. The greater our purchasing power, the more identity options from which we may choose. If it was once said the winner is the one who winds up with the most toys, today's winners might be identified by the number of identities they can accumulate. Ironically, whether they are buying into a caricatured and stereotyped version of what is supposed to be their own or trying someone else's on for size, many of those who are so desperately seeking an identity are actually in danger of losing sight of who they really are. In an observation that might well apply to many white subscribers to *Southern Living*, African American writer Debra Dickerson scoffed, "Kente cloth placemats and fertility mask screen savers are not Afrocentrism. That's just shopping." When the desire for group attachments supersedes the need for self-knowledge, it becomes more important to be different than to be real.

Although the hunger for group connectedness may seem to be nothing more than a fundamental human impulse, its intensity is also a function of historical context. David Riesman's *The Lonely Crowd* reflected the perceived rise of a coldly impersonal, suffocatingly conformist American mass society in the aftermath of World War II. This perception spawned a fixation on identity that fairly exploded in the 1960s as many Americans reexamined their traditional identification with the nation as a whole, eventually settling on a host of more narrowly based group attachments derived not only from region but other alternatives such as race, ethnicity, gender, or sexual preference.[30]

What began as a flight from conformity, however, has become for many a descent into it at multiple and contradictory levels. When Ralph Ellison wrote that "being a Negro American involves a *willed* . . . affirmation of self as against all outside pressure," he was not referring simply to pressure from whites. At the end of the twentieth century, Randall Kenan saw contemporary black identity as "a postmodern amalgam of borrowings and findings like Kwanzaa, media manipulations of street lingo, . . . only interested in style, newness, the expression of being other, being black." Within such a "vast cultural soup of consumeristic we-think," he realized, there is little tolerance for someone who wishes to retain his or her identification with the group but also chooses to be "other than other." In an Internet chat with a black man from Los Angeles, Kenan confessed his own ineptitude at basketball and his feelings of insecurity on the subject, only to have his cross-country conversation cut short when his new "cyberNegro" acquaintance abruptly signed off with, "Well, I got to get outta here and git wit some real niggas."[31]

Kenan observed that it is difficult "to be black on a computer screen," but the means of communication had less to do with the none-too-subtle suggestion that he was not really "black" or at least not "black enough" than the fact that he was trying to convey individuality within blackness, or more broadly, "otherness" within "otherness." Like Kenan, Henry Lewis Gates explained, "I want to be black, to know black, to luxuriate in whatever I might be calling blackness at any particular time." Yet, Gates also admitted, "I rebel at the notion that I can't be part of other groups, that I can't construct other identities through elective affinity, that race must be the most important thing about me." The difficulty here lies not so much in identifying *with* groups as identifying solely *through* groups. As Ellison's great novel made abundantly clear, human invisibility can be every bit as thorough and devastating when group otherness is consciously sought and sustained from within as when it is imposed from without, because in order to be identified with a distinctive group, we are sometimes called on to sacrifice our freedom to be distinctive as individuals.[32]

This has surely been the case with the white southerners who made the belief, first in slavery, then in racial segregation, the cardinal test of southernness and also with those who now base their claims to distinctiveness on their own superficial amalgam of lifestyle, caricature, and cultural commodification. Over the course of the South's history, the primary practitioners and beneficiaries of the politics of identity have included both the defenders of slavery and the proponents of secession, as well as those who led the way in overthrowing

Reconstruction. In the deceptively misnomered New South, identity politics proved instrumental in re-subjugating blacks socially, neutralizing the political potential of the masses of both races and throwing off any attempt to remedy these conditions for some three-quarters of a century.

African American racial pride helped to ignite the crusade against Jim Crow, but in the mid-1960s and the 1970s, the divisive politics of black identity helped not only to sap the momentum of the civil rights movement but also to fuel the mounting white backlash against it and, some think, even to undermine efforts to expand federal programs to assist disadvantaged blacks. Regardless of its radical-populist trappings, identity politics typically redounds to the ultimate benefit of elites, who can use it to divert and divide the masses and even exploit them economically. In a broader contemporary setting, the emphasis on group distinctiveness and exclusivity, as Carl Pletsch has argued, pits "this ethnic group against that race, this race against those women, these women against those men, and many identity groups against civil society as a whole." This reduction of American society into a "multichrome mosaic of monochrome identity groups," Rogers Brubaker and Frederick Cooper have argued, "hinders rather than helps the work of understanding the past and pursuing social justice in the present."[33]

As Michael O'Brien has observed, if "identity is something we are free to invent," we must ask if "southern [is] something still worth inventing, and reinventing, when American culture makes so many other more pressing demands on the stamina of invention? Is there much left over from inventing gender, or race, or post-ethnicity to be spared for the South?" The challenge of retaining or reconciling multiple group identities is suggested by the long-term trend in polling data gathered from residents of the South in the period 1991–2001. Although the percentage of respondents who identified themselves as southerners remained above 70 percent, over the decade the proportion of those giving this response declined by 7.4 percent. The most striking drop in southern identification (19 percent) came from Hispanics, followed by Asian Americans and Native Americans (9.5 percent), both groups who are likely to have become more sensitive to their ethnic identities than their regional identities in recent years. Meanwhile, the tendency to see themselves as southerners declined by less than 1 percent among whites who were lifelong residents of the South and generally, as Larry Griffin put it, "do not have ready access to competing ethnic or racial identities."[34]

Because it is such a competitive process, the politics of identity encourages exaggeration both of commonalities within groups and differences among them, as events and trends in the South and North in the final years before the Civil War illustrate all too well. Here again, further evidence that the prevailing obsession with group distinctiveness is anything but harmless abounds throughout the contemporary global scene, where, in pursuit of what has been called a "terrible singularity," cultural nationalists who cast themselves as the guardians of national or ethnic identity have rekindled smoldering prejudices and grievances that have led not only to social and political polarization but often to violence and bloodshed as well. Closer to home, leaders of the League of the South have dedicated themselves to saving "true Southerners" from "ethnic cleansing" and preserving "the historic Anglo-Celtic core culture" that has "given Dixie its unique institutions and civilization." "Should the Christian, Anglo-Celtic core be displaced," league spokesmen warned, "the South would cease to be recognizable to us and our progeny."[35]

In their move to promote southern independence, league representatives have likened themselves to separatists from Scotland to Quebec to the Balkans who have called for ethnic and cultural home rule, insisting that "American Southerners have much in common with the Scot and the Welsh in Britain, the Lombards and Sicilians in Italy and the Ukrainians in the defunct Soviet Union. All have made enormous economic, military and cultural contributions to their imperial rulers, who rewarded their loyalty with exploitation and contempt."[36]

The South absorbed 1.3 million new foreign-born residents between 1990 and 1998 alone, and like many contemporary right-wing movements around the world, the League of the South has blamed globalization for the flow of immigrants into their region. On April 24, 2002, league president Michael Hill congratulated anti-immigration National Front candidate Jean-Marie Le Pen on his stronger-than-expected showing in the first round of the French presidential elections. A league press release noted that over the past decade, "there had been a huge influx of non-white immigrants into both Europe and America that threatens to engulf our historic populations and culture." Citing the success of other rightist, anti-immigration candidates throughout Europe, Hill called for "others like Le Pen to arise in America and from every corner of Christendom in defense of the common folks who work, pay taxes and otherwise provide society's backbone. . . . [I]t's time for the deracinated globalists everywhere to be sent packing."[37]

The academics who do most of the talking for the League of the South consistently deny the racist subtext that their statements often seem to convey. Still, the language they employ is too redolent of the rhetoric that fueled a

wave of racial violence in the post-Reconstruction South and turned Europe
inside out in the 1930s for them to be laughed off as just another bunch of
professors behaving foolishly. When a Scottish journalist heard Michael Hill
describe white southerners as a "demonized" people "at war" with those who
believe they should be "eradicated," the reporter heard chilling echoes not of
Jefferson Davis or George Wallace but of the terminology employed more recently by Serbia's most notorious ethnic cleanser, Radovan Karadzic.[38]

Such rhetoric hardly encourages tolerance in a region that, in addition to a
multitude of unresolved black-white issues, has led the nation in Hispanic
population growth in recent years and attracted a growing stream of Asian
immigrants as well. (W. E. B. DuBois foresaw "the problem of the color line"
as "the problem of the Twentieth Century"; at the dawn of the twenty-first
century, that problem is increasingly compounded by the question of where
that line actually runs.) To a world where diminishing national distinctions
may make other sorts of group distinctions seem far too important and sometimes even matters of life and death, the South's experience surely says that
any identity—national, regional, cultural, or otherwise—that can be sustained
only by demonizing or denigrating other groups exacts a terrible toll, not simply on the demonized and denigrated but ultimately on those who can find
self-affirmation only by rejecting others.[39]

However admirable the intentions of its proponents, an obsessive insistence
on the importance of group distinctiveness can be intellectually constricting
as well. In the post-North, post–civil rights era, historians and other scholars,
along with a new generation of southern writers, have faced steadily decreas-
ing pressure to focus on, as David Potter put it in 1967, "the distinctive features of southern society." No longer encumbered by the obligation to explain
why things did not work out as they did in the North, they have been able to
confront southern history on its own terms, as it happened to southerners
both across and within not just racial but class and gender groupings as well.
Freed from the burden of southern distinctiveness, we can better appreciate
not only the weight but the complexity of the burden of southern history.

For all the contemporary statistical data documenting regional convergence
and the physical evidence afforded by skyscrapers, suburban sprawl, and
gridlocked expressways, I have yet to encounter anyone who has moved into

or out of the South and did not sense that, for better or worse, living here was different from living in other parts of the country. In one aspect or another, I have spent the last thirty-five years pondering the question of southern exceptionalism. Over the last decade or so, however, both in the course of researching and writing this book and of trying to pay some attention to events in the contemporary globalizing world, I have seen human beings driven again and again to extremes of both savagery and superficiality by a desire not simply to *be* different but to be *acknowledged* as such by others. This leads me to believe that continuing to focus on why the South is not like the rest of America may actually prevent southern historians from fully understanding why the South is like it is (or was like it was) and southerners themselves from knowing who they really are and, perhaps, even from becoming everything they could really be.

At the risk of sounding every bit as heretical as Hazel Motes, who championed the church without Jesus in Flannery O'Connor's *Wise Blood*, I believe the lessons of both the distant and the recent southern pasts underscore the need to consider a conception of identity without distinctiveness or at least one that emphasizes the importance of being "oneself or itself" over not being "another." Certainly, in trying to understand some of those who have struggled most thoughtfully with the idea of southern identity, nothing is so clear as the importance of their own personal connections with a particular place, family, and community to their sense not only of what it meant to be southern but, more critically, their sense of who they were as individuals. Ellen Glasgow became both herself and a southerner in Richmond; William Faulkner in Lafayette County, Mississippi; Harry Crews in Alma, Georgia; Alex Haley in Henning, Tennessee; and Randall Kenan in Chinquapin, North Carolina, all of them influenced by unwitting role models who probably spent little, if any, time worrying about whether they were like other southerners or unlike everybody else. These authors may have taught us a great deal about the South as a region, but Faulkner was surely correct, after all, when he concluded that ultimately "it is himself that every Southerner writes about."[40]

Finally, as I suggested at the outset, our historical survey definitely points to the need to rethink the association of identity with "remaining the same one . . . under varying aspects and conditions." On the contrary, as Ayers has pointed out, "the very story of the South is a story of unresolved identity, unsettled and restless, unsure and defensive." As the most adept chronicler and analyst of the continuity of southern white identity, W. J. Cash enjoyed, albeit posthumously, a phenomenal surge in credibility in the midst of the often appalling response of many white southerners to the civil rights movement. By the same token, however, Cash's characterizations have seemed increasingly out of sync with events and trends in recent decades as it has become ever more obvious that many of the traits he had identified as regional were a lot more national than he and many others had realized. Certainly, Cash's model of a monolithic and static southern mind rooted in dogged resistance to change has proven inadequate to explain the experience of most southerners, white or black, in the post–Jim Crow, post-North era. Writing at the end of the longest period of relative continuity in the region's history, he did not perceive that what he saw as the southern white mind, which he believed had already persisted for roughly a century, could actually be only a stage in an ongoing process of interaction with—and ultimate adaptation to—the forces of change. In fact, this interaction had already fostered a more flexible, sensitive, and self-critical spirit that was emerging even as he undertook a book about what Daniel Singal called "a permanent mind impervious to the forces of historical change."[41]

Cash's concerns about white southerners' behavioral and emotional pathologies, especially their exaggerated emphasis on racial values, seemed to be borne out in the ugly, violent, and utterly shameful short term. Yet, their ultimate, relatively rapid and low-key accommodation to the integration of schools and other public venues and facilities suggested that their "capacity for adjustment" was greater over the long haul than he had anticipated, just as the eagerness of many black southerners to claim the post–civil rights era South as home also came as a surprise to many observers. Ultimately, instead of destroying the "southern way of life," the overthrow of Jim Crow seemed to result in a broader, biracial effort to keep it alive, although often on dramatically different terms. Resolving some of these differences or at least learning to respect them may well be crucial to determining whether the label of "southerner" continues to have legitimate meaning and, more important, whether the South finally becomes a place where southerners can truly come to know themselves and each other.

Those of us who care about how things turn out "away down South" can certainly take heart in George Tindall's suggestion that "to change is not necessarily to lose one's identity, to change sometimes is to find it." Yet, as we have surely seen, identity is not a matter of simply deciding either to be different or remain the same. Its sources are not just internally but externally contingent as well. Just as the demise of the North against which they defined themselves left many southerners, whites especially, hard-pressed to explain who and why they are, allowing the newest New South simply to fade uncontested into a "No South" would have similar, and only marginally less severe, consequences for many others throughout the nation at large. Certainly, if its history is any guide, the southern identity of the future will reflect not just what southerners themselves have chosen to make it but what other Americans need or want it to be as well.[42]

Notes

INTRODUCTION

1. David M. Potter, "The Enigma of the South," *The Yale Review* 51 (October 1961), 142–51; U. B. Phillips, "The Central Theme of Southern History," *American Historical Review* 34 (October 1928), 30–43; U. B. Phillips, *Life and Labor in the Old South* (Boston, 1929), 3; C. Vann Woodward, "The Search for Southern Identity," *Virginia Quarterly Review* 34 (Summer 1958), 321–38. "The South" as I use it here will normally refer to the old Confederacy, plus Kentucky and Oklahoma, although there are a few references to pertinent events in Maryland as well.
2. William Faulkner, *Intruder in the Dust* (New York, 1948), 152–53; C. Vann Woodward, "The Irony of Southern History," *Journal of Southern History* 19 (February 1953), 3–19; Edward L. Ayers, "What Do We Talk about When We Talk about the South?" in Edward L. Ayers, Patricia Nelson Limerick, Stephen Nissenbaum, and Peter S. Onuf, eds., *All over the Map: Rethinking American Regions* (Baltimore, 1996), 65.
3. Joyce Oldham Appleby, *Inheriting the Revolution: The First Generation of Americans* (Cambridge, Mass., 2000), 265.
4. *Webster's Unabridged Dictionary of the English Language* (New York, 1989), 707; David R. Jansson, "Internal Orientalism in America: W. J. Cash's *The Mind of the South* and the Spatial Construction of National Identity," *Political Geography* (no monthly date, 2003), 297, 311; Susan-Mary Grant, *North over South: Northern Nationalism and American Identity in the Antebellum Era* (Lawrence, Kans., 2000), 35.
5. Jack P. Greene, *Pursuits of Happiness: The Social Development of Early Modern British Colonies and the Formation of American Culture* (Chapel Hill, 1988), 3–4.
6. Carl N. Degler, "Thesis, Antithesis, Synthesis: The South, the North and the Nation," *Journal of Southern History* 52 (February 1987), 5; Richard N. Current, *Northernizing the South* (Athens, 1983), 35.
7. Rogers Brubaker and Frederick Cooper, "Beyond Identity," *Theory and Society* 29 (February 2000), 1–47; Philip Gleason, "Identifying Identity: A Semantic Identity History," *Journal of American History* 69 (March 1983), 931.
8. Gleason, "Identifying Identity," 911. In addition to the works cited here and elsewhere throughout the book, I refer the reader to James A. Boon, *Other Tribes, Other Scribes: Symbolic Anthropology in the Comparative Study of Cultures, Histories,*

Religions, and Texts (Cambridge, 1982), and Joanne Nagel, "Constructing Ethnicity: Creating and Recreating Ethnic Identity and Culture," *Social Problems* 41 (February 1994), 152–76.

9. *Webster's Unabridged Dictionary*, 707; Lawrence W. Levine, *Black Culture and Black Consciousness: Afro-American Folk Thought from Slavery to Freedom* (New York, 1978), 5. There is always the question of how much an identity can change and remain "authentic," of course, but it is important to remember that the benchmarks of authenticity are themselves a matter of perception and that they can change as well. For that matter, if authenticity as a southerner must be linked to direct experience with the realities of southern life, then it is also necessary to point out at the beginning that those who are most authentically "southern" are generally those who have been least involved publicly either in actively constructing or contemplating southern identity.

10. George Brown Tindall, *The Ethnic Southerners* (Baton Rouge, 1976), ix; Yoder is quoted in John Shelton Reed and Dale Volberg Reed, *1001 Things Everyone Should Know about the South* (New York, 1996), 294; Cable is quoted in Fred C. Hobson, *Tell about the South: The Southern Rage to Explain* (Baton Rouge, 1983), 114.

1. CAVALIER AND YANKEE: THE ORIGINS OF SOUTHERN "OTHERNESS"

1. John Richard Alden, *The First South* (Baton Rouge, 1961), 8–9.

2. Jack P. Greene, *Pursuits of Happiness: The Social Development of Early Modern British Colonies and the Formation of American Culture* (Chapel Hill, 1988), 5.

3. Peter A. Coclanis, "Tracking the Economic Divergence of the North and South," *Southern Cultures* 6 (Winter 2000), 83, 88.

4. Ibid., 93.

5. Alden, *The First South*, 14; Jack P. Greene, *Imperatives, Behaviors and Identities: Essays in Early American Cultural History* (Charlottesville, 1992), 329–30.

6. Thomas Jefferson to Marquis de Chastellux, Paris, September 2, 1785, "Climate and American Character," The Publicly Accessible Jefferson Collection, http://extext.virginia.edu.

7. Ibid.; Alden, *The First South*, 17–18.

8. Marquis de Chastellux, *Voyages de M. le Marquis de Chastellux dans l'Amerique Septentrionale: dans les Années 1780, 1781, and 1782* (Paris, 1786), excerpted in Chastellux, *Travels in North America, 1786*, http://occawlonline.pearsoned.com/bookbind/pubbooks/nash5e_awl/chapter7/medialib/primarysources1_6_1.html.

9. Ibid.

10. Greene, *Imperatives*, 330.

11. "The United States of North America," *North American Review* 2 (November 1815), 83; Jennifer Rae Greeson, "The Figure of the South and the Nationalizing Imperatives of Early United States Literature," *The Yale Journal of Criticism* 12 (Fall 1999), 243.

12. J. Hector St. John De Crevecoeur, *Letters from an American Farmer*, reprint (Oxford, 1997), 151.

13. Ibid., 153–54.

14. Ibid., 156.

15. Ibid., 115.

16. *Pennsylvania Gazette*, January 7, 1789, item #75465, Accessible Archives, Inc., www.accessible.com.

17. Jennifer Rae Greeson, "The Figure of the South and the Nationalizing Imperatives of Early United States Literature," *The Yale Journal of Criticism* 12 (Fall 1999), 231–32; Ayers, "What Do We Talk About?" 73.

18. "A Georgia Planter's Method of Spending His Time," *American Museum* 8 (November 1790), 243–44.

19. Greeson, "The Figure of the South," 219; "Remarks on Cockfighting," *New York Magazine* 2 (March 1791), 158.

20. *Pennsylvania Gazette*, August 8, 1798, item #82491; see also March, 20, 1799, #82715; Robert Kelley, *The Cultural Pattern in American Politics: The First Century* (New York, 1979), 119.

21. Royall Tyler, *The Algerine Captive or The Life and Adventures of Doctor Updike Underhill, Six Years a Prisoner among the Algerines*, reprint (New York, 2002), 160–62.

22. Ibid., 138; Crevecoeur, *Letters from an American Farmer*, 64.

23. Kelley, *The Cultural Pattern in American Politics*, 116; Chastellux, *Travels in North America*.

24. Joseph A. Conforti, *Imagining New England: Explorations of Regional Identity from the Pilgrims to the Mid-Twentieth Century* (Chapel Hill, 2001), 95, 108.

25. Ibid., 106; Martin Bruckner, "Lessons in Geography: Maps, Spellers, and Other Grammars of Nationalism in the Early Republic," *American Quarterly* 51 (June 1999), 332.

26. Conforti, *Imagining New England*, 107, 88; David Hackett Fischer, *Albion's Seed: Four British Folkways in America* (New York, 1989), 845; Bruckner, "Lessons in Geography," 332.

27. David M. Potter, *The South and Sectional Conflict* (Baton Rouge, 1968), 62; Peter S. Onuf, "The Origins of American Sectionalism," in Ayers, Limerick, Nissenbaum, and Onuf, *All over the Map*, 25; Greene, *Imperatives, Behaviors and Identities*, 334–35, 341, 344; John Richard Alden, *The South in the Revolution, 1763–1789* (Baton Rouge, 1957), 2; Kelley, *The Cultural Pattern in American Politics*, 112.

28. Conforti, *Imagining New England*, 120, 117.

29. Onuf, "The Origins of American Sectionalism," 31; Eve Kornfield, *Creating an American Culture: A Brief History with Documents* (New York, 2001), 79.

30. *Pennsylvania Gazette*, January 20, 1790, #76413; Oct. 29, 1788, #75280.

31. Ibid., July 14, 1790, #76842; June 25, 1788, #74693; March 19, 1788, #74682.

32. See Robert McColley, *Slavery and Jeffersonian Virginia* (Urbana, 1964).

33. William Cohen, "Thomas Jefferson and the Problem of Slavery," *Journal of American History* 56 (December 1969), 506, 508.

34. Ibid., 518, n. 54, 516, 506; Peter C. Mancall, Joshua L. Rosenbloom, and Thomas Weiss, "Slave Prices and the Economy of the Lower South, 1722–1809," www.ch.net/clio/conferences/assa/jan_00/rosenbloom.shtml.

35. "The Union and the States," *North American Review* 37 (July 1833), 247.

36. Joyce Oldham Appleby, *Inheriting the Revolution: The First Generation of Americans* (Cambridge, Mass., 2000), 23, 45, 248.

37. Joseph J. Ellis, *American Sphinx: The Character of Thomas Jefferson* (New York, 1997), 265.

38. Appleby, *Inheriting the Revolution*, 266.

39. "The Spy," *North American Review* 15, New Series (July 6, 1822), 252.

40. "Ingram's Proceedings" [no date, c. 1676], quoted in Fischer, *Albion's Seed*, 207, 212.

41. W. H. Trescot, "South Carolina: A Colony and State," *DeBow's Review* 27 (December 1859), 672; "Editorial Department," *DeBow's Review* 9 (August 1850), 239; J. Quitman Moore, "Southern Civilization; or the Norman in America," *DeBow's Review* 32 (January–February 1862), 12; Frank H. Alfriend, "A Southern Republic and a Northern Democracy," *Southern Literature Messenger* 37 (May 1863), 283.

42. Louis Philippe to Charles Gayarre, 1835, quoted in William R. Taylor, *Cavalier and Yankee: The Old South and American National Character* (New York, 1961), 14; J. H. Ingraham, "The Mysterious State Room, a Tale of the Mississippi," *The Ladies Book* 24 (April 1842), 182, Accessible Archives, Inc.

43. John Pendleton Kennedy, *Swallow Barn; or a Sojourn in the Old Dominion* (Philadelphia, 1832), 27–28. Machine-readable transcript, University of Virginia *Early American Fiction Full-Text Database* (accessed through the University of Georgia Library).

44. Ibid., 28–31.

45. Ibid., 294, 74.

46. "*Swallow Barn; or a Sojourn in the Old Dominion*," *North American Review* 36 (April 1833), 519–44 and "*Swallow Barn; or a Sojourn in the Old Dominion*," *New England Magazine* 3 (July 1832), 76–80, both quoted in Howard R. Floan, *The South in Northern Eyes, 1831–1861* (Austin, 1958), 90–91.

47. "South Carolina," *New England Magazine* 2 (January 1832), 37–45; 1 (September 1831), 246–50; 1 (October 1831), 337–41, both in Floan, *The South in Northern Eyes*, 92–93; Cooper is quoted in Taylor, *Cavalier and Yankee*, 97.

48. "The United States of North America," 83; Taylor, *Cavalier and Yankee*, 96; Lorman Ratner, "Northern Concern for Social Order as Cause for Rejecting Anti-Slavery, 1831–1840," *Historian* 28 (November 1965), quoted in Susan-Mary Grant, *North over South: Northern Nationalism and American Identity in the Antebellum Era* (Lawrence, Kans., 2000), 39.

49. John Pendleton Kennedy, "Rural Life in Virginia: *The Swallow Barn*," *The International Magazine of Literature, Art, and Science* (September 4, 1851), 152.

50. James Kirke Paulding, *Westward Ho!* (New York, 1832), 44, *Early American Fiction Database*.

51. Taylor, *Cavalier and Yankee*, 156–57.

52. Ibid., 286, 293, 323; Ben Ames Williams, ed., *Mary Boykin Chesnut, a Diary from Dixie* (Boston, 1949), 238; Grant, *North over South*, 84–85.

53. "South-Carolina," *New England Magazine* 1 (September 1831), 246–50.

54. Henry F. Harrington, "The Southerner's Daughter," *The Lady's Book* 24 (January 1842), 30.

55. Grant, *North over South*, 41–42.

56. "The Debates in the Federal Convention of 1787 Reported by James Madison: August 8," www.yale.edu/lawweb/avalon/debates/808.htm.

57. Grant, *North over South*, 84–85; "United States of North America," 83–84. See also David Bertelson, *The Lazy South* (New York, 1967).

58. Frederick Law Olmsted, *The Cotton Kingdom: A Traveler's Observations on Cotton and Slavery in the American Slave States*, edited and with an introduction by Arthur M. Schlesinger (New York, 1996), 616–17.

59. Grant, *North over South*, 50–51; Floan, *The South through Northern Eyes*, 54; T. Harry Williams, *Romance and Realism in Southern Politics* (Baton Rouge, 1966), 10.

60. Charles Joyner, *Down by the Riverside: A South Carolina Slave Community* (Urbana, 1984), 191–95. See also Mechal Sobel, *The World They Made Together: Black and White Values in Eighteenth-Century Virginia* (Princeton, 1989).

61. Frederick Douglass, *My Bondage and Freedom*, Appendix, iv, "Extract from a Lecture on Slavery, December 1, 1850, at Rochester, N.Y.," 340, World Wide School Library, www.worldwideschool.org/library/books/hst/biography/MyBondageandMyFreedom/chap29.html.

62. *Narrative of the Life of Frederick Douglass, Written by Himself* (Boston, 1845), electronic edition, 14–15, 60–63, University of North Carolina at Chapel Hill Libraries, Documenting the American South, http://docsouth.unc.edu/douglass/douglass. Frederick.

63. "Letter from a Fugitive Slave: Slaves Sold under Peculiar Circumstances," Harriet A. Jacobs, 1813–1897, *New York Daily Tribune*, New York, June 21, 1853, 6.

64. John Brown, *Slave Life in Georgia*, F. N. Boney, ed. (Savannah, 1972), 20.

65. *Slavery in the United States: A Narrative of the Life and Adventures of Charles Ball, a Black Man, Who Lived Forty Years in Maryland, South Carolina, and Georgia, as a Slave under Various Masters and Was One Year in the Navy with Commodore Barney, during the Late War* (New York, 1837), 17–18, Documenting the American South, http://docsouth.unc.edu/ballslavery/menu.html.

66. Taylor, *Cavalier and Yankee*, 307; Conforti, *Imagining New England*, 108, 336, n.71; Harriett Beecher Stowe, *Uncle Tom's Cabin or Life among the Lowly*, reprint (New York, 1966), 172–73, 179.

67. Stowe, *Uncle Tom's Cabin*, 173–75, 180.

68. Ibid., 116.

69. Ibid., 19.

70. Ibid., 447, 239, 468.

71. Ibid., 329.

72. Taylor, *Cavalier and Yankee*, 311; Carl E. Krog, "Women, Slaves, and Family in *Uncle Tom's Cabin*: Battleground in Antebellum America," *Midwest Quarterly* 31 (Winter 1990), 254; Helen Waite Papashvily, *All the Happy Endings* (New York, 1956), 73–74.

73. Williams, *Chesnut: A Diary from Dixie*, 122.

74. Charles S. Sydnor, *The Development of Southern Sectionalism, 1819–1848* (Baton Rouge, 1948), 220, 338.

2. THE SOUTH BECOMES A CAUSE

1. Angelina E. Grimké, *An Appeal to the Women of the Nominally Free States* (New York, 1837), 14; Susan-Mary Grant, *North over South: Northern Nationalism and American Identity in the Antebellum Era* (Lawrence, Kans., 2000), 59–60.

2. Grant, *North over South*, 52; Howard R. Floan, *The South in Northern Eyes, 1831–1861* (Austin, 1958), 55.

3. Grant, *North over South*, 52, 59, 55; Richard N. Current, *Northernizing the South* (Athens, Ga., 1983), 39.

4. Joseph A. Conforti, *Imagining New England: Explorations of Regional Identity from the Pilgrims to the Mid-Twentieth Century* (Chapel Hill, 2001), 118, 120; David Brion Davis, *Slavery and Human Progress* (New York, 1984), 27; James M. McPherson, *Battle Cry of Freedom: The Civil War Era* (New York, 1985), 860.

5. Eric Foner, *Free Soil, Free Labor, Free Men: The Ideology of the Republican Party before the Civil War* (New York, 1970), 311.

6. Merle E. Curti, *The Roots of American Loyalty* (New York, 1946), 111; *The Great Speeches and Orations of Daniel Webster* (Boston, 1879), 583.

7. Grant, *North over South*, 131, 130.

8. Ibid., 131; William W. Freehling and Craig M. Simpson, eds., *Secession Debated: Georgia's Showdown in 1860* (New York, 1992), 122; Leonard L. Richards, *The Slave Power: The Free North and Southern Domination, 1780–1860* (Baton Rouge, 2000), 194; David M. Potter, *The South and Sectional Conflict* (Baton Rouge, 1968), 66; Grant, *North over South*, 59.

9. Current, *Northernizing the South*, 39, 44; Davis, *Slavery and Human Progress*, 262; Foner, *Free Soil, Free Labor, Free Men*, 51–52; "An Essay on American Society as Seen through the Eyes of a Southern Spectator," *Southern Quarterly Review* 9 (October 10, 1854), 379.

10. Foner, *Free Soil, Free Labor, Free Men*, 40, 51; Potter, *The South and Sectional Conflict*, 66.

11. Foner, *Free Soil, Free Labor, Free Men*, 107, 72, 316; Robert Kelley, *The Cultural Pattern in American Politics: The First Century* (New York, 1979), 223.

12. Eric J. Hobsbawm, *The Age of Capital, 1848–1875* (New York, 1975), 141, 142; Barrington Moore, Jr., *Social Origins of Dictatorship and Democracy: Lord and Peasant in the Modern World* (Boston, 1966), 116; Peter A. Coclanis, "Globalization before Globalization: The South and the World to 1950," in James C. Cobb and William Stueck, eds., *Globalization and the American South* (Athens, Ga., 2005), 218.

13. James M. McPherson, *Ordeal by Fire: The Civil War and Reconstruction*, 2nd ed. (New York, 1992), 218.

14. Gavin Wright, *The Political Economy of the Cotton South: Households, Markets, and Wealth in the Nineteenth Century* (New York, 1978), 90–97; Michael O'Brien, *All Clever Men, Who Make Their Way: Critical Discourse in the Old South* (Fayetteville, Ark., 1982), 24.

15. McPherson, *Ordeal by Fire*, 26; Harold D. Woodman, *King Cotton and His Retainers: Financing and Marketing the Cotton Crop of the South, 1800–1925* (Lexington, Ky., 1968), 135.

16. Edward Pessen, "How Different from Each Other Were the Antebellum North and South?" *American Historical Review* 85 (December 1980), 1125–26; Wright, *The Political Economy of the Cotton South,* 141; Fred Bateman and Thomas Weiss, *A Deplorable Scarcity: The Failure of Industrialization in the Slave Economy* (Chapel Hill, 1981), 111, 114, 123.

17. Pessen, "How Different," 1126.

18. McPherson, *Ordeal by Fire*, 27–28; Pessen, "How Different," 1147.

19. Bertram Wyatt-Brown, *Southern Honor: Ethics and Behavior in the Old South* (New York, 1982), xv, 20–22.

20. Pessen, "How Different," 1146, 1148.

21. William R. Taylor, *Cavalier and Yankee: The Old South and American National Character* (New York, 1961), 17–18.

22. Jack P. Greene, *Pursuits of Happiness: The Social Development of Early Modern British Colonies and the Formation of American Culture* (Chapel Hill, 1988), 1–2.

23. Rollin G. Osterweis, *Romanticism and Nationalism in the Old South* (London, 1949), 27, 94; Caroline Winterer, *The Culture of Classicism; Ancient Greece and Rome in American Intellectual Life, 1780–1910* (Baltimore, 2002), 28, 9.

24. Michael W. Fazio and Patrick A. Sandon, "Greek Revival Architecture," in William R. Ferris and Charles R. Wilson, eds., *Encyclopedia of Southern Culture* (Chapel Hill, 1989), 77; Winterer, *The Culture of Classicism*, 74–76.

25. Osterweis, *Romanticism and Nationalism in the Old South*, 41–53, 56; James M. McPherson, *Is Blood Thicker Than Water? Crises of Nationalism in the Modern World* (New York, 1998), 45.

26. Louis Philippe to Charles Gayarre, 1835, quoted in Taylor, *Cavalier and Yankee*, 14; Abel P. Upshur, "The Partisan Leader," *Southern Literary Messenger* 3 (January 1837), 80; Beverley Tucker, "A Discourse on the Genius of the Federative System of the United States," *Southern Literary Messenger* 4 (December 1838), 767.

27. James Kirke Paulding, *The Puritan and His Daughter* (New York, 1849), 144, 149–51.

28. W. H. Trescot, "South Carolina: A Colony and State," *DeBow's Review* 27 (December 1859), 672; Frank H. Alfriend, "A Southern Republic and a Northern Democracy," *Southern Literature Messenger* 37 (May 1863), 283; Osterweis, *Romanticism and Nationalism in the Old South*, 79; J. Quitman Moore, "Southern Civilization; or the Norman in America," *DeBow's Review* 32 (January–February 1862), 14.

29. Grant, *North over South*, 54, 57; "The Cavalier's Song," *Vanity Fair* 4 (July 4, 1861), 21.

30. Moore, "Southern Civilization," 14; McPherson, *Is Blood Thicker than Water?* 55–56.

31. Drew Gilpin Faust, *The Creation of Confederate Nationalism: Ideology and Identity in the Civil War South* (Baton Rouge, 1988), 10–11; McPherson, *Is Blood Thicker Than Water?* 45.

32. Quoted in Osterweis, *Romanticism and Nationalism in the Old South*, 50; McPherson, *Is Blood Thicker than Water?* 61.

33. George Fitzhugh, "Cannibals All! or Slaves without Masters," in Harvey Wish, ed., *Ante-Bellum: Writings of George Fitzhugh and Hinton Rowan Helper on Slavery* (New York, 1960), 114; Fred C. Hobson, *Tell about the South: The Southern Rage to Explain* (Baton Rouge, 1983), 24–25.

34. David Donald, "The Pro-Slavery Argument Reconsidered," *Journal of Southern History* 37 (February 1971), 13, 14.

35. Ibid., 17.

36. George Fitzhugh, *Sociology for the South or the Failure of Free Society, 1854*, reprint ed. (New York, 1965), 244, quoted in Current, *Northernizing the South*, 29; *The Proslavery Argument, as Maintained by the Most Distinguished of the Southern States, Containing Several Essays, on the Subject, of Professor Drew* (Charleston, 1852), 177–78; William Gilmore Sims, *Woodcraft; or Hawks about the Dovecote*, reprint (New York, 1882), 101–2, 290–91, quoted in Taylor, *Cavalier and Yankee*, 290–91.

37. Daniel R. Hundley, *Social Relations in Our Southern States*, edited, with an introduction by William J. Cooper, Jr. (Baton Rouge, 1979), 8, 71, 41.

38. Hundley, *Social Relations*, 170–71, 175.

39. Charles S. Sydnor, *The Development of Southern Sectionalism, 1819–1848* (Baton Rouge, 1948), 54, 336.

40. Edward R. Crowther, "Holy Honor: Sacred and Secular in the Old South," *Journal of Southern History* 58 (November 1992), 630; Christine Leigh Heyrman, *Southern Cross: The Beginnings of the Bible Belt* (New York, 1997).

41. Edward R. Crowther, *Southern Evangelicals and the Coming of the Civil War* (Lewiston, N.Y., 2000), 93–94, 104; Sydnor, *The Development of Southern Sectionalism*, 336; Crowther, "Holy Honor," 635.

42. Crowther, *Southern Evangelicals*, 159; W. J. Cash, *The Mind of the South—With a New Introduction by Bertram Wyatt-Brown*, paperback version (New York, 1991), 80; Charles R. Wilson, *Baptized in the Blood: The Religion of the Lost Cause, 1865–1920* (Athens, Ga., 1980), 25.

43. Heyrman, *Southern Cross*, 248.

44. Crowther, *Southern Evangelicals*, 93, 203; Crowther, "Holy Honor," 631; Heyrman, *Southern Cross*, 248–49.

45. Faust, *The Creation of Confederate Nationalism*, 22; Crowther, *Southern Evangelicals*.

46. Crowther, *Southern Evangelicals*, 199; Faust, *The Creation of Confederate Nationalism*, 34–35, 32, 39.

47. Don H. Doyle, *Nations Divided: America, Italy, and the Southern Question* (Athens, Ga., 2002), 39.

48. McPherson, *Ordeal by Fire*, 27–28; William R. Taylor, "Toward a Definition of Orthodoxy: The Patrician South and the Common Schools," *Harvard Educational Review* 36 (1966), 424–25.

49. Quoted in Avery O. Craven, *The Coming of the Civil War*, 2nd ed. (Chicago, 1969), 283; Craven, *The Growth of Southern Nationalism, 1848–1861* (Baton Rouge, 1953), 253.

50. Craven, *Coming of the Civil War*, 283; John S. Ezell, "A Southern Education for Southrons," *Journal of Southern History* 17 (August 1951), 327, n. 91; Potter, *The South and the Sectional Conflict*, 69 and page 69, n. 17; Ezell, "A Southern Education," 308.

51. Hinton Rowan Helper, *Impending Crisis of the South* (New York, 1857), 181, v, 23.

52. Ibid., 126, 40, 149, 186.

53. Hobson, *Tell about the South*, 56.

54. Robert E. Bonner, *Colors and Blood: Flag Passions of the Confederate South* (Princeton, 2002), 113; Alfriend, "A Southern Republic," 289–90, 288, 286.

55. Doyle, *Nations Divided*, 20, 80; E. Merton Coulter, *The Confederate States of America: 1861–1865* (Baton Rouge, 1950), 60; Emory M. Thomas, *The Confederate Nation, 1861–1865* (New York, 1979), 62.

56. Coulter, *The Confederate States of America*, 258, 58; Clement Eaton, *A History of the Southern Confederacy* (New York, 1954), 43; Faust, *The Creation of Confederate Nationalism*, 14.

57. Doyle, *Nations Divided*, 83; David R. Goldfield, *Still Fighting the Civil War: The American South and Southern History* (Baton Rouge, 2002), 17, 22; Reid Mitchell, *Civil War Soldiers: Their Expectations and Their Experiences* (New York, 1988), 22, 46.

58. James M. McPherson, *What They Fought For, 1861–1865* (Baton Rouge, 1994), 10; A. V. Huff, Jr., "The Eagle and the Vulture: Changing Attitudes toward Nationalism in Fourth of July Orations Delivered in Charleston, 1778–1860," *South Atlantic Quarterly* 73 (Winter 1974), 10–22.

59. Kenneth M. Stampp, *The Imperiled Union: Essays on the Background of the Civil War* (New York, 1980), 258, 255–56; Faust, *The Creation of Confederate Nationalism*, 101, n. 1; McPherson, *What They Fought For*, 47–48.

60. Potter, *The South and the Sectional Conflict*, 40.

61. Benedict Anderson, *Imagined Communities: Reflections on the Origins and Spread of Nationalism*, rev. ed. (London, 1995), 6; David A. Bell, *The Cult of the Nation in France: Inventing Nationalism, 1680–1800* (Cambridge, Mass., 2001), 20. On the relationship between patriotism and nationalism see Maurizio Viroli, *For Love of Country: An Essay on Patriotism and Nationalism* (Oxford, 1995).

62. Eric H. Walther, "Fire-Eaters and the Riddle of Southern Nationalism," *Southern Studies* 3 (1992), 68, 72–73; Bell, *The Cult of the Nation*, 20; McPherson, *What They Fought For*, 20; James M. McPherson, *For Cause and Comrades, Why Men Fought in the Civil War* (New York, 1991), 21, 23–24.

63. Bonner, *Colors and Blood*, 97.

64. Ibid., 180, n. 5.

65. Ibid., 108, 122–23; Gary W. Gallagher, *The Confederate War: How Popular Will, Nationalism, and Military Strategy Could Not Stave Off Defeat* (Cambridge, Mass., 1997), 87, 95–96; Robert E. Bonner, "Flag Culture and the Consolidation of Confederate Nationalism," *Journal of Southern History* 68 (May 2002), 327.

66. Potter, *The South and Sectional Conflict*, 41.

67. Judkin Browning, "Conflicting Visions of Freedom and Civilization: Forging New Identities in Beaufort, North Carolina, during the Civil War," unpublished paper presented at the 2003 meeting of the Southern Historical Association, copy in possession of the author.

68. Cash, *The Mind of the South*, 66, 104; Bonner, "Flag Culture," 325; McPherson, *For Cause and Comrades*, 97; Robert Penn Warren, *The Legacy of the Civil War* (Cambridge, Mass., 1983), 14–15; Warren, *Jefferson Davis Gets His Citizenship Back* (Lexington, Ky., 1980), 59.

69. Doyle, *Nations Divided*, 87; Carlton J. H. Hayes, *Nationalism: A Religion* (New York, 1960), 94–5; Bertram Wyatt-Brown, "W. J. Cash and Southern Culture," in Walter J. Fraser and Winfred B. Moore, eds., *From the Old South to the New: Essays on the Transitional South* (Westport, Conn., 1981), 209; William Pfaff, *The Wrath of Nations: Civilization and the Furies of Nationalism* (New York, 1993), 174.

70. David W. Blight, *Race and Reunion: The Civil War in American Memory* (Cambridge, Mass., 2001), 81; Stampp, *The Imperiled Union*, 257; Richard E. Beringer et al., *The Elements of Confederate Defeat: Nationalism, War Aims, and Religion* (Athens, Ga., 1988), 26; E. Merton Coulter, *The South during Reconstruction* (Baton Rouge, 1947), 23–24.

71. Stampp, *The Imperiled Union*, 268–69.

72. Rollin G. Osterweis, *The Myth of the Lost Cause, 1865–1900* (Hamden, Conn., 1973), 25.

73. Emory M. Thomas, "Civil War," in Ferris and Wilson, eds., *The Encyclopedia of Southern Culture*, 605; Stampp, *The Imperiled Union*, 268.

74. Ethel Moore, "Reunion of Tennesseans: Address of Welcome by Miss Ethel Moore," *Confederate Veteran* 6 (October 1898), 482, quoted in Paul M. Gaston, *The New South Creed: A Study in Southern Mythmaking*, rev. ed. (Montgomery, Ala., 2002), 172.

75. Wilson, *Baptized in the Blood*, 48.

76. Ibid., 68, 72, 73; Lawrence W. Levine, *Black Culture and Black Consciousness: Afro-American Folk Thought from Slavery to Freedom* (New York, 1978), 48; Goldfield, *Still Fighting*, 55.

77. John D. Boles, "The Discovery of Southern Religious History," in John D. Boles and Evelyn Thomas Nolen, *Interpreting Southern History: Essays in Honor of Sanford*

W. *Higginbotham* (Baton Rouge, 1987), 534; Wilson, *Baptized in the Blood*, 72, 74; Levine, *Black Culture and Black Consciousness*, 48, 40–51.

78   E. A. Pollard, *The Lost Cause* [A facsimile of the original 1866 edition] (New York, 1998), 50–51, 518, 729.

79.   Ibid., 750, 746, 750–751.

80.   E. A. Pollard, *The Lost Cause Regained* (New York, 1868), 13–14.

81.   Ibid., 165, 265; Henry Watterson, *The Compromises of Life and Other Lectures and Addresses, Including Some Observations on the Downward Tendencies of Modern Society* (New York, 1903), 97,100

82.   W. Scott Poole, "Religion, Gender, and the Lost Cause in South Carolina's 1876 Governor's Race," *Journal of Southern History* 68 (August 2002), 597–98; Blight, *Race and Reunion*, 222.

3. THE NEW SOUTH AND THE OLD CAUSE

1.   Peter A. Coclanis, "The American Civil War in Economic Perspective: Basic Questions and Some Answers," *Southern Cultures* 2 (Winter 1996), 162; see also Peter A. Coclanis, "Tracking the Economic Divergence of the North and South," *Southern Cultures* 6 (Winter 2000), 6, 99–100.

2.   David R. Goldfield, *Still Fighting the Civil War: The American South and Southern History* (Baton Rouge, 2002), 181.

3.   Paul M. Gaston, *The New South Creed: A Study in Southern Mythmaking*, rev. ed. (Montgomery, Ala., 2002), 27.

4.   David W. Blight, *Race and Reunion: The Civil War in American Memory* (Cambridge, Mass., 2001), 222; Goldfield, *Still Fighting*, 17.

5.   Clement Eaton, *The Growth of Southern Civilization, 1790–1860* (New York, 1961), 243–45; Current, *Northernizing the South*, 43; Gaston, *The New South Creed*, 44.

6.   Dwight B. Billings, Jr., *Planters and the Making of a "New South": Class, Politics, and Development in North Carolina, 1865–1900* (Chapel Hill, 1979), 88–89.

7.   Jonathan M. Wiener, *Social Origins of the New South: Alabama, 1860–1885* (Baton Rouge, 1978), 209; C. Vann Woodward, *Origins of the New South, 1877–1913* (Baton Rouge, 1951), 146; Gaston, *The New South Creed*, 70–71.

8.   Woodward, *Origins*, 146; Gaston, *The New South Creed*, 56–57, 70–71; see also Joseph Frazier Wall, *Henry Watterson: Reconstructed Rebel* (New York, 1956).

9.   Woodward, *Origins*, 14–15; Herbert Fielder, *A Sketch of the Life and Times and Speeches of Joseph E. Brown* (Springfield, Mass., 1883), 549.

10.   *The Old South: Addresses Delivered before the Confederate Survivors Association in Augusta, Georgia, on Memorial Day, by his Excellency Governor John B. Gordon and Col. Charles C. Jones, Jr., LL.D., April 26, 1887* (Augusta, Ga., 1887), 17; Gaines M. Foster, *Ghosts of the Confederacy, Defeat, the Lost Cause, and the Emergence of the New South, 1865–1913* (New York, 1987), 84, 83; Reverend R. L. Dabney, *The New South: A Discourse* (Raleigh, N.C.), 12.

11.   Woodward, *Origins*, 151, 146; E. Culpepper Clark, *Francis Warrington Dawson and the Politics of Restoration: South Carolina, 1874–1889* (Tuscaloosa, Ala., 1980);

Richard L. Wilson, "Sam Jones: Apostle of the New South," *Georgia Historical Quarterly* 47 (Winter 1973), 461–62; Jack P. Maddex, Jr., *The Reconstruction of Edward A. Pollard: A Rebel's Conversion to Postbellum Unionist* (Chapel Hill, 1974), 37, 39, 72.

12. Numan V. Bartley, *The Creation of Modern Georgia* (Athens, Ga., 1983), 86.

13. Wiener, *Social Origins*, 213; Allen P. Tankersley, *John B. Gordon: A Self Study in Gallantry* (Atlanta, 1955), 356.

14. Thomas W. Hanchett, *Sorting Out the New South City: Race, Class, and Urban Development in Charlotte, 1875–1975* (Chapel Hill, 1998), 67; Wall, *Henry Watterson*, 63.

15. W. J. Cash, *The Mind of the South—With a New Introduction by Bertram Wyatt-Brown*, paperback version (New York, 1991), 184; Gaston, *The New South Creed*, 28, 87–88.

16. Richard H. King, *A Southern Renaissance: The Cultural Awakening of the American South, 1930–1955* (New York, 1980), 30; Gaston, *The New South Creed*, 181–82; Henry Grady, *The New South: Writings and Speeches of Henry Grady*, Mills Lane, ed. (Savannah, Ga., 1971), 107–8; Fred C. Hobson, *Tell about the South: The Southern Rage to Explain* (Baton Rouge, 1983), 144.

17. David M. Potter, *The South and the Sectional Conflict* (Baton Rouge, 1989), 30; Blight, *Race and Reunion*, 292; Woodward, *Origins*, 148; Gaston, *The New South Creed*, 191–92.

18. Eric Hobsbawm, "The New Threat to History," *New York Review of Books* (December 16, 1993), 62.

19. Woodward, *Origins*, 154–55.

20. Goldfield, *Still Fighting*, 21; Joseph G. Brown, *The New South—Address Delivered at the Convention of the American Bankers' Association at New Orleans, November 11, 1902* (Raleigh, 1902), 3, quoted in Gaston, *The New South Creed*, 182.

21. Anthony Smith, "The Golden Age and National Renewal," in Geoffrey Hosking and George Schopflin, eds., *Myths and Nationhood* (New York, 1997), 50–51.

22. Ibid.

23. Thomas Nelson Page, *The Old South: Essays Social and Political* (Chautauqua, N.Y., 1919), 6; Gaston, *The New South Creed*, 173; "Henry W. Grady Dead," (*Albany News and Advertiser*), in Joel Chandler Harris, ed., *The Life of Henry Grady, including His Writings and Speeches* (New York, 1890), 552.

24. "Henry W. Grady Dead," "The South Laments" (*Middle Georgia Progress*) in Harris, *Life of Henry Grady*, 552, 578.

25. Goldfield, *Still Fighting*, 22.

26. Foster, *Ghosts of the Confederacy*, 82.

27. Quoted in Wiener, *Social Origins*, 208–209; Wilson, "Sam Jones," 462; Woodward, *Origins*, 154.

28. Gaston, *The New South Creed*, 200.

29. Ibid., 96; *Atlanta Constitution*, November 7, 1880; Henry W. Grady, "The South's Industrial Problem," "Stilled Is the Eloquent Tongue" (*Brunswick Times*), "A Mea-

sureless Sorrow" (*LaGrange Reporter*), all in Harris, *The Life of Henry Grady*, 119–20, 552, 572.

30. Woodward, *Origins*, 115.

31. Henry W. Grady, "The New South," in Harris, *Life of Henry Grady*, 88; Raymond B. Nixon, *Henry W. Grady, Spokesman of the New South* (New York, 1943), 349.

32. Francis Pendleton Gaines, *The Southern Plantation: A Study in the Development and the Accuracy of a Tradition* (New York, 1925), 63–64; Blight, *Race and Reunion*, 220.

33. C. Vann Woodward, *American Counterpoint: Slavery and Racism in the North-South Dialogue* (Boston, 1971), 6; Blight, *Race and Reunion*, 222.

34. Henry James, *The American Scene* (London, 1907), 237; John Pendleton Kennedy, *Swallow Barn; or a Sojourn in the Old Dominion* (Philadelphia, 1832), 184; David Bertelson, *The Lazy South* (New York, 1967), 185.

35. Rollin G. Osterweis, *The Myth of the Lost Cause, 1865–1900* (Hamden, Conn., 1973), 5–6.

36. Nina Silber, *The Romance of Reunion: Northerners and the South, 1865–1900* (Chapel Hill, 1993), 116, 110.

37. Blight, *Race and Reunion*, 228–29; Jennifer Ritterhouse, "Reading, Intimacy, and the Role of Uncle Remus in White Southern Social Memory," *Journal of Southern History* 69 (August, 2003), 585–622.

38. W. Fitzhugh Brundage, "Meta Warrick's 1907 'Negro Tableaux' and (Re)Presenting African American Historical Memory," *Journal of American History* 89 (March 2003), 1, 373.

39. Blight, *Race and Reunion*, 2.

40. Gaston, *The New South Creed*, 125; Blight, *Race and Reunion*, 276.

41. Eric Hobsbawm, "Introduction," in Eric Hobsbawm and Terence Ranger, eds., *The Invention of Tradition* (Cambridge, 1983), 14; Gaston, *The New South Creed*, 190–91.

42. Francis Hopkinson Smith, *Colonel Carter of Cartersville* (Boston, 1892), 11, 10.

43. Catherine W. Bishir, "Landmarks of Power: Building a Southern Past, 1885–1915," *Southern Cultures* 1 (Inaugural Edition, no monthly date, 1993), 6; Foster, *Ghosts of the Confederacy*, 124.

44. Foster, *Ghosts of the Confederacy*, 123.

45. Ibid., 46, 181, 194; W. Fitzhugh Brundage, "Whispering Consolation to Generations Unborn," in Winfred B. Moore, Jr., Kyle S. Sinisi, and David H. White, Jr., eds., *Warm Ashes: Issues in Southern History at the Dawn of the Twenty-First Century* (Columbia, S.C., 2000), 41, 341; Kathleen Clark, "Celebrating Freedom: Emancipation Day Celebrations and African American Memory in the Early Reconstruction South," in W. Fitzhugh Brundage, ed., *Where These Memories Grow: History, Memory, and Southern Identity* (Chapel Hill, 2000), 117–18; Mamie Garvin Fields, with Karen Fields, *Lemon Swamp and Other Places, a Carolina Memoir* (New York, 1983), 55–56.

46. Kathleen Clark, "Making History: African American Commemorative Celebrations in Augusta Georgia, 1865–1913," in Pamela H. Simpson and Cynthia Mills, eds., *Monuments to the Lost Cause: Women, Art, and the Landscapes of Southern Memory* (Knoxville, Tenn., 2003), 46, 50–52; Anne Elizabeth Marshall, "'A Strange Conclusion to a Triumphant War': Memory, Identity, and the Creation of a Confederate Kentucky" (Ph.D. dissertation, University of Georgia, 2004), 64; Brundage, "Whispering Consolation," 345.

47. Clark, "Making History," 47, 59–60; Brundage, "Whispering Consolation," 352.

48. Clark, "Making History," 46, 49; Pauli Murray, *Proud Shoes: The Story of an American Family* (New York, 1978), 275.

49. Julian Marie Johnson, "'Drill into Us the . . . Rebel Tradition': The Contest over Southern Identity in Black and White Women's Clubs, South Carolina, 1898–1930," *Journal of Southern History* 66 (August 2000), 551.

50. David W. Blight, "Southerners Don't Lie, They Just Remember Big," in Brundage, *Where These Memories Grow*, 349.

51. Woodward, *Origins*, 158; Blight, *Race and Reunion*, 294.

52. Sarah H. Case, "The Historical Ideology of Mildred Lewis Rutherford: A Confederate Historian's New South Creed," *Journal of Southern History* 68 (August 2002), 620.

53. Ibid.; Bishir, "Landmarks of Power," 9–13.

54. Bishir, "Landmarks of Power," 15–16.

55. Ibid., 16.

56. Ibid., 16–17.

57. Fields, *Lemon Swamp*, 57.

58. Ibid., 54; Billings, *Planters and the Making of a "New South" Class*, 87–90; Bishir, "Landmarks of Power," 31; Charles Reagan Wilson, "The Invention of Southern Tradition: The Writing and Ritualization of Southern History, 1880–1940," in Lothar Honninghausen and Valeria Gennardo Lerda, eds., *Rewriting the South: History and Fiction* (Tubingen, Germany, 1993), 13–15.

59. John W. Cell, *The Highest Stage of White Supremacy: The Origins of Segregation in South Africa and the American South* (Cambridge, 1982), 181–82. On segregation as an invented tradition, see also Wilson, "The Invention of Southern Tradition," 4–5.

60. Cell, *The Highest Stage*, 181–82.

61. Jack Temple Kirby, *Media-Made Dixie: The South in the American Imagination*, rev. ed. (Athens, Ga., 1986), 1–9.

62. Thomas Dixon, *The Leopard's Spots: A Romance of the White Man's Burden—1865–1900* (New York, 1906), 69, 283–84.

63. Billings, *Planters and the Making of a "New South,"* 85–86; Wayne Mixon, *Southern Writers and the New South Movement, 1865–1913* (Chapel Hill, 1980), 50.

64. On disfranchisement, see J. Morgan Kousser, *The Shaping of Southern Politics: Suffrage Restriction and the Establishment of the One-Party South, 1880–1910* (New Haven, 1974).

65. Henry Grady to Booker T. Washington, January 10, 1887, in *Montgomery Advertiser*, January 15, 1887; Louis R. Harlan, *Booker T. Washington: The Making of a Black Leader, 1856–1901* (New York, 1972), 165.

66. Harlan, *Booker T. Washington*, 217–20, 223; Gaston, *The New South Creed*, 212–15.

67. Harlan, *Booker T. Washington*, 227; see also Booker T. Washington, *Up from Slavery: An Autobiography* (New York, 1901).

68. Burton J. Hendrick, *The Training of an American: The Earlier Life and Letters of Walter Hines Page, 1855–1913* (Boston, 1928), 168, 176; Bruce Clayton, *The Savage Ideal: Intolerance and Intellectual Leadership in the South, 1890–1914* (Baltimore, 1972), 48; Hobson, *Tell about the South*, 164–65; W. H. Page, *The Southerner, a Novel; Being an Autobiography of Nicholas Worth* (New York, 1909), 313–15; Herbert J. Doherty, Jr., "Voices of Protest from the New South, 1875–1910," *Mississippi Valley Historical Review* 42 (June 1955), 56.

69. J. Louis Campbell III, "In Search of the New South," *Southern Speech Communications Journal* 47 (Summer 1982), 378, 361–88; Hobson, *Tell about the South*, 179, 165.

70. Charles W. Chesnutt, "The March of Progress," *Century Magazine* 61 (January 1901), 422–28.

71. Mixon, *Southern Writers*, 110; Chesnutt, "The March of Progress," 424.

72. Charles W. Chesnutt, *The Colonel's Dream* (New York, 1905), 115–16; see also Julian D. Mason, Jr., "Charles W. Chesnutt as Southern Author," *Mississippi Quarterly* 20 (Winter 1966–67), 77–89.

73. Doherty, "Voices of Protest," 48–49; W. E. B. DuBois, *The Souls of Black Folk*, reprint (New York, 1989), 74, 73.

74. DuBois, *The Souls of Black Folk*, 54–55, 57, 61.

75. Hugh C. Bailey, *Liberalism in the New South: Southern Social Reformers and the Progressive Movement* (Coral Gables, Fla., 1969), 33, 39–40; Hobson, *Tell about the South*, 106; George W. Cable, "The Silent South," *Century* 30 (September 1885), 674–91.

76. Arlin W. Turner, *George W. Cable: A Biography* (Durham, N.C., 1956), 247–48.

77. Bailey, *Liberalism in the New South*, 24; Hobson, *Tell about the South*, 119, 114.

78. George W. Cable, *John March, Southerner* (New York, 1894), 121; Morton Sosna, *In Search of the Silent South: Southern Liberals and the Race Issue* (New York, 1977), 8.

79. Gaston, *The New South Creed*, 194; Lewis Harvie Blair, *Prosperity of the South Dependent on the Elevation of the Negro* (Richmond, Va., 1891), 3–4, 7.

80. Alan Lomax, *The Land Where the Blues Began: A Transcript and Study Guide to the Film* (Jackson, Miss., 1982), 14; James C. Cobb, *The Most Southern Place on Earth: The Mississippi Delta and the Roots of Regional Identity* (New York, 1972), 284.

81. Woodward, *Origins*, 249; Bartley, *The Creation of Modern Georgia*, 89.

82. Woodward, *Origins*, 416; Doherty, "Voices of Protest," 50– 51, 59, 54.

83. Andrew Sledd, "The Negro: Another View," *Atlantic Monthly* 90 (August 1902), 69–71.

84. Clayton, *The Savage Ideal*, 82.

85. Ibid., 87, 88.

86. Ibid., 89; John Spencer Bassett, "Stirring Up the Fires of Race Antipathy," *South Atlantic Quarterly* 2 (October 1903), 299, 301.

87. Clayton, *The Savage Ideal*, 96.

88. Ibid.; Blight, *Race and Reunion*, 296.

89. Blight, *Race and Reunion*, 221; Michael O'Brien, *The Idea of the American South, 1920–1941* (Baltimore, 1979), 6.

90. Quoted in Wendell H. Stephenson, *Southern History in the Making: Pioneer Historians of the South* (Baton Rouge, 1964), 131.

4. THE SOUTHERN RENAISSANCE AND THE REVOLT AGAINST THE NEW SOUTH CREED

1. Daniel J. Singal, *The War Within: From Victorian to Modernist Thought in the South* (Chapel Hill, 1982), 8–9; C. Vann Woodward, *Thinking Back: The Perils of Writing History* (Baton Rouge, 1986), 61, 23; Wendell Holmes Stephenson, "John Spencer Bassett: Trinity College Liberal," in Stephenson, *Southern History in the Making: Pioneer Historians of the South* (Baton Rouge, 1964), 102.

2. E. Merton Coulter, "What the South Has Done about Its History," in George B. Tindall, ed., *The Pursuit of Southern History: Presidential Addresses of the Southern Historical Association, 1935–1963* (Baton Rouge, 1964), 14; Catherine W. Bishir, "Landmarks of Power: Building a Southern Past, 1885–1915," *Southern Cultures* 1 (Inaugural Edition, no monthly date, 1993), 37.

3. Coulter, "What the South Has Done," 15, 17; David D. Van Tassel, "The American Historical Association and the South, 1884–1913," *Journal of Southern History* 23 (November 1957), 471.

4. Richard D. Starnes, "Forever Faithful: The Southern Historical Society and Confederate Historical Memory," *Southern Cultures* 2 (Winter 1996), 178, 180.

5. David W. Blight, *Race and Reunion: The Civil War in American Memory* (Cambridge, Mass., 2001), 263; see also Reverend R. L. Dabney, *The New South: A Discourse* (Raleigh, N.C., 1883), 15–16.

6. Anne Elizabeth Marshall, "'A Strange Conclusion to a Triumphant War': Memory, Identity, and the Creation of a Confederate Kentucky" (Ph.D. dissertation, University of Georgia, 2004), 137–38, 216–19.

7. Blight, *Race and Reunion*, 277; Peter Novick, *That Noble Dream: The "Objectivity Question" and the American Historical Profession* (Cambridge, 1988), 292.

8. Thomas Nelson Page, *The Old South: Essays Social and Political* (Chautauqua, N.Y., 1919), 41, 45, 4.

9. Sarah H. Case, "The Historical Ideology of Mildred Lewis Rutherford: A Confederate Historian's New South Creed," *Journal of Southern History* 68 (August 2002), 608, 610.

10. William E. Dodd, "Some Difficulties of the History Teacher in the South," *South Atlantic Quarterly* 3 (April 1904), 119.

11. Blight, *Race and Reunion*, 296.

12. H. G. Askew, J. M. Brown, W. B. Walker to George W. Littlefield, May 3, 1913, George W. Littlefield Papers, Center for American History, University of Texas at Austin.

13. Fred Arthur Bailey, "Free Speech and the 'Lost Cause' in Texas: A Study in Social Control in the New South," *Southwestern Social Science Quarterly* 97 (January 1994), 465–68; "Littlefield Fund for Southern History, Second Grant, Quotations from Major Littlefield's Will," Folder, "Correspondence, Classified, 1945–1952 and Undated," 2B104, Eugene C. Barker Papers, Center for American History, University of Texas at Austin.

14. Stephenson, *Southern History in the Making*, 158.

15. Quoted in David D. Van Tassel, "The American Historical Association and the South, 1884–1913," *Journal of Southern History* 23 (November 1957), 480; Bruce Clayton, *The Savage Ideal: Intolerance and Intellectual Leadership in the South, 1890–1914* (Baltimore, 1972), 63.

16. William P. Trent, *William Gilmore Simms* (Boston, 1892), 36–41, quoted in Clayton, *The Savage Ideal*, 69; William P. Trent, *Southern Statesmen of the Old Regime* (New York, 1897), quoted in Clayton, *The Savage Ideal*, 74.

17. William E. Dodd, *The Cotton Kingdom: A Chronicle of the Old South* (New Haven, Conn., 1919), 145; Dodd, *Statesmen of the Old South or From Radicalism to Conservative Revolt* (New York, 1911), 167.

18. Peter Novick, *That Noble Dream*, 80.

19. Daniel J. Singal, "U. B. Phillips: The Old South as New," *Journal of American History* 63 (March 1977), 887; U. B. Phillips, *American Negro Slavery: A Survey of the Supply, Employment, and Control of Negro Labor as Determined by the Plantation Regime* (New York, 1918), passim; U. B. Phillips, *Life and Labor in the Old South* (Boston, 1929), passim.

20. Singal, "U. B. Phillips," 882.

21. John Herbert Roper, *U. B. Phillips: A Southern Mind* (Macon, Ga., 1984), 1.

22. Dodd, "Some Difficulties of the History Teacher in the South," 119; Phillip Alexander Bruce, *The Rise of the New South* (Philadelphia, 1905), v–vi, quoted in Paul M. Gaston, "The New South," in Arthur S. Link and Rembert W. Patrick, eds., *Writing Southern History: Essays in Historiography in Honor of Fletcher M. Green* (Baton Rouge, 1965), 319.

23. Gaston, "The New South," 318–19, 321; A. B. Hart, *The Southern South* (New York, 1910), 218.

24. Broadus Mitchell, *The Rise of the Cotton Mills in the South* (Baltimore, 1921), vii; Singal, *The War Within*, 66.

25. Broadus Mitchell, "Fleshpots in the South," in Broadus Mitchell and George S. Mitchell, *The Industrial Revolution in the South* (Baltimore, 1930), 33, 34.

26. Broadus Mitchell, "Slippers and Old Sorrel," in Mitchell and Mitchell, *The Industrial Revolution in the South*, 281–86; Singal, *The War Within*, 71.

27. Singal, *The War Within*, 81.

28. Frank L. Owsley, "The Old South and the New," *American Review* 6 (February 1936), 482; Richard H. King, *A Southern Renaissance: The Cultural Awakening of the American South, 1930–1955* (New York, 1980), 31.

29. King, *A Southern Renaissance*, 31; Paul M. Gaston, *The New South Creed: A Study in Southern Mythmaking*, rev. ed. (Montgomery, Ala., 2002), 225.

30. Frank Tannenbaum, *The Darker Phases of the South* (New York, 1924); William H. Skaggs, *The Southern Oligarchy: An Appeal in Behalf of the Silent Masses of Our Country against the Despotic Rule of the Few* (New York, 1924), quoted in Hobson, *Tell about the South*, 184–85; W. E. B. DuBois, "Georgia: Invisible Empire State," *The Nation* 120 (January 21, 1925), 65.

31. H. L. Mencken, "The Sahara of the Bozart," in H. L. Mencken, *Prejudices: Second Series* (New York, 1920), 136, 141; George B. Tindall, "Mythology: A New Frontier in Southern History," in Frank E. Vandiver, ed., *The Idea of the South* (Chicago, 1964), 5–6.

32. Fred C. Hobson, *Mencken: A Life* (New York, 1994), 101; Gerald W. Johnson, "Saving Souls," *American Mercury* 2 (July 1924), 364, 367.

33. Fred C. Hobson, *Serpent in Eden: H. L. Mencken and the South* (Chapel Hill, 1974), 101–2.

34. Charles Scruggs, *The Sage in Harlem: H. L. Mencken and the Black Writers of the 1920s* (Baltimore, 1984), 65–66.

35. Ibid., 71.

36. George Hutchinson, *The Harlem Renaissance in Black and White* (Cambridge, Mass., 1995), 330; Scruggs, *The Sage in Harlem*, 68, 75.

37. Scruggs, *The Sage in Harlem*, 61.

38. Ibid., 64.

39. Allen Tate, "The Profession of Letters in the South," *Virginia Quarterly Review* 11 (April 1925), 175–76; Warren is quoted in C. Vann Woodward, "Why the Southern Renaissance?" in C. Vann Woodward, *The Future of the Past* (New York, 1989), 216–17.

40. Reinhard Bendix, "Tradition and Modernity Reconsidered," *Comparative Studies in Society and History* 9 (1967), 293; Richard H. King, "Victorian to Modernist Thought," *Southern Literary Journal* 15 (1983), 127.

41. Thomas Wolfe to his Mother, May 1923, in John Skally Terry, ed., *Thomas Wolfe's Letters to His Mother, Julia Elizabeth Wolfe* (New York, 1943), 50; Ellen Glasgow, "The Novel in the South," *Harper's* (1928), 98.

42. Erskine Caldwell, *Tobacco Road*, reprint of the 1955 ed. (Cambridge, Mass., 1978), 118; Wayne Mixon, *The People's Writer: Erskine Caldwell and the South* (Charlottesville, 1995), 50, 52; Bryant Simon, "The Novel as Social History: Erskine Caldwell's *God's Little Acre* and Class Relations in the South," *Southern Cultures* 2 (Fall/Winter 1996), 377.

43. Clarence Cason, "Alabama Goes Industrial," *Virginia Quarterly Review* 6 (April 1930), 164, 166, 170, 167.

44. William Faulkner, "An Introduction to *The Sound and the Fury*," *Mississippi Quarterly* 16 (Summer 1973), 411.

45. Robert A. Nisbet, *Emile Durkheim* (Englewood Cliffs, N.J., 1965), 20; Dewey W. Grantham, *Southern Progressivism: The Reconciliation of Progress and Tradition* (Knoxville, 1983), 411; see also James C. Cobb, "Southern Writers and the Challenge of Regional Convergence: A Comparative Perspective," *Georgia Historical Quarterly* 63 (Spring 1989), 1–25.

46. George B. Tindall, *Emergence of the New South, 1913–1945* (Baton Rouge, 1967), 210, 209, 136.

47. Hobson, *Serpent in Eden*, 148.

48. Edwin Mims, *The Advancing South: Stories of Progress and Reaction*, reprint (Port Washington, N.Y., 1969), 315–16.

49. Paul K. Conkin, *The Southern Agrarians* (Knoxville, Tenn., 1988), 45; Fred C. Hobson, *Tell about the South: The Southern Rage to Explain* (Baton Rouge, 1983), 187–88; Hobson, *A Serpent in Eden*, 73 , 148–49; Louis D. Rubin, Jr., "The Historical Image of Modern Southern Writing," *Journal of Southern History* 22 (May 1956), 157–58.

50. Hobson, *Serpent in Eden*, 157.

51. Twelve Southerners, *I'll Take My Stand: The South and the Agrarian Tradition* (New York, 1930).

52. "Introduction: 'A Statement of Principles,'" in Twelve Southerners, *I'll Take My Stand*, reprint of the 1930 ed. (Baton Rouge, 1994), xxxvii. For a survey of criticism of the Agrarians, see Hobson, *Tell about the South*, 215–17.

53. "Introduction: 'A Statement of Principles,'" xxxviii–xxxix.

54. John Shelton Reed, "For Dixieland: The Sectionalism of *I'll Take My Stand*," in John Shelton Reed, *Surveying the South: Studies in Regional Sociology* (Columbia, Mo., 1993), 31.

55. Ibid., 41.

56. Mary Matossian, "Ideologies of Delayed Industrialization," in Jason L. Finkle and Richard W. Gable, eds., *Political Development and Social Change* (New York, 1966), 178.

57. Merton Dillon, *Ulrich Bonnell Phillips: Historian of the Old South* (Baton Rouge, 1985), 135.

58. Twelve Southerners, *I'll Take My Stand*, 3, 166, 170–71.

59. Charles A. Beard and Mary R. Beard, *The Rise of American Civilization* (2 vols., New York , 1927), 2:53–54; Frank Lawrence Owsley, "The Irrepressible Conflict," in Twelve Southerners, *I'll Take My Stand*, 74.

60. Owsley, "Irrepressible Conflict," 62–63.

61. Ibid., 63, 65, 67.

62. Bendix, "Tradition and Modernity," 334.

63. George B. Tindall, "Business Progressivism: Southern Politics in the Twenties," *South Atlantic Quarterly* 62 (Winter 1963), 92–106; Tindall, *Emergence of the New South*, 262, 265–66; Grantham, *Southern Progressivism*, 258; William J. Cooper, Jr., and Thomas E. Terrell, *The American South: A History* (New York, 1990), 560–61.

64. Bendix, "Tradition and Modernity," 344; Reed, "For Dixieland," 45.

65. Hobson, *Tell about the South*, 190; Hobson, *Serpent in Eden*, 88; H. L. Mencken, "The South Astir," *Virginia Quarterly Review* 11 (January 1935), 50, 58.

66. H. L. Mencken, "The Calamity of Appomattox," *American Mercury* 21 (September 1930), 29–31; Mencken to Odum, September 10, 1923, in Guy J. Forgue, ed., *Letters of H. L. Mencken* (New York, 1961), 262; Mencken, "The Sahara of the Bozart," 137, 139, 154.

67. Odum to Mencken, Folder 29, June 19, 1925, Howard W. Odum Papers, Southern Historical Collection, University of North Carolina at Chapel Hill; Howard W. Odum, *American Epoch: Southern Portraiture in the National Picture* (New York, 1930); Wayne D. Brazil, *Howard W. Odum: The Building Years, 1884–1930* (New York, 1988), 596; Hobson, *Tell about the South*, 193; Singal, *The War Within*, 153.

68. Singal, *The War Within*, 312; Rupert B. Vance, *Human Geography of the South: A Study in Regional Resources and Human Adequacy*, 2nd ed. (Chapel Hill, 1935), 76; Howard W. Odum, *Southern Regions of the United States* (Chapel Hill, 1936), 227.

69. Vance, *Human Geography*, 22; George B. Tindall et al., "Rupert Bayless Vance, March 15, 1899–August 25, 1975," A Memorial Presented to the Faculty Council of the University of North Carolina at Chapel Hill, October 17, 1975 (copy in possession of the author).

70. Rupert Vance to C. Vann Woodward, August 1, 9, September 20, 1949, Folder 12; Vance to Woodward, September 21, 1954, Folder 28, all in Rupert B. Vance Papers, Southern Historical Collection, University of North Carolina at Chapel Hill.

71. John Herbert Roper, *C. Vann Woodward, Southerner* (Athens, Ga., 1987), 4.

72. King, *A Southern Renaissance*, 258–59; C. Vann Woodward, *Thinking Back: The Perils of Writing History* (Baton Rouge, 1986), 22, 23.

73. Alex Matthews Arnett, *The Populist Movement in Georgia: A View of the "Agrarian Crusade" in the Light of Solid-South Politics*, reprint (New York, 1967); Woodward, *Thinking Back*, 29.

74. Woodward, *Thinking Back*, 31–32.

75. Ibid., 30.

76. King, *A Southern Renaissance*, 260–61.

77. C. Vann Woodward, "The South in Search of a Philosophy," Phi Beta Kappa Address at the University of Florida I (1938), 10–11; Woodward, "The South in Search of Philosophy," 10–11, 17, 16, 18–20.

78. Herman Clarence Nixon, "Whither Southern Economy?" in Twelve Southerners, *I'll Take My Stand*, 199; see also, Sarah Newman Shouse, *Hillbilly Realist: Herman Clarence Nixon of Possum Trot* (Tuscaloosa, Ala., 1984).

79. Herman Clarence Nixon, *Forty Acres and Steel Mules* (Chapel Hill, 1938), 9, 31–32; C. Vann Woodward, "Hillbilly Realism," *Southern Review* 4 (Spring 1939), 676; Morton Sosna, *In Search of the Silent South: Southern Liberals and the Race Issue* (New York, 1977), 89–90, 9.

80. Nixon, *Forty Acres and Steel Mules*, 9, 31–32.

81. Benjamin Burks Kendrick and Alex Matthews Arnett, *The South Looks at Its Past* (Chapel Hill, 1935), 183.

82. Richard H. Shryock, "Review of *The South Looks at Its Past*," *The Annals of the American Academy of Political Science* 185 (May 1936), 262.

83. W. E. B. DuBois, *Black Reconstruction: An Essay toward a History of the Part Which Black Folk Played in the Attempt to Reconstruct Democracy, 1860–1888* (New York, 1935); Francis B. Simkins and R. H. Woody, *South Carolina during Reconstruction* (Chapel Hill, 1932); Vernon Wharton, "Reconstruction," in Link and Patrick, eds., *Writing Southern History*, 310–11.

84. Francis B. Simkins, "New Viewpoints of Southern Reconstruction," *Journal of Southern History* 5 (February 1939), 58; Howard K. Beale, "On Rewriting Reconstruction History," *American Historical Review* 45 (July 1940), 808.

85. Joseph J. Mathews, "The Study of History in the South," *Journal of Southern History* 31 (February, 1965), 9, 12.

86. Coulter, "What the South Has Done about Its History," 3–22; Frank L. Owsley, "The Fundamental Cause of the Civil War, Egocentric Sectionalism," A. B. Moore, "One Hundred Years of Reconstruction of the South," B. B. Kendrick, "The Colonial Status of the South," all in *Journal of Southern History*, respectively, 7 (February 1941), 3–18; 8 (February 1942), 3–22; 9 (May 1943), 153–80; H. C. Nixon, "Paths to the Past: The Presidential Addresses of the Southern Historical Association," *Journal of Southern History* 16 (February 1950), 35–38.

87. Woodward, *Thinking Back*, 22, 23.

88. Donald Davidson, *The Attack on Leviathan: Regionalism and Nationalism in the United States* (Chapel Hill, 1938), 322–23.

5. SOUTHERN WRITERS AND "THE IMPOSSIBLE LOAD OF THE PAST"

1. Allen Tate, "The New Provincialism," *Virginia Quarterly Review* 21 (Spring 1945), 545–46.

2. Louis D. Rubin, Jr., "The Historical Image of Modern Southern Writing," *Journal of Southern History* 22 (May 1956), 154–55, 147–66; Richard Gray, *The Literature of Memory* (Baltimore, 1977), 3.

3. Ellen Glasgow, *A Certain Measure: An Interpretation of Prose Fiction* (New York, 1943), 13, 28; Ellen Glasgow, "The Novel in the South," *Harper's* 157 (December 1928), 95.

4. Glasgow, *A Certain Measure*, 71, 73; Ellen Glasgow, *The Romance of a Plain Man* (New York, 1909), 151.

5. Glasgow, *A Certain Measure*, 76.

6. Ellen Glasgow, *Virginia* (Garden City, N.Y., 1913), 12–13, 65, 73.

7. Glasgow, *A Certain Measure*, 90, 13, 92, 91.

8. Anne Goodwyn Jones, *Tomorrow Is Another Day: The Woman Writer in the South, 1859–1936* (Baton Rouge, 1981), 282.

9. Frances Newman, *The Hard-Boiled Virgin*, reprint (Athens, Ga., 1980), 244; Newman, *Dead Lovers Are Faithful Lovers* (New York, 1928), 25, 227.

10. Ellen Glasgow, "The Novel in the South," 99

11. Glasgow, *A Certain Measure*, 147; Joel Williamson, *William Faulkner and Southern History* (Oxford, 1993), 245; Jones, *Tomorrow Is Another Day*, 320; Darden Asbury Pyron, *Southern Daughter: The Life of Margaret Mitchell* (New York, 1992), 401, 315–17; Margaret Mitchell, *Gone with the Wind*, reprint (New York, 1993), 48–53.

12. Mitchell, *Gone with the Wind*, 600, 602.

13. Ibid., 630, 632; Willie Lee Rose, *Race and Region in American Historical Fiction: Four Episodes in Popular Culture* (Oxford, 1979), 25–28.

14. David Herbert Donald, "Look Homeward: Thomas Wolfe and the South," *Southern Review* 23 (January 1987), 246–47.

15. Richard S. Kennedy, ed., *Welcome to Our City: A Play in Ten Scenes by Thomas Wolfe* (Baton Rouge, 1983), 2, 30; Donald, "Look Homeward," 247.

16. Donald, "Look Homeward," 242, 244; Thomas Wolfe, *Look Homeward, Angel*, reprint (New York, 1929), 230, 548.

17. Thomas Wolfe, *You Can't Go Home Again* (New York, 1940), 101–2, 110.

18. Thomas Wolfe, *The Web and the Rock* (New York, 1939), 15, 183; Terry Wolfe, "Resurrecting Thomas Wolfe," *Southern Literary Journal* 33 (Fall 2000), 38.

19. Wolfe, *Look Homeward, Angel*, 5; William Faulkner, *Intruder in the Dust* (New York, 1948), 194; "When the Dam Breaks," *Time* 33 (January 23, 1939), 45–46, 48; Williamson, *Faulkner and Southern History*, 262–63.

20. Williamson, *Faulkner and Southern History*, 326–27.

21. Karl F. Zender, *The Crossing of the Ways; William Faulkner, The South, and the Modern World* (New Brunswick, N.J., 1989), 170, 70–71.

22. Frederick R. Karl, *William Faulkner: American Writer* (New York, 1989), 788, 666.

23. Faulkner is quoted in C. Vann Woodward, *The Burden of Southern History*, 3rd ed. (Baton Rouge, 1993), 279; Deborah N. Cohn, *History and Memory in the Two Souths: Recent Southern and Spanish American Fiction* (Nashville, 1999), 7, 10; Williamson, *Faulkner and Southern History*, 363.

24. William Lawson, *The Western Scar: The Theme of the Been-to in West African Fiction* (Athens, Ohio, 1982), 3; see Chinua Achebe, *Things Fall Apart* (London, 1958) and *No Longer at Ease* (London, 1960).

25. Donald, "Look Homeward," 242; William Faulkner, *Absalom, Absalom!* (New York, 1990), 303; Richard Gray, *Writing the South: Tales of an American Region* (Baton Rouge, 1997), 171; Faulkner, "An Introduction to *The Sound and the Fury*," in Faulkner, *The Sound and the Fury* (New York, 1929), 412; Walter Taylor, *Faulkner's Search for a South* (Urbana, 1983), x.

26. William Faulkner, *Sartoris* (New York, 1929).

27. Faulkner, *The Sound and the Fury*, 17.

28. Daniel Singal, *William Faulkner: The Making of a Modernist* (Chapel Hill, 1997), 18, 19.

29. Irving Howe, *William Faulkner: A Critical Study*, 3rd ed. (New York, 1975), 74; F. Garvin Davenport, *The Myth of Southern History: Historical Consciousness in Twentieth-Century Southern Literature* (Nashville, 1970), 99.

30. William Faulkner, *The Hamlet* (New York, 1940), 4–5.

31. Williamson, *Faulkner and Southern History*, 329.

32. Faulkner, *The Hamlet*, 8; Williamson, *Faulkner and Southern History*, 42.

33. Singal, *William Faulkner*, 246–55.

34. Richard Gray, *The Life of William Faulkner* (Oxford, 1994), 270.

35. Ibid.

36. Howe, *William Faulkner*, 83; Singal, *William Faulkner*, 253.

37. Williamson, *Faulkner and Southern History*, 423–24.

38. Karl, *William Faulkner*, 655.

39. William Faulkner, *Go Down, Moses and Other Stories by William Faulkner* (New York, 1942), 269.

40. Ibid., 266.

41. Ibid., 3, 299–300.

42. Ibid., 361, 278.

43. Richard H. King, *A Southern Renaissance: The Cultural Awakening of the American South, 1930–1955* (New York, 1980),130; Karl, *William Faulkner*, 667; James H. Justus, *The Achievement of Robert Penn Warren* (Baton Rouge, 1981), 325; Warren is quoted in Woodward, *The Burden of Southern History*, 288.

44. Robert Penn Warren, *All the King's Men* (San Diego, 1974), 175, 186, 162–88.

45. Warren, *All the King's Men*, 188–89, 384, 435, 438; Faulkner, *Intruder in the Dust*, 194.

46. Karl, *William Faulkner*, 655; Warren, *All The King's Men*, 436; Justus, *The Achievement of Robert Penn Warren*, 325.

47. Thadious M. Davis, "Southern Standard Bearers in the New Negro Renaissance," in Louis D. Rubin, Jr., et al., eds., *The History of Southern Literature* (Baton Rouge, 1985), 313.

48. James R. Grossman, *Land of Hope: Chicago, Black Southerners, and the "Great Migration"* (Chicago, 1989), 3–4; Joanne V. Gabbin, *Sterling A. Brown: Building the Black Aesthetic Tradition* (Westport, Conn., 1985), 42.

49. Davis, "Southern Standard Bearers," 291; Charles S. Johnson, "Black Workers and the City," *Survey Graphic* 6 (March 1925), 641–43, 718–21.

50. John Hope Franklin, "The South: Perspective for Tomorrow," in *The Future of the South, American Issues Forum I* (Durham, N.C., 1994), 7; L. D. Reddick, "The Negro as Southerner and American," in Charles Grier Sellers, Jr., ed., *The Southerner as American* (Chapel Hill, 1960), 130–34.

51. Langston Hughes, "The South," *Crisis* (June 1922), 72; Robert Bone, *Down Home: A History of African American Short Fiction from Its Beginnings to the End of the Harlem Renaissance* (New York, 1975), xix–xx.

52. Richard Wright, *Uncle Tom's Children*, reprint of 1940 ed. (New York, 1965), 27, 126; Thadious M. Davis, "Wright, Faulkner, and Mississippi as Racial Memory,"

Callaloo 9 (Summer 1986), 477; Richard Wright, *Black Boy: A Record of Childhood and Youth* (New York, 1945), 284.

53. Wright, *Black Boy*, 283; Robert Penn Warren, "Faulkner, the South, the Negro, and Time," in Robert Penn Warren, *Faulkner: A Collection of Critical Essays* (Englewood Cliffs, N.J., 1966), 259; Richard Wright, *Letters to Joe C. Brown* (Kent, Ohio, 1968), 13, quoted in Australia Tarver Henderson, *In Loathing and in Love: Black Southern Novelists' Views of the South, 1954–1964* (Ph.D. dissertation, University of Iowa, 1978), 34.

54. W. E. B. DuBois, *The Souls of Black Folk*, reprint (New York, 1989), 3.

55. Davis, "Southern Standard Bearers," 298; Henry Louis Gates, Jr., "Introduction to the Vintage Edition," in James Weldon Johnson, *The Autobiography of an Ex-Coloured Man* (New York, 1989), xii.

56. Johnson, *The Autobiography*, 46, 142, 190–91, 193, 210–11.

57. Charles T. Davis, "Jean Toomer and the South: Region and Race as Elements within a Literary Imagination," in Victor A. Kramer, ed., *The Harlem Renaissance Re-Examined* (New York, 1987), 189; Darwin T. Turner, *A Minor Chord: Three Afro-American Writers and Their Search for Identity* (Carbondale, Ill., 1971), 28; Louis D. Rubin, Jr., ed., *The Literary South* (Baton Rouge, 1979), 429.

58. Turner, *A Minor Chord*, 20; Jean Toomer, *Cane* (New York, 1923), 2, 23, 28.

59. Toomer, *Cane*, 27–35, 13.

60. Turner, *A Minor Chord*, 20, 23.

61. Toomer, *Cane*, "Introduction," xxii; Darwin T. Turner, "Introduction," in Jean Toomer, *Cane* (New York, 1993); Cynthia Earl Kerman and Richard Eldridge, *The Lives of Jean Toomer* (Baton Rouge, 1987), 296.

62. Davis, "Southern Standard Bearers," 303.

63. Zora Neale Hurston, *Dust Tracks on a Road*, reprint (New York, 1991), 98.

64. Henry Louis Gates, Jr., "Zora Neale Hurston: 'A Negro Way of Saying,' Afterword," in Hurston, *Dust Tracks on a Road*, 258; Zora Neale Hurston, *Jonah's Gourd Vine* (Philadelphia, 1934), 157–58; Hurston, *Dust Tracks on a Road*, 136.

65. Zora Neale Hurston, *Their Eyes Were Watching God*, reprint (New York, 1990), 75, 122, 183–84; Gates, "Afterword," in Hurston, *Dust Tracks on a Road*, 259; Zora Neale Huston, "How It Feels to Be Colored Me" and "Looking Things Over," in Cheryl A. Wall, ed., *Zora Neal Hurston: Folklore, Memoirs, and Other Writings* (New York, 1995), 827, 765.

66. Davis, "Southern Standard Bearers," 304.

67. Arnold Rampersad, *The Life of Langston Hughes, Vol. I, 1902–1940* (New York, 1986), 111, 160.

68. Hughes, "The South," 72; Langston Hughes, "Christ in Alabama," *CONTEMPO* (December 1, 1931), 1; Rampersad, *Life of Langston Hughes*, 225.

69. *CONTEMPO* (November 15, 1931).

70. Langston Hughes, "Mulatto," in Webster Smalley, ed., *Five Plays by Langston Hughes* (Bloomington, 1963), 30–31; "Mulatto" in Arnold Rampersad and David Roessel, eds., *The Collected Poems of Langston Hughes* (New York, 1994), 100–101.

71. Davis, "Southern Standard Bearers," 307–9; Gabbin, *Sterling A. Brown,* 90, 95; Sterling A. Brown, "Southern Road," "Ma Rainey," "Children's Children," in *The Collected Poems of Sterling A. Brown (Selected by Michael S. Harper)* (New York, 1980), 52–53, 62–63, 94.

72. Rudolph Fisher, "The South Lingers On," *Survey Graphic* 6 (March 1925), 644–47; Mark Andrew Huddle, "Harlem and the South: History and Politics of Place," unpublished paper, copy in the possession of the author; Mary Helen Washington, "Foreword," in Hurston, *Their Eyes Were Watching God,* xiii.

73. Judith Musser, "African American Women's Short Stories in the Harlem Renaissance: Bridging a Tradition," *MELUS* 23 (Summer 1998), 39; Ramona Lowe, "The Woman in the Window," *Opportunity* 18 (January 1940), 11–13.

74. Steve Watson, *The Harlem Renaissance* (New York, 1995), 93; Richard Wright, "Blueprint for Negro Writing," *New Challenge* (Fall 1937), 54; Musser, "African American Women's Short Stories," 42–43.

75. Rampersad, *The Life of Langston Hughes,* 141–40, 145, 144.

76. Watson, *The Harlem Renaissance,* 3; John F. Callahan, "American Culture Is of a Whole: From the Letters of Ralph Ellison," *The New Republic* 220 (March 1, 1999), 38; Sterling A. Brown, "Our Literary Audience," in Sterling A. Brown, *A Son's Return: Selected Essays of Sterling A. Brown* (Boston, 1996), 143.

77. Elizabeth Davey, "The Souths of Sterling A. Brown," *Southern Cultures* 5 (Summer 1999), 29, 43, 38.

78. Davey, "Souths of Sterling Brown," 38, 43; Sterling A. Brown, "Count Us In," in Rayford W. Logan, ed., *What the Negro Wants,* rev. ed. (Notre Dame, Ind., 2001), 308.

79. Ralph Ellison, "The World and the Jug," in John F. Callahan, ed., *The Collected Essays of Ralph Ellison* (New York, 1995), 169; Ralph Ellison, *Shadow and Act* (New York, 1964), 7.

80. *Atlanta Journal-Constitution,* July 14, 2002; Berndt Ostendorf, *Black Literature in White America* (Sussex, 1982), 130.

81. Ralph Ellison, "Flying Home," in John F. Callahan, ed., *Flying Home and Other Stories* (New York, 1996), 154, 160, 168; William Alexander Percy, *Lanterns on the Levee: Recollections of a Planter's Son* (New York, 1941), 293.

82. Ralph Ellison, "Working Notes for *Invisible Man,*" in Callahan, *The Collected Essays of Ralph Ellison,* 169; Ellison, *Invisible Man* (New York, 1952), 13–14.

83. Ellison, *Invisible Man,* 15–25.

84. Ellison, "Working Notes for *Invisible Man,*" 344; Ellison, *Invisible Man,* 110, 125

85. Bhoendradatt Tewarie, "Southern Elements in Ellison's *Invisible Man,*" *Journal of General Education* 35.3 (1983), 197, 199, 200–201.

86. Tewarie, "Southern Elements," 13, 436–37; Theodore R. Hudson, "Ralph W. Ellison," in Louis D. Rubin, Jr., et al., eds., *The History of Southern Literature* (Baton Rouge, 1985), 511–12.

87. Albert Murray and John F. Callahan, eds., *Trading Twelves: The Selected Letters of Ralph Ellison and Albert Murray* (New York, 2000), 45, 158, 182. "Mose" was a euphemism used by Ellison and Albert Murray for black persons in general or

for themselves in particular. Robert W. Rudnicki, *Percyscapes: The Fugue State in Twentieth-Century Southern Fiction* (Baton Rouge, 1999), 107.

88. Callahan, "American Culture Is of a Whole," 38; Ellison, *Invisible Man*, 439.

89. Louis D. Rubin, Jr., and Robert D. Jacobs, eds., *Southern Renascence: The Literature of the Modern South* (Baltimore, 1953); Sterling A. Brown, "Memphis Blues," in *The Collected Poems of Sterling A. Brown (Selected by Michael S. Harper)* (New York, 1980), 60–61.

90. Murray and Callahan, *Trading Twelves*, 117.

91. Fred Hobson, *The Southern Writer in the Postmodern World* (Athens, Ga., 1991), 3.

6. THE MIND OF THE SOUTH

1. David L. Cohn, *Where I Was Born and Raised*, a revised edition of *God Shakes Creation* (Cambridge, Mass., 1948), 201.

2. William Alexander Percy, *Lanterns on the Levee: Recollections of a Planter's Son* (New York, 1941), 149; Richard H. King, *A Southern Renaissance: The Cultural Awakening of the American South, 1930–1955* (New York, 1980), 86–95.

3. Ben Robertson, *Red Hills and Cotton: An Upcountry Memory* (New York, 1942), 161, 286, 275; Fred C. Hobson, *Tell about the South: The Southern Rage to Explain* (Baton Rouge, 1983), 292.

4. Clarence Cason, *90° in the Shade* (Chapel Hill, 1935), 121.

5. Ibid., 23, 122–24.

6. Hobson, *Tell about the South*, 255; Cason, *90°*, ix, 175–76.

7. Joseph L. Morrison, *W. J. Cash, Southern Prophet: A Biography and a Reader* (New York, 1967), 1–14.

8. Morrison, *W. J. Cash*, 12–13.

9. Bruce Clayton, *W. J. Cash: A Life* (Baton Rouge, 1991), 36–37; W. J. Cash, "North Carolina Culture," *Old Gold and Black* (October 13, 1922), www.wjcash.org./WJCash6/gold/gold-10-13-22.htm.

10. Clayton, *W. J. Cash*, 36; W. J. Cash, "The Mind of the South," *American Mercury* 18 (October 1929), 185.

11. Cash, "The Mind of the South," 191–92.

12. Morrison, *W. J. Cash*, 49; W. J. Cash, *The Mind of the South—With a New Introduction by Bertram Wyatt-Brown*, paperback version (New York, 1991), viii–ix.

13. Cash, "Mind of the South," 185; Cash to Odum, November 13, 1929, Odum to Cash, November 20, 1929, Folder 195–96, Howard W. Odum Papers, Southern Historical Collection, University of North Carolina at Chapel Hill.

14. Cash, *The Mind of the South*, ix, 5, 8.

15. Ibid., 10; Rupert B. Vance, *Human Geography of the South: A Study in Regional Resources and Human Adequacy*, 2nd ed. (Chapel Hill, 1935), 76; Howard W. Odum, *Southern Regions of the United States* (Chapel Hill, 1936), 227.

16. Cash, *The Mind of the South*, 92, 96; Ellen Glasgow, "The Novel in the South," *Harper's* (1928), 94.

17. Cash, *The Mind of the South*, 96.
18. Ibid., 14–17.
19. Ibid., 17–19.
20. Ibid., 22; Frank L. and Harriet C. Owsley, "The Economic Basis of Society in the Late Antebellum South," *Journal of Southern History* 6 (February 1940), 24–55; Frank L. Owsley, *Plain Folk of the Old South*, reprint (Baton Rouge, 1982), 133–34.
21. Cash, *The Mind of the South*, 26–27.
22. Ibid., 42–44.
23. Ibid., 134, 303.
24. Ibid., 38–39.
25. See George M. Fredrickson, *The Black Image in the White Mind: The Debate on Afro-American Character and Destiny, 1817–1914* (New York, 1971), 61, 39.
26. Cash, *The Mind of the South*, 49–50, 82; Richard Wright, *Black Boy: A Record of Childhood and Youth* (New York, 1945), 201.
27. Cash, *The Mind of the South*, 319; Percy, *Lanterns on the Levee*, 299; Wright, *Black Boy*, 283; Michael O'Brien, "W. J. Cash," in William R. Ferris and Charles R. Wilson, eds., *The Encyclopedia of Southern Culture* (Chapel Hill, 1989), 1130–131.
28. Cash, *The Mind of the South*, 86.
29. Winthrop D. Jordan, *White over Black: American Attitudes toward the Negro, 1550–1812* (Chapel Hill, 1968); see, for example, Jacquelyn Dowd Hall, *Revolt against Chivalry; Jessie Daniel Ames and the Women's Campaign against Lynching* (New York, 1993); Bryant Simon, "The Appeal of Cole Blease of South Carolina: Race, Class, and Sex in the New South," *Journal of Southern History* 62 (February 1996), 57–87; Louis D. Rubin, Jr., "General Longstreet and Me: Refighting the Civil War," *Southern Cultures* 8 (Spring 2002), 25–26
30. Hollinger F. Barnard, ed., *Outside the Magic Circle: The Autobiography of Virginia Foster Durr* (Tuscaloosa, Ala., 1985), 45.
31. Cash, *The Mind of the South*, 86, 116, 106.
32. Ibid., 115–116; John Dollard, *Caste and Class in a Southern Town* (Garden City, N.Y., 1957), 381.
33. Cash, *The Mind of the South*, 117, 65–66.
34. Ibid., 138–39; Current, *Northernizing the South*, 12–13.
35. Cash, *The Mind of the South*, 107, 134–35.
36. Cash to Odum, November 13, 1929, Odum Papers.
37. Cash, *The Mind of the South*, 106, 134; King, *A Southern Renaissance*, 166.
38. Bertram Wyatt-Brown, *Yankee Saints and Southern Sinners* (Baton Rouge, 1985), 141; Wyatt-Brown, "W. J. Cash and Southern Culture," 199; Bassam Tibi (trans. Clare Krojzl), *Islam and the Cultural Accommodation of Social Change* (Boulder, 1990), 53.
39. Cash, *The Mind of the South*, 219; James C. Cobb, *The Selling of the South: The Southern Crusade for Industrial Development, 1936–1990* (Urbana, 1993), 71–76; David R. Goldfield, *Still Fighting the Civil War: The American South and Southern History* (Baton Rouge, 2002), 8.

40. Cash, *The Mind of the South*, 219.

41. Clayton, *W. J. Cash*, 218; Cash, *The Mind of the South*, 200.

42. Wilson Follett, "Review of Cash, *The Mind of the South*," *The Atlantic Monthly* 167 (April 1940), 4, 7; Clayton, *The Mind of the South*, 165–68.

43. Clement Eaton, "Review of Cash, *The Mind of the South*," *American Historical Review* 47 (January 1942), 376; C. Vann Woodward, "Review of Cash, *The Mind of the South*," *Journal of Southern History* 7 (August 1941), 400–401.

44. Daniel J. Singal, *The War Within: From Victorian to Modernist Thought in the South* (Chapel Hill, 1982), 373.

45. Hobson, *Tell about the South*, 257–58; Cash, *The Mind of the South*, vii.

46. Cash to Odum, November 13, 1929: Cash, *The Mind of the South*, 376.

47. Alfred A. Knopf, Incorporated, "Authors Form A, 4–29–36," Typescript, Folder 56; "Application for a John Simon Guggenheim Memorial Fellowship," October 1936, Folder 56; W. J. Cash to Alfred Knopf, September 8, 1940, Typescript, Folder 59; "Application for a John Simon Guggenheim Memorial Fellowship," October 1940, Folder 59; all in Box 5, Joseph L. Morrison Papers, #3787, Southern Historical Collection, University of North Carolina at Chapel Hill.

48. "Application for a Guggenheim Memorial Fellowship," October 1936; "Application for a Guggenheim Memorial Fellowship," October 1940; Morrison, *W. J. Cash*, 223.

49. Cash, *The Mind of the South*, 379, 377.

50. Ibid.; David L. Cohn, "Tissues of Southern Culture," *Saturday Review* 23 (February 22, 1941), 17.

51. Alfred A. Knopf, Incorporated, "Authors Form A, April 8, 1940," Folder 58, Cash Correspondence, November 1938–June 1940, Box 5, Morrison Papers, Southern Historical Collection, University of North Carolina at Chapel Hill; Cash, *The Mind of the South*, 377.

52. William Faulkner, "An Introduction to *The Sound and the Fury*," *Mississippi Quarterly* 16 (Summer 1973), 412.

53. Clayton, *W. J. Cash*, 162, 119; King, *A Southern Renaissance*, 146.

54. Cash, *The Mind of the South*, 428–29.

55. Ibid., 429; Clayton, *W. J. Cash*, 174, 186–88.

7. THE SOUTH OF GUILT AND SHAME

1. W. J. Cash, *The Mind of the South—With a New Introduction by Bertram Wyatt-Brown*, paperback version (New York, 1991), 429; Morton Sosna, "More Important than the Civil War? The Impact of World War II on the South," in James C. Cobb and Charles R. Wilson, eds., *Perspectives on the American South: An Annual Review of Society, Politics, and Culture*, Volume 4 (New York, 1987), 145–61; Ralph W. McGill, *The South and the Southerner* (Boston, 1964), 159.

2. John Dollard, *Caste and Class in a Southern Town*, reprint (Madison, Wis., 1988), 33; Numan V. Bartley, *The New South, 1945–1980* (Baton Rouge, 1995), 28, 30; Morton Sosna, *In Search of the Silent South: Southern Liberals and the Race Issue*

(New York, 1977), 19; Virginius Dabney, *Below the Potomac: A Book about the New South* (New York, 1942), 300–304.

3. John Egerton, *Speak Now against the Day: The Generation before the Civil Rights Movement in the South* (New York, 1994), 327.

4. C. Vann Woodward, *Thinking Back: The Perils of Writing History* (Baton Rouge, 1986), 102; Sosna, *In Search*, 205.

5. William Faulkner, *Go Down, Moses and Other Stories by William Faulkner* (New York, 1942), 286, 260; Richard Gray, *The Life of William Faulkner* (Oxford, 1994), 275.

6. James C. Cobb, "World War II and the Mind of the Modern South," in Neil McMillen, ed., *Remaking Dixie: The Impact of World War II on the American South* (Jackson, 1997), 37.

7. Frederick R. Karl, *William Faulkner: American Writer* (New York, 1989), 709, 644, 708.

8. William Faulkner, *Intruder in the Dust* (New York, 1948), 153, 203–4, 217, 154, 204.

9. "A Way Out of the Swamp?" *Time* 52 (October 4, 1948), 111–12; "William Faulkner's Reply to the Civil Rights Program," *The New Yorker* 23 (October 1948), 106, 110; Maxwell Geismar, "Ex-Aristocrat's Emotional Education," *Review of Literature* 31 (September 25, 1948), 9.

10. Malcolm Cowley, "William Faulkner's Nation," *New Republic* 119 (October 18, 1948), 22.

11. Gray, *The Life of William Faulkner*, 300; Joseph Blotner, *Faulkner: A Biography*, reprint (New York, 1991), 617–18.

12. Walter Taylor, *Faulkner's Search for a South* (Urbana, 1983), 157; James C. Cobb, *The Most Southern Place on Earth: The Mississippi Delta and the Roots of Regional Identity* (New York, 1972), 210.

13. Hodding Carter, *Southern Legacy* (Baton Rouge, 1950), 175, 89–90.

14. Gunnar Myrdal, *American Dilemma: The Negro Problem and Modern Democracy* (New York, 1944), 65–66.

15. Egerton, *Speak Now against the Day*, 325; Elizabeth Davey, "The Souths of Sterling A. Brown," *Southern Cultures* 5 (Summer 1999), 43; Numan V. Bartley, *The New South, 1945–1980* (Baton Rouge, 1995), 14; Frederick D. Patterson, "The Negro Wants Full Participation in the American Democracy," in Rayford W. Logan, ed., *What the Negro Wants*, rev. ed. (Notre Dame, 2001), 265.

16. Egerton, *Speak Now against the Day*, 325; Rampersad, *Life of Langston Hughes*, Volume 2 (New York, 1988), 36, 46, 50.

17. Ralph Ellison, "In a Strange Country," in John F. Callahan, *Flying Home and Other Stories* (New York, 1996), 137–46.

18. Robert E. Hemenway, *Zora Neale Hurston: A Literary Biography* (Urbana, Ill., 1977), 287, 288, 294, 295.

19. Michel Fabre, *The Unfinished Quest of Richard Wright*, 2nd ed. (Urbana, 1993), 223–27; Richard Wright, *Black Boy: A Record of Childhood and Youth* (New York, 1945), 201.

20. Fabre, *The Unfinished Quest*, 280–82.

21. "*Black Boy*: A Negro Writes a Bitter Autobiography," *Life* (June 4, 1945), 87.

22. Katharine Du Pre Lumpkin, *The Making of a Southerner*, reprint (Athens, Ga., 1992), 130, 132, 215–22.

23. Ibid., 233–34; Fred C. Hobson, *Tell about the South: The Southern Rage to Explain* (Baton Rouge, 1983), 314–15.

24. Sosna, *In Search*, 186, 191; Ralph Ellison, "A Party Down at the Square," in Callahan, *Flying Home*, 9; Lillian Smith, *Strange Fruit* (New York, 1944), 348–49.

25. Lillian Smith to Richard Wright, June 12, 1944, in Margaret Rose Gladney, *How Am I to Be Heard? Letters of Lillian Smith* (Chapel Hill, 1993), 84; Lillian Smith, *Killers of the Dream* (New York, 1949), 15, 17–18.

26. Lillian Smith to Alfred Knopf, September 26, 1949, Box 57, Folder 18, Alfred Knopf Papers, Harry Ransom Humanities Research Center, University of Texas at Austin; Smith to George Brockway, July 3, 1965, in Gladney, *How Am I to Be Heard?* 323.

27. Smith, *Killers of the Dream*, 90, 158–59.

28. Fred C. Hobson, *But Now I See: The White Southern Racial Conversion Narrative* (Baton Rouge, 1999), 31; Smith, *Killers of the Dream*, 151, 143.

29. Smith, *Killers of the Dream*, 147–48, 149.

30. Lillian Smith to George Brockway, July 3, 1965; Lillian Smith to Lawrence Kubie, October 10, 1957, in Gladney, *How Am I to Be Heard?*, 323; Lillian Smith, "The Right Way Is Not the Moderate Way," in Michelle Smith, ed., *The Winner Names the Age* (New York, 1978), 68.

31. Stetson Kennedy, *Southern Exposure* (Garden City, N.Y., 1946), 78.

32. Dollard, *Caste and Class*, 33; John Gunther, *Inside U.S.A.* (New York, 1947), 657–58.

33. Daniel J. Singal, *The War Within: From Victorian to Modernist Thought in the South* (Chapel Hill, 1982), 373.

34. Alfred A. Knopf to W. J. Cash, May 26, 1941; to John W. Cash, September 9–10, 1941, both in Wilbur J. Cash Collection, Wake Forest University Library, www.wfu. edu/Library/rarebook/cash/index.html; Lillian Smith to Alfred Knopf, September 26, 1949, Box 57, Folder 18, Alfred Knopf Papers, Harry Ransom Humanities Research Center, University of Texas at Austin.

35. Smith to George Brockway, July 3, 1965; William A. Koshland to Dewey W. Grantham, Jr., June 1, 1961, Box 302, Folder 2, Knopf Papers.

36. *New York Times Book Review*, February 7, 1960; Jack Temple Kirby, *Media-Made Dixie: The South in the American Imagination*, rev. ed. (Athens, Ga., 1986), 80.

37. Cash, *The Mind of the South*, 122–23.

38. Bob Smith, "A Prisoner in Time," *Red Clay Reader*, Volume 4 (1967), 16.

39. Edwin M. Yoder, "W. J. Cash after a Quarter Century," in Willie Morris, ed., *The South Today: 100 Years after Appomattox* (New York, 1965), 92; Hobson, *Tell about the South*, 247.

40. McGill, *The South and the Southerner*, 217.

41. Ibid., 217, 236.

42. Pat Watters, *The South and the Nation* (New York), 286; Pat Watters, *Down to Now: Reflections on the Southern Civil Rights Movement* (New York, 1971), 30.

43. James C. Cobb, "On the Pinnacle in Yankeeland: C. Vann as a [Southern] Renaissance Man," *Journal of Southern History* 67 (November 2001), 729; Woodward, *Thinking Back*, 65, 63, 64.

44. C. Vann Woodward, *Origins of the New South, 1877–1913* (Baton Rouge, 1951), 211.

45. C. Vann Woodward, "New South Fraud Is Papered by Old South Myth," *Washington Post*, July 9, 1961; Woodward, *Thinking Back*, 42; David Donald, "After Reconstruction," *The Nation* 124 (May 15, 1952), 484.

46. Donald Davidson, *The Attack on Leviathan: Regionalism and Nationalism in the United States* (Chapel Hill, 1938), 323; C. Vann Woodward, "Why the Southern Renaissance?" in Woodward, *The Future of the Past* (New York, 1989), 236.

47. "The Background to the Abandonment of Reconstruction," Box 2, Folder, "NAACP Segregation Case," "Segregation in Historical Perspective," Box 7, Folder, "Unpublished Papers, 1960–1973," C. Vann Woodward Papers, Manuscripts and Archives, Yale University, New Haven, Conn.; C. Vann Woodward, *The Strange Career of Jim Crow*, 2nd ed. (London, 1966), xii–xiii.

48. Woodward, *Thinking Back*, 87, 83.

49. Richard H. King, *A Southern Renaissance: The Cultural Awakening of the American South, 1930–1955* (New York, 1980), 271; Woodward, *The Strange Career of Jim Crow*, 163.

50. Rayford W. Logan, "Review of C. Vann Woodward, *The Strange Career of Jim Crow*," *American Historical Review* 61 (1955), 212; E. Franklin Frazier, Ibid., *Saturday Review* 38 (June 11, 1955), 13; Rufus E. Clement, Ibid., *Journal of Southern History* 21 (November 1955), 557.

51. Woodward, *Thinking Back*, 92

52. Margaret Just Butcher, "*Gone with the Wind*," *New Republic* 135 (December 3, 1956), 21.

53. Stanley Elkins, *Slavery: A Problem in American Institutional and Intellectual Life* (Chicago, 1959).

54. Bernard A. Weisberger, "The Dark and Bloody Ground of Reconstruction Historiography," *Journal of Southern History* 25 (1957), 429, 477.

55. John Hope Franklin, *Reconstruction: After the Civil War*, reprint (Chicago, 1994), 147.

56. "Provocative Revisionist," *Time* (April 23, 1965), 107; Harry V. Jaffa, "Reconstruction, Old and New," *National Review* 17 (April 20, 1965), 332.

57. Clement Eaton, "Professor James Woodrow and the Freedom of Teaching in the South," in George B. Tindall, ed., *The Pursuit of Southern History: Presidential Addresses of the Southern Historical Association, 1935–1963* (Baton Rouge, 1964), 449.

58. James W. Silver, "Mississippi: The Closed Society," in Tindall, *The Pursuit of Southern History*, 491.

59. David M. Potter, "On Understanding the South," *Journal of Southern History* 30 (February 1964), 454.

60. Ibid.; David M. Potter, "C. Vann Woodward and the Uses of History," in Don E. Fehrenbacher, ed., *History and American Society: Essays of David M. Potter* (New York, 1973), 166.

61. Robert Coles, *Flannery O'Connor's South* (Athens, Ga., 1993), 50; Hobson, *But Now I See*, 130.

62. Eudora Welty, *The Collected Stories of Eudora Welty* (San Diego, 1980), xi, 604.

63. Walker Percy, "Mississippi, The Fallen Paradise," in Patrick Samway, ed., *Signposts in a Strange Land* (New York, 1991), 39, 40.

64. Robert Penn Warren, "The Briar Patch," in Twelve Southerners, *I'll Take My Stand*, 264, 246, 254, 251.

65. Robert Penn Warren to Allen Tate and Caroline Gordon, May 19, 1930, in William Bedford Clark, ed., *Selected Letters of Robert Penn Warren* (Baton Rouge, 2000), 186; "Warren on the Art of Fiction," in Floyd C. Watkins, et al., eds., *Talking with Robert Penn Warren* (Athens, Ga., 1920), 33, 384.

66. Robert Penn Warren, *Who Speaks for the Negro?* (New York, 1965), 12.

67. Ibid.

68. Watkins, *Talking with Robert Penn Warren*, 34.

69. Robert Penn Warren, *Brother to Dragons: A Tale in Verse and Voices: A New Version* (New York, 1979), 110, 117, 118, 132.

70. Watkins, *Talking with Robert Penn Warren*, 33; Robert Penn Warren, *Segregation, The Inner Conflict in the South* (New York, 1956), 63, 65–66.

71. Warren, *Who Speaks for the Negro?* 428.

72. Ibid., 12, 13.

73. Hobson, *But Now I See*, 129; Warren, *Segregation*, 51–52; Willie Morris, *North Toward Home*, reprint (Oxford, Miss., 1982), 437; Larry King, *Confessions of a White Racist* (New York, 1971), 149, 155.

74. King, *Confessions of a White Racist, 149, 155*.

8. NO NORTH, NO SOUTH? THE CRISIS OF SOUTHERN WHITE IDENTITY

1. Robert Penn Warren, *Who Speaks for the Negro?* (New York, 1965), 334.

2. Grace Elizabeth Hale, *Making Whiteness: The Culture of Segregation in the South, 1890–1940* (New York, 1998), 9; C. Vann Woodward, *Origins of the New South, 1877–1913* (Baton Rouge, 1951), 353; U. B. Phillips, "The Central Theme of Southern History," *American Historical Review* 34 (October 1928), 31; Walker Percy, "Red, White and Blue-Gray," in Patrick Samway, ed., *Signposts in a Strange Land* (New York, 1991), 80.

3. Harry S. Ashmore, *An Epitaph for Dixie* (New York, 1958), 15, 22, 188.

4. William H. Nicholls, *Southern Tradition and Regional Progress* (Chapel Hill, 1960), 130.

5. Nichols, *Southern Tradition*, 183, 163, 5.

6. Frank E. Smith, *Look Away from Dixie* (New York, 1965), 88, 9.

7. Joseph B. Cumming, Jr., "Been Down Home So Long It Seems Like Up to Me," *Esquire* 76 (August 1971), 84; Hodding Carter III, "The End of the South," *Time* 136 (August 1990), 82.

8. Hale, *Making Whiteness*, 242; Henry Miller, *The Air-Conditioned Nightmare*, Volume 1 (New York, 1945), 283–84; Curtis Wilkie, *Dixie: A Personal Odyssey through Events that Shaped the Modern South* (New York, 2001), 36, 38.

9. Roy Blount, Jr., *Now Where Were We?* (New York, 1988), 161; William Faulkner, *Intruder in the Dust* (New York, 1948), 152–53.

10. Faulkner, *Intruder in the Dust*, 152; Richard N. Current, *Northernizing the South* (Athens, Ga., 1983), 12. On "the North" as the rest of the United States, see John Egerton, *The Americanization of Dixie: The Southernization of America* (New York, 1974), xix.

11. Current, *Northernizing the South*, 35, 82.

12. A. B. Hart, *The Southern South* (New York, 1910), 2–3, 64–65; Phillips, "The Central Theme of Southern History," 31; John T. Westbrook, "Twilight of Southern Regionalism," *Southwest Review* 42 (Summer 1957), 234.

13. Joseph Cumming, Jr., "A Final Farewell," *Georgia* 15 (June 1972), 35; James C. Cobb, "An Epitaph for the North: Reflections on the Politics of Regional and National Identity at the Millennium," *Journal of Southern History* 66 (February 2000), 6.

14. Jack Temple Kirby, *Media-Made Dixie: The South in the American Imagination*, rev. ed. (Athens, Ga., 1986), 134; Lewis Chester, Godfrey Hodgson, and Bruce Page, *An American Melodrama: The Presidential Campaign of 1968* (New York, 1969), 652; C. Vann Woodward, "The Irony of Southern History" and "A Second Look at the Theme of Irony," in C. Vann Woodward, *The Burden of Southern History* (Baton Rouge, 1993), 190, 214.

15. Kevin Phillips, *The Emerging Republican Majority* (New Rochelle, N.Y., 1969), 437; *New York Times*, January 16, 1972.

16. Egerton, *Americanization of Dixie*, xix; C. Vann Woodward, "From the First Reconstruction to the Second," in Willie Morris, ed., *The South Today: 100 Years after Appomattox* (New York, 1965), 14; and "The South Tomorrow," *Time* 108 (September 22, 1976), 98–99.

17. Larry King, "We Ain't Trash No More," *Esquire* 126 (November 1976), 88.

18. Ibid.

19. C. Vann Woodward, *American Counterpoint: Slavery and Racism in the North-South Dialogue* (Boston, 1971), 6; Sheldon Hackney, "The South as Counterculture," *American Scholar* 42 (Number 2, Spring 1973), 21.

20. James Peacock, "The South in a Global World," *Virginia Quarterly Review* 78 (Autumn 2002), 582–83; Sheldon Hackney, "Southern Violence," *American Historical Review* 74 (February 1969), 924–25.

21. John Shelton Reed, *The Enduring South: Subcultural Persistence in Mass Society* (Lexington, Mass., 1972), 88–90.

22. John Shelton Reed, *The Enduring South*, rev. ed. (Chapel Hill, 1986), 91, 101.

23. Edward L. Ayers, "What Do We Talk about When We Talk about the South?" in Ayers, Patricia Nelson Limerick, Stephen Nissenbaum, and Peter S. Onuf, eds., *All over the Map: Rethinking American Regions* (Baltimore, 1996), 65.

24. John Shelton Reed, *Southerners: The Social Psychology of Sectionalism* (Chapel Hill, 1983), 109.

25. C. Vann Woodward, "The Search for Southern Identity," *Virginia Quarterly Review* 34 (Summer 1958), 46; Larry J. Griffin and Ashley B. Thompson, "Enough about the Disappearing South: What about the Disappearing Southerner?" *Southern Cultures* 9 (Fall 2003), 56.

26. Reed, *Southerners*, 111, 114.

27. C. Vann Woodward, "The Search for Southern Identity," *Virginia Quarterly Review* 34 (Summer 1958), 12; Woodward, "From the First Reconstruction to the Second," in Willie Morris, ed., *The South Today: 100 Years after Appomattox* (New York, 1965), 14; Woodward, "Look Away, Look Away," *Journal of Southern History* 59 (August 1993), 504; David R. Goldfield, *Black, White, and Southern: Race Relations and Southern Culture, 1940 to the Present* (Baton Rouge, 1990), 169–73.

28. Basam Tibi, *Islam and the Cultural Accommodation of Social Change* (Boulder, Colo., 1990), 54; Hackney, "Southern Violence," 924–25; James McBride Dabbs, *Who Speaks for the South?* (New York, 1964), 320; Current, *Northernizing the South*, 83.

29. "*Southern Living*: In Tune with Today's South," *Southern Living* 1 (February 1966), 4.

30. John Shelton Reed, *One South: An Ethnic Approach to Regional Culture* (Baton Rouge, 1982), 122; Diane Roberts, "Living Southern in *Southern Living*," in Richard H. King and Helen Taylor, eds., *Dixie Debates: Perspectives on Southern Cultures* (London, 1996), 86.

31. Lemann is quoted in John Shelton Reed and Dale Volberg Reed, *1,001 Things Everyone Should Know about the South* (New York, 1996), 294; Sam G. Riley, *Magazines of the American South* (Westport, Conn., 1986), 240, quoted in Roberts, "Living Southern," 86.

32. Jack Temple Kirby, *The Countercultural South* (Athens, Ga., 1995), 74; "Bubba Joins the Electronic World," *North Carolina State University Libraries Newsletter*, 21 (September 1993), www.lib.ncsu/stacks/n/nc/n/-v21no2-editor-bubbal.txt.

33. "Bubba Joins the Electronic World," 75; www.southernness.com.

34. Ibid.

35. Jim and Susan Erskine, *The Southerner's Instruction Book* (Gretna, La., 1994), n.p.

36. "Lewis Grizzard Live! The Goodwill Tour from Moreland to Macon," Southern Tracks Records, 1996; Lewis Grizzard, *I Haven't Understood Anything since 1962 (And Other Nekkid Truths)* (New York, 1992), 152–53, 31–32.

37. Kirby, *Countercultural South*, 71.

38. Ibid., 72; V. S. Naipaul, *A Turn in the South* (New York, 1989), 207–8; Kirby, *Countercultural South*, 71.

39. Kirby, *Countercultural South*, 73.

40. Robert Kelley, "Redneck Chic: A New Honky-Tonk Craze Sweeps the City," *Highpoint*, 4–17 (December 1992), 1, 8.

41. *Atlanta Journal-Constitution*, September 17, 1995.

42. Edwin M. Yoder, Jr., "Thoughts on the Dixiefication of Dixie," in John B. Boles, ed., *Dixie Dateline: A Journalistic Portrait of the Contemporary South* (Houston, 1983), 151, 162.

43. *Atlanta Journal-Constitution*, September 5, 1993.

44. Peter Applebome, *Dixie Rising: How the South Is Shaping American Values, Politics, and Culture* (New York, 1996), 286.

45. James C. Cobb, "Does Mind No Longer Matter? The South, the Nation, and *The Mind of the South*, 1941–1991," *Journal of Southern History* 57 (November 1991), 716; *Atlanta Journal-Constitution*, December 30, 1990.

46. John Shelton Reed, "Of Collard Greens and Kings," in *Minding the South* (Columbia, Mo., 2003), 99–100; Alex Haley, "Foreword," in William R. Ferris and Charles R. Wilson, eds., *Encyclopedia of Southern Culture* (Chapel Hill, 1989), xi.

47. David A. Bell, "Paris Blues," *New Republic* 217 (September 1, 1997), 32; Steven Englund, "The Ghost of the Nation Past," *Journal of Modern History* 64 (June 1992), 317.

48. *Atlanta Journal-Constitution*, September 5, 1993; Richard H. King, "Reflections on Southern Intellectuals," *Southern Cultures* 1 (Spring 1995), 337.

49. *New Orleans Times Picayune*, August 13, 1995.

50. *New York Times*, August 5, 6, 1995; *New Orleans Times Picayune*, August 13, 1995; *Oxford Eagle*, July 30, 1996; "Then Sings My Soul," Elvis and the Sacred South, flier in possession of the author. For criticism of the "pop culture" emphasis at the first Elvis Conference, see the *New York Times*, August 6, 1995.

51. *Jackson Clarion Ledger*, August 2, 1996; *Oxford Eagle*, July 30, 1996.

52. *Anderson Independent*, August 10, 1998.

53. Edwin M. Yoder, Jr., "A Dixieland Reverie," *Saturday Review* 47 (May 30, 1964), 40; Yoder, "Thoughts on the Dixiefication of Dixie," 164; *U.S.A. Today*, August 13, 1997; Dr. Michael Hill and Dr. Thomas Fleming, "The New Dixie Manifesto—States' Rights Will Rise Again," "The Southern League Position on Secession," "Frequently Asked Questions," Compiled for Dixienet by Mr. James C. Langcuster, The Southern League of Alabama, copies in possession of the author; *The Washington Post*, Sunday, October 29, 1995; *Jackson Clarion Ledger*, August 2, 1996.

54. Hill and Fleming, "New Dixie Manifesto." The web site of the League of the South is available at www.dixienet.org; *U.S.A. Today*, August 13, 1997; "Paleo-Federalist/Southern Nationalist F.A.Q.—Frequently Asked Questions," Compiled for Dixienet by Mr. James C. Langcuster, The Southern League of Alabama State, available at http://www.dixienet.org/faqs/pf_snfaq.html; "The Southern League Position on Secession," manuscript copy in possession of the author; *Southern Patriot, The Official Bi-Monthly Journal of the League of the South* 1 (September/October 1994), http://dixienet.org/spatriot/vol1no1/ourgov1.html; *Atlanta Journal-Constitution*, August 15, 1998; Tony Horwitz, *Confederates in the Attic: Dispatches from the Unfinished Civil War* (New York, 1998), 69, 86.

55. *Atlanta Journal-Constitution*, April 21, 1996; "League of the South Summer Institute Sponsored by the L. S. Institute for the Study of Southern History and Culture," manuscript copy in possession of the author; *Atlanta Journal-Constitution*, August 16, 1998; "League of the South Grand Strategy," manuscript copy in possession of the author.

56. Anthony P. Cohen, *The Symbolic Construction of Community* (Chichester, England, 1985), 115; C. Vann Woodward, "The Narcissistic South," *New York Review of Books* 36 (October 26, 1989), 13.

57. *Atlanta Journal-Constitution*, April 2 and October 24, 30, 1993.

58. *New York Times*, February 9 and October 6, 1993.

59. Fox News Channel, October 23, 2002, www.foxnews.com/story/o.2933,6652700.html; Horwitz, *Confederates in the Attic*, 283; *Atlanta Journal-Constitution*, July 28, 1995.

9. "SUCCESSFUL, OPTIMISTIC, PROSPEROUS, AND BLAND": TELLING ABOUT THE NO SOUTH

1. Fred C. Hobson, *The Southern Writer in the Post-Modern World* (Athens, Ga., 1991), 8; Hobson, *Tell about the South: The Southern Rage to Explain* (Baton Rouge, 1983), 352.

2. Woodward, "The South Tomorrow," *Time* 108 (September 22, 1976), 99; William Lee Miller, *Yankee from Georgia: The Emergence of Jim Crow* (New York, 1978).

3. George B. Tindall, *The Ethnic Southerners* (Baton Rouge, 1976), ix–xi; Tindall, "Other Voices," *Time* 108 (September 27, 1976), 99; Paul M. Gaston, "Sutpen's Door: The South since the Brown Decision," in Ernest J. Lander, Jr., and Richard J. Calhoun, eds., *Two Decades of Change: The South since the Supreme Court Desegregation Decision* (Columbia, S.C., 1975), 101–2; Joseph B. Cumming, Jr., "Been Down Home So Long It Seems Like Up to Me," *Esquire* 76 (August 1971), 110.

4. Horace Sutton, "The South as New America," *Saturday Review* 3 (September 4, 1976), 8.

5. *New York Times*, February 11, 1976; James C. Cobb, *The Selling of the South: The Southern Crusade for Industrial Development, 1936–1990* (Urbana, 1993), 185.

6. Bobby Braddock, copyright, 1973, Tree Publishing Company.

7. "Reverse Migration" and "The Good Life," *Time* 108 (September 27, 1976), 50, 32.

8. Jack Temple Kirby, *Media-Made Dixie: The South in the American Imagination*, rev. ed. (Athens, Ga., 1986), 146; James C. Cobb, "From Muskogee to Luckenbach: Country Music and the Southernization of America," *Journal of Popular Culture* 16 (Winter 1982), 87.

9. Rubin is quoted in Dewey W. Grantham, ed., *The South and the Sectional Image: The Sectional Theme since Reconstruction* (New York, 1967), 2.

10. Eudora Welty, *One Writer's Beginnings* (Cambridge, Mass., 1983), 44; Thomas Wolfe, *The Web and the Rock* (New York, 1939), 246; William Faulkner, *Intruder in the Dust* (New York, 1948), 152–53.

11. William Faulkner, *Absalom, Absalom!* (New York, 1990), 174; Hobson, *Tell about the South*, 15; Walker Percy, "Southern Comfort," *Harper's* 258 (January 1979), 80, 83.

12. Hobson, *The Southern Writer*, 6; Percy, "Southern Comfort," 83, 80.

13. Willie Morris, *North toward Home*, reprint (Oxford, Miss., 1982), 77–78, 90.

14. Ibid., 140–41.

15. Hobson, *The Southern Writer*, 6; Willie Morris, *New York Days* (Boston, 1993), 368.

16. Willie Morris, *Terrains of the Heart and Other Essays* (Oxford, Miss., 1981), 12.

17. Willie Morris, *The Courting of Marcus Dupree* (Garden City, N.Y., 1983), 420.

18. Willie Morris, *Yazoo, Integration in a Deep-Southern Town* (New York, 1971), 150.

19. Morris, *Terrains of the Heart*, 38; Morris, *New York Days*, 368, 371.

20. Ralph Ellison, "Richard Wright's Blues," in John F. Callahan, *The Collected Essays of Ralph Ellison* (New York, 1995), 129.

21. Morris, *New York Days*, 368; n.a., *Remembering Willie* (Jackson, Miss., 2000), 84.

22. William Faulkner, *Requiem for a Nun*, reprint (New York, 1975), 4; Faulkner, *Intruder in the Dust*, 119–20.

23. Flannery O'Connor, "The Displaced Person," in Flannery O'Connor, *The Complete Stories* (New York, 1971), 405–20.

24. Robert Coles, *Flannery O'Connor's South* (Athens, Ga., 1993), 29.

25. Eudora Welty, *Losing Battles*, reprint (New York, 1990), 240.

26. Ibid., 228, 235.

27. Ibid., 231, 287.

28. Suzanne Marrs, "Eudora Welty: The Southern Context," in James C. Cobb and Charles R. Wilson, eds., *Perspectives on the American South*, Volume 4 (1987), 19–38.

29. Flannery O'Connor, "The Fiction Writer and His Craft," in Granville Hicks, ed., *The Living Novel: A Symposium* (New York, 1957), 159.

30. John Egerton, *The Americanization of Dixie: The Southernization of America* (New York, 1974), xx; Marshall Frady, "Gone with the Wind," *Newsweek* 86 (July 28, 1975), 11.

31. Frady, "Gone with the Wind," 11.

32. Hodding Carter III, "The End of the South," *Time* 136 (August 1990), 82.

33. Flannery O'Connor, "Everything that Rises Must Converge," in O'Connor, *The Complete Stories*, 405–20.

34. Walker Percy, "A Southern View," "Red, White, and Blue-Gray," in Patrick Samway, *Signposts in a Strange Land* (New York, 1991), 93, 81.

35. Walker Percy, *The Last Gentleman*, reprint (New York, 1968), 150.

36. Ibid., 26; Walker Percy, *The Moviegoer* (New York, 1961), 145.

37. Walker Percy, *Lancelot* (New York, 1977), 219–20.

38. Percy, "Southern Comfort, 81; "Walker Percy, Interview with Jan Nordby Gretlund, January 2, 1981," *The South Carolina Review* 13 (Spring 1981), 12.

39. Ralph Ellison, *Invisible Man* (New York, 1952), 581, 577; Robert W. Rudnicki, *Percyscapes: The Fugue State in Twentieth-Century Southern Fiction* (Baton Rouge, 1999), 122.

40. Walker Percy, *The Message in the Bottle: How Queer Man Is, How Queer Language Is, and What One Has to Do with the Other* (New York, 1975), 58; "Ellison, Ralph." (ca. 1950–1990), Folder 14, Walker Percy Papers, Southern Historical Collection, University of North Carolina at Chapel Hill.

41. Roberta S. Maguire, "Walker Percy and Albert Murray: The Story of Two 'Part Anglo-Saxon Alabamians,'" *Southern Quarterly* 41 (Fall 2002), 20; Walker Percy, Letter to the Editor, *Harper's* 234 (May 1967), 11.

42. Walker Percy, *Love in the Ruins: The Adventures of a Bad Catholic at a Time Near the End of the World* (New York, 1971), 107–8, 112, 388.

43. Percy, "Southern Comfort," 79; Malcolm Jones, "Moralist of the South," in Lewis A. Lawson and Victor A. Kramer, eds., *More Conversations with Walker Percy* (Jackson, Miss., 1993), 170.

44. Cleanth Brooks, "The Southernness of Walker Percy," *South Carolina Review* 13 (Spring 1981), 34–38; Jay Tolson, *Pilgrim in the Ruins: A Life of Walker Percy* (New York, 1992), 377; Michael Kubre, "New South Diagnosis: Remembering Walker Percy," *Creative Loafing Summer Book Quarterly*, Creative Loafing Online, http://archivecln.com/charlotte/newsstand/c0617001cover.htm.

45. Arno Weller, "Within and Beyond the Southern Tradition: Walker Percy," in Lothar Hönnighausen and Valeria Gennaro Lerda, eds., *Rewriting the South: History and Fiction* (Tübirgen, Germany, 1993), 371; Percy, "Southern Comfort," 83.

46. W. Hampton Sides, "Interview, Richard Ford: Debunking the Mystique of the Southern Writer," *Memphis* 10 (February 1986), 42, 49.

47. Richard Ford, *The Sportswriter* (New York, 1986), 115.

48. Hobson, *The Southern Writer*, 55; *Washington Times*, September 21, 1988.

49. Josephine Humphreys, *Dreams of Sleep*, reprint (New York, 1985), 136; Josephine Humphreys, *Rich in Love*, reprint (New York, 2000), 5, 11.

50. Humphreys, *Dreams of Sleep*, 136–39, 162.

51. Ibid., 178, 182.

52. Josephine Humphreys, "A Disappearing Subject Called the South," in Dudley Clendenin, ed., *The Prevailing South: Life and Politics in a Changing Culture* (Atlanta, 1988), 218.

53. Hobson, *The Southern Writer*, 11; Bobbie Ann Mason, *In Country* (New York, 1985), 226; Bobbie Ann Mason, "Airwaves," in *Love Life* (New York, 1989), 185.

54. Lee Smith, *Oral History* (New York, 1983), 1, 2, 11, 292.

55. Hobson, *The Southern Writer*, 29–30; Lee Smith, *Saving Grace* (New York, 1995), 243.

56. Tim McLaurin, *Keeper of the Moon: A Southern Boyhood* (New York, 1991), 16, 49; Larry Brown, *Dirty Work* (Chapel Hill, 1989), 33.

57. Dorothy Allison, *Bastard Out of Carolina* (New York, 1993), 3.

58. Rick Bragg, *All Over But the Shoutin'* (New York, 1997), 297.

59. Harry Crews, *A Childhood: The Biography of a Place* (New York, 1978), 40.

60. Ibid., 43.

61. Harry Crews, *A Feast of Snakes* (New York, 1976).

62. Larry Brown, *Joe* (Chapel Hill, 1991).

63. Larry Brown, *Fay* (Chapel Hill, 2000), 86–87.

64. Erik Bledsoe, "The Rise of Southern Redneck and White Trash Writers," *Southern Cultures* 6 (March 2000), 82; Tim McLaurin, *Woodrow's Trumpet* (New York, 1989).

65. Harry Crews, "The Mythic Mule," *Southern Magazine* (January 25, 1987), 22.

66. Bragg, *All Over But the Shoutin'*, 309.

67. Brown, *Joe*, 73, 90–91; Jan Nordby Gretlund, *Frames of Southern Mind: Reflections on the Stoic, Bi-racial and Existential South* (Odense, Denmark, 1998), 237.

68. Janisse Ray, *Ecology of a Cracker Childhood* (Minneapolis, 1999), 13, 4; McLaurin, *Keeper of the Moon*, 316.

69. McLaurin, *Woodrow's Trumpet*, 157.

10. BLACKNESS AND SOUTHERNNESS: AFRICAN AMERICANS LOOK SOUTH TOWARD HOME

1. Charlayne Hunter-Gault, *In My Place* (New York, 1992), 178–79, 253.

2. "Transcript of the American Academy Conference on the Negro American, May 14–15, 1965," *Daedalus* (Winter 1966), 441.

3. Merle Black and John Shelton Reed, "Blacks and Southerners: A Research Note," *Journal of Politics* 44 (February 1982), 169; Larry J. Griffin and Ashley B. Thompson, "Enough About the Disappearing South: What About the Disappearing Southerner?" *Southern Cultures* 9 (Fall 2003), 59.

4. *New York Times*, July 31, 1994.

5. *San Francisco Chronicle*, March 30, 1998; *Washington Post*, May 5, 2001; *New York Times*, July 31, 1994; William H. Frey, "Migration to the South Brings Blacks Full Circle," *Population Today* (May/June 2001), http://www.prb.org/Content/NavigationMenu/PT_articles/April–June_2001/Migration_to_the_South_Brings_U_S__Blacks_Full_Circle.htm; Gavin Wright, "The Persistence of the South as an Economic Region," *Journal of Atlanta History* 44 (Winter 2001), 78; Sandra Yin, "Southern Comfort," *Forecast* 21 (July 16, 2001), 1.

6. *Washington Post*, May 5, 2001; Yin, "Southern Comfort," 1–3; Edward L. Glasser and Jacob L. Vigdor, "Racial Integration in 2000 Census: Promising News," The Brookings Institution Survey Series (Washington, D.C., April 15, 2001).

7. Randall Kenan, *Walking on Water: Black American Lives at the Turn of the Century* (New York, 1999), 569.

8. Peter Applebome, *Dixie Rising:How the South Is Shaping American Values, Politics, and Culture* (New York, 1996), 341; Fred Powledge, *Journeys through the South: A Rediscovery* (New York, 1979), 18.

9. *Atlanta Constitution*, August 15, 1993.

10. Chalmers Archer, Jr., *Growing Up Black in Rural Mississippi: Memories of a Family, Heritage of a Place* (New York, 1992), 147, 139.

11. Anthony Walton, *Mississippi* (New York, 1997), 258, 275; Walton, "Chicago as the Northernmost County of Mississippi," *Southern Cultures* 8 (Spring 2002), 52, 54, 55.

12. Thadious M. Davis, "Expanding the Limits: The Intersection of Race and Region," *Southern Literary Journal* 20 (Spring 1988), 6; C. Vann Woodward, "Look Away, Look Away," *Journal of Southern History* 59 (August 1996), 496.

13. James Morgan, "Going Home," *American Way* 106 (September 15, 1993), 106; Henry Louis Gates, Jr., *America behind the Color Line: Dialogues with African Americans* (New York, 2004), 143.

14. David R. Goldfield, *Black, White, and Southern: Race Relations and Southern Culture, 1940 to the Present* (Baton Rouge, 1990), 170; Alice Walker, *In Search of Our Mothers' Gardens* (New York, 1983), 143.

15. Walker, *In Search*, 145; Gates, *America behind the Color Line*, 143.

16. *Atlanta Journal-Constitution*, February 28, 1997; Jerry Ward, "A Writer for Her People: An Interview with Dr. Margaret Walker Alexander," *Mississippi Quarterly* 42 (Winter 1989), 42, 514, 519.

17. Applebome, *Dixie Rising*, 339; William R. Ferris and Charles R. Wilson, eds., *Encyclopedia of Southern Culture* (Chapel Hill, 1989), xi.

18. Ann Hawthorne, "Alex Haley: At Home in the Hills of East Tennessee," *Appalachia* (Winter 1992), 37.

19. Hunter-Gault, *In My Place*, 232; "Transcript of the American Academy Conference," 441.

20. Nikki Giovanni, *Gemini: An Extended Autobiographical Statement on My First Twenty-Five Years of Being a Black Poet* (New York, 1971), 12; Giovanni, *Black Feeling, Black Talk, Black Judgment* (New York, 1970), 58; Giovanni, *Knoxville, Tennessee* (New York, 1994).

21. Helen Taylor, *Circling Dixie: Contemporary Southern Culture through a Transatlantic Lens* (New Brunswick, N.J., 2001), 173.

22. Walker, *In Search*, 20–21; John Oliver Killens, "Introduction," in John Oliver Killens and Jerry W. Ward, Jr., eds., *Southern Black Voices: An Anthology of Fiction, Poetry, Drama, Nonfiction, and Critical Essays* (New York, 1992), 2.

23. Robert E. Hemenway, *Zora Neale Hurston: A Literary Biography* (Urbana, 1977), vii–xiii.

24. Raymond Andrews, *Appalachee Red* (Athens, Ga., 1987), iv, vii–viii, 214; "Black Boy and Man in the Small Town South," in Dudley Clendenin, ed., *The Prevailing South: Life and Politics in a Changing Culture* (Atlanta, 1988), 180.

25. Walker, *In Search*, 261–62.

26. Alice Walker, *The Color Purple* (New York, 1985).

27. Jack Temple Kirby, *Media-Made Dixie: The South in the American Imagination*, rev. ed. (Athens, Ga., 1986), 183–88.

28. Endesha Ida Mae Holland, *The Mississippi Delta: A Memoir* (New York, 1997); Holland, "Memories of the Mississippi Delta," *Michigan Quarterly Review* 26 (Winter 1987), 201–19, 246–47.

29. "Tina McElroy Ansa," in Clendenin, *The Prevailing South: Life and Politics in a Changing Culture* (Atlanta, 1988), 184; *Atlanta Constitution*, July 8, 1993; Tina McElroy Ansa, *Ugly Ways* (New York, 1993), 149, 275–76.

30. Tina McElroy Ansa, *The Hand I Fan With* (New York, 1996), 454–55.

31. Dori Sanders, *Clover* (Chapel Hill, 1990), 1.

32. Dori Sanders, *Her Own Place* (Chapel Hill, 1993), 164.

33. Walker, *In Search*, 19; Ernest J. Gaines, "Miss Jane and I," *Callaloo* 1 (May 1978), 25–27.

34. Gaines, "Miss Jane and I," 23–28; Ernest J. Gaines, *The Autobiography of Miss Jane Pittman*, reprint (New York, 1979).

35. Ernest J. Gaines, *A Gathering of Old Men* (New York, 1983), 138, 146, 208.

36. Ibid., 92.

37. "Randall Kenan Is 1997 Grisham Writer in Residence," *The Southern Register*, University of Mississippi (Fall 1997), 16; *Charleston News and Courier*, October 20, 1991.

38. Frank Shelton, "Of Machines and Men: Pastoralism in Gaines' Fiction," in David C. Estes, ed., *Critical Reflections on the Fiction of Ernest J. Gaines* (Athens, Ga., 1994), 28–29; Fred C. Hobson, *The Southern Writer in the Post-Modern World* (Athens, Ga., 1991), 101.

39. Hobson, *The Southern Writer*, 101; Walker, *In Search*, 17.

40. Clifton L. Taulbert, *Once Upon a Time When We Were Colored* (Tulsa, Okla., 1989), 5–6. See also Onita Estes-Hicks, "The Way We Were: Precious Memories of the Black Segregated South," *African American Review* 27 (Spring 1993), 9–17.

41. Belle Gayle Chevigny, "Still It's a Fight for Power," *Nation* (August 22/29, 1994), 196; *New York Times*, July 31, 1994.

42. Jacqueline Joan Johnson, "Rememory: What There Is for Us," in Malaika Dero, ed., *Up South: Stories, Studies, and Letters of This Century's Black Migrations* (New York, 1993), 107; Barbara Shircliffe, "We Got the Best of that World: A Case for the Study of Nostalgia in the Oral History of School Segregation," *Oral History Review* 28 (Summer–Fall 2001), 67, 70–71, 77.

43. Belle Gayle Chevigny, "Mississippi Stories I: The Fruits of Freedom Summer," *Nation* (August 15, 1994), 157; Henry Louis Gates, Jr., *Colored People: A Memoir* (New York, 1994), 213.

44. Ray Furlong, "Germans Flock to Nostalgia Film," http://news.bbc.co.uk/1/hi/entertainment/film/2836215.stm.

45. "The Salon Interview: Randall Kenan," *Salon* (February 24, 1999), www.salon.com/books/int/1999/02/cov24int2.html; H. B. Grace, "Meet Randall Kenan: Southern Writing Is Changing; It Has to Change," www.bookpage.com/BPinterviews/kenan492.html; Randall Kenan, "The Foundations of the Earth," in Randall Kenan, *Let the Dead Bury Their Dead* (New York, 1992), 49–72; Randall Kenan, *A Visitation of Spirits* (New York, 1989); V. Hunt, "A Conversation with Randall Kenan," *African American Review* 29 (Autumn 1995), 413.

46. Toni Morrison, *Beloved* (New York, 1987), 13–14.

47. "American Academy Conference Transcript," 440; Eddy L. Harris, *South of Haunted Dreams: A Ride through Slavery's Back Yard* (New York, 1993), 361, 139; Michelle

Orecklin, "The Pulse of America: The Twist on Tradition," www.time.com/reports,Mississippi/literature/html.

48. Killens, "Introduction," 3; Deborah H. Barnes, "Myth, Metaphor, and Memory in Toni Morrison's Reconstructed South," *Studies in the Literary Imagination* 31 (Fall 1998), 29.

49. Toni Morrison, *Song of Solomon*, reprint (New York, 1987), 328, 332, 336–37; Gay Wilentz, "Civilizations Underneath: African Heritage as Cultural Discourse in Toni Morrison's *Song of Solomon*," *African American Review* 26 (Spring 1992), 61–76.

50. Barnes, "Myth, Metaphor, and Memory," 33; see also Catherine Carr Lee, "The South in Toni Morrison's *Song of Solomon*: Initiation, Healing, and Home," *Studies in the Literary Imagination* 31 (Fall 1998), 109, 123; Patricia Yeager, *Dirt and Desire: Reconstructing Southern Women's Writing, 1930–1990* (Chicago, 2000), 56; 139; Harris, *South of Haunted Dreams*, 361, 139.

51. Harris, *South of Haunted Dreams*, 171, 192–93.

52. "Randall Kenan Is 1997 Grisham Writer," 16; Kenan, *Walking on Water*, 610, 612.

53. Kenan, *Walking on Water*, 7.

54. Ibid., 6–7, 612; Orecklin, "The Pulse of America."

55. Davis, "Expanding the Limits," 7; *Washington Post*, January 5, 1997; *Washington Post*, February 1, 1998.

56. *Washington Post*, January 5, 1997, February 1, 1998.

57. *New York Times*, April 5, 1992; *Washington Post*, October 5, 9, 1994, June 7, 2001; see also *Washington Post*, February 19, 1999.

58. *Washington Post*, January 5, 1997.

59. Lynn Casmier-Pas, "Heritage Not Hate? Collecting Black Memorabilia," *Southern Cultures* 9 (Spring 2003), 46, 56, 53, 44; *Houston Chronicle*, February 15, 2002.

60. Jack Hitt, "Confederate Chic," *Gentleman's Quarterly* 67 (November 1997), 266.

61. Adolph Reed, Jr., "Dangerous Dream," *The Village Voice*, April 16, 1996, 26; Casmier-Pas, "Heritage Not Hate?" 46, 56, 53, 44.

62. Taulbert, *Once upon a Time*, 10–11.

63. Henry Louis Gates, Jr., *Colored People: A Memoir* (New York, 1994), 53, 62, 93; Reed, "Dangerous Dream," 24; U.S. Census Bureau Historical Income, Table F-3a, "Mean Income Received by Each Fifth and Top Five Percent of White Families, 1966 to 2001," http://www.census.gov/hhes/income/histinc/f03a.html; Table F-3b, "Mean Income Received by Each Fifth and Top 5 Percent of Black Families, 1966–2001," http://www.census.gov/hhes/income/histinc/f03b.html.

64. Walker, *In Search*, 17; Liane Gay Rozzell, Letter to *The New Yorker*, "The Mail," *The New Yorker* (March 17, 2003), 18.

65. James Alan McPherson, "Preserving a Sense of Community in the Suburban South," *Atlanta Journal-Constitution*, August 1, 1996, A-17.

66. Adrian Walker, "America's Economic Divide Not Strictly a Black-White Issue," *Atlanta Journal-Constitution*, January 21, 2004, A-11. For other expressions of concern on this point, see Gates, *America behind the Color Line*, passim, and Kenan, *Walking on Water*, 627.

67. Elizabeth Fortson Arroyo, "The Asterisk Southerner," *Oxford American* (August/ September 1996), 26, 28.

11. DIVIDED BY A COMMON PAST: HISTORY AND IDENTITY IN THE CONTEMPORARY SOUTH

1. W. J. Cash, *The Mind of the South—With a New Introduction by Bertram Wyatt-Brown*, paperback version (New York, 1991), 49–50; Peter Applebome, *Dixie Rising: How the South Is Shaping American Values, Politics, and Culture* (New York, 1996), 339; Charlayne Hunter-Gault, *In My Place* (New York, 1992), 253.

2. Jimmie L. Franklin, "Black Southerners, Shared Experience and Place; a Reflection," *Journal of Southern History* 59 (February 1994), 4; "A Southern Sense of Place: Notes of a Native Son," an address Delivered at the Seventh Annual Authors Dinner at the University of Alabama at Tuscaloosa, April 13, 1993.

3. "The Asterisk Southerner," *Oxford American* (August/September 1996), 27.

4. See Charles Joyner, *Shared Traditions: Southern History and Folk Culture* (Urbana, 1999); *Southern Focus Poll Reports, Southern Crosstabulations,* Fall 1999, Spring 2000, Spring 2001, and *Non-Southern Crosstabulations,* Fall 1999, Spring 2000, The Odum Institute for Research in the Social Sciences, University of North Carolina at Chapel Hill, http://www2.irss.unc.edu/irss/researchdesignservices/researchdeslinks/sfpreports.asp.

5. David R. Goldfield, *Black, White, and Southern: Race Relations and Southern Culture, 1940 to the Present* (Baton Rouge, 1990), 1; Franklin, "Black Southerners," 4; *Birmingham Post Herald*, March 11, 1993.

6. C. Vann Woodward, "The Search for Southern Identity," *Virginia Quarterly Review* 34 (Summer 1958), 16, 19.

7. Kevin Thornton, "The Confederate Flag and the Meaning of Southern History," *Southern Cultures* 2 (Winter 1996), 237–38.

8. James C. Cobb, *Georgia Odyssey* (Athens, Ga., 1997), 110–11; John Walker Davis, "An Air of Defiance; Georgia's State Flag Change of 1956," *Georgia Historical Quarterly* 82 (Summer 1998), 305–30.

9. Cobb, *Georgia Odyssey*, 110–11, 89; Thornton, "The Confederate Flag," 240; *Atlanta Journal-Constitution*, March 29, August 2, 1992, and January 29, 13, 1993; Richard Hyatt, *Zell, the Governor Who Gave Georgia Hope* (Macon, Ga., 1997), 132.

10. *Atlanta Journal-Constitution*, March 7, 1993; *Southern Focus Poll*, Fall 1994, Codebook Number 74-0972, Vol. 6, http//irss.unc.edu/cgi-bin/Poll/search.link.cgi.

11. John Shelton Reed, "South Polls" and "Confederate Agents in the Ivy League," manuscript transmitted via e-mail, both copies in possession of the author.

12. John Shelton Reed, "The Banner that Won't Stay Furled," *Southern Cultures* 8 (Spring 2002), 99; www.cnn.com/2003/ALLPOLITICS/11/01/elec04.prez.dean.confederate.flag/.

13. Tony Horowitz, *Confederates in the Attic: Dispatches from the Unfinished Civil War* (New York, 1998), 102–3.

14. Ibid., 110–12.

15. Ibid., 112–13.

16. Tony Horwitz, "A Death for Dixie," *The New Yorker* (March 18, 1996), 63; *Charlotte Observer*, May 18, 1996; *Atlanta Journal-Constitution*, February 27, April 13, 1997.

17. Pauli Murray, *Proud Shoes: The Story of an American Family* (New York, 1978), 275; Eddy L. Harris, *South of Haunted Dreams: A Ride through Slavery's Back Yard* (New York, 1993), 124–25.

18. *New York Times*, November 27, 1996; *Atlanta Journal-Constitution*, March 21, 1993; Reed, "The Banner that Won't Stay Furled," 94.

19. Walker Percy, "Red, White, and Blue-Gray," in Patrick Samway, ed., *Signposts in a Strange Land* (New York, 1991), 80; Shelby Foote to Walker Percy, June 15, 1970, in Jay Tolson, ed., *The Correspondence of Shelby Foote and Walker Percy* (New York, 1997), 144.

20. Hodding Carter III, "Looking Back," *Southern Cultures* 2 (Number 3/4, 1996), 286; Reed, "The Banner that Won't Stay Furled," 88; Hodding Carter III, "The End of the South," *Time* 136 (August 1990).

21. *Chattanooga Times*, January 26, 1998; *New York Times*, July 29, 2000; Miranda Green, *The Sun Gods of Ancient Europe* (London, 1991), 46–48.

22. *Atlanta Journal-Constitution*, March 23, 1997.

23. Douglas Lederman, "Old Times Not Forgotten," *Chronicle of Higher Education*, October 20, 1993, A-51; *Memphis Commercial Appeal*, March 1, 1997; *Atlanta Journal-Constitution*, May 20, 2003.

24. Thornton, "The Confederate Flag," 236; "Marchers Want Confederate Flag to Fly Again in Alabama," www.cnn.com/2000/us/03/03/confederate.rally/.

25. *New Orleans Times-Picayune*, May 7, 1994; *Rock Mountain News*, December 4, 1994; *Atlanta Journal-Constitution*, August 31, 1994, November 27, 1996; *Pittsburg Post-Gazette*, December 3, 1996; *The Guardian*, November 28, 1996; *New York Times*, November 27, 1996.

26. *New York Times*, November 28, 1996.

27. *Atlanta Journal-Constitution*, January 18, 19, 2000.

28. *The Australian*, May 25, 2000; *New York Times*, November 9, 2002.

29. *Atlanta Journal-Constitution*, November 10, 2000; *Athens Banner Herald and Daily News*, January 24, 25, 2001.

30. *Athens Banner Herald*, January 25, 2001.

31. *Atlanta Journal-Constitution*, May 10, 2003; March 3, 5, 2004.

32. *Atlanta Journal-Constitution*, January 10, 2001; *U.S.A. Today*, October 27, 2000; *Christian Science Monitor*, October 23, 2000; *New York Times*, April 22, 2001.

33. Andrew Ferguson, "When Lincoln Returned to Richmond," Part III, http://www.weeklystandard.com/Content/Public/Articles/000/000/003/541wlouy.asp?pg=2; *The Guardian*, June 5, 1999.

34. *Atlanta Journal-Constitution*, February 15, 2003; *Washington Post*, January 9 and February 11, 2003.

35. *Atlanta Journal-Constitution*, November 27, 1997; *Greensboro News and Record*, January 20, 1998; *New York Times*, February 9, 1998.

36. Derek H. Alderman, "A Street Fit for a King: Naming Places and Commemoration in the American South," *Professional Geographer* 52 (November 2000), 676; *Atlanta Journal-Constitution*, February 16, 1990, March 3, April 3, 1994; *Memphis Commercial Appeal*, July 5, 1991; *Birmingham News*, March 28, 1993.

37. Paul Hemphill, *Leaving Birmingham: Notes of a Native Son* (New York, 1993), 10.

38. Ibid., 4; Carter, "The End of the South," 82.

39. *New York Times*, July 21, 1990.

40. *Atlanta Journal-Constitution*, February 25, 2001; William Dusinberre, *Them Dark Days: Slavery in the American Rice Swamps* (New York, 1996), 429.

41. *Atlanta Journal-Constitution*, January 27, 2004.

42. Melton A. McLaurin, "Commemorating Wilmington's Racial Violence of 1898: From Individual to Collective Memory," *Southern Cultures* 6 (Winter 2000), 35–57; *Atlanta Journal-Constitution*, January 24, 2004.

43. *New York Times*, October 18, 1994, October 11, 1994.

44. *New York Times*, June 22, 2000; *Baltimore Sun*, December 21, 1995.

45. *Savannah Morning News*, December 2, 2001, February 4 and March 28, 2001; Edward Beasley, "Matters of Fact," *The Call*, Internet edition, June 14, 2002, www.kccall.com/news/2002/editorial/035.html.

46. Harris, *South of Haunted Dreams*, 148.

47. *Christian Science Monitor*, June 20, 2001.

48. *The Scotsman*, June 8, 2000.

49. *Baltimore Sun*, July 17, 2003.

50. *Greensboro News and Record*, January 20, 1998.

51. W. Fitzhugh Brundage, ed., *Where These Memories Grow: History, Memory, and Southern Identity* (Chapel Hill, 2000), 19; *The Financial Times*, May 18, 2001; *Seattle Times*, September 7, 2002.

52. Berndt Ostendorf, *Black Literature in White America* (Sussex, England, 1982), 128; *The Irish Times*, April 5, 1997; *New Orleans Times-Picayune*, April 16, 2001.

53. *Atlanta Journal-Constitution*, January 21, 2001, March 18, 2003; Georgia Chamber of Commerce, "Put the Focus on the Future . . . Not the Past," mailing in possession of the author.

54. *Atlanta Journal-Constitution*, April 19, 2001; James C. Cobb, *The Selling of the South: The Southern Crusade for Industrial Development, 1936–1990* (Urbana, 1993), 122–50; *Washington Post*, March 25, 2001; Reed, "The Banner that Won't Stay Furled," 84.

55. Cobb, *The Selling of the South*, 148–50; Paul Luebke and Joseph Schneider, "Economic and Racial Ideology in the North Carolina Elite," in James C. Cobb and Charles R. Wilson, eds., *Perspectives on the American South: An Annual Review of Society, Politics, and Culture*, Vol. 4 (New York, 1987), 129–44.

56. David Brion Davis, "Slavery and the Post–World War II Historians," *Daedalus* 103 (Spring 1974), 10.

57. Daniel Patrick Moynihan, *The Negro Family in America: The Case for National Action* (Washington, D.C., 1965), xvii; Kenneth S. Lynn, "The Regressive Historians," *American Scholar* 47 (Autumn 1978), 495.

58. John W. Blassingame, *The Slave Community: Plantation Life in the Antebellum South* (New York, 1972), vii.

59. Rawick, *From Sundown to Sunup: The Making of the Black Community* (Westport, Conn., 1972), 3, 9.

60. Ibid., 11–12; Thomas L. Webber, *Deep Like the Rivers: Education in the Slave Quarter Community, 1831–1865* (New York, 1978), 262.

61. Alex Haley, *Roots: The Saga of an American Family* (Garden City, N.J., 1976); Helen Taylor, *Circling Dixie: Contemporary Southern Culture through a Transatlantic Lens* (New Brunswick, N.J., 2001), 64; Willie Lee Rose, *Race and Region in American Historical Fiction: Four Episodes in Popular Culture* (Oxford, 1979), 10.

62. Jack Temple Kirby, *Media-Made Dixie: The South in the American Imagination*, rev. ed. (Athens, Ga., 1986), 7; Taylor, *Circling Dixie*, 65.

63. Rose, *Race and Region*, 8; Taylor, *Circling Dixie* 64, 74.

64. Blassingame, *The Slave Community*, 48–49; Henry Bibb, *The Life and Adventures of Henry Bibb, an American Slave*. Reprint (Madison, Wis., 2001), 27–28.

65. David Brion Davis, "Review of Herbert G. Gutman, *The Black Family in Slavery and Freedom, 1750–1925*," *American Historical Review* 82 (June 1977), 744–45; Lynn, "The Regressive Historians," 495.

66. Peter Kolchin, *American Slavery, 1619–1877* (New York, 1993), 148–49.

67. Bertram Wyatt-Brown, "The Mask of Obedience: Male Slave Psychology in the Old South," *American Historical Review* 93 (December 1988), 1230; Clarence E. Walker, *Deromanticizing Black History: Critical Essays and Reappraisals* (Knoxville, Tenn., 1991), xvii, viii; Dusinberre, *Them Dark Days*, 436.

68. Peter Kolchin, "Slavery in United States History Textbooks," *Journal of American History* 84 (March 1998), 1434. See also 1434, n. 18.

69. Edward L. Ayers et al., *American Passages: A History of the United States* (Belmont, Calif., 2004), 87, 307; Robert A. Divine, et al., *America Past and Present* (New York, 1999), 382, 406.

70. *Washington Post*, November 4, 2000.

71. *New York Times*, September 29, 2000, May 10, 1996; *Memphis Commercial Appeal*, May 10, 1996.

72. Peter Novick, *That Noble Dream: The "Objectivity Question" and the American Historical Profession* (Cambridge, 1988), 488–89; Henry Louis Gates, Jr., *America behind the Color Line: Dialogues with African Americans* (New York, 2004), 109.

73. Eric J. Hobsbawm, *Nations and Nationalism since 1780: Programme, Myth, Reality*, 2nd ed. (Cambridge, 1982), 12.

74. William Pfaff, *The Wrath of Nations: Civilization and the Furies of Nationalism* (New York, 1993), 58.

75. C. Vann Woodward, "New South Fraud Is Papered by Old South Myth," *Washington Post*, July 9, 1961.

12. THE SOUTH AND THE POLITICS OF IDENTITY

1. John Egerton, *The Americanization of Dixie: The Southernization of America* (New York, 1974), ii.

2. William J. Cooper, Jr., and Thomas E. Terrill, *The American South: A History* (New York, 1990), 778.

3. James C. Cobb, "Does Mind No Longer Matter? The South, the Nation, and *The Mind of the South*, 1941–1991," *Journal of Southern History* 57 (November 1991), 711–13; *Atlanta Constitution*, December 11, 1990.

4. Michael Lind, "The Southern Coup," *New Republic* 212 (June 19, 1995), 20; James N. Gregory, "Southernizing the American Working Class: Post-War Episodes of Class Transformation," *Labor History* 39 (May 1998), 135–54.

5. Alan Draper, "Congress Is Dominated by Southern Dixiecrats Using Republican Front," *Buffalo News*, June 16, 1996, p. G-3; Stephen D. Cummings, *The Dixiefication of America: The American Odyssey into the Conservative Economic Trap* (Westport, Conn., 1998), 10.

6. James C. Cobb, "GOP's Southern Exposure: Talk of Inclusion May Irk Loyalists; Balancing Act May Be Required to Craft New Republican Image," *Atlanta Journal-Constitution*, January 5, 2003, E-6.

7. *The Pew Research Center for the People and the Press, Survey Report, The 2004 Political Landscape: Evenly Divided and Increasingly Polarized, Part 5, Social and Political Attitudes about Race*, http://people-press.org/reports/display.php3?PageID=754; *Southern Focus Poll Reports, Southern Crosstabulations*, Fall 1999, *Non-Southern Crosstabulations*, Fall 1999, The Odum Institute for Research in the Social Sciences, University of North Carolina, Chapel Hill, http://irss.unc.edu.

8. C. Vann Woodward, "Southern Styles: A Typology," typescript, Box 73, folder 130, Woodward Papers; Larry J. Griffin, "Southern Distinctiveness Yet Again or Why America Still Needs the South," *Southern Cultures* 6 (Fall 2000), 57–58, 68; Peter Applebome, "What Did We Just Learn? America's Blind Spot on Race," *New York Times*, December 22, 2002, Section 4, p. 3.

9. Peter Applebome, *Dixie Rising: How the South Is Shaping American Values, Politics, and Culture* (New York, 1996), 20, 195–96; Helen Taylor, *Circling Dixie: Contemporary Southern Culture through a Transatlantic Lens* (New Brunswick, N.J., 2001), 9; Joshua Zeitz, "Dixie's Victory," *American Heritage* (Aug./Sept. 2002), 46–55.

10. Ken Tucker, "Study Has Good News for Country Radio," *Billboard* 116 (July 31, 2004), 35.

11. *New York Times*, November 26, 1995.

12. Matthew Benjamin, "Life in the Fast Lane," *U. S. News and World Report* 137 (November 22, 2004), 64–66.

13. Michael O'Brien, "The Apprehension of the South in Modern Culture," *Southern Cultures* 4 (Winter 1998), 11; "Debunking the 'NASCAR Dad' Myth," http://www.thecarpetbaggerreport.com/archives/001280.html.

14. Howard Zinn, *Southern Mystique* (New York, 1964), 223; David R. Jansson, "Internal Orientalism in America: W. J. Cash's *The Mind of the South* and the Spatial Construction of National Identity," *Political Geography* (no monthly date, 2003), 311.

15. John B. Judis, "War Resisters: The Numbers Are In and the 'Nays' Are Growing," *The American Prospect*, October 7, 2002 (www.prospect.org/print/V13/18/judis-j.html); Death Penalty Information Committee, "Regional Murder Rates, 2001–2002" (www.deathpenaltyinfo.org/article.php?scid=12&did=169).

16. *Southern Focus Poll Reports, Southern Crosstabulations*, Fall, 1999, *Non-Southern Crosstabulations*, Fall, 1999; Clarence Page, "How Bush Improved His Black Vote," http://www.southernillinoisan.com/articles/2004/11/14/opinions/columnists/page/doc41971e1e2794e191249572.txt; www.fuckthesouth.com.

17. "Integrated Communications and Marketing Plan for Sewanee: The University of the South," http://www.sewaneeconnection.com/marketingplan.htm (copy in possession of the author); *Atlanta Journal-Constitution*, November 30, 2004.

18. Zinn, *The Southern Mystique*, 263; Taylor, *Circling Dixie*, 8; Griffin, "Southern Distinctiveness," 68.

19. Edward L. Ayers, "What Do We Talk about When We Talk about the South?" in Ayers, Patricia Nelson Limerick, Stephen Nissenbaum, and Peter S. Onuf, eds., *All over the Map: Rethinking American Regions* (Baltimore, 1996), 65–66; *Atlanta Journal-Constitution*, December 18–19, 2003.

20. Jansson, *Internal Orientalism*, 307–308.

21. Robert Coles, *Flannery O'Connor's South* (Athens, Ga., 1993), 50; *New York Times*, February 20, 1999; University of Connecticut, "New England Poll," www.news.uconn.edu/2004/may2004/rel104062.htm.

22. *New York Times,* February 9, 1998.

23. Taylor, *Circling Dixie*, 11; O'Brien, "The Apprehension of the South," 6.

24. Don H. Doyle, *Nations Divided: America, Italy, and the Southern Question* (Athens, Ga., 2002), 3; William Faulkner, *Requiem for a Nun*, reprint (New York, 1975), 80; James C. Cobb, "European Scholars Can't Get Enough of the American South," *Georgia Magazine* 82 (June 2003), 33–37.

25. Anne Goodwyn Jones, "Sushi South: Teaching Southern Culture in Japan," *Southern Cultures* 4 (Winter 1998), 21.

26. Richard H. King, "Review of *Not Like Us: How Europeans Have Loved, Hated, and Transformed American Cultures since World War II*," *Southern Cultures* 4 (Winter 1988), 81.

27. David Rieff, "Multiculturalism's Silent Partner: It's the Newly Globalized Consumer Economy, Stupid," *Harper's* 287 (August 1993), 62; Marilyn Halter, *Book Review*, "Shopping for Identity: The Marketing of Ethnicity," *Publishers Weekly* 247 (July 24, 2000), 76.

28. "Design as Cultural Marketing," *Malaysian Business* (October 1, 1997), 12; *The (Glasgow) Herald*, December 11, 1935; *Sunday (London) Times*, March 28, 1999; *Atlanta Journal-Constitution*, July 30, 2000.

29. Author's personal observations.

30. Jamie Glazov, "The End of Blackness," *FrontPageMagazine.com*, February 20, 2004, http://www.frontpagemag.com/Articles/ReadArticle.asp?ID=12273; David Riesman, *The Lonely Crowd: A Study of the Changing American Character* (New Haven, Conn., 1950); Philip Gleason, "Identifying Identity: A Semantic Identity History," *Journal of American History* 69 (March 1983), 926–29.

31. John F. Callahan, ed., *The Collected Essays of Ralph Ellison* (New York, 1995), 178; Randall Kenan, *Walking on Water: Black American Lives at the Turn of the Century* (New York, 1999), 625, 623.

32. Henry Louis Gates, Jr., *Colored People: A Memoir* (New York, 1994), xv.

33. Carl Pletsch, "Class, Nationalism, and Identity Politics," *Peace Review* 11 (June 1999), 197; Rogers Brubaker and Frederick Cooper, "Beyond 'Identity,'" *Theory and Society* 29 (February 2000), 33.

34. O'Brien, "The Apprehension of the South," 13; Larry J. Griffin and Ashley B. Thompson, "Enough about the Disappearing South: What about Disappearing Southerners?" *Southern Cultures* 9 (Fall 2003), 55–60.

35. Brubaker and Cooper, "Beyond 'Identity,'" 1.

36. "The New Dixie Manifesto—States Rights Will Rise Again," Copyright 1995, The Southern League, Inc., Dr. Michael Hill and Dr. Thomas Fleming, *The Washington Post*, Sunday, October 29, 1995.

37. "Alarm over Immigration Effects French Presidential Election," For Immediate Release, April 24, 2002, www.dixienet.org//s-press-release; "Freedom of Association and Preserving the South's Core Anglo-Celtic Culture," www.dixienet.org/positions/free-ac-htm.

38. *The Scotsman*, June 8, 2000.

39. W. E. B. DuBois, *The Souls of Black Folk*, reprint (New York, 1989), xxxi.

40. *Webster's*, 707; Faulkner is quoted in Thadious M. Davis, "Wright, Faulkner, and Mississippi as Racial Memory," *Callaloo* 9 (Summer 1986), 474.

41. Oxford English Dictionary, s.v. "Identity," in Gleason, "Identifying Identity," 911; Edward L. Ayers, "What We Talk About," 81; Daniel J. Singal, "Review of Bruce Clayton, *W. J. Cash, a Life*," *Journal of Southern History* 59 (February 1993), 166.

42. George Brown Tindall, *The Ethnic Southerners* (Baton Rouge, 1976), 21; Clayton, *W. J. Cash*, 162, 119.

Index